MW01073339

Praise for *The Mind of Benedict XVI*

"DeClue's survey of Benedict's thought and legacy is truly exceptional. The most comprehensive accessible overview of this beloved pope's theology available, it will lead a wide range of readers toward a deeper appreciation of Benedict's incomparable brilliance and enduring relevance."

—**Matthew Ramage**, Professor of Theology and Co-director of the Center for Integral Ecology at Benedictine College

"Unlike many other books on the theology of Pope Benedict, this work seeks to piece together the many occasional publications and public addresses of Ratzinger / Benedict XVI into a more systematic framework. It will be of great value to theology students as well as being accessible to a general readership. The early sections of the work on Ratzinger's Bavarian childhood are the best accounts of this period of his life I have read."

—**Tracey Rowland**, St. John Paul II Chair of Theology, University of Notre Dame (Australia)

"This book is a wonderful introduction to the theology of Joseph Ratzinger that is both accessible to anyone interested in his thought and a great addition to any serious student of Ratzinger's theology. It will be an excellent overview for anyone who wants to study and to understand the thought of this theological giant. DeClue is able to highlight the notion of communion as the consistent note that brings unity and harmony to Ratzinger's theological symphony, which consists of movements made up of fundamental theology, dogmatics, liturgy, and moral theology."

—**Roland Millare**, Vice President of Curriculum and Director of Clergy Initiatives for the St. John Paul II Foundation, author of *A Living Sacrifice: Liturgy and Eschatology in Joseph Ratzinger*

The MIND *of* BENEDICT XVI

The MIND of BENEDICT XVI

A THEOLOGY *of* COMMUNION

RICHARD G. DECLUE, JR.

FOREWORD BY FR. EMERY DE GAÁL

Published by Word on Fire, Elk Grove Village, IL 60007
© 2024 by Word on Fire Catholic Ministries
Printed in the United States of America
All rights reserved

Cover design, typesetting, and interior art direction by Nicolas Fredrickson,
Clark Kenyon, and Rozann Lee

Scripture excerpts are from the New Revised Standard Version Bible: Catholic
Edition (copyright © 1989, 1993), used by permission of the National
Council of the Churches of Christ in the United States of America. All rights
reserved worldwide.

Excerpts from the English translation of the *Catechism of the Catholic Church*
for use in the United States of America copyright © 1994, United States
Catholic Conference, Inc.—Libreria Editrice Vaticana. Used by permission.
English translation of the *Catechism of the Catholic Church: Modifications from
the Editio Typica* copyright © 1997, United States Conference of Catholic
Bishops—Libreria Editrice Vaticana.

Excerpts from Joseph Ratzinger, *Introduction to Christianity* (© 1990, 2004)
and *Milestones: Memoirs 1927–1977* (© 1998) reprinted by permission from
Ignatius Press through Copyright Clearance Center, Inc. Excerpts from
Joseph Ratzinger, *Eschatology: Death and Eternal Life* (© 1988) reprinted by
permission from The Catholic University of America Press through Copyright
Clearance Center, Inc.

First printing, April 2024

ISBN: 978-1-68578-988-6

Library of Congress Control Number: 2022943558

Contents

Foreword

Fr. Emery de Gaál, PhD

Pope Benedict XVI's oeuvre is vast. His bibliography contains more than fifteen hundred titles. Dr. Richard DeClue presents us with a most readable, unifying synopsis of Ratzinger's writings, which permits us to easily access the central thoughts of "the Mozart of Theology," as Joseph Ratzinger is sometimes called. The terms "unity" and "whole" repeatedly occur in DeClue's excellent study. Structured in ten organically organized chapters, the author convincingly shows us that Ratzinger's thinking is characterized by an overarching coherence, a recurring *leitmotif*. DeClue argues that there is a *cantus firmus*, a unifying melody to all his writings.

Why unity? Is not postmodernity unity-resistant? Does it not delight in the fragmentary, scattered, and unreconciled? In the wake of Jean-François Lyotard (1924–1998), postmodernity rejects overarching grand narratives. To phrase it in language less familiar to our age's sensibilities: Can the multifarious and contingent, in principle, approximate the absolute and noncontingent God? And, vice-versa, can God communicate with mere mortals? These are valid questions that have been pondered by numerous serious minds throughout the centuries.

Ratzinger's theology is eminently concerned about the unity of God and humankind—a unity that signals the redeemability of creation. The God who created this world also mercifully restores it, after the fall, to a redeemed unity, from the Eucharistic altar until the Second Coming of the Lord, which will render it most real. To render unity real is the work of redemption. Being a Christian, a priest, and a theologian means partaking in this unity and enabling such unity to come about tangibly for all. Pope Benedict XVI lived for this high-minded purpose.

Striving for unity is both primordial to the human condition and internal to the theological enterprise. Human thought in general, time and time again, has sought unity of some kind. Heraclitus (c. 540–c. 480 BC) apprehended the world as a constant interaction of a multitude of contraries. To him, this vibrant process is grounded in the one *Logos* that enables both cosmic vitality and integrity.[1] The *Logos* brings about a coherent symphony that allows every constituent its particular note. Plato (c. 428–c. 348 BC), in his enigmatic and challenging dialogue *Parmenides,* expanded on how the simple, common, and unitarian allows the multitude to come about: unity of the form guarantees for the human mind the recognizability of the particular in its specificity.[2] Perhaps echoing his teacher Plato, Aristotle (384–322 BC) seems to demonstrate in the *Metaphysics* the necessity of a whole in order for diversity, in its determinacy, to be appreciated at all.[3]

To the Christian imagination, Jesus Christ is the Heraclitan *Logos*, who brings about reconciliation with the source of all being: the Blessed Trinity.

According to the Church Fathers, the unity of the dynamic and creative Godhead somehow ineluctably longs to be mirrored in the redeemed world. In 1962, Ratzinger delivered a much-noted lecture on this very topic at the University of Salzburg. In and through the rich ethnic and cultural diversity of the

---

1. Heraclitus, *Fragments*, in *Die Vorsokratiker*, ed. Laura Gemelli Marciano (Darmstadt, DE: Wissenschaftliche Buchgesellschaft, 2007), 1:300–307.

2. Plato, *Parmenides* 137c–166c.

3. Aristotle, *Metaphysics* 998b–999a.

nations, a deep, underlying harmony resides, and must be lived in order for peace to come about.[4]

Ratzinger's lodestar, Augustine (354–430), is indebted to Plato's understanding of unity. The Bishop of Hippo argues that all being is constituted from an underlying oneness. This unity is not explained simply from ontological abstractions, but concretely and personally from the Eucharist. Fallen human nature partakes sacramentally in a unity with the crucified and exalted Lord, and is thereby called to live such unity in discipleship with fellow human beings.[5] It is unity with the Eucharistic Lord that brings about unity in theology, the Church, humankind, and salvation history. Ratzinger unfolds this salient feature of Christianity early on in *The Meaning of Christian Brotherhood* (1960).[6] The human and philosophical quest for unity, integrity, and wholeness finds in Jesus Christ both its enabling ground and its fulfillment.

This is completely unlike the great synthesizer and philosopher Georg Wilhelm Friedrich Hegel (1770–1831). He strove for a forced and ersatz unity in the form of an absolute spirit—one lacking both personhood and mercy, and wholly incapable of evoking adoration and virtue. Less self-assured than Hegel, Immanuel Kant (1724–1804) had earlier postulated that unity is the synthetizing achievement of the human mind that provides the condition for the possibility of insight in the first place.[7] Probably unbeknownst to Kant, he echoes Thomas Aquinas (1225–1274), who had considered unity a transcendental.[8]

Ratzinger builds upon these insights when rejecting the French scientist Jacques Monod's (1910–1976) hypothesis that the world is the chance result of a giant lottery and, therefore,

4. Joseph Ratzinger, *The Unity of the Nations: A Vision of the Church Fathers* (Washington, DC: The Catholic University of America Press, 2015).

5. Augustine, *Sermo* 227 and 272.

6. Joseph Ratzinger, *The Meaning of Christian Brotherhood*, 2nd ed. (San Francisco: Ignatius, 1993).

7. Immanuel Kant, *Critique of Pure Reason*, B 412–413.

8. Thomas Aquinas, *De Veritate* 1.1.

that the cosmos is void of personal meaning.[9] The Christian alternative of an undergirding unity to reality sounds at first vague, but Ratzinger finds it confirmed by another modern scientist: the German theoretical physicist and Nobel laureate Werner Heisenberg (1901–1976). Heisenberg, in his book *Das Teil und das Ganze* (1969), had discussed extensively, from the perspective of the natural sciences, the indispensable connection and interplay between the part and the whole.[10]

The director of Ratzinger's dissertation, Gottlieb Söhngen (1892–1971), had penned the 1952 book *The Unity of Theology*,[11] and in Ratzinger's eulogy for his director, he captures the essence of his own view of theology: "In the breadth of his thinking lay his greatness. . . . For he asks questions so comprehensively without presenting a closed synthesis. . . . He always tried to see the whole in the fragment [*das Ganze im Fragment*], to think the fragments from the whole and to design them as reflections of the whole."[12] It was precisely in seeing the whole as the vivifying source of all being, without reducing theology to a rationalistic system, that Söhngen showed himself both a believer and a scholar. The affirmation of the fragmentary nature of theology elevates the human imagination to higher plateaus.

Likewise, Ratzinger's conscious disavowal of the grand systems advanced by Hegel and neo-Scholasticism allows the greatness of his accomplishments to shine forth more luminously. Serving the "whole in fragment" permits the divine to enter into

9. Joseph Ratzinger, '*In the Beginning . . .*': *A Catholic Understanding of the Story of Creation and the Fall*, trans. Boniface Ramsey (Huntington, IN: Our Sunday Visitor, 1990).

10. Cf. the English edition, which features a somewhat misleading title: Werner Heisenberg, *Physics and Beyond: Encounters and Conversations*, trans. Arnold J. Pomerans (New York: Harper and Row, 1971).

11. Gottlieb Söhngen, *Die Einheit der Theologie, Gesammelte Abhandlungen, Aufsätze, Vorträge* (Munich: Karl Zink, 1952).

12. Joseph Ratzinger, "Der Glaube ist es der das Fragen ermöglicht," *30 Giorni*, February 1, 2006, http://www.30giorni.it/articoli´_id_10221_15.htm.

contingent reality, "unveiling and veiling yet more"[13] the divine truth. The fragment as fragment intimates the whole without taking control of it. From the Eucharist, the whole is suggested and, at the same time, is fully present in the *communio* of believers.

In DeClue's comprehensive study we encounter Ratzinger's gift of intimating and approximating the whole without reducing it to a suffocating, airtight system. This is the signal hallmark of Ratzinger's theology: a systematician without a closed system. It is this that our author Richard DeClue most ably shares with us. He felicitously demonstrates that for Ratzinger, the unity of being does not translate into a rigid theological system, as was typical of university curricula well into the mid-twentieth century. Ratzinger thereby produced a "Symphony of Truth and Charity in Freedom."[14] In the final analysis, DeClue shows us how the richness of the Blessed Trinity is "completely incompletely" refracted in his theology. This constitutes the greatness of Joseph Ratzinger / Pope Benedict XVI, qualifying him to be declared, one joyful day, a Doctor of the Church.

---

13. A celebrated line coined by Romano Guardini (1885–1968), one of the formative thinkers for the student Ratzinger in Munich. Cf. Romano Guardini, *Vom Lob des Buches*, 3rd ed. (Mainz: Matthias Grünewald, 1963).

14. Kurt Koch, "Symphonie von Wahrheit und Liebe in Freiheit," *Forum katholische Theologie* 39 (2023): 81–102.

Introduction

Aim and Outline

Joseph Ratzinger's theological corpus is massive. Before he became Pope Benedict XVI,[1] he wrote at least fifty books and penned hundreds of articles. His productivity continued after his papal election. He issued encyclicals and apostolic exhortations; he authored (though as a private theologian) the three-volume *Jesus of Nazareth* series; and he delivered numerous public addresses. Moreover, his papal and pre-papal writings collectively cover nearly every major area of theology.

However, Ratzinger never published a complete work of systematic theology that lays out how his thoughts on each topic cohere with each other. Nevertheless, it is my contention that despite the enormous breadth of his work, Ratzinger's thought is fundamentally cohesive. Accordingly, this book provides a summary of his thought on several theological topics and attempts to demonstrate their inner relation. This aim is achieved through a very intentional order of presentation.

The first couple of chapters provide background information that prepare the reader to better understand the topical chapters that follow. The first chapter considers how certain themes in Ratzinger's theological work have roots in his life experiences. In fact, some hallmarks of his more developed thought are already seen in germ during his childhood. Before delving into specific

1. The names "Ratzinger" and "Benedict XVI" will both be used throughout this book. The choice is at the author's discretion. In general, Ratzinger is used when referencing works written before his election to the papacy, while Benedict XVI is used for works written thereafter. If a description of his thought could apply to both periods, either name may be employed.

1

theological topics, it is valuable to grasp Ratzinger's overall approach to theology. Hence, the second chapter offers insights into his theological method.

In the remaining chapters, a holistic vision of Ratzinger's thought is proposed. In order to help the reader see how the various topics form a whole, I have—to the best of my ability—arranged the chapters to produce a logical flow. In this schema, the Trinity is the foundation and goal of everything else. In fact, it is my contention that the Triune God is the source of the key leitmotif undergirding Ratzinger's theology: *communion*. Everything else comes from, relates to, and is ordered back toward the loving communion of the Father, the Son, and the Holy Spirit. Ratzinger's views on creation; human nature and personhood; divine revelation; the Incarnation and salvation through the Passion, Death, and Resurrection of Christ; the Church; the liturgy and sacraments; the moral life; and the four last things, especially heaven, are all best understood through the lens of *communion*, which has its origin and end in the Triune God.[2]

As the chapters progress, I will offer comments elucidating the connections between them, especially how one chapter leads to or flows from another as well as how a given chapter either harkens back to prior chapters or anticipates aspects of following chapters. By the end, it is my hope that the reader will understand these logical connections, which I will succinctly outline in the conclusion. The unity of theology through the analogy of faith is the key principle in this enterprise. Hopefully as a consequence, the reader will gain a greater understanding of the thought of

---

2. Rather than offer a separate chapter on Mariology, this book follows the example of Vatican II insofar as it includes its discussion of Mary in other chapters, showing how she relates to various aspects of salvation history. For fuller expositions of Ratzinger's Mariology, see especially two of his books: Joseph Ratzinger, *Daughter Zion: Meditations on the Church's Marian Belief*, trans. John M. McDermott (San Francisco: Ignatius, 1983); and Hans Urs von Balthasar and Joseph Ratzinger, *Mary: The Church at the Source*, trans. Adrian J. Walker (San Francisco: Ignatius, 2005), 13–95.

Benedict XVI and—through his theology—a better grasp of the Catholic faith itself.

1

Biographical Highlights

There is no shortage of Pope Benedict XVI biographies. They are well worth the read. A comprehensive presentation of his life is thus not necessary here. Nevertheless, this chapter will discuss highlights from his life that give significant insight into his thought. Rather than sticking to a strictly chronological order, key themes in Benedict's life will be presented in thematic categories.

PIETY AND HUMILITY

Pope Benedict XVI is widely regarded for his intellectual acumen. One of the things that makes him special, however, is how his intellectual life always remained rooted in the soil of piety and humility. In this regard, Thomas Rausch recalls something noteworthy about his first meeting with Ratzinger. In 1976, when Ratzinger was still a professor at Regensburg, Rausch visited Ratzinger at home. Rausch writes, "As our visit drew to a close, he [Ratzinger] said that he had to excuse himself as he was taking part in a *Mai Andacht*. . . . It was a special devotion to Mary in the month of May, and I remember thinking that for a professor he was quite pious."[1] Ratzinger's humble and pious disposition

1. Thomas P. Rausch, *Pope Benedict XVI: An Introduction to His Theological Vision* (New York: Paulist, 2009), 8.

4

did not dwindle, even when he gained academic notoriety and rose through the ranks of the hierarchy. As Franz Niegel reports, "The pomp of being cardinal has never gone to his head. I believe he tries to live in a saintly way. There are people who are ruined by the world of scholarship, who become strange, and that was never the case with him."[2]

Ratzinger's humility was also reflected in his finances. He came from a family of meager means, and the frugality he acquired at home continued. "Later on," writes Seewald:

> Ratzinger also lived with monastic simplicity, without any luxury, and in an atmosphere that ignored and was indifferent to the essentials of comfort. When he was Prefect of the Congregation for the Doctrine of the Faith, Lufthansa once offered him a new suitcase, as his shabby old one was bad for business. In his papal apartment he decisively rejected a new desk. "He always gave away a lot of his salary," Peter Kuhn, Ratzinger's academic assistant in Tübingen, reported. When he discovered a student or young priest in financial straits, his reaction was: "Write your account number on this paper." After that, according to Kuhn, "a bank transfer was paid in every month."[3]

For Ratzinger, rising in prominence was not an excuse to dispense with humility.

The value of humility is something Ratzinger encountered in his youth. In 1934, when Ratzinger was seven years old, Brother Konrad of Parzham (1818–1894) was canonized. He had been a porter at a Capuchin monastery in Altötting, near where Ratzinger grew up. Ratzinger was impressed with the

---

2. Peter Seewald, *Benedict XVI: An Intimate Portrait*, trans. Henry Taylor and Anne Englund Nash (San Francisco: Ignatius, 2008), 101.

3. Peter Seewald, *Benedict XVI: A Life*, trans. Dinah Livingstone (London: Bloomsbury, 2020), 1:71.

celebrations surrounding this canonization. Speaking of St. Konrad, Ratzinger writes:

> In this humble and thoroughly kind man we saw what is best in our people embodied and led by faith to its most beautiful possibilities. I have often reflected since then on this remarkable disposition of Providence: that, in this century of progress and faith in science, the Church should have found herself represented most clearly in very simple people, in a Bernadette of Lourdes, for instance, or even in a Brother Konrad. . . . Is it a sign that the clear view of the essential, which is so often lacking in the "wise and prudent" (see Mt 11:25), is given in our days, too, to little ones?[4]

The contrast seen here between the "wise and the learned," on the one hand, and the faith of simple people, on the other, was also reflected in Ratzinger's experience of the rise of the Nazi regime. During that time, it was often the well-educated—doctors, lawyers, politicians, and professors—who were seduced by the malicious ideology. "But in those days," writes Ratzinger, "such rhetorical formulas hardly impressed the sober mentality of Bavarian farmers."[5]

"For a long time," Seewald reports, "the Nazis found it difficult to gain a significant number of followers in strongly Catholic rural areas."[6] Ratzinger's home region, Bavaria, was one such area. Speaking of Bavaria, Aidan Nichols relates, "There was the traditional Catholicism of an area where, by an almost exact inversion of the general pattern in Germany, nearly seventy per cent of the population had retained the old religion."[7]

4. Joseph Ratzinger, *Milestones: Memoirs 1927–1977*, trans. Erasmo Leiva-Merikakis (San Francisco: Ignatius, 1998), 9.

5. Ratzinger, 16.

6. Seewald, *Benedict XVI: A Life*, 1:39.

7. Aidan Nichols, *The Thought of Benedict XVI: An Introduction to the Theology of Joseph Ratzinger* (New York: Burns & Oates, 2005), 13.

Despite the immense power of the Nazi regime, in the end, it was the Church that perdured. For young Ratzinger, this experience confirmed his faith. Speaking of himself and his fellow seminarians after the war, he writes:

> No one doubted that the Church was the locus of all our hopes. Despite many human failings, the Church was the alternative to the destructive ideology of the brown [i.e., Nazi] rulers; in the inferno that had swallowed up the powerful, she had stood firm with a force coming to her from eternity. It had been demonstrated: The gates of hell will not overpower her. From our own experience we now knew what was meant by "the gates of hell", and we could also see with our own eyes that the house built on rock had stood firm.[8]

Hence, from a young age, Ratzinger learned the wisdom of humble, pious people and the power of faith in the face of immense evil. In his work as a theologian, he never forgot the value of piety and humility.

LITURGY

Ratzinger's piety was fed by formative liturgical experiences, which began from the day of his birth. He was born on April 16, 1927. It was Holy Saturday, and the infant Joseph was baptized almost immediately after birth with the freshly blessed water. (In those days, the Easter Vigil was celebrated on Holy Saturday morning.)

Ratzinger saw significance in the timing of his birth. "I have always been filled with thanksgiving for having had my life immersed in this way in the Easter mystery, since this could only be a sign of blessing. To be sure, it was not Easter Sunday but Holy Saturday, but, the more I reflect on it, the more this seems to

---

8. Ratzinger, *Milestones*, 42.

be fitting for the nature of our human life: we are still awaiting Easter; we are not yet standing in the full light but walking toward it full of trust."[9]

Ratzinger's parents continued to foster liturgical devotion throughout his childhood. His parents used a missal-based children's prayerbook to help him and his siblings understand the Mass. Over time, he received his own liturgical books: one for children, one for Sundays and feasts, and eventually a daily missal. From a young age, then, Ratzinger became enthralled with the beauty of the liturgy. When he was only seven years old, he wrote a letter to the Child Jesus in anticipation of Christmas in which he asked for "the *Volks-Schott* [missal], a green Mass vestment and a JESUS heart."[10] His own words speak to the profound love for the liturgy he had even as a child:

> Every new step into the liturgy was a great event for me. Each new book I was given was something precious to me, and I could not dream of anything more beautiful. It was a riveting adventure to move by degrees into the mysterious world of the liturgy, which was being enacted before us and for us there on the altar. It was becoming more and more clear to me that here I was encountering a reality that no one had simply thought up, a reality that no official authority or great individual had created. This mysterious fabric of texts and actions had grown from the faith of the Church over the centuries. It bore the whole weight of history within itself, and yet, at the same time, it was much more than the product of human history. . . . I started down the road of the liturgy, and this became a

---

9. Ratzinger, 8.

10. Archive of the Pope Benedict XVI Institute, Regensburg, quoted in Seewald, *Benedict XVI: A Life*, 1:31. On the same page, Seewald notes that on the flip side of that letter, Joseph's siblings Maria and Georg wrote their letters to the Child Jesus as well. Prefiguring his later work as a cathedral choirmaster, Georg asked for "church music and, parallel to his brother, a white Mass vestment, so they could play at being priests together," which is another foreshadowing of their lives; eventually, they would be ordained to the priesthood on the same day.

continuous process of growth into a grand reality transcending all particular individuals and generations, a reality that became an occasion for me of ever-new amazement and discovery. The inexhaustible reality of the Catholic liturgy has accompanied me through all phases of life, and so I shall have to speak of it time and again.[11]

And speak of it time and again he did. His theology of liturgy and sacraments will be explored in chapter 8. One would do well to keep in mind while reading that chapter that his thoughts about the liturgy grew from a profound love for liturgy since his youth. In fact, around the age of fourteen, Ratzinger began to translate liturgical texts from the original Latin into his native German "in an improved and more vital way."[12]

THE WAY OF BEAUTY

As attested to in the above reflections, Ratzinger saw the liturgy as beautiful. Beauty, for him, is a way of encountering the transcendent, and hence, a way of becoming aware of God. This process is sometimes called the *via pulchritudinis*, the way of beauty.[13] In his youth, Ratzinger encountered beauty in many forms: nature, music, art, and architecture.

The Ratzingers lived in rural Bavaria in southeast Germany, near the Austrian border. The youngest child, Joseph, was born in Marktl am Inn, a village that borders the Inn River (hence its name). The family had moved three times by the time Joseph was

11. Ratzinger, *Milestones*, 19–20.

12. Ratzinger, 29. Ratzinger's proficiency with languages was largely due to his schooling, which was based upon classical languages. In addition to his translation of Latin liturgical texts, while still a young student, he "had begun translating the Greek original of the Gospels into German, in order to take in the material in his own way" (Seewald, *Benedict XVI: A Life*, 1:72).

13. For a reflection on the relation between beauty and truth, see Joseph Ratzinger, "The Feeling of Things, the Contemplation of Beauty," August 24–30, 2002, vatican.va: "The beautiful is knowledge certainly, but, in a superior form, since it arouses man to the real greatness of the truth."

ten years old: to Tittmoning (1929), to Aschau am Inn (1932), and to Hufschlag on the edge of Traunstein (1937).[14] As Ratzinger recalls, their "moves occurred within a limited radius—in the triangle formed on two sides by the Inn and Salzach rivers, whose landscape and history marked my youth."[15]

Geographically, as Nichols describes, "The region is one of wooded hills, small lakes, and waterways."[16] The Ratzingers went on hikes together as a family and would sometimes cross the border into Austria. "In the fields in the fall we looked for wild lettuce, and by the Salzach in the meadows Mother showed us how to find many useful things for our nativity scene, of which we were particularly fond. . . . We often went with our parents to nearby Salzburg, where we never failed to make the pilgrimage up to Maria Plain, visit the glorious churches, and breathe in the atmosphere of this unique city."[17] In Hufschlag on the outskirts of Traunstein, their old farmhouse was bordered by a large meadow; cherry, apple, pear, and plum trees; a grove of oak trees; a pine forest; and a view of two mountains.[18] The beauty of creation that surrounded him as well as the piety of the Bavarian people made their impressions on Joseph. "In this setting, almost impossibly picture-book as it is, the young Ratzinger became aware of a possible vocation to the Catholic priesthood while still a boy. No doubt this sense was mediated by the fervent piety of the region."[19]

The grandeur of the well-designed buildings also impacted the young Ratzinger. Baroque and Salzburg-style architecture decorated his second hometown, Tittmoning, which Ratzinger describes as "my childhood's land of dreams. There is the big, even majestic, town square with its noble fountain, bordered by

14. See Rausch, *Pope Benedict XVI*, 11.
15. Ratzinger, *Milestones*, 7.
16. Nichols, *Thought of Benedict XVI*, 5.
17. Ratzinger, *Milestones*, 11–12, 24.
18. See Ratzinger, 21–22.
19. Nichols, *Thought of Benedict XVI*, 5.

the Laufen and Burghausen Gates, surrounded by the proud old houses of burghers—truly a square that would do great honor to bigger cities."[20]

A monastic church and the Ponlach Chapel, both examples of beautiful Baroque architecture, also fascinated Ratzinger. The Ponlach Chapel sat on top of a hill in the woods above the river valley. There, the natural and architectural beauty mixed with religious devotions to help form the future pontiff. "Near it [the chapel] you can hear the clear waters of the Ponlach rushing down to the valley. We three children would often make a little pilgrimage with our dear mother to this spot and allow the peace of the place to have its effect on us."[21]

These are more than mere biographical details. Looking at his childhood memories through the lens of his later works, one can see seeds of important issues in his theology. The fact that he was immersed in an almost idyllic natural landscape, which points toward the beauty of the Creator, leads him later on to recognize and to lament the antithesis: the rise of atheism in industrialized cities.[22] Similarly, the impact of beautiful architecture—especially that of churches, chapels, and shrines—foreshadows Ratzinger's later works on the liturgy and the importance of art and architecture for the life of faith. In a multitude of ways, then, the young Ratzinger saw how external beauty—natural and artistic—can move the heart, which, in turn, raises the mind to divine realities. In other words, Ratzinger's own faith developed profoundly through the *via pulchritudinis*.

Sacred music was also influential in Ratzinger's youth. After the annexation of Austria into the German Reich, Georg and Joseph Ratzinger were able to get tickets to the world-renowned Salzburg Music Festival, where they heard, among other things, Mozart's

20. Ratzinger, *Milestones*, 10.

21. Ratzinger, 11.

22. Ratzinger's observations about the impact of industrial and urban life on belief in God will be discussed in the chapter on divine revelation.

Mass in C-minor as well as a concert by the Regensburg Cathedral's boys' choir.[23] It is well known that Ratzinger remained a lifelong Mozart fan and even played piano. "Mozart, so to speak, permeated us right through; he has always moved me profoundly because he is so light and at the same time so deep."[24]

A particularly vivid expression of Joseph Ratzinger's love for sacred music is found in his book *Im Angesicht der Engel: Von der Musik im Gottesdienst* (*In the Presence of the Angels: Music in the Liturgy*): "When a Mozart Mass was sung on feast days in our Traunstein parish church, then for me as a little country boy, it was as if the heavens opened. Ahead in the sanctuary, pillars of incense rose, which the sun broke into. On the altar, the sacred rites were performed which we knew opened heaven for us. And the choir sang music that could only have come from heaven. Music which conveyed to us the angels' rejoicing over God's beauty. It brought something of that beauty down into our midst."[25] No doubt those early experiences with sacred music formed Ratzinger's notions of what is suitable for the liturgy.

As is now clear, Pope Benedict had a lifelong appreciation for beauty. He saw it as a way of expressing and encountering the divine. Thus, for him, it is something to be fostered and promoted in the Church's art, architecture, music, and liturgy.

INTELLECTUAL INFLUENCES

Shortly after the end of the war, Joseph and his brother, Georg Ratzinger, entered major seminary. This period of priestly formation was foundational for Ratzinger's intellectual development.

---

23. See Ratzinger, *Milestones*, 25.

24. Seewald, *Benedict XVI: A Life*, 1:62.

25. Quoted in Seewald, 1:182. The original work is Joseph Ratzinger, *Im Angesicht der Engel: Von der Musik im Gottesdienst* (Freiburg im Breisgau: Herder, 2008).

A wide variety of authors and professors left their mark upon his thought. As he recounts:

> We wanted not only to do theology in the narrower sense but to listen to the voices of man today. We devoured the novels of Gertrud von Le Fort, Elisabeth Langgässer, and Ernst Wiechert. Dostoevsky was one of the authors everyone read, and likewise the great Frenchmen: Claudel, Bernanos, Mauriac. We also followed closely the recent developments in the natural sciences. We thought that, with the breakthroughs made by Planck, Heisenberg, and Einstein, the sciences were once again on their way to God. . . . In the domain of theology and philosophy, the voices that moved us most directly were those of Romano Guardini, Josef Pieper, Theodor Häcker, and Peter Wust.[26]

Ratzinger was also enthralled by the literary works of Hermann Hesse, such as his *Glass Bead Game* (*Glasperlenspiel*) and *The Steppenwolf* (*Der Steppenwolf*), as well as by Aldous Huxley's *Brave New World* and George Orwell's *1984*.[27]

The philosopher and physicist from Munich, Aloys Wenzl, informed Ratzinger's studies on the intersection between philosophy, science, and religion. "Wenzl had tried to show that the deterministic world view of classical physics, which left no more room for God, had been superseded."[28] Wenzl and the giants of science mentioned above (Planck, Heisenberg, and Einstein) were not the only ones offering an enlivening rapprochement between faith and science. "Didn't the findings of leading researchers sound completely different from the Enlightenment mantras, which proclaimed that progress in the sciences meant the end of the old faith in God? Physicists like the German Pascual Jordan,

---

26. Ratzinger, *Milestones*, 42–43.
27. See Seewald, *Benedict XVI: A Life*, 1:180–187, 189–191.
28. Seewald, 1:167.

the co-founder of quantum mechanics, were suddenly talking about a 'creator God.'"[29] Such educational experiences fueled his later rebuttals to scientific reductionism, busting the myth of a conflict between science and faith.

The desire for a holistic approach to education that incorporates literature, science, philosophy, and theology is part of Ratzinger's genius as a thinker. His thought is characterized by concern both for maintaining a solid foundation in Catholic tradition and for addressing the problems and questions of contemporary humanity.

In order to understand the world of today, Ratzinger saw the need to engage with modern philosophy, and he was eager to do so. In this pursuit, Ratzinger gained an important mentor in Alfred Läpple, a prefect at the seminary in Freising who was working on a dissertation about Cardinal Newman's understanding of conscience.

Through Läpple, Newman influenced Ratzinger as well.

> Newman's teaching on conscience became an important foundation for theological personalism, which was drawing us all in its sway. Our image of the human being as well as our image of the Church was permeated by this point of departure. . . . Precisely because Newman interpreted the existence of the human being from conscience, that is, from the relationship between God and the soul, was it clear that this personalism is not individualism.[30]

Newman's understanding of conscience, then, was formative for Joseph Ratzinger's own thought. For Newman and Ratzinger alike—in contrast to misconceptions prevalent in our own

---

29. Seewald, 1:167.

30. Joseph Ratzinger, "Discorso introduttivo alla III giornata del Simposio di Newman," *Euntes Docete* 43 (1990): 432–433, quoted in Andrzej Proniewski, "Joseph Ratzinger's Philosophical Theology of the Person," *Rocznik Teologii Katholickiej* 17, no. 3 (2018): 222–223.

day—the importance of conscience cannot be reduced to mere personal tastes or inclinations. As Pablo Blanco Sarto explains, "This appeal to the voice of conscience on Newman's part does not suppose taking refuge in one's own subjectivity, but is, rather, a constant search for truth in the light of reason itself."[31]

Läpple's influence on Ratzinger was multifaceted, extending far beyond introducing him to Newman. "With his far-ranging knowledge of the history of philosophy and his taste for argumentation, Läpple became a great stimulus for us."[32] Läpple's dissertation director was Theodor Steinbüchel, who had written two volumes on the philosophical foundations of moral theology.

Through the works of Theodor Steinbüchel, Ratzinger "found a first-rate introduction to the thought of Heidegger and Jaspers as well as to the philosophies of Nietzsche, Klages, and Bergson."[33] Steinbüchel "gave a comprehensive overview of contemporary philosophy, which I sought to understand and inhabit."[34] Ratzinger also studied Edmund Husserl, Jean Anouilh, and Jean-Paul Sartre.[35]

Above all, Steinbüchel offered a foray into the realm of personalism, which was then augmented by the works of Martin Buber, a Jewish thinker. "This encounter with personalism was for me a spiritual experience that left an essential mark, especially since I spontaneously associated such personalism with the

31. Pablo Blanco Sarto, *La Teología de Joseph Ratzinger: Una introducción* (Madrid: Pelícano, 2011), 19. Translations from foreign language sources, unless otherwise noted, are my own. N.b.: I think that Pablo Blanco Sarto's book is among the best secondary resources available on the thought of Pope Benedict XVI. It covers a wider range of topics than many others, and—although following a different order of presentation than this book—it is organized intentionally and logically.

32. Ratzinger, *Milestones*, 43.

33. Ratzinger, 43.

34. Benedict XVI and Peter Seewald, *Last Testament: In His Own Words*, trans. Jacob Phillips (London: Bloomsbury, 2016), 75–76.

35. See Seewald, *Benedict XVI: A Life*, 1:164–165.

thought of Saint Augustine, who in his *Confessions* had struck me with the power of all his human passion and depth."[36]

Personalism became an important aspect of Ratzinger's own thought. In personalism, Ratzinger found a way to synthesize elements of medieval and modern thought as well as to address his own questions. In an interview with Peter Seewald, Ratzinger remarked that "just as I had my questions, my doubts, and didn't simply want to learn and take on a closed system, I also wanted to understand the theological thinkers of the Middle Ages and modernity anew, and to proceed from this. This is where personalism . . . particularly struck me, and seemed to be the right starting point of both philosophical and theological thought."[37]

Martin Buber's dialogical personalism influenced Ratzinger's own works about God. "Ratzinger shared Buber's approach when he constantly stressed that God did not come to people as an abstract definition: God was a 'You'. God accepted people, communicated with them, either in prayer or in the liturgy."[38] The I–You relation is an important theme in Ratzinger's works on God and the Church, as we shall see.

Like his predecessor as the bishop of Rome, John Paul II, Ratzinger had a fondness for the thought of Max Scheler, a convert to Catholicism from orthodox Judaism. Scheler thought depersonalization was a main force behind contemporary people's sense of separation from God and that humanity's glory is found precisely in cooperating with God. Scheler contrasted his thought with Kant and "was excited by Edmund Husserl's ideas, finally getting back to the 'objective' and the 'essence' of things."[39]

Ratzinger's philosophical education was also greatly enhanced by a four-semester course taught by Jakob Fellermeier, "who provided us with a comprehensive overview of the intellectual

36. Ratzinger, *Milestones*, 44.
37. Benedict XVI and Seewald, *Last Testament*, 76.
38. Seewald, *Benedict XVI: A Life*, 1:174–175.
39. Seewald, 1:162.

struggle, beginning with Socrates and the pre-Socratics up until the present. This gave me a foundation in philosophy for which I am still grateful today."[40]

Unfortunately, Ratzinger did not have such a good experience with the philosophy of St. Thomas Aquinas. As Tracey Rowland reports, "Ratzinger was never enchanted by pre-conciliar Thomism and he has been quite frank about this in several interviews."[41] The extent to which Ratzinger's struggles with Aquinas were rooted in the Angelic Doctor's works themselves or due to the manner in which they were taught is not entirely clear; perhaps it was both. As Ratzinger himself openly admits:

> I had difficulties in penetrating the thought of Thomas Aquinas, whose crystal-clear logic seemed to me to be too closed in on itself, too impersonal and ready-made. This may also have had something to do with the fact that Arnold Wilmsen, the philosopher who taught us Thomas, presented us with a rigid, neoscholastic Thomism that was simply too far afield from my own questions. . . . His enthusiasm and deep convictions were impressive, but now it seemed that he himself no longer asked questions but limited himself to defending passionately, against all questions, what he had found.[42]

Thus, the Thomism Ratzinger encountered stood in stark contrast to the personalism and openness to new questions that were so important for his own thinking.

It is safe to say, then, that Benedict XVI is not a Thomist. As will be discussed in more detail later, Ratzinger's thought is much more deeply rooted in St. Augustine and St. Bonaventure than in St. Thomas Aquinas. However, it would be an

40. Ratzinger, *Milestones*, 45.

41. Tracey Rowland, *Ratzinger's Faith: The Theology of Pope Benedict XVI* (New York: Oxford University Press, 2008), 2.

42. Ratzinger, *Milestones*, 44.

over-exaggeration—if not downright false—to say that Ratzinger is *anti-*Thomist.

In this connection, Joseph Ratzinger would treat the question of the relationship between Bonaventure, Augustine, Aristotle, and Aquinas in his *Habilitationsschrift*,[43] where he makes the claim (contra Étienne Gilson) that St. Bonaventure was not anti-Thomist.[44] The same can be said of Ratzinger himself. As Fergus Kerr notes, "'Non-Thomistic' is one thing; to regard Ratzinger as 'anti-Thomist' would, of course, be absurd."[45] Thus, Joseph Ratzinger's preference for the thought of St. Augustine and St. Bonaventure does not mean he rejects St. Thomas Aquinas' thought in itself.

On the contrary, Ratzinger's work with the writings of St. Thomas Aquinas was not entirely negative. In fact, "His first work was a German translation of the *Quaestio disputata* of St Thomas on charity, put together in 1946, and throughout his studies he makes reference to the stance of St Thomas whenever he thinks there is a valuable insight. He is not shy about using Aquinas as a source."[46]

Again, Alfred Läpple was influential here. Läpple was the one who assigned the translation of Aquinas' *Quaestio disputata de caritate* ("Disputed Questions on Charity") to the young Ratzinger. At that time, there was no German edition of that work.[47] The final text was about one hundred pages, and Ratzinger learned a lot from the project. He was grateful to Läpple for the benefits the assignment afforded him. As Seewald relates, "Through it he learned how Thomas constructed his writings, how he formulated

43. In Germany, after one completes a doctorate, it is common to seek a postdoctoral degree: a *Habilitation*. It is achieved through writing and successfully defending what amounts to a second dissertation, called a *Habilitationsschrift*.

44. See Joseph Ratzinger, *The Theology of History in St. Bonaventure*, trans. Zachary Hayes (Chicago: Franciscan Herald, 1989), 136.

45. Fergus Kerr, *Twentieth-Century Catholic Theologians: From Neoscholasticism to Nuptial Mystery* (Malden, MA: Blackwell, 2007), 187.

46. Rowland, *Ratzinger's Faith*, 4.

47. See Seewald, *Benedict XVI: A Life*, 1:164.

ideas and argued. Five decades later, he wrote to Läpple: 'By giving me the job of translating St. Thomas' *Quaestio disputata* on love, you . . . led me into the sources and taught me to create from first hand and be schooled by the Masters themselves.'"[48] This methodology of working with the masters themselves would become a hallmark of the *ressourcement* movement in which Ratzinger was a key figure.

In addition to assigning Ratzinger the translation of Aquinas' work and introducing him to Steinbüchel's thought, Läpple and Ratzinger also shared literary interests. In particular, they both had an appreciation for Romanticism. That fact should not be surprising, given Ratzinger's own sensitivity and interest in the whole person, not just pure logic. One book that Ratzinger and Läpple discussed with each other positively was Rilke's *Stundenbuch* (*Book of Hours*). As Läpple recalls, "With Rilke it was also that softness, almost too soft, the emotional side, which attracted us."[49] Goethe, especially *Faust*, was another favorite for them.

Arguably the most important influence that Alfred Läpple had on Joseph Ratzinger was introducing him to the works of Henri de Lubac. "In the fall of 1949, Alfred Läpple had given me *Catholicism*, perhaps Henri de Lubac's most significant work, in the masterful translation by Hans Urs von Balthasar.[50] This book was for me a key reading event. It gave me not only a new and deeper connection with the thought of the Fathers but also a new way of looking at theology and faith as such. Faith had here become an interior contemplation and, precisely by thinking with the Fathers, a present reality."[51] The impact of de Lubac upon Ratzinger would be hard to overestimate. "With de Lubac, whom

48. Seewald, 1:165–166.

49. Seewald, 1:177. Seewald's quote comes from a personal interview with Läpple.

50. About twenty-three years later, in 1972, Joseph Ratzinger cofounded the journal *Communio* along with both Henri de Lubac and Hans Urs von Balthasar. For a timeline of Pope Benedict XVI's life, see *The Pope Benedict XVI Reader* (Park Ridge, IL: Word on Fire Institute, 2021), xiii.

51. Ratzinger, *Milestones*, 98.

he [Ratzinger] described as his most important and formative theologian (besides Hans Urs von Balthasar), he had experienced the joy 'of being able to see Christianity released from its rather stale formulations and newly embedded in modern life.'"[52]

De Lubac particularly impacted Ratzinger's ecclesiology. Through de Lubac, Ratzinger gained a greater appreciation for the communal/social dimension of the Christian faith. Through another book by de Lubac, *Corpus Mysticum*, Ratzinger found the deep roots of this *communio* ecclesiology, "in which a new understanding of the unity of Church and Eucharist opened up to me beyond the insights I had already received."[53]

After two years of studies devoted mostly to philosophy,[54] which ended in the summer of 1947, Ratzinger had to make a decision about where to go for the higher theological studies portion of his priestly formation. Normally, the seminarians would study with the theology faculty in Freising. However, Ratzinger "decided to ask the bishop to allow me to study in Munich. . . . My hope was to become more fully familiar with the intellectual debates of our time by working at the university, so as some day to be able to dedicate myself completely to theology as a profession."[55]

There in Munich, Ratzinger met Hubert Luthe, a fellow student who was the same age. Later, Luthe became the secretary for Cardinal Joseph Frings, who was responsible for getting Ratzinger appointed as an official *peritus* at the Second Vatican Council. Thus, Luthe and Ratzinger's working relationship extended beyond their student years.[56]

Ratzinger's main subjects were fundamental theology and

---

52. Seewald, *Pope Benedict XVI: A Life*, 1:233.

53. Ratzinger, *Milestones*, 98.

54. I say "mostly" philosophy, because, as Seewald notes, "The subjects in Joseph's philosophy course were general philosophy, history of philosophy, secular history, biology, educational theory, and psychology" (Seewald, *Pope Benedict XVI: A Life*, 1:145).

55. Ratzinger, *Milestones*, 47.

56. See Seewald, *Benedict XVI: A Life*, 1:208.

dogmatic theology. Of course, he also took courses in other theological fields, such as biblical theology. During his theological
studies in Munich, Ratzinger gained further influences, both positive and negative.

Friedrich Wilhelm Maier, professor of New Testament in
Munich, was formative for Ratzinger. According to Ratzinger,
biblical exegesis—especially of the New Testament—is the soul
of theology. He learned a great deal about scriptural interpretation from Maier, even if he was cognizant of Maier's weaknesses as well. Positively, Maier helped Ratzinger see value in the
historical-critical method. On the other hand, Ratzinger also perceived the limitations of that liberal method. He saw in Maier
someone who viewed dogma as a shackle to which he submitted
begrudgingly. By contrast, Ratzinger saw dogma "as the living
source that made knowledge of the truth possible in the first
place."[57] Thus, Ratzinger sought a fruitful balance between approaches to exegesis, as we will discuss in more detail in chapter 2.

For Old Testament studies, Ratzinger learned from Friedrich
Stummer. Through those studies, the Old Testament became precious to Ratzinger, and he began to see the inherent link between
the two testaments. "The New Testament," writes Ratzinger, "is
nothing other than an interpretation of 'the Law, the Prophets,
and the Writings' found from or contained in the story of Jesus."[58]

Josef Pascher, a pastoral theologian, led Ratzinger to be
more open to the liturgical movement, about which he had been
quite skeptical initially. "In many of its representatives I sensed a
one-sided rationalism and historicism that . . . exhibited a remarkable coldness. . . . I was bothered by the narrow-mindedness of
many of the movement's followers, who wanted to recognize only
_one form of the liturgy as valid."[59] Despite these concerns, Pascher

---

57. Ratzinger, *Milestones*, 57.

58. Ratzinger, 53.

59. Ratzinger, 56–57. Perhaps in this statement against seeing only one form of the liturgy
as valid, we can detect an early premonition of one reason Pope Benedict XVI allowed for greater

won him over to the liturgical movement through his instruction and "the reverential manner in which he taught us to celebrate the liturgy in keeping with its deepest nature. . . . Just as I learned to understand the New Testament as being the soul of all theology, so too I came to see the liturgy as being its living element, without which it would necessarily shrivel up."[60] The Scriptures and the liturgy continued to be major emphases of Ratzinger's theology throughout his life and into his pontificate.

Some of the early reticence he had about the liturgical movement, however, also wound up being accurate. He was quite forlorn about how the liturgy would be treated after the Second Vatican Council in unexpected ways. What he saw in the Vatican II document on the liturgy, *Sacrosanctum Concilium*, and what he observed in the concrete reforms actually enacted were not the same in his estimation. The latter, in his view, had dire consequences. "I was not able to foresee that the negative sides of the liturgical movement would afterward reemerge with redoubled strength, almost to the point of pushing the liturgy toward its own self-destruction."[61]

On a more positive note, Gottlieb Söhngen was arguably the most important figure in Ratzinger's theological formation. He directed both Ratzinger's doctoral dissertation and *Habilitationsschrift*. The former was a work in ecclesiology on *The People and the House of God in Augustine's Doctrine of the Church* (*Volk und Haus Gottes in Augustins Lehre von der Kirche*). The latter was originally on St. Bonaventure's understanding of revelation and theology of history, but it wound up being drastically reduced to *The Theology of History in St. Bonaventure*, omitting the parts on revelation for reasons to be discussed in more detail later. Through his intense work on those two massive projects under the direction of Söhngen, Ratzinger gained a greater mastery and lifelong

access to the Extraordinary Form of the Mass.

60. Ratzinger, 57.
61. Ratzinger, 57.

appreciation for St. Augustine and St. Bonaventure. They have always remained central figures in his theology.

Söhngen was somewhat of an eclectic figure with interests that ranged widely. Ratzinger himself would also become a fairly eclectic theologian, drawing from a wide range of sources. The ability to bring those varied sources to bear in a unified way is part of his genius. No doubt Söhngen's example helped form Ratzinger, who has emulated Söhngen's method. "Characteristic of Söhngen above all was the fact that he always developed his thought on the basis of the sources themselves, beginning with Aristotle and Plato, then on to Clement of Alexandria and Augustine, Anselm, Bonaventure, and Thomas, all the way to Luther and finally the Tübingen theologians of the last century. Pascal and Newman, too, were among his favorite authors. . . . He always asked the question concerning the truth of the matter and hence the question concerning the immediate reality of what is believed."[62] We will discuss Ratzinger's theological method more in the next chapter, but this description of Söhngen does provide an apt foretaste.

The affinity for St. Augustine and St. Bonaventure that Ratzinger developed in his studies provided a counterbalance to other approaches to theology that were more common at the time, such as neo-Scholasticism. As Rowland describes Ratzinger's thought, "The Augustinian-Bonaventurian emphasis on love provides an antidote to the tendency of some scholastics, particularly the late nineteenth-century Neo-Scholastics, so heavily influenced by the intellectualism of Aristotle, to neglect this dimension."[63] Because his dissertation on St. Augustine and his *Habilitationsschrift* on St. Bonaventure were formative for his own thinking, it is important to mention the biographical details of both.

---

62. Ratzinger, 56.
63. Rowland, *Ratzinger's Faith*, 3.

First, Ratzinger did not choose the topic of his doctoral dissertation. Each year, the theology faculty proposed a theme as part of a competition. Students who entered the competition were given nine months to complete a dissertation on the specified theme. The winner would receive a small sum of money and—more importantly—an automatic acceptance of the dissertation with the distinction *Summa cum laude*. In 1950, Gottlieb Söhngen chose the topic "The People and the House of God in Augustine's Doctrine of the Church," and he encouraged Joseph to enter the competition. Ratzinger had already taken Söhngen's seminar on Augustine and felt confident he could do the work.[64]

He worked on the draft intensely during a semester break from July to October 1951. At the end of October, he was ordained to the subdiaconate and diaconate and then had to engage intensely with final preparations for priestly ordination, while still working on the dissertation. It was a lot to accomplish at the same time. His siblings were a great help to Joseph. His brother took care of most of the practical details for their ordination and first Masses, while his sister prepared a typed copy of his work, enabling him to submit the dissertation before the deadline.[65] The hard work paid off, as Joseph Ratzinger won the competition.

Ratzinger related to the writings of St. Augustine, who grappled personally with difficult questions and feverishly sought after the truth with a tremendous humility, due to the recognition of his own many grave sins. He combined philosophical genius with poetic expression to generate deep reflections on the truth about God and humanity. "St. Augustine was a passionate seeker of truth. . . . Philosophy, especially that of a Platonic stamp, led him even closer to Christ, revealing to him the existence of the *Logos* or creative reason," Pope Benedict XVI remarks. "Augustine converted to Christ who is truth and love, followed him throughout

64. See Ratzinger, *Milestones*, 97.
65. See Ratzinger, 99.

his life and became a model for every human being, for all of us in search of God. . . . Even today, as in his time, humanity needs to know and above all to live this fundamental reality: God is love, and the encounter with him is the only response to the restlessness of the human heart."[66] Benedict XVI was always attracted to the cooperation of a robust intellectual search for truth with the full force of a loving heart expressed in profoundly personal terms that he found in St. Augustine. The symbiosis of mind and heart, of intellect and will, of truth and love is a characteristic shared by St. Augustine and Benedict XVI alike.

His early work on Augustine's ecclesiology is important for understanding Ratzinger's theology. In his conversion process, Augustine wrestled with philosophical questions, including questions about skepticism and authority. In response, faith became a determinative aspect of Augustine's thought. Love also played a large role. "Here Ratzinger identifies two main elements that form the *Ansätze*, 'starting-points' of Augustinian ecclesiology. Augustine's reflections on the concept of faith will be vital for his understanding of the Church as *people* of God. By contrast, his concept of love is more important for his portrait of the Church as the *house* of God: the other wing of the diptych which the title of Ratzinger's thesis evokes."[67] The issues of faith, charity (love), and ecclesial unity have remained an integral part of Ratzinger's own ecclesiology.

Additionally, Ratzinger is keen to maintain the integration of both metaphysical and salvation-historical views in the realm of theology. Both aspects are found in Augustine's corpus. Most importantly, Ratzinger adopts from Augustine "the union in the Church of 'inner' and 'outer', holiness and visible—even governmental—structure, the key to which union is the Eucharist."[68]

---

66. Benedict XVI, General Audience, February 27, 2008, vatican.va.

67. Nichols, *Thought of Benedict XVI*, 32–33.

68. Nichols, 37. Nichols notes that Ratzinger sees Tertullian as influencing Augustine on this point but without the dualism that led to Tertullian's eventual rupture with the Catholic

Eucharistic ecclesiology, as we will see in a later chapter, is the best description of Ratzinger's understanding of the Church. Both Augustine and de Lubac were highly influential on Ratzinger in this regard. "The Christian is the *communicator*, conjoined with Christ in the unity of the body of Christ, itself at once the Church and the eucharistic sacrament."[69]

A key element in Ratzinger's Eucharistic ecclesiology is the Church's universality, which is reflective of Augustine's own emphasis. "Augustine's defence of the Catholic Church against the Donatists consisted in the claim that the true Church must be *ecclesia omnium gentium*, the 'Church of all nations.'"[70] With these examples, it becomes clear how Ratzinger's dissertation on Augustine is reflected in Ratzinger's own later works in ecclesiology, which are among the best and most well-known of his theological writings.

Shortly after turning in his dissertation, Ratzinger was ordained to the priesthood alongside his brother, Georg, on the Feast of Sts. Peter and Paul, June 29, 1951. On August 1 of the same year, Ratzinger began his assignment as an assistant pastor in the Munich parish of the Precious Blood. The pastor was Fr. Blumschein, who was a good example to the newly ordained priest, especially in his servant mentality.

Fourteen short months after beginning his parish assignment, the young priest was reassigned back to the academy, beginning on October 1, 1952. He became an instructor to seminarians in their final year. This transition back into higher education led to interior ambivalence for Ratzinger. "On the one hand, this was the solution I had desired, the one that would enable me to return to my theological work, which I loved so much. On the other

faith via his adoption of Montanism. Cyprian was helpful to that end by his emphasis on the unity of the Church through hierarchical structure. Alas, Ratzinger also sees a devolution in Eucharistic ecclesiology starting with Cyprian that led to the loss of a robust Eucharistic ecclesiology in the later Middle Ages. See Nichols, 38–39.

69. Nichols, 38.

70. Nichols, 41. Dan. 2:35 and Luke 24:46–47 serve as biblical bases here.

hand, I suffered a great deal, especially in the first year, from the loss of all the human contacts and experiences afforded me by the pastoral ministry. In fact, I even began to think I would have done better to remain in parish work."[71]

Ratzinger did have some pastoral work alongside his academic duties. He presided over liturgies at the cathedral and heard confessions. So, Ratzinger was not totally removed from the care for souls. But his main work was to finish his doctorate. With the dissertation long behind him, Ratzinger still had to complete a series of oral and written examinations. Finally, in July of 1953, Ratzinger completed his studies and became an official Doctor of Theology.

As if earning a doctorate is not hard enough, in Germany, there is a further degree called a *Habilitation*. It basically involves writing a second dissertation, called a *Habilitationsschrift* (habilitation writing). Ratzinger began this work almost immediately.

Since Ratzinger had written his dissertation on a Church Father (St. Augustine) in the area of ecclesiology, Söhngen recommended that, for his *Habilitationsschrift*, Ratzinger should write on a medieval, Scholastic theologian in the area of fundamental theology. Doing so would expand Ratzinger's expertise regarding theological specialties and allow him to engage with different eras of Catholic thought. St. Bonaventure was determined to be a fitting choice, and so Ratzinger began to work on St. Bonaventure's understanding of revelation and theology of history. His investigation into St. Bonaventure's thought proved illuminating for Ratzinger: "New worlds opened up as I made progress with my work."[72] He turned in his first typed draft to the theology faculty of the University of Munich in the fall of 1955.[73]

Söhngen read Ratzinger's work and gave his enthusiastic approval. Ratzinger's *Habilitationsschrift* still needed to go through

71. Ratzinger, *Milestones*, 102.
72. Ratzinger, 104.
73. See Ratzinger, 105.

a reader, in this case, Michael Schmaus. Schmaus told Ratzinger that "he had to reject my *habilitation* thesis because it did not meet the pertinent scholarly standards."[74]

One naturally wonders what "scholarly standards" Schmaus deemed Ratzinger to have failed to meet. After all, Ratzinger was a star pupil, and his academically accomplished *Habilitation* director, Söhngen, found the work to be exemplary. Unfortunately, Schmaus' specific criticisms will never be known in detail. He had written them directly on the typed copy of the work itself, which he gave to Ratzinger. That copy with Schmaus' handwritten critical notes no longer exists; Ratzinger burned it in an oven.[75]

Despite not accepting Schmaus' criticisms of the original work, Ratzinger—again exemplifying his humility—saw the trial of passing his postdoctoral degree as somehow good for him personally.[76] As he told Seewald, "I believe that it is dangerous for a young person simply to go from achieving goal after goal, generally being praised along the way. So it is good for a young person to experience his limit, occasionally to be dealt with critically, to suffer his way through a period of negativity, to recognize his own limits himself, not simply to win victory after victory. . . . Then he will not simply judge others hastily and stay aloof, but rather accept them positively, in his labours and his weaknesses."[77] In other words, experiencing such humiliation helps keep one grounded and less prone to being egotistical; it also enables one to be more sympathetic and merciful to others and their failures.

In the end, the faculty of the university had decided that Ratzinger would be given an opportunity to revise the text to bring it up to the expected standards. Ratzinger made an important observation that gave him an easy way around the problem. The vast majority of Schmaus' criticism was levied against the

---

74. Ratzinger, *Milestones*, 107.
75. See Benedict XVI and Seewald, *Last Testament*, 95.
76. See Ratzinger, *Milestones*, 112–113.
77. Benedict XVI and Seewald, *Last Testament*, 95.

first two parts of his work, which discussed Bonaventure's understanding of revelation. The third and final part, which focused on Bonaventure's theology of history, was relatively unscathed. Hence, Ratzinger simply removed the earlier parts and with some revision used the third part as the core of the whole work. Ratzinger's new plan made it possible to be done in only about two weeks, surprising the faculty. He submitted it in October and found out the following February that it had been accepted.[78]

JOSEPH RATZINGER'S ACADEMIC AND ECCLESIAL CAREERS

Shortly thereafter, Ratzinger took a lecturer position at the nearby University of Munich, before returning to Freising as a professor of dogmatic and fundamental theology in January 1958.[79] In 1959, Ratzinger took a chair in fundamental theology at the University of Bonn, near Cologne. In 1963, he moved to the University of Münster until 1966. From 1966 to 1969, Ratzinger taught at the University of Tübingen. Ratzinger's final and longest stint as a professor was at the University of Regensburg, in his beloved home region of Bavaria (1969–1977). On March 24, 1977, Ratzinger was consecrated as the Archbishop of Munich and Freising, being designated as a cardinal by Pope Paul VI on June 27 of the same year.[80]

Ratzinger's humility made him hesitant about accepting the appointment as archbishop, which he had not anticipated, expected, or even wanted. The apostolic nuncio informing him of his appointment allowed Ratzinger to consult with his confessor before rendering his decision. "So," Ratzinger writes, "I went to Professor Auer, who had very realistic knowledge of my limitations, both theological and human. I surely expected him to

78. See Ratzinger, *Milestones*, 110–111.
79. See Ratzinger, 112.
80. See *Benedict XVI Reader*, xiii.

advise me to decline. But to my great surprise he said without much reflection: 'You must accept.'"[81] Still uneasy with the prospect, Ratzinger accepted.

Ratzinger's outlook for the work he had and would later undertake is encapsulated in the episcopal motto he chose: "Co-workers of the Truth." This motto means, in Ratzinger's own words, "to follow the truth, to be at its service. And, because in today's world the theme of truth has all but disappeared, because truth appears to be too great for man and yet everything falls apart if there is no truth, for these reasons this motto also seemed timely in the good sense of the word."[82]

As if being named a cardinal-archbishop were not enough, in short order the pope wanted to promote him even higher within the Church's hierarchy. A mix of his humility and his concern for the Bavarian people under his care led Ratzinger to resist such promotion. He felt that it would be unfair to the people of his diocese to lose their archbishop after such a short period of time. Thus, Ratzinger turned down a call to head the Congregation for Catholic Education. Eventually, however, Pope John Paul II, despite Ratzinger's objections, appointed the Bavarian cardinal as the prefect for the Congregation for the Doctrine of the Faith on November 25, 1981.[83]

After this, Ratzinger's elevations continued. In 2002, Ratzinger was made Dean of the College of Cardinals. Then, on April 19, 2005, Ratzinger was elected as the 265th pope, taking the name Benedict XVI.[84] This, too, was something Ratzinger had not expected or wanted.

Famously, Benedict XVI shocked the world when, on February 11, 2013, he declared his intention to resign the papacy,

81. Ratzinger, *Milestones*, 152.
82. Ratzinger, 153.
83. See Seewald, *An Intimate Portrait*, 212.
84. See *Benedict XVI Reader*, xiii.

which went into effect on February 28 of the same year. What are we to make of that surprising decision?

First, it is illuminating to note that his resignation announcement was not the first time he had tried to retire to a life of research, writing, and prayer. In fact, on multiple occasions, Ratzinger had tried to retire as Prefect for the Congregation of the Doctrine of the Faith. In 1986, he made the case that since he had served for five years, his term was up. John Paul II dismissed the idea. Then, in 1991, after suffering a brain hemorrhage, he again pleaded to be dismissed from his onerous role. Yet again, John Paul II denied the request. Later, the pope preemptively told Ratzinger to not even bother asking, insisting that as long as he was pope, he would not allow Ratzinger to leave his post.[85] I think this is important, because, after becoming pope, the only person who could deny his request to retire would be himself. Eventually, he granted himself the permission to do what he had already wanted to do for a very long time: retire, study, and prepare his soul for eternity.

Additionally, as mentioned before, Ratzinger never wanted to become pope. He was perhaps one of the few people who did not see it as a real possibility during the conclave that elected him. "Of course I'd been mentioned a lot beforehand. But I really wasn't able to take it seriously. I thought it couldn't happen, that it was unreasonable."[86] When he was elected, he compared that moment to an execution: "The thought of the guillotine occurred to me: Now it falls down and hits you."[87]

I think Pope Benedict XVI's humility—which we have highlighted repeatedly in this book—also played a role. In the end, I think he felt that he needed the Church more than the Church

85. See Benedict XVI and Seewald, *Last Testament*, 174–175.

86. Benedict XVI and Seewald, 183.

87. Benedict XVI and Peter Seewald, *Light of the World: The Pope, the Church, and the Signs of the Times*, trans. Michael J. Miller and Adrian J. Walker (San Francisco: Ignatius, 2010), 3. See also Benedict XVI and Seewald, *Last Testament*, 184–185.

needed him. Still more, I think he saw himself as being a hindrance, honestly thinking that someone younger would be better able to manage the huge task of leading the Church throughout the world. He genuinely thought he was doing what was best for the Church.

In this regard, I think Benedict XVI exhibited a virtue complementary to that embodied by his predecessor Pope St. John Paul II. The latter was an example of perseverance and endurance, carrying on to the very bitter end. John Paul II's example of working tirelessly even as he contended with the deteriorating effects of Parkinson's disease was certainly a holy example of faithful long-suffering. In many ways, it evokes the image of Jesus carrying his own cross on the way to Calvary. Benedict XVI, on the other hand, evokes another image, found in John the Baptist's humble words: "He must increase, but I must decrease" (John 3:30). Benedict was asking himself in all humility whether he remained the best person for the role of chief shepherd of the Church, or whether it would be better to pass the baton on to another who could better serve the Church. Together, both pontiffs show how different persons can exemplify different virtues according to their unique personalities and self-awareness.

Benedict XVI passed away on December 31, 2022. Given his sentiments about his birth, I think he would have found it very appropriate that he died "on the last day."

JOSEPH RATZINGER AT THE SECOND VATICAN COUNCIL

On January 25, 1959, Pope John XXIII announced his intention to convoke an ecumenical council, and more than three years of preparation ensued. A few months after this unexpected announcement, Ratzinger moved to the University of Bonn, near Cologne. The Archbishop of Cologne at the time was Cardinal

Josef Frings, one of the eldest and most senior ranking members of the College of Cardinals. Cardinal Frings and Ratzinger developed a good rapport with one another, and Frings relied heavily upon Ratzinger both prior to and during the Second Vatican Council.

Cardinal Frings was asked to give a speech comparing the situation and circumstances of Vatican I with those of the upcoming council. Frings asked Ratzinger to write a draft to help him prepare. Frings was deeply impressed with Ratzinger's text and decided to use it—in Italian translation from Ratzinger's German—as his own speech, which he gave on November 20, 1961, in Genoa, Italy. Before delivering the speech, Frings gave copies of the German version to "his fellow German bishops at their meeting at Fulda, August 29–30, 1961."[88]

Pope John XXIII read the Italian version, much to his delight. He "summoned Card. Frings to a private audience to thank and commend him for setting forth ideas which agreed with ways in which he, Pope John, saw the situation and tasks of the coming Council."[89] This shows that Ratzinger's thought aligned well with the purposes for which the pope had called the council.

Cardinal Frings was eventually appointed as a member of the Central Preparatory Commission (CPC) for Vatican II. As the time for the council approached, Frings' dissatisfaction with the preparations increased. In order to help mitigate such frustrations, Frings recommended to the CPC that an introductory constitution be prepared to explain the council's goals. He asked Ratzinger to write just such a draft, which Ratzinger completed

---

88. Jared Wicks, "Six Texts by Prof. Joseph Ratzinger as *Peritus* before and during Vatican Council II," *Gregorianum* 89, no. 2 (2008): 234. From 1945 to 1965, Cardinal Frings was the Chairman of the Fulda Conference of Catholic Bishops, redesignated in 1966 as the German Bishops' Conference (*Deutsche Bischofskonferenz*).

89. Wicks, "Six Texts," 235. For a presentation of the text, including an outline and summary of its contents with English translations of select portions, see Wicks, "Six Texts," 253–261. For the full German text, see Joseph Ratzinger, *Joseph Ratzinger: Gesammelte Schriften* [henceforth, JRGS] 7/1, ed. Gerhard Ludwig Müller (Freiburg: Herder, 2012), 73–91.

in June of 1962.[90] While no such introductory constitution was adopted by the council, its contents are a valuable resource for understanding Vatican II and Ratzinger's perspectives about its purpose.

A couple of months after Ratzinger finished that draft, Cardinal Frings once again sought Ratzinger's assistance. In August of 1962, seven preparatory schemas were sent to the members of the council for them to review and offer their impressions and recommendations before the commencement of the council in October. Frings sent his copy of the schemas to Ratzinger and asked him to review them. Ratzinger submitted his analyses of the texts (in Latin) to Frings on September 14, 1962. Only three days later, Cardinal Frings—sufficiently pleased with Ratzinger's evaluations—submitted their contents to Cardinal Cicognani (the papal secretary of state).[91]

In Ratzinger's opinion, out of the seven draft schemas, only two of them were suited for the council without significant revision. Additionally, some of his remarks regarding a draft text (or schema) on revelation (*De Fontibus Revelationis*) echo elements of the original version of his *Habilitationsschrift* that had been rejected by Schmaus. In his criticism of that schema, Ratzinger made a number of suggestions that Vatican II did end up employing in *Dei Verbum*, the Dogmatic Constitution on Divine Revelation.[92] Ratzinger followed up his evaluations of the draft schemas with a more detailed explanation of his rationale that he gave to Cardinal Frings on October 3, 1962.[93] We will go into

---

90. See Wicks, "Six Texts," 237. Ratzinger's draft of an introductory constitution was first published in Wicks, 262–264 (in English translation) and 293–295 (in the original Latin).

91. See Wicks, 240.

92. See Jared Wicks, *Prof. Ratzinger at Vatican II: A Chapter in the Life of Pope Benedict XVI* (New Orleans: Loyola University Press, 2012), 7. Here, Wicks does not suggest that Ratzinger was the sole cause of these changes; he merely highlights that some of Ratzinger's recommendations correspond to the final document of the council.

93. See Jared Wicks, "Light from Germany on Vatican Council II," *The Catholic Historical Review* 99, no. 4 (Fall 2013): 734n22. For the German text of Ratzinger's rationale for his recommended changes, see Joseph Ratzinger, "Begründung der Änderungsvorschläge zu Band I der Schemata »Constitutionum et Decretorum«," in JRGS 7/1, 142–156.

some of the details of Ratzinger's analyses of the draft texts later in this book. For now, it suffices to highlight the fact that Ratzinger had a profound impact on Cardinal Frings, who himself was one of the most vocal and widely respected members of the council during its deliberations.

A week after giving the expanded rationale for his comments on the schemas, on October 10, 1962—the day before the council officially opened—Ratzinger gave a lecture to German-speaking bishops expressing his views on revelation by means of a lengthy criticism of *De Fontibus Revelationis*. This speech delivered to the very active German-speaking contingent at Vatican II is important, because, as Kurt Koch writes, "Theological criticism and reorientation in the Council through the cooperation of Joseph Ratzinger become visible primarily and most palpably in his opinions on the prepared schema, '*De fontibus revelationis*.'"[94] It also indicates the fact that, despite being left out of his final *Habilitationsschrift*, Ratzinger's research on St. Bonaventure's theology of divine revelation was providentially given a means to be much more influential than he, or Schmaus, could have imagined.

Once the council began, Ratzinger continued to act as an advisor to Cardinal Frings. Ratzinger's role was expanded as he was also named an official *peritus* (theological expert) of the council itself through Frings' influence.

During the council, Ratzinger worked intensively to move the discussions forward through a number of ways. As one example, Ratzinger wrote his own alternate schema on revelation, which he read in the presence of seven cardinals on October 25, 1962, at a meeting arranged by Cardinal Frings.[95]

94. Kurt Koch, "Ein konsequenter Papst des Konzils: Joseph Ratzinger—Benedikt XVI. und das Zweite Vatikanum," *Internationale Katholische Zeitschrift: Communio* 43, no. 4 (2013): 385.

95. See Wicks, *Prof. Ratzinger*, 9. See also Ratzinger, *Milestones*, 128. A German translation is presented alongside the Latin original in JRGS 7/1, 177–182. The title was "*De voluntate Dei erga hominem*" ("The will of God for man") [henceforth "*De voluntate Dei*"].

Around the time of that presentation, Ratzinger teamed up with Karl Rahner, who had written his own version of a draft text, and the two German scholars blended their works together into a short text, *The Revelation of God and Man in Jesus Christ*.[96] This combined draft had a much wider circulation than the seven cardinals who listened to Ratzinger's solo draft, having been distributed in around two thousand copies.[97] "This second text," Ratzinger admits, is "much more Rahner's work than my own."[98] It also did not seem to have much impact on the council, so its value is limited to those interested in Rahner's thoughts on revelation during the council.

Of more import, however, is a speech written by Ratzinger but delivered by Frings during oral interventions at the council. Because he missed part of the text in the first speech on November 14, 1962, Frings added the other portion on November 17. These were not the only speeches of Frings that Ratzinger helped to draft. In fact, there were at least ten speeches by Frings that Ratzinger was directly involved with generating. Through Frings, Ratzinger was able to have a broad influence on Vatican II's work. As Jared Wicks notes, speaking of Frings, "His speeches in St. Peter's had a notable impact since as a senior Cardinal he was often among the first to address a topic. Also, his promotion of development aid by the West German church for third-world and especially Latin American churches had gained him many grateful friends among the bishops of those areas, who would listen carefully to the points he made when speaking in St Peter's."[99]

Between the first two sessions of Vatican II, in the spring of 1963, twelve schemas were sent to the council fathers. Once

---

96. See Wicks, *Prof. Ratzinger*, 9. The Latin with an English translation can be found in Brendan J. Cahill, *The Renewal of Revelation Theology (1960–1962): The Development and Response to the Fourth Chapter of the Preparatory Schema "De deposito Fidei"* (Rome: Editrice Pontificia Università Gregoriana, 1999), 300–317.

97. See Wicks, *Prof. Ratzinger*, 9.

98. Ratzinger, *Milestones*, 128.

99. Wicks, *Prof. Ratzinger*, 11.

again, Frings gave a copy of the schemas to Ratzinger, asking for his input. Ratzinger obliged via handwritten comments in the margins, which Frings brought with him to Rome. On June 8 and June 15 of 1963, Rahner sent some letters to Ratzinger asking for his thoughts on the new schemas. Ratzinger wrote a response on June 19. In that letter, Ratzinger tried to recreate the substance of the marginal notes he had given to Frings, to the best of his recollection.[100] Without going into details here, once more, some of Ratzinger's comments are echoed in subsequent drafts of the documents, especially the later drafts on revelation, including the final document, *Dei Verbum*.[101]

Ratzinger also had a more direct mode of contributing to the council. He "was drawn into the service of Commissions of the Council in their work of entering revisions into draft texts to make them ready for voting and promulgation as final Vatican II documents."[102] He assisted the doctrinal commission in its work on the constitution on the Church, especially in the sections that produced paragraphs 21 through 23 of *Lumen Gentium*. He also assisted the doctrinal commission with work on *Dei Verbum*, particularly chapter 6 on "Sacred Scripture in the Life of the Church." Additionally, he worked on a subcommission of the council's commission on the missions, where he helped formulate the doctrinal basis of the Church's missionary activity, which is presented in *Ad Gentes*. Thus, Ratzinger was directly employed by the council to assist with three of the council's documents.

Following the various sessions of the council as well as after the end of the council, Ratzinger offered helpful reports and

---

100. A copy of that letter is available in Joseph Ratzinger, "Brief von Joseph Ratzinger," in "Texte im Umfeld des Zweiten Vatikanischen Konzils," in *Mitteilungen Institut Papst Benedikt XVI.*, (Regensburg: Schnell & Steiner, 2012), 5:13–16.

101. For comparisons of various drafts leading to the promulgation of *Dei Verbum*, see Francisco Gil Hellín, *Constitutio dogmatica de divina revelatione Dei Verbum: Concilii Vaticani II synopsis in ordinem redigens schemata cum relationibus necnon patrum orationes atque animadversiones* (Vatican City: Libreria Editrice Vaticana, 1993).

102. Wicks, *Prof. Ratzinger*, 2.

reflections on its proceedings and documents. He is among the most respected commentators on Vatican II.

Ratzinger's writings have been a source of inspiration for theologians and the common faithful alike. By exploring the breadth and depth of his vast theological corpus, his ideas can be better understood both individually and in their mutual relation.

2

Ratzinger's
Theological Method

Pope Benedict XVI is undoubtedly one of the most influential Catholic theologians of the twentieth and early twenty-first centuries. The range of theological topics that he has treated throughout his career is impressive. The variety of literary genres represented in his works is also remarkable. He has written numerous full-length books; short, reflective monographs; academic articles; homilies; speeches; commentaries; and theological dictionary entries. As pope, he has also penned encyclicals, apostolic constitutions, exhortations, and more. Additionally, he has published multiple book-length interviews.

The German publisher Herder has been in the process of publishing the most central works of Ratzinger's immense corpus in a series of sixteen volumes. Since some of those volumes are split into sub-volumes, the grand total of bound books in this massive collection is twenty-four. In truth, that number is low, given the fact that Ratzinger wrote at least fifty books in German along with hundreds of journal articles and contributions to collected works. His full body of writing is so large that his bibliography will be printed separately in the final volume of his collected works (alongside an index for all the volumes).

Many of his writings have been translated into multiple

languages, further expanding his readership and influence. His works have inspired countless other thinkers, leading to presentations of his thought in secondary literature, including books by authors around the globe and innumerable academic articles that engage his ideas.

What is perhaps more impressive than the extent and variety of his written work is the scope of Benedict XVI's readership. Members of his audience span multiple generations and cross confessional lines.[1] He is read by the young, the old, Catholics, Protestants, and even non-Christians. His readership includes individuals across a spectrum from top-rate scholars to people of simple faith.

It might be asked: What is it about his theology that captivates such a variety of people? I submit that—at least in part—it is his approach to theology and the style in which he expresses it. These attributes combine to offer compelling insights into the faith, making it at once better understood and more deeply loved.

Thus, before we delve into the specific contents of Benedict XVI's thought in subsequent chapters, we would do well to consider first the principles that guide his theology.

SACRED SCRIPTURE AS THE SOUL OF THEOLOGY

For Ratzinger, Sacred Scripture, especially the New Testament, is the soul of theology.[2] That fact is especially noteworthy given that Ratzinger is a fundamental and dogmatic theologian. All too often, dogmatic (or systematic) theologians are far removed from direct work with Sacred Scripture. There is always some scriptural background to the major categories of Catholic doctrine

---

1. See Tim Perry, ed., *The Theology of Benedict XVI: A Protestant Appreciation* (Bellingham, WA: Lexham, 2019). This book is a collection of essays by more than a dozen Protestant scholars showing their appreciation for Pope Benedict XVI's thought.

2. See Joseph Ratzinger, *Milestones: Memoirs 1927–1977*, trans. Erasmo Leiva-Merikakis (San Francisco: Ignatius, 1998), 53, 57.

that make up the subspecialties within dogmatics, but it is quite common for dogmatic theologians to maintain this connection in a merely tangential or distally derivative way.

Such is not the case with Ratzinger. As he states and as his body of work confirms, "Exegesis has always remained for me the center of my theological work."[3] The Lutheran exegete Eckart Schmidt appreciates Ratzinger's work in this regard: "Joseph Ratzinger . . . throughout all his work has devoted himself so intensively to exegesis and biblical hermeneutics like few other systematic theologians (of both great Christian confessions)."[4]

Even as a dogmatic theologian, then, Ratzinger engaged in scholarly biblical interpretation as the foundation and center of his theology. In turn, this means that his method of exegesis—his biblical hermeneutic—greatly impacts his theological conclusions. It is therefore necessary to treat—at least in broad strokes—Ratzinger's understanding of the proper interpretation of Sacred Scripture.

Ratzinger was concerned about many issues occurring in the field of biblical theology. He was opposed to the errors of modernism that often found their biggest influence in Scripture studies. In this regard, Ratzinger rejects the works of figures such as Alfred Loisy (1857–1940) and George Tyrrell (1861–1909), whom he describes as "men who thought they could not save the faith without throwing away the inner core along with the expendable shell. Such figures and their tragic schizophrenia show

3. Ratzinger, *Milestones*, 52–53. He thanks a professor at his seminary in Freising, Friedrich Wilhelm Maier, for this. For an excellent example of how to apply Pope Benedict XVI's hermeneutics to difficult passages of Sacred Scripture, see Matthew J. Ramage, *Dark Passages of the Bible: Engaging Scripture with Benedict XVI and St. Thomas Aquinas* (Washington, DC: The Catholic University of America Press, 2013). For an exploration of Benedict XVI's method of biblical interpretation in comparison and contrast with others' uses of the historical-critical method, especially with respect to the question of the Jesus of faith and the historical Jesus, see Matthew J. Ramage, *Jesus, Interpreted: Benedict XVI, Bart Ehrman, and the Historical Truth of the Gospels* (Washington, DC: The Catholic University of America Press, 2017).

4. Eckart Schmidt, ». . . *das Wort Gottes immer mehr zu lieben« Joseph Ratzingers Bibelhermeneutik im Kontext der Exegesegeschichte der römisch-katholischen Kirche* (Stuttgart: Katholisches Bibelwerk, 2015), 5. Schmidt is another example of how Ratzinger's admirers transcend confessional lines.

forth the mortal danger that threatened Catholicism at the first outbreak of the modern mind."[5]

In the development of his own approach to Scripture, Ratzinger found inspiration from the Church Fathers. Ratzinger holds that the Fathers' understanding of Sacred Scripture remains—and always will remain—important for sound Catholic theology. He appeals to the Magisterium in support of his position: "Vatican Council I expressly followed the Council of Trent in decreeing that in ecclesiological matters and in matters of faith that meaning is to be accepted as the true meaning of Scripture 'which Holy Mother Church has held and still holds. She has the right to judge concerning the true sense and interpretation of the Sacred Scriptures. No one, therefore, is permitted to interpret Sacred Scripture contrary to this sense or contrary to the unanimous consent of the Fathers.'"[6] Showing how this teaching is also echoed in Vatican II, Ratzinger cites *Dei Verbum* 23, which says that the Church "'strives to reach day by day a more profound understanding of the Sacred Scriptures in order to provide her children with food from the divine words. For this reason also she duly fosters the study of the Church Fathers, both Eastern and Western.'"[7] The patristic understandings of Sacred Scripture are, therefore, keys for a properly Catholic interpretation of the Bible.

Why? Ratzinger explains that the Church Fathers' interpretations of Scripture are fundamental for a proper reading of the Bible because they are "witnesses to the text" and "members of an age that was relatively close to the origin of the Scriptures."[8] The New Testament canon was established in the patristic era.

---

5. Joseph Ratzinger, *Theological Highlights of Vatican II*, trans. Henry Traub, Gerard C. Thormann, and Werner Barzel (New York: Paulist, 2009), 41.

6. Joseph Ratzinger, *Principles of Catholic Theology: Building Stones for a Fundamental Theology*, trans. Mary Frances McCarthy (San Francisco: Ignatius, 1987), 135. The English translation of Ratzinger's quote of Vatican I comes from "Dogmatic Constitution *Dei Filius*, on the Catholic Faith," in *Documents of Vatican Council I, 1869–1870*, trans. John F. Broderick (Collegeville, MN: Liturgical, 1971), 9, 43.

7. Ratzinger, *Principles*, 135.

8. Ratzinger, 136–137.

Therefore, the way that the Fathers understood the Bible cannot be separated from the very existence of the New Testament as Scripture. For Ratzinger, then, patristics is integral to biblical exegesis.

Ratzinger does not, thereby, believe that Catholic biblical scholarship should be reduced to reading and citing the Fathers alone. Rather, he thinks the works of Catholic theologians from every age can be useful for contemporary exegesis. The Fathers, the Scholastics, and even some modern scholars have valuable insights into the meaning of the sacred page. "Certainly the richness of scriptural exegesis through the ages can help every age to a deeper understanding of the breadth of the biblical testimony."[9]

The broader context of Ratzinger's treatment of biblical interpretation involves conflicts over what is called the historical-critical method of exegesis. As Thomas Rausch explains, "Behind this exegetical approach lies the attempt to find in matters biblical or theological the same kind of certainty that might be found in the natural sciences; indeed they give the appearance of 'a quasi-clinical-scientific certainty.'"[10] With the advent of this approach to reading the Bible, some scholars ignore patristic exegesis and withhold submission to ecclesiastical authority and Tradition. Instead, they base their interpretation on a supposedly scientific method that comes to conclusions on its own terms, applying developments in historical and literary analysis to Scripture. Such a method, so it is argued, should lead to more accurate

---

9. Ratzinger, 138.

10. Thomas P. Rausch, *Pope Benedict XVI: An Introduction to His Theological Vision* (New York: Paulist, 2009), 71. Here, Rausch quotes Ratzinger's Erasmus Lecture given in New York on January 27, 1988. Various texts of the lecture are available in different places under slightly different titles. Rausch refers to the title as "Biblical Interpretation in Crisis: On the Question of the Foundations and Approaches of Exegesis Today." See also Joseph Ratzinger, "Biblical Interpretation in Conflict: On the Foundations and the Itinerary for Exegesis Today," in *Opening Up the Scriptures: Joseph Ratzinger and the Foundations of Biblical Interpretation*, ed. José Granados, Carlos Granados, and Luis Sánchez-Navarro (Grand Rapids, MI: Eerdmans, 2008). Transcripts of the lecture are also available on the websites of EWTN and *First Things* Magazine.

and certain readings of the Bible. As a result, it should also lead to broader consensus among biblical scholars.

Ratzinger, however, calls for a criticism of this kind of biblical criticism. He argues that the method has not, in fact, attained its intended goal. During his pontificate, he wrote a series of books on Jesus of Nazareth that are brilliant reflections on various aspects of Jesus' life as revealed to us in the Gospels. In the first volume of that series, he wrote:

> As historical-critical scholarship advanced, it led to finer and finer distinctions between layers of tradition in the Gospels, beneath which the real object of faith—the figure [*Gestalt*] of Jesus—became increasingly obscured and blurred. At the same time, though, the reconstructions of this Jesus . . . became more and more incompatible with one another. . . . If you read a number of these reconstructions one after the other, you see at once that far from uncovering an icon that has become obscured over time, they are much more like photographs of their authors and the ideals that they hold. . . . All these attempts have produced a common result: the impression that we have very little certain knowledge of Jesus.[11]

Thus, rather than produce a field-wide consensus on the authentic meaning of Sacred Scripture through "scientific" exegesis, the result has been a vast array of contradictory interpretations that reflect the divergent images of their authors' agendas. That is the definition of *eisegesis* (reading into the text), not *exegesis* (reading from the text). For example, speaking of scholars J. Hick and P. Knitter, Ratzinger remarks, "It is not a case of exegesis providing

---

11. Benedict XVI, *Jesus of Nazareth*, vol. 1, *From the Baptism in the Jordan to the Transfiguration*, trans. Adrian J. Walker (New York: Doubleday, 2007), xii. See also Joseph Ratzinger, *Behold the Pierced One: An Approach to a Spiritual Christology*, trans. Graham Harrison (San Francisco: Ignatius, 1986), 44.

evidence that supports a philosophy; rather, it is a matter of a philosophy that produces the exegesis."[12]

Additionally, a narrowly applied historical-critical reading of the Bible cannot attain the intended purposes of the very work it studies. "But this idea which identifies God's revelation with literature and employs the dissecting knife of the literary critic to lay bare to us the inmost secrets of God, misreads both the nature of God and that of literary science," and would lead to a reading of Scripture that is wholly unscriptural since "the Bible itself never implies anything like that. In the Bible the act of faith by which a person receives revelation is by no means a comparison between the book and the individual's analytic reasoning."[13] The reduction of biblical reading to the minutiae of historical and literary analysis misses the whole point of the Bible. Thus, some applications of the historical-critical method are woefully incongruous with understanding the texts themselves.

A further limitation of the historical-critical method is that—by the very nature of its approach—it treats portions of the Bible apart from the rest of the Bible. "Ultimately, it considers the individual books of Scripture in the context of their historical period, and then analyzes them further according to their sources."[14]

While this technique has its benefits, there is a limit to the fruit that it can bear. If done properly, historical-critical investigation enhances one's understanding of the intended meaning of a given human author in a particular text, and to that extent, also aids an understanding of what God is revealing. At the same time, since God is the primary author of the entire Bible, the various parts are meant to be understood in their cohesive unity. On its own, the historical-critical method cannot provide such a

12. Joseph Ratzinger, *Truth and Tolerance: Christian Belief and World Religions*, trans. Henry Taylor (San Francisco: Ignatius, 2004), 132. In a footnote to this comment, Ratzinger gives a further example exhibited by the conflict between Adolf Schlatter and Adolf von Harnack.

13. Joseph Ratzinger, "The Church and Scientific Theology," *Communio* 7, no. 4 (1980): 339.

14. Benedict XVI, *Jesus of Nazareth*, 1:xvii.

holistic vision. "The unity of all of these writings as one 'Bible,' however, is not something it [the historical-critical method] can recognize as an immediate historical datum."[15] Precisely because the unity of Scripture is willed by God from his eternal perspective, the meaning of any individual text can only be understood fully through its relation to the whole, which transcends any specific historical context, providing a unified vision of the whole of salvation history.

Despite the limitations of the method and the errors of many historical-critical exegetes, it ought to be remembered that *abusus non tollit usum* (abuse does not cancel use). In other words, the historical-critical method is not, in itself, completely devoid of value, even if many of its practitioners misuse it. As Ratzinger remarks, "The historico-critical method is essentially a tool, and its usefulness depends on the way in which it is used, i.e., on the hermeneutical and philosophical presuppositions one adopts in applying it."[16] Ratzinger does think the method can be used effectively and fruitfully. In fact, he claims further "that there is no longer a way to pass by the historical-critical method and that as such it corresponds to the demand of the subject of theology itself."[17]

There is real value in considering the literary genres of the various sections of Sacred Scripture. Much can be gained by philological investigations into the meaning of words and idioms as they were used when the texts were written. Learning more about the cultural, historical, and religious contexts of specific books or passages can make the intended meaning of the biblical authors clearer. "The legitimacy, indeed the necessity of the

---

15. Benedict XVI, 1:xvii.

16. Ratzinger, *Behold the Pierced One*, 43.

17. Joseph Ratzinger, "Einleitung," in *Einleitung und Kommentar zum Vorwort und zu Kapitel I, II und VI der Offenbarungskonstitution "Dei Verbum,"* in *Lexikon für Theologie und Kirche*, Erg.-Bd. II (1967), 498–528, 571–581, at 499.

historical research of Scripture," explains Rudolf Voderholzer, "is thus based on the character of Scripture as historical witness of revelation."[18]

Ratzinger, then, takes a balanced approach to the discipline of scriptural scholarship. He affirms the value and enduring usefulness of historical-critical methods while also calling for an honest assessment of their inherent limits and an admission of the sheer fact of widespread instances of their misapplication.

Benedict XVI calls for a complementary set of methods that together lead to better interpretation of the Bible.[19] Relating back to the unity of Scripture mentioned earlier, Pope Benedict speaks favorably of the "canonical exegesis" movement that was led by American scholars. "The aim of this exegesis is to read individual texts within the totality of the one Scripture, which then sheds new light on all the individual texts."[20]

Benedict believes this approach is valid because it is something intrinsic to the Bible. This method is not extrinsic to Scripture but is reflected in Scripture itself. Later portions of the Bible often refer back to prior sections. This approach gives the older Scriptures "added depth and breadth of meaning."[21] Take, for example, the comparison of the Red Sea crossing to the saving waters of Baptism. Without the latter, the significance of the former would remain limited. In light of Baptism, however, the divinely intended significance of the miracle at the Red Sea is clearer. At

18. Rudolf Voderholzer, "Der Grundduktus innerhalb der Fundamentaltheologie von Joseph Ratzinger," in *Zur Mitte der Theologie im Werk Joseph Ratzinger/Benedikt XVI.*, ed. Maximilian Heim and Justinus C. Pech, in *Ratzinger-Studien* (Regensburg: Friedrich Pustet, 2013), 6:52.

19. See Benedict XVI, *Jesus of Nazareth*, 1:xviii. There, Benedict XVI says that the historical-critical method is intrinsically open to such complementary methods. Ratzinger's approach is often referred to as "Method C," which is a sort of hybrid between the patristic and Scholastic approach (Method A) and the historical-critical approach (Method B). For more on this theme, see Gregory Vall, *Ecclesial Exegesis: A Synthesis of Ancient and Modern Approaches to Scripture* (Washington, DC: The Catholic University of America Press, 2022).

20. Benedict XVI, *Jesus of Nazareth*, 1:xviii. This approach is also commended by Vatican II in *Dei Verbum* 12, November 18, 1965, in *The Word on Fire Vatican II Collection*, ed. Matthew Levering (Park Ridge, IL: Word on Fire Institute, 2021), 28–29.

21. Benedict XVI, *Jesus of Nazareth*, 1:xviii–xix.

the same time, the older event provides a type that helps us grasp the new. They are mutually enriching and illuminating. The same can be said for the manna from heaven in Exodus and the true bread (Christ himself) that came down from heaven as described in John 6. Without Baptism and the Holy Eucharist, the Old Testament could not, on its own, convey the providential plan of God being fulfilled. At the same time, the Old Testament archetypes provide insights into the realities of the New Covenant.

The human authors of the Old Testament books were not necessarily aware of God's further intentions for the events' significance. But God weaves them together according to his will and plan for salvation. Thus, Ratzinger "insists on the fundamental unity and continuity of the two Testaments, 'an inner unity-in-diversity,' an insight he attributes to his teacher at Munich, Gottlieb Söhngen."[22] In this view, "canonical exegesis" is a must for authentic biblical interpretation.[23]

In 1959, Henri de Lubac published the first volume of his three-volume series on medieval exegesis. The subject of the volumes was the four senses of Scripture.[24] Given that he was very close to Henri de Lubac, it is no surprise that Ratzinger is also an advocate of retrieving the four senses of Scripture that were a hallmark of high Scholastic theology (although it has roots in earlier periods).

For those readers who are not familiar, the four senses of Scripture are comprised of one literal sense (the basis for the

22. Rausch, *Pope Benedict XVI*, 76. Here, Rausch draws from Joseph Ratzinger, *Many Religions—One Covenant* (San Francisco: Ignatius, 1999) and Joseph Ratzinger, *The Spirit of the Liturgy* (San Francisco: Ignatius, 2000), 49, 67.

23. See Benedict XVI, *Jesus of Nazareth*, 1:xix.

24. See Henri de Lubac, *Medieval Exegesis: The Four Senses of Scripture*, vol. 1, trans. Mark Sebanc (Grand Rapids, MI: Eerdmans, 1998). The French original is *Exégèse médiévale: Les quatre sens de l'écriture*, vol. 1 (Paris: Éditions Montaigne, 1959). This work by de Lubac is just one of many counterarguments to the fallacious charges levied by some that de Lubac was a modernist and anti-Scholastic. In a time when the historical-critical method (and bad implementations thereof) was rampant, de Lubac intentionally responded with a call to retrieve authentic Scholasticism as an important corrective to misguided biblical hermeneutics. By extension, this defense is valid for Balthasar and Ratzinger as well.

others[25]) and three spiritual senses: the allegorical sense, the moral (or tropological sense), and the anagogical sense. Benedict refers to the object of each sense through a pithy medieval expression: "Littera facta docet. Quid credas allegoria. Moralis quid agas. Quo tendas anagogia."[26] Here is one way to translate this phrase: "The letter [i.e., the literal sense] teaches what happened, allegory what you [should] believe, moral what you [should] do, the anagogical where you are going." As the *Catechism of the Catholic Church* explains, "The *literal sense* is the meaning conveyed by the words of Scripture and discovered by exegesis, following the rules of sound interpretation."[27] The allegorical sense refers to how the various parts of Scripture are related to Christ in some way, such as promise and fulfillment. The allegorical sense is also called typology. The moral sense refers to the way that Scripture teaches us how to act rightly. The anagogical sense refers to the eternal or eschatological significance of a given passage of Scripture.[28]

For Pope Benedict XVI, it is important to see these four senses in their unity: "The four senses of Scripture are not individual meanings arrayed side by side, but dimensions of the one word that reaches beyond the moment."[29]

The principle of seeing the part in light of the whole extends beyond the canon of Scripture. In addition to canonical exegesis, there is also "the need for taking account of the living tradition of the whole Church and of the analogy of faith (the intrinsic correspondences within the faith)."[30] In other words, Benedict holds that the doctrines that are distilled from Scripture and Tradition

---

25. See Thomas Aquinas, *Summa theologiae* 1.1.10 ad. 1.

26. Benedict XVI, "Grace and Vocation without Remorse: Comments on the Treatise *De Iudaeis*," *Communio* 45 (Spring 2018): 167. Other renderings of this phrase have *gesta* in place of *facta*.

27. *Catechism of the Catholic Church* 116 [hereafter, *CCC*].

28. See *CCC* 117.

29. Benedict XVI, *Jesus of Nazareth*, 1:xx. Pope Benedict XVI also speaks about the four senses of Scripture in *Verbum Domini* 37, September 30, 2010, vatican.va.

30. Benedict XVI, *Jesus of Nazareth*, 1:xviii. This principle is also reflected in *Dei Verbum* 12.

must be understood in their mutual relation. How does the Incarnation affect our understanding of the Church? How are both
related to Catholic doctrine on the Eucharist?

Ratzinger's stress on the need to read Sacred Scripture as a
whole and in light of the unity of the faith is connected to another exegetical principle. On his understanding, the Bible belongs to and must be read within the Church as the people of
God on its pilgrim way through history toward eternal life. Thus,
Ratzinger seeks "an exegesis rooted in the living reality . . . of the
Church of all ages."[31] The Bible, for him, is no ordinary piece of
literature. It comes from God and arises within the Church, is
addressed to the Church and to her individual members, and is
understood rightly only within the communion of the Church's
faith, sacraments, and life. "The Scripture emerged from within
the heart of a living subject—the pilgrim People of God—and
lives within this same subject."[32] Therefore, as Tracey Rowland
reports, he insists that "the scriptures must be interpreted from
within the horizon of faith itself and, from Ratzinger's point of
view, the institution of the Church and her interpretations of the
passages, forms part of that horizon."[33] The texts of Scripture are
to be understood within the context of the Church. This theme
of the ecclesial dimension of biblical interpretation will recur in
later chapters on divine revelation and ecclesiology, once again
highlighting the inner unity of Ratzinger's thought.

31. Joseph Ratzinger, "Assessment and Future Prospects," in *Looking Again at the Question
of the Liturgy with Cardinal Ratzinger: Proceedings of the July 2001 Fontgombault Liturgical Conference*, ed. Alcuin Reid (Farnborough, UK: Saint Michael's Abbey Press, 2003), 148. See also
Rausch, *Pope Benedict XVI*, 80–82.

32. Benedict XVI, *Jesus of Nazareth*, 1:xx. See also p. xxi.

33. Tracey Rowland, *Benedict XVI: A Guide for the Perplexed* (New York: T&T Clark,
2010), 60.

THE SUBORDINATE ROLE OF THE THEOLOGIAN

Understanding the Bible as the Church's book leads directly into another prominent theme in Ratzinger's theological methodology: the role of the theologian, which he describes as an *ecclesial* vocation. By ecclesial vocation, he means that theologians are subject to the Magisterium.

At this point, a potential conflict arises. While it is true that theology is an ecclesial vocation, is it not also an academic—or even "scientific"—discipline? Does not the theologian, then, require the academic freedom to follow the results of scholarly, scientific investigations wherever they may lead? Ratzinger himself poses the problem thusly: "Ecclesiastical authority appears to be a tribunal wholly foreign to the nature of scientific scholarship, whose inner logic in and of itself would preclude the existence of such an authority. Scientific scholarship—so it seems—can obey only its own laws, which dictate, however, that it recognize as valid nothing except reasonable, objective argument."[34]

Does submitting to magisterial authority call into question theology's academic credentials and scientific rigor? A seemingly inescapable dichotomy thus appears: "A church without theology impoverishes and blinds, while a churchless theology melts away into caprice."[35] How can we avoid both dangers and resolve the apparent contradiction?

Ratzinger's solution is to explore the *intrinsic connection*[36] between the Church (including the Magisterium) and theology. In doing so, he aims to show that true academic freedom—insofar as theology is concerned—requires the Magisterium.

Why does Ratzinger consider the role of theologians to be an ecclesial vocation subject to magisterial teaching and authority?

---

34. Joseph Ratzinger, *The Nature and Mission of Theology: Approaches to Understanding Its Role in the Light of Present Controversy*, trans. Adrian J. Walker (San Francisco: Ignatius, 1995), 47.

35. Ratzinger, *Nature and Mission*, 48.

36. See Ratzinger, 48.

The traditional definition of theology is "faith seeking under-standing," and faith, Ratzinger argues, is an inherently ecclesial reality. He treats this concept in a number of places, including chapter 2 of his well-known book *Introduction to Christianity*, which is entitled "The Ecclesiastical Form of Faith."[37]

There, Ratzinger notes that the earliest professions of faith were baptismal creeds, especially the double threefold renuncia-tion and adherence formulas posed as questions to the candidates for Baptism. His main point here is that no one baptizes oneself. One is baptized by the Church into the faith and community of the Church. Ratzinger believes that this understanding of Bap-tism is reflected in Romans 6:17: "But thanks be to God that you, having once been slaves of sin, have become obedient from the heart *to the form of teaching* to which you were entrusted" (emphasis added). Ratzinger sees in this passage a description of "baptism as an experience of being committed to *the standard of doctrine*; the subjective response to this transaction, in which one is handed over into a common sphere of knowledge, is an obedi-ence coming from the heart."[38]

From the very start, then, one's profession of faith is an ec-clesial reality.[39] As he insists, "Belief is not the result of lonely meditation in which the 'I', freed from all ties and reflecting alone on the truth, thinks something out for itself; on the contrary, it is the result of a dialogue, the expression of a hearing, receiving, and answering that guides man through the exchanges of 'I' and 'You' to the 'We' of those who all believe in the same way."[40]

Furthermore, the communion of the faithful as believing subjects—and ultimately as the one believing subject of the Church—is a reflection of the very object of the faith: the Triune

---

37. See Joseph Ratzinger, *Introduction to Christianity*, trans. Mary Frances McCarthy (San Francisco: Ignatius, 1987), 82–100.

38. Ratzinger, *Nature and Mission*, 53 (emphasis added).

39. See Ratzinger, *Introduction*, 87–90.

40. Ratzinger, 90.

God. Inspired by Henri de Lubac's work in this regard, Ratzinger writes in *Principles of Catholic Theology* that "to believe in the Trinity means to become *communio*. Historically, this means that the 'I' of the credo-formulas is a collective 'I', the 'I' of the believing Church, to which the individual 'I' belongs as long as it believes. . . . The 'I' of the Church is a structural precondition of the creed: this 'I' utters itself only in the *communio* of the Church; the oneness of the believing subject is the necessary counterpart and consequence of the known 'object'."[41]

In simpler terms, the communion of the Most Holy Trinity (that which is believed in, the object of faith) calls for the communion of believers (those who believe, the subject of faith) in the one Church. These words already foreshadow aspects of chapter 3 (on the Triune God) and chapter 7 (on ecclesiology), again highlighting the interconnectedness of the various facets of Ratzinger's thought.

How is the role of the theologian tied to the ecclesiastical form of faith? Unlike a scholar of religious studies, who does not necessarily have to be a believer in any of the religions studied, the theologian is—*by definition*—supposed to be a believer and thus a member of the Church. In order to fulfill one's task as a theologian, therefore, one must be rooted in the faith of the Church. The Magisterium ensures that this faith is knowable, certain, and unified.

Theology is not merely the exposition of one's personal opinions. Indeed, it can and ought to be a very personal endeavor, but it ought never to be an individualistic enterprise. It is the Church's faith that one is seeking to understand and to elucidate. Perhaps more precisely, the individual theologian's faith and the faith of the Church ought to be one and the same.

Again, the faith is not the theologian's private possession. The theologian is not the leader of a private cult who is attempting to

41. Ratzinger, *Principles*, 23.

gain followers for oneself. The theologian is tasked with strengthening the bonds of faith by leading others to a deeper understanding of the contents of the Church's faith, which necessarily presupposes and accepts the deposit of faith as its condition of possibility. Along these lines, Ratzinger states quite bluntly that "theology either exists in the church and from the church, or it does not exist at all."[42] In fact, the Magisterium's teachings about the faith are precisely key objects of theological investigation; magisterial "proclamation is the measure of theology, and not vice versa."[43]

Thus, Ratzinger argues that the Magisterium is not—despite how it may *seem*—the enemy of theological freedom but its condition of possibility. He insists that "the liberty of theology consists in its bond to the church and that any other freedom is a betrayal both of itself and of the object entrusted to it. . . . There can be no office of teaching theology if there is no ecclesiastical magisterium."[44] It is the Magisterium that guarantees the correctness of the doctrines of the faith. Without the judgments of the Magisterium, then, there is no certainty regarding the contents of faith and thus no basis upon which to build one's theology *as* faith seeking understanding. The scientific (i.e., *noetic*) investigation of the faith presupposes knowledge of the contents of faith as a necessary precondition. This foundation is supplied and safeguarded precisely through the authority bestowed upon the Church's Magisterium by God.

There is a further reason that theology is an ecclesial vocation.

42. Joseph Ratzinger, *Nature and Mission*, 45. Leading up to this quote, Ratzinger gives the example of a Protestant theologian during the rise of Nazism (1935) who came to similar conclusions: Heinrich Schlier. Schlier eventually became Catholic. Ratzinger gives other examples of similar stories, including that of Erik Peterson, an Evangelical exegete who became Catholic. He also notes the experiences of Romano Guardini. Karl Barth is similarly referred to, although, in this case, he remained Protestant, while emphasizing the need for the Church for theology, especially in his great work, aptly named *Church Dogmatics*. The heading of the section of Ratzinger's book in which all this takes place reflects our current theme quite explicitly: "The Spiritual Basis and Ecclesial Identity of Theology," 45–72.

43. Ratzinger, *Nature and Mission*, 63.

44. Ratzinger, 45–46.

A theologian's work should not be conducted solely for one's own gain or glory. Rather, a theologian's work is meant to benefit others, to help them better understand the faith of the Church so that it can be more effective in their lives. In short, a theologian's task is to enhance the faith of others.

In this regard, Ratzinger holds to the notion of the primacy of the faith of the simple, which the Magisterium is tasked with safeguarding.[45] This view is important, because it reverses the charge of a sort of tyranny of the Magisterium over academic freedom. The Magisterium is not a tyrant. Quite the contrary, it is tasked with protecting the common belief of nonexperts from the tyranny of academic elites, who might otherwise try to usurp their role, casting doubts in the minds of the average person of faith. I understand Ratzinger to mean that the right of the members of the Church to sound teaching trumps the so-called "freedom" of academic theologians to present their theses as if they were more certain than the doctrines of the faith themselves. The Magisterium, then, has the right—nay, the obligation—to set the boundaries of orthodoxy precisely as a means of making the truth of the faith more surely and securely known by *all* the faithful. It must, then, exercise authority over theologians, who could otherwise lead others astray.

Obviously, all these points relate to the theology of divine revelation as well as to ecclesiology, which will be discussed in later chapters in more detail. They are, however, important for understanding the very essence of theological study and exposition, and thus needed to be treated here. Again, all the chapters are related. Thus, this sort of repetition is not only unavoidable but also desirable for making this fact more obvious.

45. See Ratzinger, 63.

THE RELATIONSHIP BETWEEN PHILOSOPHY AND THEOLOGY

While Ratzinger is not a philosopher in the strict sense of the term, the question of philosophy's role in theology (and vice versa) was an important one throughout his career. His inaugural lecture at the University of Bonn (June 24, 1959) was on "The God of Faith and the God of the Philosophers,"[46] a title shared with the third chapter of part one of *Introduction to Christianity*,[47] which was first published in 1968. He addressed the topic again in 1993 with the publication of *The Nature and Mission of Theology*, which opens with a chapter titled "Faith, Philosophy and Theology."[48] There are other examples, but these highlight the fact that Ratzinger repeatedly considered the question of the relationship between theology and philosophy over the course of several decades.

In *The Nature and Mission of Theology*, Ratzinger provides an overview of various approaches to the question from a historical perspective before putting forth his own views on the issue. He notes that, in early Christianity, philosophy and theology were united.[49] Similarly, in his original *Habilitationsschrift*, he writes, "For them [the Church Fathers] Christianity was *the* philosophy, the true philosophy in contrast with the false philosophy of the heathens."[50]

Heeding the command of 1 Peter 3:15 to "always be ready

---

46. Patricia Pintado-Murphy has translated this lecture into English, and it is expected to be published in a forthcoming issue of the English edition of *Nova et Vetera*.

47. See Ratzinger, *Introduction*, 137–150.

48. See Ratzinger, *Nature and Mission*, 13–29. This chapter has its origins in an address Ratzinger gave on two different occasions in 1984, the first of which was in English at the College of Saint Thomas in St. Paul, Minnesota, and published in *Communio* 11, no. 4 (1984): 350–363. A German version of the speech was delivered in Fulda and published in *Internationale katholische Zeitschrift Communio* 14 (1985): 56–66. The English text found in *The Nature and Mission of Theology* is a translation of the German text, rather than a reprint of the original English version found in *Communio*.

49. See Ratzinger, 13.

50. Joseph Ratzinger, *Das Offenbarungsverständnis und die Geschichtstheologie Bonaventuras: Habilitationsschrift und Bonaventura-Studien*, in JRGS 2, ed. Gerhard Ludwig Müller (Freiburg, DE: Herder, 2009), 379.

to make a defense to anyone who demands from you an accounting for the hope that is in you," the Church Fathers took up the task of showing the reasonableness of Christianity. In this regard, Ratzinger remarks, "Christian mission contributed forcefully to demythologizing the thinking of the world and strengthened the course of *logos* against *mythos*. . . . Christianity accepted the rational philosophy as a partner in its labor for souls."[51]

After the patristic era, changes in perspective began to take place. Gradually, philosophy and theology began to be increasingly divided. Aquinas made a clear distinction between philosophy and theology. A more radical separation followed in the later Middle Ages, until the modern period began positing an even more radical opposition between philosophy and theology.[52]

By the early modern period, philosophers and theologians alike were arguing for the incompatibility between philosophy and theology. Philosophers such as Martin Heidegger and Karl Jaspers held that the two disciplines could have no meaningful relationship with one another. The theologian Martin Luther—in criticizing the standard Catholic use of philosophy—also argued for such opposition. As Ratzinger notes:

> Martin Luther inaugurated a new era of antagonism to philosophy for the sake of the unadulterated Word of God. His battle cry, "*sola scriptura*", was a declaration of war not merely against the classical interpretation of Scripture advanced by tradition and the Magisterium of the Church but also against Scholasticism, that is, the use of Aristotle and Plato in theology. For Luther, the incorporation of philosophy into theology automatically destroys the message of grace, hence, the gospel itself in its very heart. . . . On this reading, philosophy is the sheer corruption of theology.[53]

51. Ratzinger, "The Church and Scientific Theology," 338.
52. See Ratzinger, *Nature and Mission*, 16–18.
53. Ratzinger, 18–19.

The Swiss Calvinist theologian Karl Barth advanced a similar perspective, especially with his rejection of the analogy of being.[54] Another Swiss Reformed theologian, Emil Brunner, "considered the patristic synthesis of the God of faith and the God of reason a fundamental evil."[55] Accordingly, Brunner "deems . . . any philosophical doctrine of God fundamentally incompatible with the Christian belief in God."[56]

Ratzinger summarizes the modern opposition of philosophy and theology as follows: "On the one hand, philosophy defends itself against the prior given which faith implies for thinking; it feels that such a given inhibits the purity and freedom of its reflection. Theology, on the other hand, defends itself against the prior given of philosophical knowledge as a threat to the purity and novelty of faith."[57] Can this apparent impasse be overcome? Ratzinger believes so.

Ratzinger rejects the portrayal of philosophy and theology as mutually exclusive. He does so on both historical and rational grounds. In reaction to the erroneous rejection of a mutually enriching relationship between philosophy and theology, he writes:

> In reality, however, the pathos of such denials cannot be maintained to the end. How could philosophical thinking make a beginning at all without prior givens? Since Plato, philosophy has always thrived on critical dialogue with some great religious tradition. Its own standing has always been bound to the status of the traditions which lie at the starting point

54. See Ratzinger, 19. For a fuller discussion of Barth's rejection of the *analogia entis*, see Hans Urs von Balthasar, *The Theology of Karl Barth*, trans. Edward T. Oakes (San Francisco: Ignatius, 1992), 161–167.

55. Felix Resch, "Der Gott des Glaubens und der Gott der Philosophen: Zur fundamentaltheologischen Bedeutung der philosophischen Gotteslehre in Joseph Ratzingers Bonner Antrittsvorlesung (1959)," in *Mitteilungen Institut Papst Benedikt XVI.*, ed. Rudolf Voderholzer et al. (Regensburg: Schnell & Steiner, 2014), 7:65. See also Joseph Ratzinger, *Der Gott des Glaubens und der Gott der Philosophen: Ein Beitrag zum Problem der theologia naturalis* (Munich: Schnell & Steiner, 1960), 22n2.

56. Resch, "Der Gott des Glaubens," 67.

57. Ratzinger, *Nature and Mission*, 19.

of its struggle for truth. Whenever it discontinues such dialogue, it quickly dies out even as pure philosophy. Conversely, in reflecting upon the revealed Word, theology simply cannot avoid proceeding in a philosophical manner. As soon as it no longer repeats, no longer merely gathers historical marginalia, but endeavors to understand in the proper sense of the word, it enters into the realm of philosophical thinking. As a matter of fact, neither Luther nor Barth managed to divest himself of philosophical thinking and of a certain philosophical patrimony, and the very least that can be said is that the history of Evangelical theology is no less profoundly shaped by exchange with philosophy than that of its Catholic counterpart.[58]

Theology is faith seeking understanding. As such, it necessarily involves rational reflection, which inherently involves some sort of philosophical thinking. Even those opposed to it have not been able to avoid it. It is therefore foolish to think that one can conduct theology completely purified of any philosophical notions.

Ratzinger holds that such an endeavor would not lead to a true "purification" of theology at all but would instead weaken it and hamper the attainment of its objectives. Christian theology, he notes, "wishes to make a reasonable statement," and therefore, theology is "a rationality that is inherent in the faith and that makes explicit the inner coherence of the faith. This explains the peculiar phenomenon that, at the time of its beginning, Christian faith found its ally not among the other religions but in the great philosophy of the Greeks."[59] One of Christianity's most significant assets in its missionary activity was precisely its ability to show how irrational paganism was and—by way of contrast—how rational the Christian faith is. Greek philosophy provided natural tools that could be used for supernatural ends, leading

58. Ratzinger, 19–20.
59. Ratzinger, "The Church and Scientific Theology," 337.

to the conversions of many who would otherwise have remained pagan. Philosophy was a key part of the success of Christianity's missionary efforts.

Unfortunately, there is a common presumption in contemporary society that theology is incompatible with rational discourse, whether philosophical or scientific. We ought not to concede this point. Rather, we ought to continue to insist on the rationality of faith. As Ratzinger himself contends, "It can hardly be disputed that as a consequence of the division between philosophy and theology established by the Thomists, a juxtaposition has gradually been established which no longer appears adequate. There is, and must be, a human reason *in* faith."[60]

Ratzinger points out that even the Protestant opposition to the so-called "Hellenization" of theology had its limits. After all, Protestant orthodoxy submits to the creeds of the early ecumenical councils, which are suffused with Greek philosophical terminology, particularly with respect to metaphysical categories. The irony is that metaphysics (especially that of Plato and Aristotle) is what the likes of Luther and Barth objected to the most. Yet, "the dogma of the ancient Church itself appears as the epitome of the hellenization and ontologization of faith. It is a fact that both the doctrine of the triune God and the profession of faith in Christ as true God and true man had moved the ontological content of the Bible's utterances to the center of Christian thought and belief."[61] At the Council of Nicaea—whose teaching is accepted by Catholics, Orthodox, and mainline Protestants alike—"the Council Fathers used philosophy in order to clarify, beyond the possibility of misunderstanding, the belief that is the essence of Christianity."[62] Ratzinger strongly defends the use—and usefulness—of

---

60. Joseph Ratzinger, "The Dignity of the Human Person" in *Commentary on the Documents of Vatican II*, ed. Herbert Vorgrimler, trans. W.J. O'Hara (New York: Herder, 1969), 5:120.

61. Ratzinger, *Nature and Mission*, 20–21.

62. Ratzinger, *Principles*, 115.

philosophy for theology. He is especially insistent on the necessity of metaphysics as a vital part of both philosophy and theology. Against those who reject metaphysics, Ratzinger counters that "no one can exclude the question of metaphysics from philosophical inquiry. . . . To cease asking about the origin and goal of the whole of reality is to leave out the characteristic element of philosophical questioning itself."[63]

As devastating as the loss of metaphysics would be to philosophy, it would be even more destructive of theology. "If the door to metaphysical knowledge remains barred . . . then faith will necessarily atrophy, simply for lack of breathing space."[64] A loss of metaphysics would also hamper the Church's missionary activity. As Emery de Gaál reports, "Ratzinger asserts that if Christianity were to surrender the metaphysical dimensions of the Judeo-Christian understanding of God, then invariably it would simultaneously give up its claim to universality."[65]

Because metaphysics is crucial for both philosophy and theology alike, it serves as a point of intersection between them.[66] After all, "the question of metaphysics and the question of God are fundamentally the same. The problem of God is not a supplementary section of metaphysics, but is posited simultaneously with the question of being itself, while conversely, the question of being implies the question of God."[67] Just as the question of God is inherent to metaphysics, so too, the question of metaphysics is inherent to Christian faith and theology. For, "faith advances a philosophical, more precisely, an ontological claim when it professes the existence of God, indeed, of a God who has power over

63. Ratzinger, *Nature and Mission*, 21.

64. Ratzinger, *Truth and Tolerance*, 135.

65. Emery de Gaál, "Pope Benedict XVI's Early Contributions to Fundamental Theology—1955–1956," *Josephinum Journal of Theology* 21, no. 2 (Summer/Fall 2014): 273.

66. See Ratzinger, *Nature and Mission*, 22: "We held that both disciplines [philosophy and theology] need this dimension of thought [metaphysics] and that it is here that they find themselves indissolubly associated."

67. Ratzinger, "Commentary on Introductory Article and Chapter I of *Gaudium et Spes*," in *Commentary on the Documents of Vatican II*, 132–133.

reality as a whole. . . . The scope of the assertion that there is a God who is the creator and savior of the whole universe reaches beyond the religious community which makes it. It is . . . a statement about reality as it is in itself."[68] Following Ratzinger's line of thought, Matthew Levering explains that "the theologian needs philosophy—especially metaphysics—to be able to formulate the testimony of faith. Metaphysics is required to defend theology's claim that God exists and acts with power over the whole of reality."[69]

The universal and metaphysical significance of theology's claims is already found in the Old Testament[70] and developed even further in the New Testament. The ancient Jewish faith's claim to rationality provided the foundation for the synthesis between divine revelation and philosophy. This synthesis is especially evident in the Gospel of John. As Ratzinger argues:

> For this reason, it is incorrect to reduce the concepts of *logos* and *aletheia*, upon which John's Gospel centers the Christian message, to a strictly Hebraic interpretation, as if *logos* meant "word" merely in the sense of God's speech in history, and *aletheia* signified nothing more than "trustworthiness" or "fidelity". For the very same reason, there is no basis for the opposite accusation that John distorted biblical thought in the direction of Hellenism. On the contrary, he stands in the classical sapiential tradition. It is precisely in John's writings that one can study, both in its origins and in its outcome, the inner movement of biblical faith in God and biblical Christology toward philosophical inquiry.[71]

68. Ratzinger, *Nature and Mission*, 24.

69. Matthew Levering, "Jesus and Metaphysics: Knowledge of God according to Joseph Ratzinger/Pope Benedict XVI," *Josephinum Journal of Theology* 21, no. 2 (Summer/Fall 2014): 309.

70. See Ratzinger, *Nature and Mission*, 24.

71. Ratzinger, 24–25.

As evident here, Ratzinger's argument for the proper use of philosophy (especially metaphysics) in theology is not only based on history and reason; it is also biblical.

In Ratzinger's theological method, then, Sacred Scripture and philosophy both have a place. They do not just stand side by side, however; they work symbiotically. "We have to strive toward such a renewed process of dialogue between faith and philosophy, for each has need of the other. Without faith, philosophy cannot be whole, but faith without reason cannot be human."[72] As de Gaál explains, speaking about biblical faith and metaphysics in Ratzinger's thought, "In relatedness to the other, both disciplines gain their respective contours, acquire greater depth and achieve their 'requisite purification and transformation.'"[73]

This is a fitting alliance because both metaphysics and theology seek knowledge about the same reality: the one God knowable by human reason and through divine revelation. There is thus significant overlap between the two. As an example, one can cite the perfections predicated of God (e.g., eternity, truth, and omnipotence), "which are common to the God of Israel and to the concept of natural reason. In this way, the possibility of a universal communicability of biblical faith is opened, whereby the absolute perfection of the God of Israel can be explained. This missionary-apologetic tendency is strengthened with the transition from Judaism to the essentially more expansive Christianity."[74]

At the heart of Christianity's missionary mandate is its claim to universal validity. This requires theology to be "oriented beyond the symbolism of the religious toward an answer meant for all, an answer which also appeals to the common reason of mankind. . . . The question of God, therefore, obliges theology

---

72. Ratzinger, *Truth and Tolerance*, 136.

73. De Gaál, "Pope Benedict," 274. De Gaál cites here from Joseph Ratzinger, *Der Gott des Glaubens und der Gott der Philosophen. Ein Beitrag zum Problem der theologia naturalis*, 2nd expanded German edition, ed. Heimo Sonnemans (Leutesdorf: Johannes, 2005), 35.

74. Resch, "Der Gott des Glaubens," 69.

to take a position in the philosophical debate."[75] Conversely, philosophy—if it is to be true and honest—must be open to faith's rational claims.[76] As Ratzinger contends, "Christian faith is characterized by its desire to unlock real knowledge and as such has direct relevance to intellectual reasoning."[77] De Gaál echoes this rationale when he speaks about the complementarity of philosophy and faith in Ratzinger's thought: "The historical horizon of the philosophical quest for God is ultimately open to the same God as the one proclaimed by Judeo-Christian revelation. The truth of humankind's existential and intellectual search is welcomed and transformed by the true God in his self-communication. . . . Philosophical truth becomes personal, divine-human truth in Jesus Christ as the *Logos*."[78]

There is yet another reason why Ratzinger holds that the use of philosophy is legitimate in theology. Faith seeks understanding because the believer's love for God includes a desire to know and understand God more.[79] This justification goes beyond utility and rational argumentation to the very heart of the theologian's interior impetus. "Love is the desire for intimate knowledge, so that the quest for intelligence can even be an inner requirement of love. Put another way, there is a coherence of love and truth which has important consequences for theology and philosophy."[80] As Ratzinger expresses it elsewhere, "Faith is life because it is relation, that is to say, it is knowledge which becomes love, love which comes from knowledge and which leads to knowledge."[81]

It is critical to highlight just how important Ratzinger holds

75. Ratzinger, *Nature and Mission*, 25.

76. See Ratzinger, 25.

77. Ratzinger, "The Church and Scientific Theology," 338.

78. De Gaál, "Pope Benedict," 275.

79. See Joseph Ratzinger, "Faith, Philosophy and Theology," *Communio* 11, no. 4 (Winter 1984): 361, where Ratzinger attributes this thought to St. Bonaventure.

80. Ratzinger, *Nature and Mission*, 27.

81. Ratzinger, "Sources and the Transmission of the Faith," *Communio* 10, no. 1 (Spring 1983): 17–34.

the cooperation of philosophy and theology to be, not just for theology but for humanity as a whole. He is concerned that if the two fields remain radically separated, humankind will stop asking fundamental questions about reality. In other words, theology helps keep philosophical questions alive. As Levering notes, Ratzinger "proposes that the testimony of faith enables the philosopher to continue raising the deepest questions rather than giving up in despair."[82] Rather than being opposed to philosophy, "Faith thus supports and requires philosophy's dynamic of fruitful questioning about ultimate questions."[83]

Faith need not be afraid of philosophical questions; faith ought to welcome and encourage such questions. It is the cessation of questioning, of seeking the truth, that faith should fear. As Ratzinger insists, "Faith needs philosophy because it needs man who questions and seeks. It is not questioning, in fact, which places obstacles to faith but that closure which no longer wants to question and holds truth to be unreachable or not worth striving for. Faith does not destroy philosophy, it champions it. Only when it takes up the cause of philosophy does it remain true to itself."[84]

THE ESSENCE OF THEOLOGY

Ratzinger contrasts two Scholastic ways of viewing theology, exemplified by St. Thomas Aquinas and St. Bonaventure. "According to Ratzinger, Aquinas views theology as a science of inference, meaning that it starts from the truths of the faith and deduces new insights from them. Bonaventure sees it differently. For the Seraphic Doctor, theology is to be understood principally as the

---

82. Levering, "Jesus and Metaphysics," 309.

83. Levering, 310.

84. Ratzinger, *Nature and Mission*, 29.

external expression of the faith."[85] In other words, Ratzinger sees Aquinas as exemplifying a deductive, logically inferential mode of theology, which seeks to draw new conclusions from the prior givens of sacred doctrine. For Bonaventure, however, "it does not behoove theology to bring forth new thoughts; rather it behooves it only to find the right words for thoughts, which derive not from it but from God himself. Its task would thus be simply to hear the kerygma, to understand, and then to recast it in scientific conceptual language."[86]

The emphasis therefore is on rightly grasping and communicating to others what one has received from God, rather than curiously pondering what else one can figure out. Understanding what God has revealed is the focus. Thus, receptivity is the fundamental posture of a good theologian. "For Ratzinger, the result of this reflection is that theology must first and foremost be listening, believing, and praying; it must be listening to God."[87]

Prescinding from whether the contrast between Aquinas and Bonaventure is entirely accurate or hyperbolic (I leave that to scholars of medieval thought), it is in any case an interesting dichotomy. It is fair to say that—here, as elsewhere—Ratzinger's own approach is more akin to his description of Bonaventure. Throughout Ratzinger's works, one gets the sense that he follows Bonaventure's model. He first believes, then tries to understand, and only then tries to explain what he has understood. It is not primarily deducing further truths but unpacking the truth of the faith itself that is important for Ratzinger.

Now that we have explored Ratzinger's theological method in some detail, we can turn to his thoughts on specific theological topics. Of course, we will continue to show how each topic relates

85. Richard DeClue, "Joseph Ratzinger's Theology of Divine Revelation" (SThD diss., The Catholic University of America, 2021), 244, https://cuislandora.wrlc.org/islandora/object /cuislandora:223939. See Ratzinger, *Offenbarungsverständnis*, 204–205.

86. Ratzinger, *Offenbarungsverständnis*, 205.

87. Emery de Gaál, *The Theology of Pope Benedict XVI: The Christocentric Shift* (New York: Palgrave MacMillan, 2010), 61.

to other topics throughout the following chapters. This relationality of the various Christian doctrines and theological specialties will be clearer through the order of presentation. Fittingly, we will start with the origin of all things: the Triune God.

3

The Triune God

We now turn to the first and most foundational area of Ratzinger's theological unity: the Triune God.

THE QUESTION OF GOD

The typical neo-Scholastic approach to fundamental theology would begin by offering proofs of God's existence in precise, logically constructed arguments. Ratzinger, preferring the personalism exemplified by the likes of St. Augustine,[1] starts with a different consideration: the condition of the person questioning. There is a certain wisdom to his approach. You can be as rational, objective, and logical as you wish, but the receptivity of the person to whom you are speaking (or the receptivity of the person asking the question for oneself) is a prior condition affecting one's ability to see or to accept the results of the intellectual inquiry.

We see here a hint of that primacy of the will that is commonly attributed to the Franciscan tradition in contradistinction to the Dominican tradition's emphasis on knowledge. These two great Scholastic traditions are exemplified by St. Bonaventure and St. Thomas Aquinas, respectively. Pope Benedict XVI himself speaks about their different approaches while affirming the legitimacy of

1. See Pablo Blanco Sarto, *La Teología de Joseph Ratzinger: Una introducción* (Madrid: Pelícano, 2011), 125ff.

both: "Along these lines we could also say that the loftiest category for St. Thomas is the true, whereas for St. Bonaventure it is
the good. It would be mistaken to see a contradiction in these two
answers. For both of them the true is also the good, and the good
is also the true; to see God is to love and to love is to see. Hence it
was a question of their different interpretation of a fundamentally
shared vision."[2] For both Aquinas and Bonaventure, the intellect
and the will work together, and so the fact that one prioritizes
knowledge of the truth and the other prioritizes love of the good
should not—as Pope Benedict has argued—lead one to speak of a
radical contradiction but rather a difference in emphasis.

Nevertheless, in this case, as elsewhere, Benedict tends in
the more Bonaventurian direction. He notes the influence of
Pseudo-Dionysius on St. Bonaventure with respect to knowledge
and love. For Pseudo-Dionysius, "In the ascent toward God one
can reach a point in which reason no longer sees. But in the night
of the intellect love still sees[;] it sees what is inaccessible to reason. Love goes beyond reason, it sees further, it enters more profoundly into God's mystery."[3] These reflections are reminiscent of
one of the Beatitudes: "Blessed are the pure in heart, for they will
see God" (Matt. 5:8). Purity of heart and will determines how
much we can see and thus how much we can know. A pure heart
includes an openness to the truth, a humility of reception without which we may be incapable or unwilling to seek or to accept
the truth. This view is also found in Pauline literature, as Benedict XVI noted in what has come to be called his "Regensburg
Address." In that address, the Holy Father expressed both the
surpassing quality of love's perception over mere rationality and
the remaining unity between love and reason that is rooted in the
object of that love: God himself. "Certainly, love, as Saint Paul
says, 'transcends' knowledge and is thereby capable of perceiving

---

2. Benedict XVI, General Audience, March 17, 2010, quoted in Benedict XVI, "St.
Bonaventure," in *Great Teachers* (Huntington, IN: Our Sunday Visitor, 2011), 104.

3. Benedict XVI, *Great Teachers*, 106.

more than thought alone (cf. *Eph* 3:19); nonetheless it continues to be love of the God who is *Logos*."[4]

In these remarks, one can glimpse the personalist approach of Pope Benedict. He does not view theology as taking place primarily according to the cold logic of mathematics. The human spirit is a dynamic, complex reality that is affected by a plethora of circumstances, and the individual person's condition affects their vision. As Ratzinger writes:

> These considerations also show us one fundamental aspect of the question of man's knowledge of God. We see that, ultimately, the knowledge of God is not a purely theoretical matter: it depends on the relationship that a man establishes between himself and the world and between his own self and his life. . . . On a deeper level, this depends on prior decisions taken in the relationship. . . . Is he [God] a competitor, a danger, or a reason for confidence? And this in turn determines whether man in the long run is compelled to contradict this Witness or to say Yes to him in reverence and thankfulness.[5]

In other words, the acceptance of God's revelation in faith is not just a matter of logical proof. "It is my view," writes Ratzinger, "that the neoscholastic rationalism that was trying to reconstruct the *praeambula fidei*, the approach to faith, with pure rational certainty, by means of rational argument that was strictly independent of any faith, has failed."[6]

For Ratzinger, then, the question of God is not just a matter

---

4. Benedict XVI, "Faith, Reason, and the University: Memories and Reflections," Apostolic Journey of His Holiness Benedict XVI to München, Altötting and Regensburg, September 12, 2006, vatican.va.

5. Joseph Ratzinger, *The God of Jesus Christ: Meditations on the Triune God*, trans. Brian McNeil (San Francisco: Ignatius, 2008), 17.

6. Joseph Ratzinger, *Truth and Tolerance: Christian Belief and World Religions*, trans. Henry Taylor (San Francisco: Ignatius, 2004), 136. Ratzinger thinks that Karl Barth was correct to critique such a use of philosophy in a manner totally independent of faith as somehow a means to establish faith, even if Barth went too far in the opposite direction of seeing faith as inher-

of intellectual curiosity, but it is—for every person who honestly confronts the question—an intimately personal issue with profound implications. "This reflection leads us to the real starting point of the question of God, which is much more basic than the dispute about proofs of God's existence."[7]

Furthermore, there is no opting out of the question. Everyone must take a stance on the question of God, either explicitly and intentionally or implicitly and by the default of inaction. It is inescapable; for, even if one attempts to ignore the question, one must still act either as if God does or does not exist.

Relatedly, it would be a false presumption to think that only those who believe in God are plagued by doubt, as if unbelief is immune from doubt. "Just as the believer knows himself to be constantly threatened by unbelief, which he must experience as a continual temptation, so for the unbeliever faith remains a temptation and a threat to his apparently permanently closed world."[8] It is an illusion to think that the unbeliever has—by default—more certainty than the believer. "In other words, both the believer and the unbeliever share, each in his own way, doubt *and* belief, if they do not hide from themselves and from the truth of their being. Neither can quite escape either doubt or belief; for the one, faith is present *against* doubt; for the other, *through* doubt in the *form* of doubt."[9] In a way, not believing in God is still a belief subject to doubt.

In contemporary times, there is a tendency to pit science and faith against one another. This tendency can give nonbelievers a false sense of security but only if they remain unreflective and at

---

ently contrary and independent of reason. See Ratzinger, *Truth and Tolerance*, 136. For a brief synopsis of Ratzinger's approach to apologetics, see Richard DeClue, "Joseph Ratzinger," in *The New Apologetics: Defending the Faith in a Post-Christian Era*, ed. Matthew Nelson (Park Ridge, IL: Word on Fire Institute, 2022), 106–111.

7. Ratzinger, *God of Jesus Christ*, 17.

8. Joseph Ratzinger, *Introduction to Christianity*, trans. Mary Frances McCarthy (San Francisco: Ignatius, 1987), 45.

9. Ratzinger, *Introduction*, 46–47.

a superficial level. The modern tendency to reduce knowledge solely to that which we can do or make is a grave error. Ratzinger calls this epistemological reductionism *Machbarkeitswissen*[10] (the knowledge of makeability or doability). I see it as related to the ancient Greek category of *techne*.

In our own day, technological achievements have been viewed as evidence for the success of the scientific endeavor and thus have led to confidence in the power and possibilities of science. The recognition of scientific potential is not bad in itself, of course. However, danger arises when one tries to nullify the affirmation of any other type of knowledge or to reject the significance of anything other than scientific facts.

But when one digs deeper, one begins to unearth the startling truth: science and technology are not self-sufficient. They do not provide their own foundations, and they certainly do not suffice to establish meaning for human life.

I would like to offer an example to illustrate Ratzinger's point. Imagine that there are two chemical compounds—A and B—that, when they interact, lead to result C. On the level of pure fact, it does not matter what A and B are, let alone the result. However, the mere facts of the chemical reaction between A and B are not nearly as important as understanding that compound A is an antidote to poison B that results in the saving of human life (C).

Thus, even in the arena of the medical sciences (arguably one of the most successful areas of scientific advancement), the value of the very science itself is dependent upon a level of meaning that scientific positivism itself does not and cannot provide. The judgment that a particular technology is good or bad is not a scientific judgment; it is a value judgment or even a *moral* judgment. Science is not the source of its own value. Without a *telos*,

10. See Ratzinger, 63–69, especially 66.

without a goal that has value, even science and technology would be worthless.

That is also why it is a scary proposition for all knowledge to be reduced to the hard sciences alone. Doing so would lead to a form of agnosticism about every other area that touches upon human existence, including and especially moral issues. It is a twisted form of irony that in the age of overconfidence in scientific knowledge, there is a simultaneous preponderance of relativism that denies the objectivity of truth. Yet, Ratzinger thinks this strange coexistence is inevitable in a reductionistic worldview. "By thinking only of the practicable, of what can be made, [man] is in danger of forgetting to reflect on himself and on the meaning of his existence."[11]

In contrast to the reduction of all knowledge to factual *techne*, faith opens up a level of knowledge that is at once higher and deeper. Faith "does not belong to the relationship of 'know-make' . . . but is much better expressed in the quite different relationship of 'stand-understand.'"[12]

Man is capable of so much more than knowledge of scientific facts. The human mind can perceive the more important level of understanding, which sees the meaning behind the facts. Data is one thing; what the data means is something greater. One must take a stand, and where one decides to stand has ramifications for what one makes of the data. In this perspective, "Faith in God appears as a holding on to God through which man gains a firm foothold for his life. Faith is thereby defined as taking up a position, as taking a stand trustfully on the ground of the word of God."[13] By contrast, "'If you do not believe, then you do not understand, either.'"[14]

It is important to note that the choice between the two stances

11. Ratzinger, 71.
12. Ratzinger, 68.
13. Ratzinger, 69.
14. Ratzinger, 69. The quote inside this citation is a reference to Isa. 7:9.

is not equal. Faith leads to understanding, while unbelief leads to a lack of understanding. Why is that? One may reasonably come to this conclusion: either one affirms that understanding (i.e., meaning) is *real* and thus has a *real* foundation, or one denies understanding and sees meaning as a mere illusion resulting from random interactions of subatomic particles. The power of belief, in this case, is that it actually makes *sense* of everything else.

This view is reflected in Ratzinger's response to a question about creation and evolution posed to him during a radio interview in 1968:[15] "Of course the question remains open whether being, understood in such a way as a path—that is, evolution as a whole—has a meaning, and it cannot be decided within the theory of evolution itself; for that theory this is a methodologically foreign question, although of course for a live human being it is the fundamental question of the whole thing. Science rightly acknowledges its limits in this regard and declares that this question, which is indispensable for man, cannot be answered within science, but only within the framework of a 'faith system.'"[16]

Science does not explain everything. Such an idea is an illusion. The truth is that humans cannot really live without meaning. Taken to the extreme, scientific reductionism thus leads inevitably to dissatisfaction. As Ratzinger observes, "The world of planned economy, of research, of exact calculation and experiment is quite obviously not enough to satisfy people."[17] Knowing facts about the universe may be interesting, but it does not grant meaning and value to life. Truth is not reducible to that

15. See Joseph Ratzinger, "Schöpfungsglaube und Evolutionstheorie," in *Wer ist das eigentlich—Gott?* ed. H.J. Schulz (Munich: Suhrkamp, 1969), 232–245. Also in Joseph Ratzinger, *Dogma und Verkündigung*, 4th ed. (Donauwörth: Wewel, 2005), 152–156. In what follows, we will be quoting from a translation of large sections of this interview found in Christoph Schönborn, foreword to *Creation and Evolution: A Conference with Pope Benedict XVI in Castel Gandolfo*, trans. Michael J. Miller (San Francisco: Ignatius, 2008), 7–23.

16. Ratzinger, "Schöpfungsglaube," quoted in Schönborn, "Foreword," 12. For a book-length treatment of the question of evolution from the perspective of Pope Benedict XVI, see Matthew J. Ramage, *From the Dust of the Earth: Benedict XVI, the Bible, and the Theory of Evolution* (Washington, DC: The Catholic University of America Press, 2022).

17. Joseph Ratzinger, *Faith and the Future* (Chicago: Franciscan Herald, 1971), 25–26.

which we can do or make; rather, all our activity has its basis on something prior that sustains its significance. "Through faith," explains Aidan Nichols, "we acknowledge that a meaning adequate to making sense of experience can only be received. . . . In saying *credo*, we declare that in this world the receiving of meaning is prior to its making by man. . . . So far from being irrational, faith is therefore a movement toward meaning and truth, toward the *logos*."[18]

Reducing all knowledge to facticity and to what we can do through technology impoverishes human life and thought. The temptation to this error is sometimes based on a false perception of the real extent of what science knows. There can exist an ironic fideism in science's explanatory power. If one thinks about it more deeply, however, the illusion can be dispersed. For man "is insecure most of all at the point where exact science abandons him, and it is the measure of his abandonment that first makes him aware of how narrow the slice of reality is in which science gives him security."[19] Science accounts for very little of the most important aspects of human existence. Despite popular perceptions to the contrary, even some of the most well-established scientific facts (e.g., gravity) are only descriptions of what we observe rather than true understandings of how and why they are the case. For example, we know *that* the forces of nature exist and can roughly describe their effects. That does not mean that we know how or why they work the way that they do. Saying that a messenger particle conveys the information may sound like an explanation, but—at bottom—it is only a superficial description that does not give a satisfactory explanation for the observed phenomena. The limits of science are even more pronounced with respect to the most important aspects of our lives. Thus, if science is the only

18. Aidan Nichols, *The Thought of Benedict XVI: An Introduction to the Theology of Joseph Ratzinger* (New York: Burns & Oates, 2005), 108.

19. Ratzinger, *Faith and the Future*, 28.

thing we trust or believe in, then we have very little confidence in or basis for most aspects of our lived existence.

If mere scientific fact is all that one accepts, then everything else seems to be an illusion. But such a stance does not explain our experience; it explains it away. It does not give meaning; it denies the existence of meaning. Yet, when one sees the cosmos not as a random, unexplainable fact but as the creation of God endowed with a purpose, then meaning has a foundation, and a rational one at that. Taking a stand in faith, then, makes more sense out of everything—including science—which is itself a reason to believe.

Notice how Ratzinger's approach to the question of God is vastly different than logical argumentation about necessary being. That is not to say that proofs of God are without value, or that Aquinas' "Five Ways" have no place in fundamental theology. They certainly do. Nevertheless, Ratzinger demonstrates that there are other, complementary ways of confronting the question of God. He considers the human condition and how it might affect the results of one's inquiry. He challenges would-be skeptics to reflect more deeply about the ramifications of the stance they might choose to take. He leads one to the realization that faith is no mere blind wish but has real explanatory power in which everything makes more sense, because the meaning we long for and naturally intuit *as real* has a firm basis only if the universe has its origin and goal in the Creator. Faith makes *more sense* out of the world, and that is nothing to take lightly.

THE GOD OF FAITH AND THE GOD OF THE PHILOSOPHERS

A person must—explicitly or implicitly—take a stance on the question of God, and the stance one takes either serves as a ground upon which meaning and understanding are affirmed or serves as a reason to reject the reality of meaning and thus of understanding.

Such considerations are more of a reflection on the origins and significance of the question of God than a direct answer to the question. Furthermore, no real content has yet been given to the concept of God. We will begin to explore what is meant by "God" both from a biblical/faith perspective as well as how that perspective correlates to or deviates from the classical philosophical notion of God. Ratzinger's presentation and comparison of the biblical data with the philosophical concept is an example of his method's principles outlined in the previous chapter.

In the first place, Ratzinger considers the significance of various references to God in salvation history as evidenced in Sacred Scripture. Prior to the Exodus, Israel's God was primarily referred to as El or Elohim. The significance of these appellations is manifold. It was common in those days for "gods" to be connected with a specific place, to be a "god of this place" in contrast to a "god of that place." This is not so with El. El and Elohim evoke the social and personal character of Israel's God, who is not connected to or limited by a specific location. Rather, *El* is the God of a certain people: the God of Abraham, Isaac, and Jacob. "The God upon whom they decided is characterized by the fact that, in the language of religious typology, he is a *numen personale* (personal god), not a *numen locale* (local god)."[20] At this point, Ratzinger's oft-repeated motif of the I–You relation makes another appearance. In Israel's faith, "God is seen on the plane of I and You, not on the plane of the spatial. He thus moves away into the transcendence of the illimitable and by this very fact shows himself to be he who is always (not just at one point) near, whose power is boundless."[21]

The connection between God as personal and God as

20. Ratzinger, *Introduction*, 122.
21. Ratzinger, 123.

boundless leads to another aspect of the God of Israel that Ratzinger believes is significant. God is not just a powerful being alongside other powerful beings. El is the highest and greatest power of all, "that power alone which embraces in itself all power and stands above all individual powers."[22] Added to this, the God of Israel is also the God of the promise, who can be the basis of hope, because he has a plan for the future: there is meaning, a goal, to history.[23]

There is also significance to the fact that Israel most often referred to God as Elohim, which is technically the plural of El, even though they affirmed that God is one and only one. "He is one, but as the exceeding great, entirely Other, he himself transcends the bounds of singular and plural; he lies beyond them. Although in the Old Testament . . . there is certainly no kind of revelation of the Trinity, nevertheless in this process there is latent an experience that points toward the Christian concept of the triune God. . . . While God is indeed radically One, he cannot be forced into our categories of singular and plural; rather, he stands above them."[24]

With the theophany of the burning bush experienced by Moses, another appellation for God appears. It is—at one and the same time—both a name and yet a refusal to give a name. The origin of the precise meaning of the name Yahweh is not entirely certain, and there are many ways of rendering its possible meaning. What stands out is that it is given to Moses after Moses asks who he is supposed to say sent him. Rather than give a unique, delimited name to distinguish him from the gods with other names in a manner that would put him on their level, the answer given is more mysterious: "I Am Who I Am" or "I Am." The translators of the Septuagint saw a connection between this self-designation of God and the God of the ancient Greek

22. Ratzinger, 124.
23. See Ratzinger, 124.
24. Ratzinger, 125.

philosophers, who understood God as being itself. On the other hand, many biblical scholars see the "I Am" as also indicating "I am here for you" and thus not just ultimate Being-in-itself but as the relational Being-for.[25]

All of these aspects of the divine name are taken up and extended in the New Testament, especially in the Johannine tradition. There, Jesus is associated with both Moses and the burning bush. He is the one who reveals the name of God (John 17:6, 11, 12, and 26), precisely as the one in whom God is revealed: "Since in the view of the fourth Gospel Jesus unites in himself, applies to himself, the 'I am' of Exodus 3 and Isaiah 43, it becomes clear at the same time that *he himself* is the name, that is the 'invocability' of God. . . . The name is, no longer merely a word, but a person: Jesus himself."[26]

These reflections reveal a two-sided presentation of God in Sacred Scripture: (1) God is the highest being, the source of all things, and existence itself that stands above time and space *as well as* (2) the one who makes himself invocable, revealing himself as the one who is most near to us as being *for* us, to such a degree that he has—in Jesus Christ—become one of us.[27] Both dimensions are indispensable for the biblical understanding of God. Moreover, Judeo-Christian faith insists that this God is also the only real God. The God of Israel is, in truth, the God of all, God alone.[28] The biblical God is incomparable to various gods spoken of in pagan myths. The God of faith is affirmed precisely as the God of reality. This is a metaphysical claim, as we saw in the prior chapter.

Here, then, a point of contact is established between the God of faith and the God of the philosophers. As Nichols explains, "For all the differences between the religious philosophy of the

---

25. See Ratzinger, 126–130.
26. Ratzinger, 133.
27. See Ratzinger, 135.
28. See Ratzinger, 136.

Greek sages and the Jewish prophetic and sapiential movements, both constitute a striving toward the *logos*: a critique of myth."[29] The commonality between the faith of ancient Israel and the position of ancient philosophers is noteworthy. "Contemporary scholarship," writes Ratzinger, "is coming to see more and more clearly that there are quite amazing parallels in chronology and content between the philosophers' criticism of the myths in Greece and the prophets' criticism of the gods in Israel."[30]

The early Church Fathers were conscious of this similarity. When considering Marcus Terrentius Varro's (116–27 BC) three categories of theology, St. Augustine places Christianity in the category of the natural theology of the philosophers in contrast with both the myth-based mystical theology of the poets and the civic cults ordered toward political utility. As Tracey Rowland notes, "Christianity . . . has its antecedents in philosophical rationality, not in mythical cults which have their ultimate justification in their political usefulness."[31] Rowland continues: "Christianity understood itself as the triumph of knowledge over myth."[32] Thus, Ratzinger states quite explicitly that "early Christianity boldly and resolutely made its choice and carried out its purification by deciding for the God of the philosophers and *against* the gods of the various religions."[33] The God of faith has much more similarity to ancient Greek philosophy's notion of God than to the pagan notions of "god" or "gods."

In turn, it is precisely Christianity's claims to rationality that support its universal missionary efforts (in addition to the divine mandate, of course). Christianity "had to be taken forth to all peoples not as a specific religion elbowing its way among others,

---

29. Nichols, *Thought of Benedict XVI*, 113.

30. Ratzinger, *Introduction*, 139.

31. Tracey Rowland, *Benedict XVI: A Guide for the Perplexed* (New York: T&T Clark, 2010), 115.

32. Rowland, 115.

33. Ratzinger, *Introduction*, 137.

not through any sort of religious imperialism, but as truth which makes illusion superfluous."[34]

This missionary aspect of Christian faith is also a reason why philosophy was employed by the early Church Fathers. As Hansjürgen Verweyen explains, "With the crossing over of the 'horizon of Jerusalem' to the whole world, the biblical proclamation inevitably had to carry out a translation into terms that are fundamentally understandable to all people."[35] Christianity insisted on its universal validity and thus believed it could use human reason as a tool for converting the nations. Seeing in certain philosophers the presentation of fundamental truths, the earliest Christian theologians viewed them as allies in the fight against the myths of paganism.

Philosophy is, then, a much-needed tool for theology. At the same time, faith provides benefits to philosophy, that is, to human reason. "By no means the least important practical function of faith is to offer healing for the reason as reason, not to overpower it or to remain outside it, but in fact to bring it to itself again"; once "faith has set it on the right path again—reason can once more see properly for itself."[36] In other words, to say that the God of faith and the God of the philosophers is one and the same does not mean that the precise contents of what is known about this one God is exactly the same, as if knowledge gained through revelation and faith added nothing to what is known about God through unaided human reason (philosophy).

On the contrary, while faith does insist that the God knowable through reason as pure Being-itself is the same God believed in by Christian faith, more has been revealed about and by this God than could be known through human reason alone. So, on

34. Joseph Ratzinger, "The Truth of Christianity" (address, University of Sorbonne, November 27, 1999), trans. Maria Klepacka, quoted in Rowland, *Benedict XVI*, 115.

35. Hansjürgen Verweyen, *Joseph Ratzinger–Benedikt XVI.: Die Entwicklung seines Denkens* (Darmstadt: WBG, 2007), 31.

36. Ratzinger, *Truth and Tolerance*, 136.

the one hand, "he [God] does not thereby cease to be what they [the philosophers] had discovered," but, on the other hand, "the God of the philosophers is quite different from what the philosophers had thought him to be," for he is "at one and the same time the God of faith, the God of men."[37] The fact that this uncaused cause, the first mover, is also the God who has revealed himself in history makes all the difference. "By deciding exclusively in favor of the God of the philosophers and logically declaring this God to be the God who speaks to man and to whom one can pray, the Christian faith gave a completely new significance to this God of the philosophers, removing him from the purely academic realm and thus profoundly transforming him."[38]

While ancient philosophy had acknowledged that there must be one God, the basis of all existence, the uncaused cause, etc., it also seemed unfitting for this God to be concerned with the world too directly since only God himself was a "worthy" object of God's intellect. With divine revelation, however, "this God who had been understood as pure Being or pure thought, circling around forever closed in upon itself without reaching over to man and his little world; this God of the philosophers, whose pure eternity and unchangeability had excluded any relation with the changeable and transitory, now appeared to the eye of faith as the God of men, who is not only thought of all thoughts, the eternal mathematics of the universe, but also *agape*, the power of creative love."[39] When considered in light of St. Anselm of Canterbury's ontological argument, which understands God as "that than which no greater can be conceived," what is noteworthy here is that revelation has not subtracted from the greatness of the concept of God (philosophically speaking) but indeed added to it.

The fact that this God, knowable as the first cause and sustainer of all existence, has also taken an interest in *us* reveals this

37. Ratzinger, *Introduction*, 144.
38. Ratzinger, 143.
39. Ratzinger, 143.

God as being even more wonderful than rationally conceived. Ratzinger points us to another author's beautiful way of expressing this truth: "the aphorism with which Hölderlin prefaced his *Hyperion* will serve to recall the Christian image of the true greatness of God: 'Non coerceri maximo, contineri tamen a minimo, divinum est' (Not to be encompassed by the greatest, but to let oneself be encompassed by the smallest—that is divine). The boundless spirit who bears in himself the totality of Being reaches beyond the 'greatest' . . . and he reaches into the smallest, because to him nothing is too small."[40]

There is a reversal of values here. There are those who would argue that divine revelation is foolish since, compared with all the rest of the cosmos, man occupies such a small, infinitesimal fraction, that it is sheer arrogance to think we matter to supreme being itself. To such sentiments, one can simply reply that quantity is not as important as quality. "To him who as spirit upholds and encompasses the universe, a spirit, a man's heart with its ability to love, is greater than all the milky ways in the universe. Quantitative criteria become irrelevant; other orders of magnitude become visible, according to which the infinitely small is the truly embracing and truly great."[41]

Once again, we see here the primacy of love reflected in Ratzinger's presentation. As he also says, "The message of the Gospel, and the Christian picture of God contained in it, corrects philosophy and lets us know that love is higher than mere thought. Absolute thought is a kind of love."[42]

One poignant example of how revelation—and thus the God of faith—corrects and augments the understanding of God known only through philosophy arises with the question of divine impassibility. Margaret Turek offers a helpful presentation of this question in her book on atonement. There, she expresses

40. Ratzinger, 146.
41. Ratzinger, 146–147.
42. Ratzinger, 147.

what Christian faith and philosophy have in common with respect to divine impassibility along with an important caveat gained through divine revelation. Along with philosophy, Christian faith affirms that "God is *not passible* (not naturally subject to suffering) in that God is not subject to suffering by way of being involuntarily overpowered from the outside. Neither is God passible insofar as the term signifies being subject to blameworthy passions. . . . God is *not mutable* (not naturally subject to change) by way of increasing or decreasing in perfection (cf. Jas 1:17). . . . Nevertheless, 'God loves us with the love of friendship, and he wishes to be loved by us in return. When this love is offended, Sacred Scripture speaks of suffering on the part of God. On the other hand, it speaks of his joy when the sinner is converted (cf. Lk 15:7).'"[43]

While in ancient philosophy, the idea that God must be impassible was used to support the conclusion that God must not be directly interested in us, revelation says the exact opposite. Here, the true character of impassibility comes to the fore. Following the research of a patristics scholar, Turek writes, "Gavrilyuk makes clear that for the Church Fathers, divine impassibility does not denote the absence of affectivity; it does not mean that God is aloof from and unconcerned about his creatures. Rather, impassibility denotes God's perfect control over his affectivity, such that it is expressive only of pure selfless love."[44]

Thus, while the God of faith is aligned with the God of the philosophers, the God of faith also transcends the limits of

---

43. Margaret M. Turek, *Atonement: Soundings in Biblical, Trinitarian, and Spiritual Theology* (San Francisco: Ignatius, 2022), 34–35. Here, Turek quotes from International Theological Commission, "Theology, Christology, Anthropology," in *International Theological Commission: Texts and Documents, 1969–1985*, ed. Michael Sharkey and Thomas Weinandy (San Francisco: Ignatius, 2009), 226. Turek's book is an attempt to advocate for an atonement soteriology drawing from the tradition according to four theologians: John Paul II, Joseph Ratzinger/Benedict XVI, Hans Urs von Balthasar, and Norbert Hoffmann. Turek insists that all four are in substantial agreement even if different nuances are present in each.

44. Turek, *Atonement*, 247. This quote comes from Appendix B of her book, titled, "On God's Impassible Passion of Love."

philosophical knowledge of God in two important ways. First, the God of philosophy was self-centered, thinking only about himself, whereas God has revealed himself as fundamentally relational and concerned with humankind. As Ratzinger affirms, "The highest mode of Being includes the element of relationship."[45] Flowing from this, we come to the second way in which the God of faith transcends the limits of philosophical knowledge of God. God is not—as philosophy understood him—pure thought alone but also love: "The *logos* of the whole world, the creative original thought, is at the same time love; in fact this thought is creative because, as thought, it is love, and, as love, it is thought. It becomes apparent that truth and love are originally identical."[46]

Still more, the revelation of God as Triune (one God in three persons) has further implications for purifying philosophy. Because (according to ancient Greek philosophy) the three transcendentals of being were unity (oneness), truth, and goodness, relationality was left out of that category, and thus out of the philosophical concept of God. Aristotle, for instance, thought that relation exists only where there is multiplicity, which was understood as an imperfection. As Pablo Blanco Sarto notes, "The ancients believed that only unity was divine. Multiplicity, on the other hand, seemed to them to be something secondary, something excessively human: multiplicity comes from disintegration and tends toward it."[47] Consequently, multiplicity and relationality were quite low on the metaphysical ranking system. As Ratzinger puts it, "Greek thought always regarded the many individual creatures, including the many individual human beings, only as individuals, arising out of the splitting up of the idea in matter."[48] The truly real was what was most absolute, the most general. The multiplication of

---

45. Ratzinger, *Introduction*, 148.

46. Ratzinger, 148.

47. Blanco, *Teología de Joseph Ratzinger*, 132. See also Ratzinger, *Introduction*, 178.

48. Ratzinger, *Introduction*, 160.

individuals was seen as a kind of imperfection upon which relation is based.

With the revelation that the one God is, in fact, a relation of three divine persons, a whole new understanding of relation is made possible. "The Christian confession of God as one and three (of the one who is at the same time . . . unity and multiplicity par excellence) reveals the conviction that divinity transcends our categories of unity and multiplicity."[49] As Ratzinger himself puts it, "Not only unity is divine; plurality, too, is something primordial and has its inner ground in God himself. Plurality . . . corresponds to the creative fullness of God, who himself stands above plurality and unity, encompassing both."[50]

Thus, relationality is no longer a low-level metaphysical category reserved for finite, imperfect beings but is rooted in God himself. As Aidan Nichols explains, "The Trinitarian dogma makes it clear that *relation*, which for Aristotle had been simply among the 'accidents' or contingent circumstances of being, by contrast with 'substance', the sole sustaining form of the real, in fact stands beside substance as an 'equally primordial form of being'."[51]

As Nichols notes, *relation* is no longer considered to be an "accident" in the Aristotelian sense. Ratzinger comes to the same conclusion, drawing directly from St. Augustine. With respect to the Trinity, "Augustine could attempt, at least in outline, to show the interplay between threeness and unity by saying, for example . . . (in God there is nothing accidental, but only substance and relation). Relation is here recognized as a third specific fundamental category between substance and accident, the two great categorical forms of thought in Antiquity."[52] Unlike accidents,

49. Blanco, *Teología de Joseph Ratzinger*, 132. See also, Ratzinger, *Introduction*, 178.

50. Ratzinger, *Introduction*, 178–179.

51. Nichols, *Thought of Benedict XVI*, 119. Here, Nichols points the reader to Augustine, *De Trinitate* 5.5.6 and Ratzinger, *Introduction*, 131.

52. Joseph Ratzinger, "Concerning the Notion of Person in Theology," trans. Michael Waldstein, *Communio* 17, no. 3 (Fall 1990): 444–445. This was originally published as Joseph Ratzinger, "Zum Personenverständnis in der Theologie," in *Dogma und Verkündigung*, 205–223.

relation is an inherent part of God's being. Relation, then, is an aspect of the highest metaphysical reality. God as personal is God as interpersonal and not merely as an absolute individual unrelated to everything or anyone else. Far from being a sign of imperfection, relation is part of the perfection of personhood.

As Ratzinger puts it, "If it is the case that the person is more than the individual, that the many is something real and not something secondary, that there exists a primacy of the particular over the universal, then oneness is not the unique and final thing; plurality, too, has its own and definitive right."[53] Being-in-relation is divine and thus also a perfection, not just the residue of the limitation of finite, material being. "In this vision of the world, the person is not the mere individual, a monad, an exemplar born of matter from the division of an idea."[54]

Ratzinger thinks this is the real distinction between the God of faith and the God of Greek philosophy, which also has implications for our understanding of humanity. "The Christian sees in man, not an individual, but a person; and it seems to me that this passage from individual to person contains the whole span of the transition from antiquity to Christianity, from Platonism to faith."[55] The concept of person expands mere individuality precisely through its relational character. "The unrelated, unrelatable, absolutely One could not be person. There is no such thing as person in the categorical singular."[56]

Ratzinger sees the concept of person founded upon the Trinity as the most important contribution of faith and theology to philosophy. Prior to the dogma of the Trinity, the concept of person was relatively rare and of little importance to philosophy.

53. Ratzinger, *Introduction*, 161.

54. Blanco, *Teología de Joseph Ratzinger*, 129.

55. Ratzinger, *Introduction*, 160. Of course, personhood is not obtained through any type of relation whatsoever. Inanimate objects and other subrational creatures also have relations. Personal relation involves intellect and will, as we shall see in our later treatment of theological anthropology.

56. Ratzinger, 180.

Speaking about two important questions—"what is God" and "who is Christ"—Ratzinger makes this very point when he says, "'In order to resolve these two questions, which arose immediately with reflection on the faith, this thinking made use of the word *prosopon* (person), until then without philosophical relevance and actually very little used; it gave it a new meaning and opened a new dimension to human thought.' Here begins, according to Gilson and Ratzinger, a great revolution in thought."[57]

As we already saw in the last chapter when discussing the importance of the concept of *communio*, interpersonal relation is at the origin and end of all reality. It is, in many ways, the leitmotif of Christian faith and as such the key to Catholic theology. This truth leads directly into the topic for our next section: God as Three-in-One.

GOD AS THREE-IN-ONE

The revelation of God as three-in-one has profound implications for our understanding of metaphysics (especially the category of relation) and for various aspects of theology. Relationality is not—as philosophers supposed—a low level of existence resulting from the finite character of lesser beings. Rather, relationality is at the heart of the God who is both self-subsisting being and the ground of all beings. Relationality is an intimate aspect of perfect, divine being. "The experience of the God who conducts a dialogue, of the God who is not only *logos* but also *dia-logos*, not only idea and meaning but speech and word in the reciprocal exchanges of partners in conversation—this experience exploded the ancient division of reality into substance, the real thing, and accidents, the merely circumstantial. It now became clear that

<hr />

57. Blanco, *Teología de Joseph Ratzinger*, 128. Blanco quotes here from Joseph Ratzinger, *Palabra en la Iglesia* (Salamanca: Sígueme, 1976), 165, which is a Spanish translation of *Dogma und Verkündigung*.

the dialogue, the *relatio*, stands beside the substance as an equally primordial form of being."[58]

For Ratzinger, this makes perfect sense when we consider that God is love. God is Father, Son, and Holy Spirit, and "it is only thus that the affirmation that he is 'love' becomes meaningful. If he is not love in himself, he is not love at all. But if he is love in himself, he must be 'I' and 'Thou', and this means that he must be triune."[59]

One may ask how saying that God must be "I" and "Thou" means that he must be a Trinity. "I" and "Thou" are only two terms, not three. Ratzinger himself asks this question: "Why a Trinity? We have grasped that God is two. . . . But where does this third Person suddenly come from?"[60]

Ratzinger's answer to the question is reminiscent of St. Augustine's famous psychological analogy for the Trinity. Ratzinger explains at length:

> The Father and the Son do not become one in such a way that they dissolve into each other. They remain distinct from each other, since love has its basis in a "vis-à-vis" that is not abolished. If each remains his own self, and they do not abrogate each other's existence, then their unity cannot exist in each one by himself: rather, their unity must be in the fruitfulness in which each one gives himself and in which each one is himself. They are one in virtue of the fact that their love is fruitful, that it goes beyond them. In the third Person in whom they give themselves to each other, in the Gift, they are themselves, and they are one.[61]

58. Ratzinger, *Introduction*, 183.
59. Ratzinger, *God of Jesus Christ*, 37.
60. Ratzinger, 34.
61. Ratzinger, 35.

The perichoresis of the Father, Son, and Holy Spirit explains how Being-itself is love. The highest love is not self-love. Mutual love of each other and the shared love of two for a third are more perfect still. So, as supreme being, God must also be supreme love, and supreme love involves three. Quite apart from the Aristotelian notion that God must be thinking about himself and loving himself as a monad, which would involve a self-enclosed love or self-love, the ground of all existence subsists in the loving relation of three divine persons. It is precisely this unity-in-relation, then, that characterizes the highest possible being. *Communio* is divine.

Once again, these thoughts show how faith informs reason. "The trinitarian doctrine was not born from speculation about the divinity, from a philosophical investigation about the origin of all being; but, it is the result of a laborious synthesis of certain historical experiences: specifically, from the struggle of Christian intellectuals against the trinitarian and christological heresies. It is also a concept that is found in scripture itself."[62] We cannot know that God is triune without revelation, but once this truth has been revealed, it makes *more* sense than what reason could know on its own. Knowledge of God through revelation makes *more* sense than the knowledge of God by reason alone. The truth about the God of faith is more rational than the limits of the God of philosophy, even if the Trinity can only be understood to a limited degree and is, in this sense, beyond reason. The God of faith understood as triune is more perfect than the concept of God as pure monad. By comparison with the Trinity, then, the God of the philosophers could not be "that than which no greater can be conceived."

Understanding God as a Trinity of three divine persons certainly supports and enhances Ratzinger's attraction toward personalism. Some commentators assert that the doctrine of the Trinity—and the notion of person flowing from it—is the basis

62. Blanco, *Teología de Joseph Ratzinger*, 131.

for Ratzinger's theology in general. This would make sense, given that it is the foundation of the Christian faith itself. As Ratzinger notes, "God *is*—and the Christian faith adds: God is as Father, Son, and Holy Spirit, three and one. This is the very heart of Christianity."[63] Because Ratzinger's theology is founded upon the faith of the Church, it is no surprise that the Trinity is also the ground of his own theology. "'The concept of person,' affirms Schumacher, 'obtained from the Trinitarian faith is the foundation that sustains the form of Ratzinger's theological thought.'"[64]

In order to avoid an individualistic conception of personhood, however, I would add to this last quote that it is the notion of person *as relation* that is the basis of Ratzinger's theological structure. For him, the relation between "I" and "You" is constitutive of what it means to be a person, as we saw earlier. For Ratzinger's theology of God and theological anthropology alike, the relationality of personhood is indispensable.

Relationship is so central to personhood that it is even part of the definition of the divine persons. As Ratzinger insists, "It is just as essential to the Father to say 'Son' as it is essential to the Son to say 'Father'."[65] This notion is, of course, completely commensurate with Aquinas' definition of the divine persons of the Trinity as "subsistent relations." One can only be a Father in relation to a child, and one is a son or daughter *of* one's parents. This means that the relation between the persons is not something additional or extrinsic but inherent to their personhood. As Ratzinger insists, "In God, person means relation. Relation, being related, is not something superadded to the person, but it *is* the person itself."[66]

---

63. Ratzinger, *God of Jesus Christ*, 29 (emphasis added).

64. Blanco, *Teología de Joseph Ratzinger*, 127. Here, Pablo Blanco Sarto quotes from Ferdinand Schumacher, "Creo en la resurrección de los muertos. El fin de los tiempos en la teología de Joseph Ratzinger," in *El teólogo Joseph Ratzinger*, ed. Frank Meier-Hamidi and Ferdinand Schumacher (Barcelona: Herder, 2007), 145.

65. Ratzinger, *God of Jesus Christ*, 34.

66. Ratzinger, "Concerning the Notion," 444.

At this point, it is fitting to consider each of the persons of the Trinity in Ratzinger's thought. We will consider them in the traditional order: Father, Son, and Holy Spirit. When treating the Son, we will limit our discussion of the Incarnation because that will be treated in the chapter on Christology. Thus, in the section on the second person of the Trinity, we will focus on God the Son within the Trinity itself.

GOD THE FATHER

First, let us speak about God the Father. What does it mean to profess faith in "God, the Father Almighty"? As mentioned above, "Father" is only understandable in relation to "the Son." Thus, the first article of the Creed already anticipates the second article's proclamation of belief in God the Son.[67] Again, the relationality of the Trinity comes to the fore.

It is important to note that because each divine person is understood *as* relation, they must coexist eternally in reference to one another. Their mutual relations are not additions to their personhood but define it. "Put more concretely," Ratzinger writes, "the first person does not generate in the sense that the act of generating a Son is added to the already complete person, but the person [i.e., the Father] *is* the deed of generating, of giving itself, of streaming itself forth. The person is identical with this act of self-donation."[68]

Further, Ratzinger wants us to be cognizant of the fact that when we call God "Father," we are not extrapolating from human experience and projecting it onto the divine; it is quite the reverse. "The biblical Father is not a heavenly duplicate of human fatherhood. Rather, he posits something new: he is the divine

---

67. See Ratzinger, *Introduction*, 149.
68. Ratzinger, "Concerning the Notion," 444.

critique of human fatherhood. God establishes his own criterion."[69] In other words, the extent to which one is a good human father is judged based upon God's fatherhood and not the other way around. As Ratzinger notes, "While we have different earthly fathers, we all come from one single Father, who is the measure and source of all fatherhood."[70]

That principle is important to help overcome potential roadblocks to understanding God as Father. Poor experiences of human fatherhood can make it difficult to understand or relate to God as Father. Ratzinger believes there is a crisis in fatherhood in the world today, and this travesty can hinder our understanding of God. "Human fatherhood can give us an inkling of what God is; but where fatherhood no longer exists, where genuine fatherhood is no longer experienced as a phenomenon that goes beyond the biological dimension to embrace a human and intellectual sphere as well, it becomes meaningless to speak of God the Father."[71]

As pope, he made similar remarks during a 2013 general audience, highlighting various ways in which authentic human fatherhood is hindered in our own day and how this can make it difficult for us to relate to God as our Father. He writes:

> It is not always easy today to talk about fatherhood, especially in the Western world. Families are broken, the workplace is ever more absorbing, families worry and often struggle to make ends meet and the distracting invasion of the media invades our daily life: these are some of the many factors that

---

69. Ratzinger, *God of Jesus Christ*, 33. See also Ratzinger, *Dogma und Verkündigung*, 94–98, 101–104.

70. Benedict XVI, *Jesus of Nazareth*, vol. 1, *From the Baptism in the Jordan to the Transfiguration*, trans. Adrian J. Walker (New York: Doubleday, 2007), 141. Benedict XVI continues this thought by citing a couple of biblical passages. "As Saint Paul says: 'I bow my knees before the Father, from whom every fatherhood in heaven and on earth is named' (Eph. 3:14–15). In the background we hear the Lord himself speaking: 'Call no man your father on earth, for you have one Father, who is in heaven' (Matt. 23:9)."

71. Ratzinger, *God of Jesus Christ*, 29.

can stand in the way of a calm and constructive relationship between father and child. At times communication becomes difficult, trust is lacking and the relationship with the father figure can become problematic; moreover, in this way even imagining God as a father becomes problematic without credible models of reference.[72]

The effects of original and actual sin are at the origin of this problem. Man was made in the image of God; man *is* the image of God. But insofar as this image has been tarnished, it fails to reflect the one of whom man is the image. This extends to fatherhood as well. If one understands a father to be a domineering, egotistical tyrant, then one misunderstands what a father should be. At the other extreme, a disinterested, aloof father who gives hardly any guidance nor sets any boundaries whatsoever also distorts authentic fatherhood. As Benedict admits, "It is not easy for those who have experienced an excessively authoritarian and inflexible father or one who was indifferent and lacking in affection, or even absent, to think serenely of God and to entrust themselves to him with confidence."[73]

However, even experiences of bad fathers can help point us toward understanding what a good father should be by way of negation. For those who have not had good relationships with their own fathers, there is a feeling that something is wrong and that it should be otherwise. God the Father shows us how he is different from those domineering or absent fathers. He is the father that we truly need. "If human existence is to be complete," writes Ratzinger,

we need a father, in the true meaning of fatherhood that our faith discloses, namely, a responsibility for one's child that does

---

72. Benedict XVI, "General Audience," January 30, 2013, vatican.va.
73. Benedict XVI, "General Audience."

not dominate him but permits him to become his own self. This fatherhood is a love that avoids two traps: the total subjugation of the child to the father's own priorities and goals, on the one hand, and the unquestioning acceptance of the child as he is, under the pretext that this is the expression of freedom, on the other. Responsibility for one's child means the desire that he realize his own innermost truth, which lies in his Creator.[74]

We can see this sort of fatherhood in salvation history. God the Father provides for his children, who are often rebellious. He tells them what is good for them and even chastises those who act poorly. Yet he does not constrain their freedom entirely. He neither controls them as a puppeteer works a marionette nor as a tyrant who enslaves his people. He guides and disciplines but does not control every aspect of our lives. Nevertheless, as a good Father, God wants what is best for us, which can only be found in that which corresponds to the truth of our existence. He reveals that truth to us, so that we can follow the path to authentic humanity. The Ten Commandments, for instance, are not arbitrary rules of some tyrannical dictator who wishes to see how many hoops he can make us jump through. Rather, they impart the wisdom of our heavenly Father, who reveals what constitutes authentic human goodness. At the same time, he allows us to make our mistakes, even to rebel if we so choose. But he is always there to forgive and to reconcile with his prodigal children when they turn back in repentance and love.

God can be our Father—and, as such, be the exemplar for all earthly fathers to imitate—because he is already a Father in his very being. "Before the world was made, God is already the

---

74. Ratzinger, *God of Jesus Christ*, 29–30.

love of Father and Son. He can become our Father and the criterion of all fatherhood precisely because he himself is Father from eternity."[75]

We see here a correspondence between the immanent and economic Trinity. Who God the Father is within the Godhead is reflected in his relation to humanity. It is no coincidence that Jesus, the eternal Son of God, is the one who taught us the Our Father. As Ratzinger remarks, "In Jesus' prayer, the Father becomes visible and Jesus makes himself known as the Son. The unity that this reveals is the Trinity. Accordingly, becoming a Christian means sharing in Jesus' prayer. . . . Becoming a Christian means saying 'Father' with Jesus and, thus, becoming a child, God's son. . . . Being a Christian means looking at the world from this central point, which gives us freedom, hope, decisiveness and consolation."[76]

The good news is precisely that God is love, both within the inner-Trinitarian life and in relation to us. Despite our sinful rejection of God, we can recognize "the plan of the Father who, moved by love (cf. *Jn* 3:16), sent his only-begotten Son into the world to redeem man."[77] Even depictions of God's anger can be understood in light of the Father's love for us. Fathers are often angry at their children when their children harm themselves by choosing the wrong path. It is *because* the Father loves us that anger is enkindled. It is not anger *against* us but *for* us. Thus, Christians, "immersed like everyone else in the dramatic complexity of historical events . . . remain unshakably certain that God is our Father and loves us."[78]

What is more, the fatherhood of God is no less real than human biological fatherhood. On the contrary, "God's fatherhood is more real than human fatherhood, because he is the ultimate

75. Ratzinger, 34.
76. Ratzinger, 35.
77. Benedict XVI, *Deus Caritas Est* 19, encyclical letter, December 25, 2005, vatican.va.
78. *Deus Caritas Est* 38.

source of our being; because he has thought and willed us from all eternity; because he gives us our true paternal home, which is eternal. And if earthly fatherhood divides, heavenly fatherhood unites."[79]

GOD THE SON, THE ETERNAL WORD

We encounter God the Father through Jesus Christ, who has revealed the Father to us (see Matt. 11:27, John 14:6–11, and John 17:25–26). In this section, I will limit discussion as much as possible to God the Son within the Godhead, although that cannot be done absolutely. While this book tries to follow the order of ontology, the way that we know is usually in the reverse direction. In this case, what is first known is the man Jesus. As the synoptic Gospels show, the disciples only came to recognize Jesus' divinity gradually. We only know the Trinity through salvation history, especially through the Life, Death, Resurrection, and Ascension of Jesus and the descent of the Holy Spirit at Pentecost. As David Bonagura explains, "The inner dialogue of the Trinity is revealed by the experience 'from below' that the disciples had of Jesus' prayer to the Father, which continues in his humanity the dialogue—the prayer—of the Father and Son for all eternity."[80]

In other words, it was through God's self-revelation in history—above all in the life and saving work of Jesus of Nazareth—that we gained access to knowledge of God as the Trinity. As Ratzinger remarks, "The doctrine of the Trinity did not arise out of speculation about God, out of an attempt by philosophical thinking to figure out what the fount of all being was like; it developed out of the effort to digest historical experiences. . . . In the formative period of the New Testament comes a completely unexpected event in which God shows himself from a hitherto

79. Benedict XVI, *Jesus of Nazareth*, 1:141–142.

80. David Bonagura, "Joseph Ratzinger/Benedict XVI's Christology of Jesus' Prayer and Two Contemporary Theological Questions," *Nova et Vetera* 12, no. 1 (Winter 2014): 290–291.

unknown side: in Jesus Christ one meets a man who at the same time knows and professes himself to be the Son of God."[81]

For this reason, we must keep in mind that when we choose to speak first about the immanent Trinity in our order of presentation, we are speaking about that which was known subsequent to the encounter with the economic Trinity. With respect to the knowledge of God the Son, herein lies the well-known distinction between a Christology from below and a Christology from above.[82] It is sometimes said that the synoptic Gospels present a Christology from below; that is, they start with the encounter with Jesus in his humanity before coming to a conclusion about his divinity. In contrast, the Gospel of John starts with a Christology from above: "In the beginning was the Word, and the Word was with God, and the Word was God" (John 1:1). Only after this does John say, "And the Word became flesh and lived among us" (John 1:14).

Even though our knowledge of God the Son is consequent upon our knowledge of Jesus in his humanity, it is still important to consider him in his eternal life as the second person of the Trinity. Ratzinger thinks this is imperative in order to combat modern temptations to reduce Jesus to the status of a mere human being. In this respect, he asks, "But if [Jesus] was really only a man like any of us, what was happening then, and what happens now? Can one expect that an enthusiasm for a Jesus of that kind will last?"[83] Ratzinger then answers his own questions as follows: "Karl Jaspers . . . has attempted to retain the importance of Jesus by seeing him as the definitive man; but what remains is in reality only an exceptional existence that cannot offer any

81. Ratzinger, *Introduction*, 163.

82. Sometimes authors may equate Christology from below with low Christology and Christology from above with high Christology. However, I would caution against this. "From below" and "from above" indicate the starting point of one's presentation of who Jesus is, while "low Christology" and "high Christology" refer to whether one emphasizes Jesus' humanity or divinity in one's Christological reflections. It is possible to have a low Christology from above or a high Christology from below.

83. Ratzinger, *God of Jesus Christ*, 87.

direct guidance for the lives of other men. What remains is empty and ultimately has nothing to say to us. This applies to every form of veneration based on the man Jesus alone: where all that is left is the man, men themselves cannot remain," and thus, Ratzinger concludes, "That which makes Jesus important and irreplaceable in every age is precisely the fact that he was and is the Son, that in him God has become man."[84] Jesus' significance is fundamentally rooted in *who* he is: God the Son, the eternal Word.

Perhaps this is why the Nicene Creed first speaks of Jesus as the second person of the Trinity before professing belief in the Incarnation. Jesus is first of all "the only Son of God, eternally begotten of the Father, God from God, Light from Light, true God from true God, begotten, not made, consubstantial with the Father." As Ratzinger notes, "These statements in the Creed remain in the sphere that lies before the time of our world."[85]

As the order of topics in this book reflects, everything in this world comes from the eternal Trinity and is ordered back to it. Thus, the importance of the immanent Trinity is the foundation of everything else. As Ratzinger himself insists, "We must first be reminded of the inviolable majesty of the One from whom all things come, for where this is lost to sight, the descent of God, too, loses its greatness and is absorbed into the general monotony of those events that recur in aimless cycles. Where this majesty is not seen, the drama of history, the drama of human existence, loses all tension and all meaning."[86] For Ratzinger, then, one must affirm the full divinity of Christ prior to the Incarnation as utterly essential for understanding his relevance in his temporal mission in the world as man.

The first ecumenical council, the Council of Nicaea (AD 325), was convoked precisely to address the question of Jesus' identity prior to the Incarnation. Arius had taught that Jesus was

84. Ratzinger, 87.
85. Ratzinger, 59.
86. Ratzinger, 61.

the Word, but that this Word was not eternal; it was, so to speak, the first thing created; the Word did not exist from all eternity. The Word was *like* God but was not God. In response, the fathers of the Council of Nicaea condemned the Arian heresy and professed that Jesus is God the Son, God from God, *homoousios* with the Father from all eternity.

Ratzinger holds that, in general, the council fathers sought to speak as fishermen rather than as philosophers.[87] Still, they inserted this "one single philosophical term into the Creed: *homoousios*."[88] Its use was significant, and the fathers of Nicaea employed it for a very specific reason. *Homoousios* "affirms something very simple, namely, that 'Son' is not a mere comparison, but literal reality. . . . The Word is literally true—*that* is what is meant by calling Jesus 'consubstantial' with the Father. That is not placing philosophy on an equal footing with the Bible: on the contrary it protects the Bible from attack by philosophy."[89] The use of *homoousios* is a profession of the *reality*—the metaphysical truth—of who Christ is from all eternity.[90] This assertion is part of Christianity's claim to universal validity and significance.

Jesus is no mere religious figure or moral guide: he is God. That fact makes all the difference. "The Christian position . . . is put emphatically by Tertullian when he says with splendid boldness: 'Christ called himself the truth, not custom.'. . . Christianity

---

87. See Ratzinger, 86–87. Reflecting Ratzinger's notion of the primacy of the faith of the simple, he writes of the Nicene Fathers, "They were interested in the simple basic questions of simple people" (87).

88. Ratzinger, 85. Here, we see support for Ratzinger's insistence that philosophy—especially metaphysics—is useful for theology. The very first ecumenical council, even one generally concerned with the faith of simple people, found it necessary to employ some philosophical terminology in order to protect the truth of the apostolic faith.

89. Ratzinger, 89–90.

90. See Joseph Ratzinger, *Behold the Pierced One: An Approach to a Spiritual Christology*, trans. Graham Harrison (San Francisco: Ignatius, 1986), 36: "The Council of Nicaea, in interpreting the word 'Son' philosophically by means of the concept 'of one substance,' is saying that 'Son' is to be understood here, not in the sense of religious metaphor, but in the most real and concrete sense of the word. The central word of the New Testament, the word 'Son,' is to be understood literally." See also Bonagura, "Joseph Ratzinger/Benedict XVI's Christology," 292, and Benedict XVI, *Jesus of Nazareth*, 1:320, 355.

thus put itself resolutely on the side of truth and turned its back on a conception of religion satisfied to be mere outward cere-monial."[91] Christianity is a truth claim. Its fundamental truth is the very truth of God. "The Son is truly the Son. The martyrs died for this truth, and Christians of all ages live on the basis of this truth."[92]

This emphasis on the truth about God leads us to consider what it means for God the Son to be referred to as the divine Logos. The Greek term *Logos* is, of course, where we get the word logic. It pertains to rationality. To speak about the divine and eternal Logos is to speak about God's own thinking, divine ra-tionality. But what does John the Evangelist mean when he refers to Jesus as the Word, the Logos, and insists that this Logos was and is God?

Ratzinger holds that John's usage of the word *Logos* is an ap-propriation of that term's meaning—as it was understood in both Greek and Jewish thought—to the person of Jesus. At the same time, Ratzinger also thinks John is augmenting those implicit understandings with new content, a content that reflects the *re-lationality* that we have seen as a recurring theme in Ratzinger's theology as a whole and his theology of the Trinity in particular. As Ratzinger writes:

> *Logos* does not mean simply the idea of the eternal rationality
> of being, as it did essentially in Greek thought. By its applica-
> tion to Jesus of Nazareth, the concept of *logos* acquires a new
> dimension. It no longer denotes simply the permeation of all
> being by meaning; it characterizes this man: he who is here
> is "Word". The concept of *logos*, which to the Greeks meant
> "meaning" (*ratio*), changes here really into "word" (*verbum*).
> He who is here is Word; he is consequently "spoken" and,

91. Ratzinger, *Introduction*, 140–141.
92. Ratzinger, *God of Jesus Christ*, 90.

hence, the pure relation between the speaker and the spoken to. Thus *logos* Christology, as "word" theology, is once again the opening up of being to the idea of relationship.[93]

These reflections on the Gospel of John's use of *logos* relate to another reflection, this time on words from the Gospel of Matthew: "No one knows the Son except the Father, and no one knows the Father except the Son and anyone to whom the Son chooses to reveal him" (Matt. 11:27). Commenting on this passage, Ratzinger writes, "First of all, it says something very simple and clear: God can be known only through God. No one other than God himself can know God. This act of knowing, in which God knows himself, is God's giving of himself as Father and God's receiving of himself and giving back of himself as Son, the exchange of eternal love, both the eternal gift and the eternal return of this gift."[94]

In these words, we see how Ratzinger unites the themes of the second person of the Trinity as both God the Son and the eternal, divine Word. He makes this connection elsewhere, when speaking about the eternal Word. He writes, "It [the eternal Word] is first of all Son, proceeding in eternal origin from the Father, God's interiority eternally comprehending itself."[95]

The appellation of Logos for the second person of the Trinity indicates something further about the Triune God. As Bonagura explains, "Within the God who is *logos*—the creative original thought who is speech, meaning, and Word—there exists a *dia-logos* that is a 'reciprocal exchange of word and love' between the divine Persons," which is "the inner dialogue of the Father and Son from all eternity."[96]

93. Ratzinger, *Introduction*, 189.

94. Ratzinger, *God of Jesus Christ*, 90–91.

95. Joseph Ratzinger, *Das Offenbarungsverständnis und die Geschichtstheologie Bonaventuras: Habilitationsschrift und Bonaventura-Studien*, in JRGS 2, ed. Gerhard Ludwig Müller (Freiburg, DE: Herder, 2009), 133.

96. Bonagura, "Joseph Ratzinger/Benedict XVI's Christology," 289. Here, Bonagura cites from Ratzinger, *Introduction*, 183.

Here again we encounter the divine grounds for the categories of relation and personhood. Just as the Father can only be understood in relation to the Son, so too the Son can only be understood in relation to the Father. At the same time, the Father and the Son are intimately united. There is one God and only one God, and yet the Father and the Son are distinct persons.

In order to treat this unity-in-distinction, Ratzinger juxtaposes two references to Jesus in the Gospel of John. On the one hand, John refers to Jesus as "Son." On the other hand, Jesus is described as "one with the Father." About this juxtaposition, Ratzinger writes:

> On the face of it, a contradiction arises when the same Christ says of himself in St. John: "I and the Father are one" (10:30). But anyone who looks more closely will see at once that in reality the two statements are complementary. In that Jesus is called "Son" and is thereby made "relative" to the Father, and in that Christology is ratified as a statement of relation, the automatic result is the total reference of Christ back to the Father. Precisely because he does not stand in *himself*, he stands in *him*, constantly one with him.[97]

Ratzinger offers another profound meditation on this relation between the Father and the Son. It is a reflection that illuminates the inner core of the procession of the Son *from* the Father as well as the significance this has in his being *for* us. It thus provides a bridge between God the Son within the Trinity and Jesus as the Incarnate Word of God "for us men and our salvation."

> The Son as Son, and insofar as he is Son, does not proceed in any way from himself and so is completely one with the Father; since he is nothing beside him, claims no special position

97. Ratzinger, *Introduction*, 185.

of his own, confronts the Father with nothing belonging only to him, makes no reservations for what is specifically his own, therefore he is completely equal to the Father. The logic is compelling: If there is nothing in which he is just he, no kind of fenced-off private ground, then he coincides with the Father, is "one" with him. It is precisely this totality of interplay that the word "Son" aims at expressing. To John, "Son" means being from another; thus, with this word he defines the being of this man as being from another and for others, as a being that is completely open on both sides, knows no reserved area of the mere "I". When it thus becomes clear that the being of Jesus as Christ is a completely open being, a being "from" and "toward", which nowhere clings to itself and nowhere stands on its own, then it is also clear at the same time that this being is pure relation (not substantiality) and, as pure relation, pure unity.[98]

With these words, we already see a foreshadowing of the significance of the inner-Trinitarian life for the work of the economic Trinity. It prefigures the Incarnation as well as ecclesiology. As Ratzinger remarks, "Parallel to the logic that makes Christ say, 'I and the Father are one,' we find here the petition 'that they may be one, even as we are one' ([John] 17:11 and 22). The significant difference from Christology comes to light in the fact that the unity of Christians is expressed."[99] The unity of the Father and the Son is what enables Christ to unite us to the Father, which is at the same time a call to be united with one another.

Yet again, we see here the cohesion of Ratzinger's thought. His Trinitarian theology has import for his Christology, soteriology, and ecclesiology. We shall see in a later chapter that Ratzinger's theology of divine revelation is also based in the Trinity, an idea

98. Ratzinger, 186–187.
99. Ratzinger, 186.

that he draws from St. Bonaventure.[100] It also relates to Ratzinger's theology of creation, including his theological anthropology.

Before we get into Ratzinger's theology of creation and theological anthropology, however, we must complete our consideration of his Trinitarian theology. We thus now turn to the topic of the third person of the Blessed Trinity: the Holy Spirit.

THE HOLY SPIRIT

With only slight hyperbole, the Holy Spirit is sometimes referred to as the forgotten person of the Trinity. As Ratzinger notes, "While we are able to say rather a lot about the Father and the Son, the Holy Spirit has largely remained the unknown God."[101] Hopefully, this section will help the reader come to a better understanding of the Holy Spirit through a consideration of Ratzinger's pneumatology.

Above, we discussed God the Father and God the Son as being mutually determinative, meaning that the Father is such in relation to the Son and vice versa. Additionally, we noted a quote in which Ratzinger appears to reflect the Augustinian analogy of the Trinity. That quote ended with the following words: "In the third Person in whom they give themselves to each other, in the Gift, they are themselves, and they are one."[102] Ratzinger thus identifies the Holy Spirit as the bond of unity between the Father and the Son, as the gift of the Father and the Son to each other.

In another work, Ratzinger makes his use of Augustine's doctrine of the Trinity even more explicit in this regard. The title of the pertinent article reflects the same notion of the Holy Spirit as the bond between the Father and the Son and simultaneously

---

100. See Ratzinger, *Offenbarungsverständnis*, 131, where, speaking of St. Bonaventure, Ratzinger writes: "Thus, the saint's speculation about revelation reaches into the middle of his doctrine of the Trinity and finds there its real foundation."

101. Ratzinger, *God of Jesus Christ*, 105.

102. Ratzinger, 35.

reflects the leitmotif of Ratzinger's theology, which is *communio*: "The Holy Spirit as *Communio*: Concerning the Relationship of Pneumatology and Spirituality in Augustine."[103]

Therein, Ratzinger presents the main outlines of Augustine's pneumatology. Augustine, writes Ratzinger, "proceeds to try to grasp the essence of the Holy Spirit by interpreting his customary names."[104] The names considered are "the Holy Spirit," "love," and "gift."

First, according to Ratzinger, Augustine's analysis suggests that the name "Holy Spirit" indicates the unique character of the third person of the Trinity.[105] Yet this unique character consists precisely in being that which is not absolutely unique but common. Mysteriously, the uniqueness is the lack of uniqueness, in contrast with the more specified descriptions of the Father and the Son. "Unlike 'Father' and 'Son,' the name of the third Divine Person is not the expression of something specific. It designates that which is common in the Godhead."[106]

What does Ratzinger mean by this? Paradoxically, what indicates the third person's unique character is precisely the fact that the name "Holy Spirit" also serves as an accurate description of the other two persons as well as of God in general: "Each of the two other Persons of the Trinity could be named in this way. Above all, God himself and as such could be named this way since John 4:24 also states: 'God is spirit.' Being spirit and being holy is the essential description of God. That is what identifies him as God."[107]

For Ratzinger and Augustine, it is significant that the third person of the Trinity is designated with a name that—in and of

103. Joseph Ratzinger, "The Holy Spirit as *Communio*: Concerning the Relationship of Pneumatology and Spirituality in Augustine," *Communio* 25, no. 2 (Summer 1998): 324–337.

104. Ratzinger, 326.

105. See Ratzinger, 326–327.

106. Ratzinger, *God of Jesus Christ*, 109.

107. Ratzinger, "Holy Spirit as *Communio*," 326.

itself—is descriptive of the other persons as well as of God *qua* God. "When he [the Holy Spirit] is named by that which is the divinity of God, by what the Father and the Son have in common, then his essence is just that, the *communio* of Father and Son. The particularity of the Holy Spirit is evidently that he is what the Father and the Son have in common. His particularity is being unity. The general name 'Holy Spirit' is the most appropriate way to express him in the paradox characteristic of him—mutuality itself," and further, "The Spirit is Person as unity, unity as Person."[108]

Once again, we see relationality as an inherent part of Ratzinger's Augustinian notion of person. In this case, the third person of the Trinity is person precisely as the relational unity between the other two divine persons; he *is* divine *communio*. The proper character of the Holy Spirit is that "he is that which is common, the unity of the Father and the Son, the unity in Person. . . . It is in the third Person, in the fruitfulness of their act of giving, that they [the Father and the Son] are One."[109]

In another work, Ratzinger discusses the Holy Spirit by reflecting on the meaning of the word "spirit."[110] There, Ratzinger posits a distinction between "mind" and "spirit," which are often treated as synonyms.[111] "Today," writes Ratzinger, "we encounter 'spirit' chiefly as the rational mind that calculates and deals with the kind of stored-up knowledge that the computer can collect and manipulate. . . . Mind, then," he continues, "is the sum of the receptive, logical, and pragmatic powers of consciousness."[112]

---

108. Ratzinger, 326.

109. Ratzinger, *God of Jesus Christ*, 109.

110. Joseph Ratzinger, "The Holy Spirit: Mind, Spirit, and Love: A Meditation on Pentecost," in *Credo for Today: What Christians Believe*, trans. Michael J. Miller et al. (San Francisco: Ignatius, 2009), 121–127. This was previously published in Joseph Ratzinger, *Dogma and Preaching*, trans. Matthew J. O'Connell (Chicago: Franciscan Herald, 1985), 66–71. Henceforth cited as Ratzinger, *Credo for Today*, with relevant pagination.

111. "Mind" and "spirit" as synonyms is particularly true for German-speakers, since the word *Geist* can mean either one.

112. Ratzinger, *Credo for Today*, 122–123.

Following Pierre-Henri Simon, however, Ratzinger thinks we should speak about "spirit" separately from mere "mind." He is concerned that reducing spirit to mind leads to an abhorrent positivism that reduces humanity to that which is eminently calculable.[113] Such hyper-rationalization of the human spirit is destructive to an authentic grasp of what spirit means. Spirit is more than the intellect and precise mathematical or scientific calculation. In contrast to mind, "Spirit . . . discovers the order of values that lies beyond facts, the freedom that transcends law, the kind of existence in which justice has priority over self-interest."[114]

How does this view of spirit relate to the *Holy* Spirit? Ratzinger makes the connection through a comparison between the Tower of Babel and Pentecost. The Tower of Babel prefigures modern man's hubris in trusting too much in the power of technology. Referring to those who built the tower, Ratzinger says, "They believed that by their own powers of planning and constructing they could even build a bridge to heaven, make heaven accessible to themselves by their own efforts, and turn man into a deity. The result of their effort was the confusion of tongues. The human race, which seeks only itself and looks for salvation in the satisfaction of a ruthless egoism by means of economic power, suffers instead the consequence of egoism, which is the radical opposition of each to his fellows."[115] In the Acts of the Apostles, by contrast, man's salvation is not self-made but is given as a gift. It is not man raising himself to God through human effort. Rather, it is God descending upon man.

Accordingly, the results of Pentecost are the precise opposite of the Tower of Babel. At Pentecost, Ratzinger writes, "The disciples were touched by fiery tongues and found themselves

---

113. Notice how this relates directly with his concerns about reducing knowledge to mere fact known through the hard sciences.

114. Ratzinger, *Credo for Today*, 123. Here, Ratzinger references P.-H. Simon, *Woran ich glaube* (Tübingen: Leins, 1967), 175–183.

115. Ratzinger, 125.

speaking in a manner that . . . people from all parts of the then known world, heard the disciples speaking in his own tongue."[116] Rather than divide humanity by race and language, for those open to the working of the Holy Spirit, people from across the globe are united in God's self-communication. The Holy Spirit, who is the loving union of the Father and the Son, is sent upon man in order to impart the bonds of charity. The Spirit brings union, *communion*.

Once again appealing to St. Augustine, Ratzinger notes the significance of Pentecost. "World history, he [Augustine] says, is a struggle between two kinds of love: self-love to the point of hatred for God, and love of God to the point of self-renunciation. This second love brings the redemption of the world and the self."[117] Here, the Holy Spirit is connected with the bringing of love. This should not be surprising, since the bond between the Father and the Son is a loving unity, and the Holy Spirit is defined as the unity between the Father and the Son. For this reason, it is no wonder that one of the Holy Spirit's other names is "love." Recalling that the term "Holy Spirit" is specific to the third person as well as common to both the other two persons and to God as one, we can recognize a parallel regarding the appellation "love." Just as the Gospel of John states that "God is spirit" (John 4:24), so too does the First Letter of John state that "God is love" (4:16). Once again, what is common to God is also designated as specific to the Holy Spirit. Referring to the statement that God is love, "Augustine determines that, first of all and fundamentally, this statement pertains completely to God as the undivided Trinity but still expresses the unique property of the Holy Spirit."[118]

Augustine supports his thesis by comparing three verses of 1 John 4 (12, 16b, and 13). These passages speak about God abiding in those who abide in love. This mutual abiding of the human

116. Ratzinger, 125.
117. Ratzinger, 126.
118. Ratzinger, "Holy Spirit as *Communio*," 328.

who loves and the God who is love is accomplished through the gift of the Holy Spirit: "We recognize that we abide in him and he in us because he has given us of his spirit" (1 John 4:13). Ratzinger presents his version of the argument thusly: "The Holy Spirit, of whom he has given us, causes us to abide in God, and God in us. But love does this. He is, therefore, the God who is love."[119]

To this Johannine evidence, Augustine adds Pauline support with Romans 5:5. According to Ratzinger, this passage "states that the love of God is poured out through the Holy Spirit who is given to us. . . . The gift of God is the Holy Spirit. The gift of God is love."[120]

Ratzinger augments this view via 1 John 4:7 and 16.[121] He writes, "Verse 16 states that God is love. Verse 7 reads: 'Love is from God.' Love is on the one hand 'God,' on the other hand 'from God.' If you put the two together, love is equally 'God' and 'from God'; in other words, love is 'God from God.'"[122]

All of this leads quite directly to the other name for the third divine person: gift. God is both the giver and the gift. The Holy Spirit given as love is the gift of God himself to us. Here, we see the link between the Holy Spirit within the immanent Trinity— the love between the Father and the Son—and the Holy Spirit in the economy of salvation: the gift of God himself as divine love abiding within us.

Understanding the Holy Spirit as gift is crucial for differentiating the third person of the Trinity from the second. When one first reads Ratzinger's reference to Augustine's understanding of the Spirit as "God from God" quoted above, one's initial reaction might be that that phrase is usually applied to God the Son rather

119. Ratzinger, 328.
120. Ratzinger, 328.
121. N.b.: Pope Benedict XVI's very first encyclical begins by quoting 1 John 4:16, and thus, as usual, the title of the encyclical is drawn from the opening words: "God is Love" (*Deus Caritas Est*). See Benedict XVI, *Deus Caritas Est* 1.
122. Ratzinger, "Holy Spirit as *Communio*," 329.

than to the Holy Spirit. That is not to deny that it would be and is appropriate, but it raises the question of how these two divine persons are distinct. Ratzinger raises and answers that question in his article, and the key is found through the "name" of "gift." Quoting Augustine's *De Trinitate*, Ratzinger writes, "'He [the Holy Spirit] comes from God not as born but as given. . . . Therefore he is not called son because he is neither "born" like the "first-born" nor "created" as we are. . . .' He [Augustine] distinguishes three modes of origin from God: being born, being given, and being created. . . . If one can best describe the essence of the Son, his own status with regard to the Father, with the concept of generation, then that of the Spirit is 'giving.'"[123]

As noted earlier, the fact that the Holy Spirit is the mutual giving of the Father and the Son to one another is the immanent-Trinitarian basis for his being given in the economy of grace. As Ratzinger understands Augustine's view, "The Holy Spirit always is in his essence the gift of God, God as the self-donating, God as the self-distributing, as gift. The inner ground for creation and salvation history already lies in this mode of being of the Holy Spirit, being *donum* and *datum*. . . . On the one hand, the 'immanent' doctrine of the Trinity is opened wholly to the 'economic.' On the other hand, salvation history is referred back to theo-logy. The *gift* of God is God himself."[124]

Yet again, we see the importance of Trinitarian theology and pneumatology for other subspecialities, such as theology of creation and soteriology. Additionally, in this same article, Ratzinger points to the connection between pneumatology and other areas, including ecclesiology, eschatology, sacramental theology, and Christology.

At present, however, it is of greater import to discuss the connection between the three names of the third person of the

123. Ratzinger, 330.
124. Ratzinger, 331.

Trinity: Holy Spirit, love, and gift. Ratzinger addresses that issue directly. Quoting Augustine, Ratzinger writes, "'Because he [the Holy Spirit] is the one common to both [Father and Son], his own name is what they have in common.' This statement also establishes the inner unity of the designations 'love' and 'gift' with the main designation 'Holy Spirit.' In this manner, he [Augustine] shows the legitimacy of this unity and integrates the whole into a mutually interpreting unity."[125]

Yet again we see this theme of unity, integration, wholeness. As we have mentioned repeatedly, these related themes are at the foundation and heart of Ratzinger's theology, which he finds here rooted in *the* mystery: the Holy Trinity. Everything else flows from (*exitus*) and/or leads back to (*reditus*) the Trinitarian reality of the Godhead. All of the other subspecialties in theology must relate to the Trinity, precisely in order to be *theo*-logy: a word about God.

Now that we have discussed God *ad intra* here, we shall start exploring what God does *ad extra*, beginning with a consideration of God's creation, including the apex of God's creative action, the humanity made in God's image and likeness.

---

125. Ratzinger, 331.

4

Creation and Theological Anthropology

God has created that which is not God: the universe and everything in it. The fact that God is Trinity affects our understanding of creation.

How? To answer this question, we must recall that God is *unity-in-relation* (and thus *personal*), that God is *Logos* (the Son), and that God is the bond of love and gift (the Holy Spirit). As Pablo Blanco Sarto reminds us, for Ratzinger, "This God—who is truth, spirit, and thought—is 'Verbo,' is 'Word,' and thus, is also 'relationship' [*Zuwendung*]. . . . Once again, God is, therefore, truth and love, reason and relation."[1] Insofar as creation reflects the Creator, there is a relational aspect to all existence.

The universe does not proceed from an indifferent, impersonal first principle but from the utter interpersonal unity of eternal reason and divine love. Therefore, the world has meaning. "As the German professor [Ratzinger] frequently put it, when God is called 'the Logos,' it means that 'in the beginning there was a God who is thought and meaning [*Sinn*], that is, a creative Logos, a

---

1. Pablo Blanco Sarto, *La Teología de Joseph Ratzinger: Una introducción* (Madrid: Pelícano, 2011), 320.

thought that has called the world into existence out of love and that, with that call and at that very moment, gives it meaning.'"[2]

To say that God is the Creator is not just to say something about God, it is to say something about the world that comes from God. It means that we see the universe precisely as a *creation*, something that has an intended existence and is thus not a meaningless happenstance. This view can help us avoid nihilistic despair that sees life as a tragic accident. As Ratzinger insists, "The universe is not the product of darkness and unreason. It comes from intelligence, freedom, and from the beauty that is identical with love. Seeing this gives us the courage to keep on living, and it empowers us, comforted thereby, to take upon ourselves the adventure of life."[3]

We saw earlier that Ratzinger opposes scientism or epistemological reductionism. He insists that belief in creation is not wishful thinking; it is reasonable and rational. In fact, he believes that it is much more reasonable than the alternative. In this connection, Ratzinger recounts a lecture given by the scientist and atheist Jacques Monod wherein Monod argues that the world came about through some combination of chance and necessity. During the course of the lecture, he admitted that his view was absurd, but since he had preemptively (*a priori*) chosen to exclude God as a consideration, he was left with no alternative. François Mauriac's quite understandable reaction to this lecture was as follows: "What this professor wants to inflict on us is far more unbelievable than what we poor Christians were ever expected to believe."[4]

Contrary to Monod, Ratzinger holds that the reasonableness and rationality of the world points to its origin in the divine

2. Blanco, 320.

3. Joseph Ratzinger, *'In the Beginning...': A Catholic Understanding of the Story of Creation and the Fall*, trans. Boniface Ramsey (Grand Rapids, MI: Eerdmans, 1995), 25.

4. Ratzinger, *In the Beginning*, 24. Ratzinger quotes here from J. Monod, *Zufall und Notwendigkeit. Philosophische Fragen der modernen Biologie* (Munich: DTV, 1973), 171, 149.

intellect. Rather than see science as explaining away belief in God the Creator, Ratzinger sees it as confirming the universe's divine origin. "The more we know of the universe the more profoundly we are struck by a Reason whose ways we can only contemplate with astonishment. In pursuing them we can see anew that creating Intelligence to whom we owe our own reason."[5] In support of his position, Ratzinger not only cites theologians such as St. Bonaventure but also modern scientific geniuses such as Werner Heisenberg[6] and Albert Einstein.[7]

Moreover, contrary to popular perception, Ratzinger believes that recent advances in modern science have—if anything— pointed *more* toward the truth of creation than against it. Prior to the Big Bang theory, for instance, the common scientific opinion was that the universe was eternal, with no beginning. That has drastically changed. Similarly, advances in microbiology show us that the mechanisms of life are vastly more complex than ever imagined, and thus, they are significantly less explainable via appeals to blind chance.[8] "Physics and biology, and the natural sciences in general," concludes Ratzinger, "have given us a new and unheard-of creation account with vast new images, which let us recognize the face of the Creator and which make us realize once again that at the very beginning and foundation of all being there is a creating Intelligence."[9]

5. Ratzinger, 23.

6. See Joseph Ratzinger, *The God of Jesus Christ: Meditations on the Triune God*, trans. Brian McNeil (San Francisco: Ignatius, 2008), 39–40.

7. See Ratzinger, *In the Beginning*, 23: "Albert Einstein once said that in the laws of nature 'there is revealed such a superior Reason that everything significant which has arisen out of human thought and arrangement is, in comparison with it, the merest empty reflection.'" Here, Ratzinger quotes from Einstein, *Mein Weltbild*, ed. Carl Seelig (Stuttgart-Zurich-Vienna: Europa, 1953), 21.

8. See Ratzinger, 23–24: "In what is most vast, in the world of heavenly bodies, we see revealed a powerful Reason that holds the universe together. And we are penetrating ever deeper into what is smallest, into the cell and into the primordial units of life; here, too, we discover a Reason that astounds us, such that we must say with Saint Bonaventure: 'Whoever does not see here is blind. Whoever does not hear here is deaf. And whoever does not begin to adore here and to praise the creating Intelligence is dumb [as in mute].'"

9. Ratzinger, 24–25.

It is worth noting that in this quote, Ratzinger refers to the *images gained through science* as means by which we can recognize God. From a Christian perspective, this is fitting. Unlike the many ancient pagan religions, "Christianity is not based on mythical images and vague notions that are ultimately justified by their political usefulness; rather, it relates to that divine presence which can be perceived by the rational analysis of reality."[10]

In other words, Ratzinger thinks that the common narrative so uncritically imbibed by many today is a false narrative: a narrative that portrays science as undermining belief in God as the Creator. Quite to the contrary, never has belief in the divine creative intelligence had a more solid basis. "Even today faith in creation is not unreal; even today it is reasonable; even from the perspective of the data of the natural sciences it is the 'better hypothesis,' offering a fuller and better explanation than any of the other theories. Faith is reasonable. The reasonableness of creation derives from God's Reason, and there is no other really convincing explanation."[11] Ultimately, Ratzinger thinks that Christianity's belief in God the Creator "means that the Christian faith concerns the whole of reality. It concerns reason. It asks a question that concerns everyone."[12]

Now that we have seen Ratzinger's general defense of the reasonableness of faith augmented by the advances of modern science, let us turn to his consideration of one particular issue at the intersection of science and belief in creation: evolution. Ratzinger dealt with this question on several occasions.[13]

10. Joseph Ratzinger, *Truth and Tolerance: Christian Belief and World Religions*, trans. Henry Taylor (San Francisco: Ignatius, 2004), 169.

11. Ratzinger, *In the Beginning*, 17.

12. Ratzinger, *God of Jesus Christ*, 38.

13. See Joseph Ratzinger, *Dogma und Verkündigung* (Munich: Erich Wewel, 1973), 133–136; reprinted in English as Joseph Ratzinger, "Creation: Belief in Creation and the Theory of Evolution," in *Credo for Today: What Christians Believe*, trans. Michael J. Miller et al. (San Francisco: Ignatius, 2009), 32–47. See also Ratzinger, "Creation and Evolution," in *In the Beginning*, 50–58; this was originally part of a series of homilies given during Lent in 1981, while Ratzinger was Archbishop of Munich and Freising. See also Ratzinger, "Christianity—the True Religion?" in *Truth and Tolerance*, 162–182. For presentations by Ratzinger's former students

Undoubtedly, there are those who try to present evolution as proof against creation. This move is typically one aspect of the larger project of epistemological reductionism so loathsome to Ratzinger. As we have seen before, he insists on the need for sound metaphysics and argued that we cannot reduce everything to the hard sciences. As Ratzinger observes, "Everything is to become 'physics' again. The theory of evolution has increasingly emerged as the way to make metaphysics disappear, to make 'the hypothesis of God' (Laplace) superfluous, and to formulate a strictly 'scientific' explanation of the world."[14] But such epistemological reductionism is not itself a scientific truth; it is, ironically, a philosophical assertion that is not grounded in the very principles it claims to uphold as the only authentic principles. Metaphysical questions are inevitable. There are questions of physics, and there are questions of metaphysics. The latter do not disappear or become obsolete simply because they are not within the scope of the former.

Ultimately, the metaphysical question is "whether reason, or rationality, stands at the beginning of all things and is grounded in the basis of all things or not. The question is whether reality originated on the basis of chance and necessity . . . and, thus, from what is irrational . . . or whether the principle that represents the fundamental conviction of Christian faith and of its philosophy remains true . . . at the beginning of all things stands the creative power of reason."[15] Thus, in this philosophical dispute, it is Christianity that is the advocate for reason and rationality over irrationality. Reason is not the accidental result of irrational processes, a chance by-product of meaningless forces. Rather, the *reality* of reason—as seen in creation—is metaphysically prior to

---

with some comments by then-Pope Benedict XVI, see *Creation and Evolution: A Conference with Pope Benedict XVI in Castel Gandolfo* (San Francisco: Ignatius, 2008); this was the result of the 2006 meeting of the so-called Ratzinger *Schülerkreis* (Student Circle).

14. Ratzinger, *Truth and Tolerance*, 178.

15. Ratzinger, 181.

the human reason with which we evaluate the world, even scientifically.

Understanding the difference between metaphysical questions and questions of physics can help clarify the question of creation and evolution. In this regard, Ratzinger thinks that the tension—or even apparent contradiction—between belief in creation and the theory of evolution takes place on distinct levels, which must thus be handled separately. He sees the first level as rather superficial once one considers the matter more thoughtfully. He acknowledges that the idea of static, unchanging species that were each created completely individually is "untenable today."[16] Ratzinger even says that "the believer must allow himself to be taught by science"[17] on this point. However, he does not really think that that is problematic for belief in creation as such, because whether each species was created independently or whether there is an evolutionary process is not essential to belief in creation. Creation and evolution answer two different questions from two different perspectives. "We cannot say: creation *or* evolution, inasmuch as these two things respond to two different realities."[18] One is asking the question "why" with regard to the totality of being, while the other is asking "how" with regard to particular beings. One is metaphysical; the other is procedural and phenomenological. Ratzinger is worth quoting at length in this regard:

> Belief in creation inquires into the fact that there is being as such; its question is why anything exists at all instead of nothing. In contrast, the idea of evolution asks why precisely these things exist and not others, whence they acquired their particularity, and how they are connected with other formations. Philosophically, then, one would say that the idea of evolution

16. Ratzinger, *Credo for Today*, 34.
17. Ratzinger, 36.
18. Ratzinger, *In the Beginning*, 50.

is situated on the phenomenological level and deals with the actually occurring individual forms in the world, whereas the belief in creation moves on the ontological level, inquires into what is behind individual things, marvels at the miracle of being itself, and tries to give an account of the puzzling "is" that we commonly predicate of all existing realities. One could also put it this way: Belief in creation concerns the difference between nothing and something, while the idea of evolution examines the difference between something and something else. Creation characterizes being as a whole as "being from somewhere else." Evolution, in contrast, describes the inner structure of being and inquires into the specific "from where" of individual existing realities.[19]

Ratzinger's point is that evolution does not really challenge belief in creation, at least on this level. For evolution does not actually provide an answer to the question that creation addresses: Why is there something rather than nothing? Evolution, then, cannot be said to be a contrasting or disproving theory vis-à-vis creation.

Conversely, the belief in creation presented in Scripture was never meant to be taken as a scientific presentation of the physical process of the development of the universe and its various parts. The biblical imagery was meant to convey a more fundamental truth about the unicity of the true God, who is the Creator, in contrast to polytheistic and pantheistic conceptions of the relation between nature and the divine. Thus, from this perspective, creation and evolution are not competing theories. "To that extent," Ratzinger maintains, "we are faced here with two complementary—rather than mutually exclusive—realities."[20]

Ratzinger also discusses a different level or aspect of the question of creation and evolution: their scope. In Ratzinger's view,

19. Ratzinger, *Credo for Today*, 34–35.
20. Ratzinger, *In the Beginning*, 50.

the scope of the theory of evolution is much narrower than that of creation. Creation suggests a much broader question. This difference in scope leads to a certain asymmetry in their relation to one another. By definition, that which is narrower cannot address that which is broader, since what is broader is beyond its scope; yet, that which is broader ought to be able to incorporate that which is narrower, at least in principle. Thus, while evolution cannot—due to its limited scope—incorporate the theory of creation *within* itself as part of its view, the question still remains whether belief in creation can incorporate the theory of evolution as an acceptable position within its own vision.[21]

In response to this question, Ratzinger makes a fundamental distinction in order to avoid unnecessary confusion. There is a difference between the worldviews within which the faith is expressed and the faith itself. In fact, the Bible often employs the language of worldviews or conceptual categories of the cosmos held by the people to whom it was originally written without thereby being absolutely beholden to those worldviews. The Bible is conveying a truth within various cultural contexts and thus makes use of ideas understandable within those culturally accepted concepts, but it is not, thereby, necessarily asserting those concepts as its own. There is an important distinction here. "But this means," Ratzinger insists, "that, even within the Bible itself,

---

21. See Ratzinger, *Credo for Today*, 36–37. The fact that evolutionary theory cannot include the question of creation within its own discipline does *not* mean that evolutionary theory negates the legitimacy of the creation question. As Ratzinger notes here, evolution "must leave open the question of whether the further inquiry proposed by faith is per se justified and possible. In any case it may regard this, in terms of a particular concept of science, as extra-scientific, but it cannot rule out the question as a matter of principle or say that man should not address the question of being as such. On the contrary: such ultimate questions will always be indispensable for man, who confronts the ultimate in his very existence and cannot be reduced to what is scientifically demonstrable." In other words, if the question of faith in creation is beyond the scope of evolutionary theory, then evolutionary theory cannot address the question one way or the other. Contrary to what some seem to presume, evolution's default position is not, therefore, *against* the question of creation but neutral to it. We also see reflected here Ratzinger's typical rejection of epistemological reductionism and scientism. Just because something does not fall within the bounds of strict scientific inquiry does not make it thereby meaningless or unworthy of asking and answering. The most important aspects of life are not demonstrable, scientifically speaking.

faith and world view are not identical: the faith *makes use* of a world view but does not coincide with it."[22]

This understanding is not new. Within the Bible itself, whose books were written over the course of a millennium at least, this is already presupposed. Furthermore, the early Church Fathers understood this just as well as we do today. That is not just true generally speaking; it is true specifically with respect to the question of creation. As Ratzinger notes, "The theologians in the early Church were confronted in principle with the same task. For the biblical world view, as expressed in the creation accounts of the Old Testament, was by no means their world view; basically it appeared to them just as unscientific as it does to us. . . . The early creation accounts express the world view of the ancient Near East, especially of Babylon; the Church Fathers lived in the Hellenistic age, to which that world view seemed mythical, prescientific, and in every respect intolerable."[23]

The reason this was not a problem for the patristic era is the same reason it should not be a problem for us today. It has to do with our understanding of biblical inspiration. For now, let it suffice to say that the Catholic understanding of the Bible is not and never has been a hyper-*literalist* view. This is obvious from early in the tradition. Many of the apparent "conflicts" between faith and science are due to misunderstandings regarding how to understand biblical literature. Whether coming from the misunderstanding of unbelievers or the misguided views of certain other Christian groups, a devotion to an overly literalist view of Scripture is at the source of a lot of problems. As Ratzinger remarks, "The sense of this internal breadth of faith began to disappear when so-called literal exegesis started to gain wide acceptance and many people lost sight of the transcendence of the

22. Ratzinger, 40.
23. Ratzinger, 40.

Word of God with respect to all of the individual forms in which it is expressed."[24]

The limits of human language dictate that some form of expression must be used, but this does not mean that every aspect of the phrasing employed is essential to the point being made. For example, if someone today speaks of sunrise or sunset, they should not be accused of holding to a false astronomical position. Neither should the use of terms like "firmament" in the Bible be understood in that way. Using common parlance or even concepts drawn from a particular time and culture is not always an assertion of some specific truth about such phrases. As Ratzinger insists, "Faith was not identical to any one of the previous world views but rather answered a question that leads back behind the world views. . . . And it is clear that faith cannot and should not be identified with our world view either."[25] As arrogant as we may tend to be in our scientific age, history should make us humbler. Just as we often look with disdain upon prior understandings of the world from a scientific perspective, future generations will likely look upon us the same way, due to our own unavoidable ignorance. Thus, we should not too hastily identify the faith with contemporary worldviews either, even if we do, nonetheless, need to express the faith in terms that modern worldviews can understand and answer the questions that they pose to us.

Much more could be said about Ratzinger's approach to the question of creation and evolution. Just as one example, we have not dealt with Ratzinger's treatment of micro- versus macro-evolution.[26] We have merely sketched the broad outlines of Ratzinger's understanding of the apparent dispute as well as the general ideas he offers as a response. His main point could perhaps be summarized in the distinction he makes between the metaphysical question and the question of physics. He encourages believers

24. Ratzinger, 41.
25. Ratzinger, 41.
26. For some discussion of this issue, see Ratzinger, *Truth and Tolerance*, 180ff.

to be open to science and to let it operate on its own proper terms, while at the same time reminding science not to overstep its boundaries by claiming to be the whole of human inquiry and knowledge. "It is the affair of the natural sciences to explain how the tree of life in particular continues to grow and how new branches shoot out from it. This is not a matter for faith. But we must have the audacity to say that the great projects of the living creation are not the products of chance and error. . . . The great projects of the living creation point to a creating Reason and show us a creating Intelligence, and they do so more luminously and radiantly today than ever before."[27]

THEOLOGICAL ANTHROPOLOGY

We turn now to one particular part of creation that is of most importance: humankind. As expected, Ratzinger's understanding of theological anthropology is intrinsically connected to other areas of theology. Man is made in the image of God and created anew through the Incarnation of the Word. Accordingly, when it comes to theological anthropology, "the concept of divine creation is thus intertwined with Christology and trinitarian theology."[28]

In fact, Ratzinger sees the concept of person itself as deriving from Trinitarian and Christological reflection. "More specifically, the concept of person arose from two questions that have from the very beginning urged themselves upon Christian thought as central: namely, the question, 'What is God?' (i.e., the God whom we encounter in Scripture); and, 'Who is Christ?'"[29]

Turning to the Scriptures and how the Church Fathers read them, Ratzinger references the works of Justin Martyr and

27. Ratzinger, *In the Beginning*, 56.

28. Blanco, *Teología de Joseph Ratzinger*, 137.

29. Joseph Ratzinger, "Concerning the Notion of Person in Theology," trans. Michael Waldstein, *Communio* 17, no. 3 (Fall 1990): 439.

Tertullian in their interpretations of key passages from Genesis.[30] Genesis 1:26 reads, "Then God said, 'Let us make humankind in *our* image, according to *our* likeness'" (emphasis added). Similarly, Genesis 3:22 says, "Then the Lord God said, 'See, the man has become like one of *us*'" (emphasis added). The Fathers saw in these passages hints toward a Trinitarian understanding of God, at least insofar as they suggest a plurality within God. As Ratzinger notes, "In *Adversus Praxean*, Tertullian writes, 'How can a person who stands by himself say, "Let us make man in our image and likeness," when he ought to have said, "Let *me* make man in my image and likeness," as someone who is single and alone for himself. . . . But he did not stand alone, because there stood with him the Son, his Word, and a third person, the Spirit in the Word.'"[31]

Without committing himself strictly to Tertullian's (and other Fathers') precise interpretation of the texts, Ratzinger nevertheless sees in these examples a key understanding of the Trinity that has import for the concept of person. In these passages, God is engaged in an intra-Trinitarian dialogue, which Ratzinger views as an essential aspect of personhood. "The idea of person expresses in its origin the idea of dialogue and the idea of God as the dialogical being. It refers to God as the being that lives in the word and consists of the word as 'I' and 'you' and 'we.'"[32]

This corresponds to what we saw in the previous chapter regarding the three divine persons: relationality is essential to personhood. Ratzinger sees that same understanding developed in other Church Fathers as well. "According to Augustine and late patristic theology, the three persons that exist in God are in their nature relations. They are, therefore, not substances that stand next to each other, but they are real existing relations, and nothing besides. . . . In God, person means relation. Relation, being

30. See Ratzinger, 440–443.
31. Tertullian, *Adversus Praxean* 12.1.3, quoted in Ratzinger, 442.
32. Ratzinger, 443.

related, is not something superadded to the person, but it *is* the person itself."[33]

Since man is created in the image of God, human personhood is to be understood similarly. Speaking about the human person, Ratzinger writes, "He is God's image in his concrete reality, which is relationship."[34] Since God is no self-enclosed monad, neither is man. "The real God is by his very nature entirely being-for (Father), being-from (Son), and being-with (Holy Spirit). Man, for his part, is God's image precisely insofar as the 'from,' 'with,' and 'for' constitute the fundamental anthropological pattern."[35] The relatedness of persons has its basis in the Trinity, and "it is at the same time the fundamental statement about what is at stake in the concept of person. It opens the concept of person into the human spirit and provides its foundation and origin."[36]

This reference to the human spirit indicates the precise locus of man's status as the image of God. The human spirit is best understood in connection with how it reflects God's own self. "It is the nature of spirit to put itself in relation, the capacity to see itself and the other."[37] Ratzinger is once again exhibiting how *communion* is at the heart of every aspect of his theological thought. Just as God is the communion of three divine persons, so too are human persons meant to exist *in relation*.

This also means that persons can go beyond themselves; there is a transcendent aspect to humanity as a spiritual creature. "The [human] spirit is that being which is able to think about, not only itself and being in general, but the wholly other, the transcendent God. This is perhaps the mark that truly distinguishes the human spirit from other forms of consciousness found in animals,

33. Ratzinger, 444.

34. Ratzinger, *God of Jesus Christ*, 30.

35. Joseph Ratzinger, "Truth and Freedom," trans. Adrian J. Walker, *Communio* 23, no. 1 (Spring 1996): 28.

36. Ratzinger, "Concerning the Notion," 447.

37. Ratzinger, 451.

namely, that the human spirit can reflect on the wholly other, the concept of God."[38]

Here, we encounter a reference to the fact that man's spiritual nature reflects God through its ability to know. Ratzinger dealt with this early on in his career, when he treated St. Bonaventure's understanding of man as the image of God. "Bonaventure places the notion of 'image' within two triads that express increasing modes of relatedness to God: shadow—vestige—image and vestige—image—likeness. Image means the same thing in each case. It differs from the lower forms of shadow and vestige in that they reflect a connection to God in terms of causality, while image bespeaks a connection to God through knowledge."[39] As Ratzinger explains, "Thus, for 'vestige' and 'shadow,' God is only '*Cause*'; for the 'image' [God is] also '*object of knowledge* (obiectum).'"[40]

What is more, it is *communion* with God that makes the human person its most complete self. "If the human person is all the more with itself, and is itself, the more it is able to reach beyond itself, the more it is with the other, then the person is all the more itself the more it is with the wholly other, with God."[41] In other words, man's ability to enter into union with God is an aspect of man's status as the image of God. His intellect and his will are aspects of man as the *imago Dei*.

Communion with God is the fulfillment of what it means to be a human person. Thus, *theological* anthropology is the ultimately *true* anthropology; what it means to be human is revealed most fully and completely through a consideration of man's relation to God.

38. Ratzinger, 451.

39. Richard DeClue, "Joseph Ratzinger's Theology of Divine Revelation" (SThD diss., The Catholic University of America, 2021), 114, https://cuislandora.wrlc.org/islandora/object/cuislandora:223939.

40. Joseph Ratzinger, *Das Offenbarungsverständnis und die Geschichtstheologie Bonaventuras: Habilitationsschrift und Bonaventura-Studien*, in JRGS 2, ed. Gerhard Ludwig Müller (Freiburg, DE: Herder, 2009), 320.

41. Ratzinger, "Concerning the Notion," 451–452.

With respect to this theme of understanding the human person as a reflection of the Trinity, Ratzinger, who is generally a devout pupil of St. Augustine, offers an important critique of Augustine's psychological analogy of the Trinity. While it is true that each human soul is created in the image of God, and thus the spiritual character of each individual human person is a reflection of God, Ratzinger is concerned that St. Augustine's analogy between the Trinity and the powers of each individual soul is missing an important aspect of how man is the image of God: not just as individuals but collectively, as a communion of persons. "In his [Augustine's] interpretation, he projected the divine persons into the interior life of the human person and affirmed that intra-psychic processes correspond to these persons. The person as a whole, by contrast, corresponds to the divine substance. As a result, the trinitarian concept of person was no longer transferred to the human person in all its immediate impact."[42]

In other words, the psychological analogy breaks down insofar as the persons of the Trinity are associated with *intra*-personal (mental and volitional) operations rather than with *inter*-personal relations between human persons. Concomitantly, the individual human person is seen to coincide with the divine nature or substance. That is to say, *human personhood* is not made analogous to being a person the way that the *divine persons* are; rather, human personhood is conceived of as being an analogy to the divine *essence* or *nature* (i.e., the unity within the Godhead). In the psychological analogy, the human person is a unity comprised of a trinity of knower, knowing, and known, or willer, willing, and willed. The relational aspect is entirely *within* the individual person. Hence, the individual person is akin to the divine nature, while the individual's mental operations are akin to the Trinity of persons. This approach disrupts the parallel between human personhood and divine personhood.

42. Ratzinger, 447.

Ratzinger is concerned that such a completely *intra*-personal analogy for the Trinity leaves out the communal dimension of man's own personhood. Ratzinger is not alone in this regard. As David L. Schindler remarks, "The shift from 'intra-psychic' processes to a community of persons in our efforts to find analogies which assist in the understanding of the Trinity lies at the very center of the theology and philosophy proposed by Joseph Ratzinger and Hans Urs von Balthasar. Indeed, it is precisely this shift that accounts for Pope John Paul's emphasis on the family as a *communio personarum* that images the divine *communio*."[43]

The reference to family as an element of humanity's reflection of the Trinity relates to another important aspect: "So God created humankind in his image, in the image of God he created them, male and female he created them" (Gen. 1:27). Although the precise relations between the persons of the Trinity is always beyond human analogues, the fact that human nature exists in man and woman in their mutual relation is a key element of the communal dimension of anthropology. As Ratzinger says, "Genesis 1:27 had portrayed mankind from the very beginning as masculine and feminine in its likeness to God, and had mysteriously, cryptically, linked its likeness to God with the mutual reference of the sexes to each other."[44] For Ratzinger, Eve "is depicted as the necessary opposite pole of man, Adam. His being without her would be 'not good' (Gen 2:18). She comes, not from the earth, but from himself: in the 'myth' or 'legend' of the rib is expressed the most intimate reference of man and woman to each

43. David L. Schindler, "The Person: Philosophy, Theology, and Receptivity," *Communio* 21, no. 1 (Spring 1994): 187. Importantly, Schindler goes on to note that "the point is not to suggest that the two different lines of analogy—'intra-psychic' (cf., e.g., Augustine) and interpersonal (cf., e.g., Richard of St. Victor)—are opposed; on the contrary, they can complement one another. The point rather is that the interpersonal analogy has remained underdeveloped in the tradition."

44. Joseph Ratzinger, *Daughter Zion: Meditations on the Church's Marian Belief*, trans. John M. McDermott (San Francisco: Ignatius, 1983), 16–17.

other. In that mutual reference the wholeness of humanity is first realized."[45]

On this basis, Ratzinger rejects popular depictions of the Old Testament as giving no significant role to women. Rather, the Old Testament "gives to woman, in its own way, an indispensable place in its own model of belief and life, corresponding to marriage on the human level. . . . The consequence of Israel's belief in God with respect to the relation of man and woman expresses itself as marriage."[46]

Additionally, women are given a prominent place in salvation history. "Sarah-Hagar, Rachel-Leah, and Hannah-Penina are those pairs of women in whom the extraordinary element in the path of the promises stands out."[47] Deborah, Esther, and Judith likewise play important roles. The latter two "personify at the same time Israel's unconquered spiritual strength . . . the embodiment of Israel's hope."[48] Ratzinger goes on to elaborate what he sees as "the proper center of the Old Testament's theology of woman: Israel herself, the chosen people, is interpreted simultaneously as woman, virgin, beloved, wife and mother. The great women of Israel represent what this people itself is. The history of these women becomes the theology of God's people and, at the same time, the theology of the covenant."[49]

Reflecting Ratzinger's understanding of the relationship between the Old Testament and the New Testament, Mary herself is seen as prefigured in these great women and in Israel itself. The development of the Old Testament "acquires its definitive meaning for the first time in the New Testament: in the woman who is herself described as the true holy remnant, as the authentic

45. Ratzinger, 16.
46. Ratzinger, 14–15.
47. Ratzinger, 18.
48. Ratzinger, 20.
49. Ratzinger, 21.

daughter Zion, and who is thereby the mother of the savior, yes, the mother of God."[50]

Just as Ratzinger has concerns about Augustine's overly *intra*-personal analogy of the Trinity, he likewise takes issue with Boethius' understanding of person "as the individual substance of a rational nature. One sees that the concept of person stands entirely on the level of substance."[51] Ratzinger prefers the concept of person as expressed by Richard of St. Victor, which Ratzinger sees as arising from within Christianity, in contrast to Boethius' concept, which stems from Western philosophy. Richard of St. Victor's view is superior, in Ratzinger's view, because it is an instance of revelation correcting natural philosophy, which—as we saw in the previous chapter—is an important aspect of Ratzinger's thought. According to Ratzinger, Richard of St. Victor defines person "as the incommunicably proper existence of spiritual nature [*unmittelbar eigene Existenz*]. This definition correctly sees that in its theological meaning 'person' does not lie on the level of essence, but of existence."[52]

---

50. Ratzinger, 24.

51. Ratzinger, "Concerning the Notion," 448.

52. Ratzinger, 449. N.b.: The present author wonders if Ratzinger is misunderstanding Boethius and thus over-contrasting him with Richard of St. Victor. Apparently, the last sentence of this quote is meant to highlight Boethius' mistake as placing "person" on the level of *essence* as opposed to Richard of St. Victor's placing "person" on the level of existence. However, Boethius' term was "substance," which had two possible meanings in Greek philosophy. While it *could* be the equivalent of essence or nature, it also had another meaning: the individual, subsisting entity. In fact, it is this latter meaning that was understood as *primary* substance, while the former was understood as *secondary* substance. Boethius' definition of person would be strange if by "substance" he meant "essence," since essence is a synonym for nature. The adage would thus mean "an individual nature of a rational nature." But that would just mean "a rational nature." Boethius clearly did not equate person here with essence but as an individual that has a rational essence. Boethius himself equated primary substance with *hypostases* or "supposits." See Marilyn McCord Adams and Richard Cross, "Aristotelian Substance and Supposits," *Proceedings of the Aristotelian Society, Supplementary Volumes*, vol. 79 (Oxford: Oxford University Press, 2005): 15–72. From this perspective, Boethius' idea and Richard of St. Victor's idea are barely distinguishable. For another argument against contrasting Boethius and Richard of St. Victor too strongly, see Antonio López, "God the Father: A Beginning without Beginning," *Communio* 36, no. 2 (Summer 2009): 219–258, esp. 255n78: "It is also important not to pit Boethius' understanding of person too strongly against that of Richard of St. Victor." As a further question, it is not clear to me how Ratzinger's distinction between the levels of essence and existence and his equation of personhood with the level of existence could be reconciled with the notion of God's essence and existence being equivalent.

This point connects to the relation between Christology and theological anthropology. Christ is fully human and fully divine, but he is not a divine person *and* a human person, which would be the case if personhood were solely determined by the level of essence. That was the mistake of the Nestorian heresy, that there are two persons in Christ corresponding to the two natures. The Catholic faith's doctrine of the hypostatic union insists on the union of the two natures in the one, divine person, God the Son.

Strictly speaking, because the person (*hypostasis*) of Christ is the second person of the Trinity, it is not proper to speak of Christ as a human person, as if this hypostasis first came into existence through the virginal conception. Nevertheless, he is a divine person with a complete human nature, body and soul. Thus, by taking on a complete human nature, Christ also reveals what it means to be human. In this way, "Christ is the archetype of the human person, in its highest dimension."[53] That is why he is referred to as the last (ultimate) Adam. From this perspective, Ratzinger insists that "the Christological concept of person is an indication for theology of how person is to be understood as such."[54]

We see here similarities with *Gaudium et Spes* 22: "The truth is that only in the mystery of the incarnate Word does the mystery of man take on light. For Adam, the first man, was a figure of Him Who was to come, namely Christ the Lord. Christ, the final Adam . . . fully reveals man to man himself."[55] As Tracy Rowland explains, "The central point of the article [*Gaudium et Spes* 22] is that the human person only understands his or her identity to the extent that he or she is open to a relationship with Christ. Christology is deemed necessary for any adequate anthropology."[56] As

---

53. Blanco, *Teología de Joseph Ratzinger*, 137.

54. Ratzinger, "Concerning the Notion," 450.

55. Second Vatican Council, *Gaudium et Spes* 22, December 7, 1965, in *The Word on Fire Vatican II Collection*, ed. Matthew Levering (Park Ridge, IL: Word on Fire Institute, 2021), 238.

56. Tracey Rowland, *Ratzinger's Faith: The Theology of Pope Benedict XVI* (New York: Oxford University Press, 2008), 32.

Ratzinger states, "In Christ, in the man who is completely with God, human existence is not canceled, but comes to its highest possibility."[57]

Furthermore, a Christological understanding of personhood already points in the direction of ecclesiology, adding yet another area of theology to the equation. "Christ, whom Scripture calls the final Adam, that is, the definitive human being, appears in the testimonies of faith as the all-encompassing space in which the 'we' of human beings gathers on the way to the Father."[58] We will explore the ecclesiological implications of this anthropology in a later chapter, but it is worth noting the connection here as a further reminder of how all the different areas of theology are related to one another as one mystery of faith in the multiplicity of doctrines, which is fitting for a theology rooted in the Triune God.

Ratzinger's Trinitarian and Christological anthropology leads to another important topic: the relation between nature and grace. Ever since de Lubac's book *Surnaturel*[59] was published, there has been an ongoing—often heated—debate over the proper understanding of the relationship between human nature and supernatural grace. As we have seen, Ratzinger's approach to anthropology views knowledge gained by revelation as essential to a proper understanding of the human person. As Rowland argues, "If Christology is a necessary component of any adequate anthropology, secular humanism is always inadequate."[60]

Thus, Ratzinger's understanding of the nature-grace relation is more closely aligned with that of de Lubac than with the neo-Scholastic view. Ratzinger and de Lubac alike are concerned about an overemphasis on the autonomy of nature vis-à-vis grace. Without completely denying the distinction, they nevertheless

57. Ratzinger, "Concerning the Notion," 452.

58. Ratzinger, 452–453.

59. Henri de Lubac, *Surnaturel: études historiques* (Paris: Aubier, 1946).

60. Rowland, *Ratzinger's Faith*, 32–33. See also Rowland, 24, and Joseph Ratzinger, "The Dignity of the Human Person," in *Commentary on the Documents of Vatican II*, ed. Herbert Vorgrimler, trans. W.J. O'Hara (New York: Herder, 1969), 5:119.

insist that man was created for supernatural beatitude, and thus, man cannot be properly understood merely from the perspective of natural reason. The *telos* (or final cause) of a creature is related to the creature's nature (or formal cause). As Ratzinger puts it, "The Alpha is only truly to be understood in the light of the Omega."[61] Eschatology, then, is also related directly to theological anthropology in Ratzinger's thought.

Ratzinger's view may be contrary to *neo*-Scholasticism, but to his mind, it is the more authentically *Scholastic* position. In fact, his position on this topic follows his reading of the great Scholastic theologian St. Bonaventure. The unity of the origin and the end as well as the unity of formal and final causes of creation, in general, and human nature, in particular, is fundamental to his view. This point relates to the *exitus-reditus* understanding of creation and salvation. The idea of flowing forth from God (creation) and returning back to God (salvation) are related to the notions of nature and grace, respectively. But they are part of one divine plan, and thus the first part (creation) is only fully understood in light of the second (salvation). God creates for the sake of man's heavenly union with God. As Ratzinger wrote in the original version of his *Habilitationsschrift*:

> The whole world is an enormous circular movement, which begins with creation and fulfills its full shape in Christ Jesus, a movement, which is first 'egress' and then 'return.' The duality natura—gratia (and thereby natura—supernaturale) is now . . . melted down in this comprehensive understanding of the world: inasmuch as things are in the movement of egress from God, he is present to them in the way of *nature*; inasmuch as they are in the movement of return, he is present to them in

---

61. Ratzinger, "Dignity of the Human Person," 121. See also Rowland, *Ratzinger's Faith*, 33–34: "For Ratzinger, the starting point of anthropology has to be the notion of Christ as the new Adam: a merely theistically coloured account of the human person is both an inadequate anthropology and an inadequate theology of creation. A full theology of creation is only intelligible in eschatology."

the three stages of *grace*. . . . In Christ, God and man, creator and creature are one and so the great circle of reality is closed. 'Nature' and 'grace' is equated with the two great branches of movement 'expressio' and 'reductio' and thereby achieves a truly astonishing 'reductio' of the nature-grace theme on the cosmic thematic of Bonaventurian work.[62]

We see in this description a distinction between nature and grace but also an intimate relation between the two. The one (nature) is ordered toward the other (graced union). Thus, following the terminology found in St. Thomas Aquinas, Ratzinger affirms that man has a natural desire for the vision of God. Additionally, Ratzinger thinks that for St. Bonaventure, man's desire for God is synonymous with man's status as an image of God. The Bonaventurian understanding of man as the image of God is a dynamic view, not a static view. Bonaventure sees in the image "a *movement*, a desire for a more complete unity with God. In this respect, the doctrine of man's divine imagery is identical with the doctrine of the natural desire of man for God."[63]

In Ratzinger's reading of St. Bonaventure, then, the image of God bespeaks man's spiritual capacities *in relation to God* and not just in the ability to know or to will in general. Bonaventure's view, "according to Ratzinger, is that the human person's soul is the image of God insofar as it has the capability to turn to God . . . and not insofar as it has the capability of turning to other objects of knowledge."[64] In the words of St. Bonaventure, "The image subsists exquisitely and primarily in the capabilities of the soul, inasmuch as they are facing God; secondarily, it subsists in it also, inasmuch as they consider the soul itself; inasmuch as they turn to lower objects of knowledge, however, they are no

62. Ratzinger, *Offenbarungsverständnis*, 316–317.
63. Ratzinger, 321.
64. DeClue, "Joseph Ratzinger's Theology of Divine Revelation," 113.

longer an image but only a vestige of the Trinity."[65] Such words lead Ratzinger to conclude thusly: "'Imago Dei' is a concept of the knowledge of God, its central concept even; one cannot be understood without the other."[66]

Ratzinger also thinks this understanding of man as the image of God has precedence in the work of St. Augustine. "With Augustine (*De Trinitate*, XIV, 8, 11) the image of God is interpreted as capacity for God, qualification to know and love God."[67] According to Ratzinger, it is precisely this understanding of *imago Dei* that *Gaudium et Spes* posits. "And that, for the [Second Vatican] Council, is the content of the doctrine that man is made to the image of God. Man stands in immediate relation to God, he does not merely have to do with God indirectly through his work and his relations with his fellow-men. He can know and love God himself."[68]

Following a traditional understanding of image and likeness, Ratzinger relates the image of God to nature and likeness to grace. Having already treated the issue of human nature in relation to man as the image of God, we now turn to the topic of divine likeness.

We find a definition of divine likeness in Ratzinger's original *Habilitationsschrift*. "'Likeness' in its special sense means . . . making similar and the alignment of man to God. It is a transformation of the 'image,' whose 'expressed similitude' now becomes expressed even more. It is thus clear, however, that a dynamic tendency must appertain to the 'likeness,' for if the deformity of the image in its ossification consists in a lack of a vital directedness toward God, then the increase of the likeness must consist in a growing vitality of the relationship with God. In fact, it can thus

---

65. Bonaventure, *Commentary on I Sentences* 3.2.1.2 c (I 83 a), quoted and translated in Ratzinger, *Offenbarungsverständnis*, 322–323.

66. Ratzinger, *Offenbarungsverständnis*, 326.

67. Ratzinger, "Dignity of the Human Person," 121.

68. Ratzinger, 123.

be said that the likeness ultimately consists in unification with God."[69] Just as we saw the image of God understood as a dynamic reality, so too do we see divine likeness being described dynamically. Yet again, relationality is central, as it is a key element both of human nature and of man's graced likeness to God.

Ratzinger wants to make it clear that the divine likeness is not to be understood as a second substance (i.e., nature or essence) that is being added to the human person. Human nature remains one and the same, but the likeness is something done to the one nature. Thus, while one may speak of an image of creation and an image of new creation, Ratzinger insists that insofar as "likeness" can be referred to as the image of the new creation, the "'image of the new creation' is merely the making-like of the old image; thus, a second image is not added to this, but only provides for it a new actual vitality."[70]

This new vitality is, ultimately, divine action upon man, upon the image of God. In fact, this "making-like" is grace.[71] Ratzinger reaffirms this in another work, where he makes the same point that divine likeness (or grace) is not a new substance. He writes that "grace is not an independent creature existing for itself, but that it constitutes an act of God *on* an already existing creature, thus that it is not itself substance but an occurrence."[72]

From this vantage point, Ratzinger understands the adage "grace presupposes nature" as an indication of the ontological status of grace rather than as a judgment about nature as such.[73]

---

69. Ratzinger, *Offenbarungsverständnis*, 334.

70. Ratzinger, 334.

71. See Ratzinger, 335.

72. Joseph Ratzinger, *Gratia praesupponit naturam: Erwägungen über Sinn und Grenze eines scholastischen Axioms*, in *Einsicht und Glaube: Festschrift für Gottlieb Söhngen zum 70. Geburtstag*, ed. Joseph Ratzinger and Heinrich Fries (Freiburg, DE: Herder, 1962), 139–140. This work is available in English translation as Joseph Ratzinger, "Gratia Praesupponit Naturam: Grace Presupposes Nature," in *Dogma and Preaching: Applying Christian Doctrine to Daily Life*, ed. Michael J. Miller, trans. Michael J. Miller and Matthew J. O'Connell (San Francisco: Ignatius, 2011), 143–161.

73. See Ratzinger, *Gratia praesupponit naturam*, 140.

In other words, what that axiom indicates is that grace is not a kind of second nature but something that presupposes a nature on which it is working.

This dynamic conception of grace is relational, since it is an outpouring of divine life upon the human person. From this perspective, Ratzinger—following Bonaventure—does not view grace in a reified way. It is not a "thing" that is possessed. Grace is an influx deriving from God operating in a continuous flow. Perhaps electrical appliances can provide an apt, contemporary example. Appliances never simply "have" electricity. Rather, they rely on a continual flow of power from an outside source in order to function. Similarly, Bonaventure "understands grace as 'esse semper in fieri': existing always in becoming. Grace 'is in the soul, but not from the soul; it is in man and yet above man, and thus never becomes man's own actual property.'"[74]

Ratzinger, following Bonaventure, connects grace with the theological virtues: faith, hope, and love. In this order, it is love that reigns supreme. Thus, Ratzinger sees the state of grace as most especially a loving relationship with God. As he writes, "The transition from the state of nature into the state of grace simultaneously and necessarily signifies the transition from the position of knowing to that of love."[75] While knowledge and love are, in some way, part of both nature (man as the image of God) and grace (man's likeness to God), the emphasis shifts from knowledge with respect to the image to love with respect to divine likeness.[76] By nature, man can know God, and thus in some natural way also love him. But by the grace of divine life acting within the human person, the loving union is elevated to something beyond the powers of mere human nature and intellection.

In summary, Ratzinger succinctly describes three ways that

---

74. DeClue, "Joseph Ratzinger's Theology of Divine Revelation," 120. Here, the quote is from Ratzinger, *Offenbarungsverständnis*, 340.

75. Ratzinger, *Offenbarungsverständnis*, 348.

76. See Ratzinger, 347.

man relates to God, his Creator: as vestige, as image, and as likeness. "For the 'vestige,' God is only cause; for the 'image,' he is a
known object; for the 'likeness' [he is] infused gift."[77] As a vestige,
man is on par with other creatures. As made in the image of God,
man surpasses other physical creatures through the capacity to
know God. Through the grace of divine indwelling, man is perfected and raised to something beyond natural capacities, a life of
supernatural beatitude, which grants one divine similitude.

When grappling with the issues of human nature and supernatural grace, another topic needs to be considered: the fall and
sin. After all, the fall came after man was created in God's image
and likeness (Gen. 1:27). So, what is the fall? What is sin? How
does it affect the human person?

As we have seen, Ratzinger understands man as the image
and likeness of God as having fundamentally relational aspects.
Sin, which removes grace (and thus divine likeness) and tar-
nishes the image of God in man, is therefore anti-relational. As
Ratzinger writes, "Human beings are relational, and they possess
their lives—themselves—only by way of relationship. . . . But sin
means the damaging or the destruction of relationality. Sin is a
rejection of relationality."[78]

Sin disrupts relationships on at least four levels: (1) it sepa-
rates us from God, (2) divides human persons and communities
from one another, (3) distorts our own relationship with ourselves,
damaging our personal integrity (making us *dis*-integrated), and
(4) disrupts our relationship with the rest of creation.[79]

Because sin is antirelational, it is never *merely* an individual
matter. In some sense, the concept of original sin includes the
notion that we are born into a disordered world, whose disorder

77. Ratzinger, 355.
78. Ratzinger, *In the Beginning*, 72–73.
79. See Ratzinger, 70: "The relationship of human beings to themselves is altered, as well
as their relationships to others. . . . The relationship to the world is altered in such a way as to
become one of destruction and exploitation."

is a consequence of sin. "Sin is loss of relationship, disturbance in relationship, and therefore it is not restricted to the individual. When I destroy a relationship, then this event—sin—touches the other person involved in the relationship. Consequently sin is always an offense that touches others, that alters the world and damages it. To the extent that this is true, when the network of human relationships is damaged from the very beginning, then every human being enters into a world that is marked by relational damage."[80] Because sin damages relationships, redemption from sin and salvation must heal relationships on all four of those levels mentioned above. This area of theological anthropology, then, will relate directly to Christology and soteriology, ecclesiology, the sacraments, and moral theology. Therefore, in the chapters dealing with those topics, this understanding of what sin is and what it does must be kept in mind. Again, all these areas of theology are interconnected.

Fundamentally, sin is man's rejection of his *creatureliness*. That is, man's desire to *be* God leads him to revolt against his inherent dependency upon the Creator and, along with this, the limitations of human nature as such. In a certain way, then, sin is man's rebellion against his own being. It is an unwillingness to accept the fact that man is not the origin of what it means to be man. Man cannot decide for himself what human nature is or is made for. Sin is, in some sense, a desire to decide for oneself what one is. Latent in this attitude is a mistrust of God's design and of God's purpose for humanity. As such, sin involves doubt about God's covenant with man, seeing it as a shackle to one's freedom rather than as the necessary condition for true freedom. Because man is not the Creator, however, sin implies a rejection of the *truth* of human nature. It is a rebellion against *reality*.[81] Ratzinger summarizes these observations when he says that "at

80. Ratzinger, 73.
81. See Ratzinger, 64–71.

the heart of every sin lies human beings' denial of their creature-liness, inasmuch as they refuse to accept the standard and the limitations that are implicit in it. They do not want to be creatures, do not want to be subject to a standard, do not want to be dependent. . . . Thus human beings themselves want to be God."[82] But man is not God. Man is, *de facto*, bound by the finiteness of human nature and of the truth of what constitutes human nature as well as of what fulfills human nature. "Sin is, in its essence, a renunciation of the truth."[83]

Given that sin is a willful rejection of the truth, the question arises: precisely what is the relationship between truth and freedom? Is a freedom exercised contrary to the truth an authentic freedom? Ratzinger thinks not. "Freedom without truth is no freedom at all."[84]

Some skeptics may reply that there is no such thing as "truth," at least with respect to human nature. This position was Sartre's. While Ratzinger disagrees with Sartre's presupposition, he never-theless acknowledges Sartre's logical consistency. If there were no truth about human nature, then freedom would not liberate but enslave. It would not make freedom a good to be relished in but a burden without a reward. "Sartre regards man as condemned to freedom. . . . Man has no nature, but is sheer freedom. His life must take some direction or other, but in the end it comes to nothing. This absurd freedom is man's hell."[85] Freedom apart from truth is directionless and thus also worthless, or still worse, a form of damnation: a series of choices with no intrinsic value that, in the end, comes to total meaninglessness. Thus, by rebel-ling against the very existence of truth, freedom is not elevated but obliterated.

The intrinsically communal character of human nature

82. Ratzinger, 70.
83. Ratzinger, 71.
84. Ratzinger, "Truth and Freedom," 24.
85. Ratzinger, 25.

sheds some light on the issue. The increasing emphasis on individual rights in the modern, liberal conception of freedom is as mistaken as the illusory Marxist promise of true freedom once absolute equality has been established. In man's misguided attempt to be God, a completely independent, absolutely free, self-determining entity, man has set up an idol, a false god. The revelation of the Trinity is key here. Once again, the "from, with, and for" of Trinitarian life is at the same time the pattern of human existence itself. Thus, individual freedom understood as radical independence is an illusion. Rather, being "from, with, and for" means that man must exist in relation. Therefore, individual freedom must be nested within a network of freedoms that includes the mutual reciprocity of human relationships. Freedom, then, must be correlated with responsibility, if it is to exist at all.[86]

For Ratzinger, responsibility means "anchoring freedom in the truth of the good, of man and of the world."[87] This conception of freedom and responsibility takes into account man's relational character, as well as the unicity of human nature present in each and every human being. Thus, any individual's freedom must be related to others. Ratzinger's insistence upon metaphysics is operative here. He writes, "There is a common truth of a single humanity present in every man. The tradition has called this truth man's 'nature.' . . . There is one divine idea, 'man,' to which it is our task to answer. In this idea, freedom and community, order and concern for the future, are a single whole."[88]

In some sense, then, authentic freedom involves a "yes" to the nature God has given to us. Human nature is *our* nature whether we accept it or reject it. Our liberty to reject it, though, does not lead to emancipation but to utter decay. It is by accepting the truth about what it means to be human that we become truly free. It means respecting our relationship with God and our

86. See Ratzinger, 26–30.
87. Ratzinger, 31.
88. Ratzinger, 32.

relations with other human persons. The Ten Commandments, which are a succinct list of basic principles of man's relation to God and neighbor, are a sound foundation for understanding authentic human freedom. It is a law that is not opposed to freedom but perfects it. "To live the Decalogue means to live our Godlikeness, to correspond to the truth of our being and thus to do the good. . . . To live the divinity of man, which is the very definition of freedom: the fusion of our being with the divine being and the resulting harmony of all with all (*CCC* 2052–2082)."[89]

With the mention of the Decalogue as an example highlighting what it truly means to be a human person created in the image of God and ordered toward divine likeness, we have already anticipated the topic for the next chapter: divine revelation. Recall that for Ratzinger, what it means to be man cannot be adequately understood from pure philosophy uninformed by revealed truth. Human nature cannot be fully comprehended apart from what God has revealed to us.

Finally, it is appropriate to consider Ratzinger's epistemology (theory of knowledge). How man knows is directly related to divine revelation.

Ratzinger makes a telling statement with regard to divergent epistemologies in the Catholic theological tradition. In short, Ratzinger prefers St. Augustine's theory of knowledge to that of St. Thomas Aquinas. "Augustine's epistemology . . . is much deeper than that of Aquinas, for it is well aware that the organ by which God can be seen cannot be a non-historical 'ratio naturalis' which just does not exist, but only the *ratio pura*, i.e. *purificata* or, as Augustine expresses it echoing the gospel, the *cor purum* ('Blessed are the pure in heart, for they shall see God')."[90] Ratzinger has a proclivity toward Augustine's epistemology, then.

At the same time, Ratzinger's most developed work on

89. Ratzinger, 33.
90. Ratzinger, "Dignity of the Human Person," 155.

epistemology treats the views of St. Bonaventure, who can be seen as a sort of middle ground between Augustine and Aquinas. Ratzinger sees both sense perception and divine illumination as aspects of Bonaventure's approach, and both components have implications for his understanding of divine revelation.[91]

As already discussed, St. Bonaventure closely links man's nature as made in the image of God with man's knowledge. Similarly, it has been repeatedly noted that, for Ratzinger, a proper anthropology must consider theological knowledge, not just pure philosophy. The same is true with respect to epistemology, precisely insofar as it is linked to man as the image of God. As Ratzinger insists:

> Reciprocally, any epistemology, which does not mistake the peculiarly human and creaturely character of human knowledge, is bound to the imago-concept. So little can the essence of man be grasped correctly apart from the imago-concept; so little can the faculty of knowledge and the process of knowledge precisely of this man be understood aright apart from this concept. And so little can there be a theologically neutral concept of being, which refrains from the creaturely character of non-divine being; so little can there be a theologically neutral epistemology, which disregards man's being the image of God. Similarly, as the wisdom-concept just as much as the doctrine of grace is a concept of epistemology, anthropology and epistemology, being and knowledge, philosophy and theology are also indissolubly linked with one another in the imago-concept.[92]

---

91. For a fuller treatment of the nuances of these issues, see DeClue, "Joseph Ratzinger's Theology of Divine Revelation," 124–135. N.b.: According to Ratzinger, Aquinas' epistemology also includes a form of divine illumination, albeit one that differs from St. Bonaventure's. See Joseph Ratzinger, *The Theology of History in St. Bonaventure*, trans. Zachary Hayes (Chicago: Franciscan Herald, 1989), 137.

92. Ratzinger, *Offenbarungsverständnis*, 354. See also DeClue, "Joseph Ratzinger's Theology of Divine Revelation," 126.

Essentially, Ratzinger is saying that even though we only know that man was created in the image of God through divine revelation, that truth about man conveys substantial information about the nature of human knowing, and thus, no purely philosophical theory of knowledge will be adequate to get an accurate understanding of human knowledge. In that sense, Ratzinger's epistemology—or at least his understanding of St. Bonaventure's epistemology—is *theological*, and necessarily so. As a spiritual being, man already occupies a space somewhere between a state of pure nature and a supernatural state.[93]

However, man is not *solely* a spiritual being; he is an embodied spirit. Furthermore, he is only the image of God with respect to the highest part of the soul, as discussed earlier. Thus, man's manner of knowing is multivalent. As a bodily creature, man's knowing involves the senses. Concrete things encountered through man's sense perception, then, are truly principles of knowledge. The soul abstracts knowable content from sensible objects.[94] St. Bonaventure is very close to Aquinas on this point. At the same time, man relies upon the eternal reasons, which act as a divine light, in order to obtain certainty in the act of knowing. While explaining thirteenth-century Franciscan views of divine illumination (including St. Bonaventure's argumentation), *The Stanford Encyclopedia of Philosophy* states, "Certain knowledge requires steadfast unchangeability. Since that can be found only in the divine mind, and since we have access to the divine mind only through illumination, certain knowledge requires illumination."[95] Ratzinger summarizes this twofold character of human knowledge as follows: "The objective content of knowledge (in this respect Bonaventure is an Aristotelian) is gained through

93. See Ratzinger, 356.

94. See Ratzinger, 357.

95. Robert Pasnau, "Divine Illumination," *The Stanford Encyclopedia of Philosophy* (Spring 2020 edition), revised February 10, 2020, ed. Edward N. Zalta, https://plato.stanford.edu/archives/spr2020/entries/illumination.

abstraction out of the reality present at hand; the formal element of certainty (by contrast, Augustinian) is derived from divine illumination."[96]

Without getting into specifics, it is worth noting that Ratzinger sees in Bonaventure a distinction between *natural* illumination that is operative in man's everyday knowledge of natural realities and *supernatural* illumination that involves knowledge of things beyond man's natural capacities. In short, Ratzinger holds that natural illumination is made possible by the fact that created realities reflect their Creator. This reflection of the divine light in created realities "is accessible at any time and to all . . . and thus it may be said about them that the '*naturalia* in rationibus aeternis cognoscuntur *naturali* iudicatorio rationis' [*natural things* are known in the eternal reasons by the *natural* judgment of reason]."[97]

While the complex details of such an epistemology are beyond the scope of this book, it is nevertheless important to make note of this twofold aspect of knowledge, because it will come up again in Ratzinger's treatment of St. Bonaventure's understanding of divine revelation.

The importance of this twofold manner of knowing is made clearer in light of the effects of sin on the ability for man to know. After the fall, there is a hindrance to knowledge both on the part of the objects of knowledge and on the part of the human subject who knows. Prior to the fall, creation reflected God more clearly than after the fall. Creation was a kind of "book" that one could read to see the Creator. Similarly, humans were better able to perceive the reflection of God in created realities, because their minds were more acute; their vision was clearer.

Thus, in the post-lapsarian state, humanity needs a twofold remedy that corresponds to the twofold (objective and subjective)

96. Ratzinger, *Offenbarungsverständnis*, 357.
97. Ratzinger, 360.

deterioration of vision inaugurated through sin. Thus, writes Ratzinger:

> The deficiency of the "first book" [Creation] demands a compensation, which is achieved through the addition of a second witness, the "book of scripture." However, this new book only remedies the objective deficiency, which consists in the eclipse of the mirror of creation. The subjective deficiency of the darkening of the human eye remains. It cannot be remedied through a new external witness but only through a new, internal light. . . . The illumination coming from God himself, which is part of the human process of knowledge.[98]

According to this logic, divine revelation involves both an external, objective dimension and an interior divine illumination that heals and elevates man's ability to know God.

98. Ratzinger, 363–364.

5

Divine Revelation

Chapter 3 of this book treated Ratzinger's theology of the Trinity as the fundamental doctrine of the faith. Because all things proceed from God and are ordered toward a return to God (*exitus-reditus*), everything else in theology is related to the Triune God. In chapter 4, we began our exploration into the first movement: the *exitus* from God. That investigation involved Ratzinger's theology of creation, in general, and his theological anthropology, more specifically. Since it was argued that God created in order to bring humanity into relation with himself, the final end of man was considered as part of a proper understanding of the human person, of human nature as such. We discussed man as the image of God, the meaning of divine likeness, sin and the fall, as well as human epistemology. All of those things led to this chapter's entry into the *reditus* of man back to God. Divine revelation gives man access to reunion with God and is thus clearly a step toward enabling man's eternal union with him.

There are a variety of aspects of Ratzinger's theology of divine revelation. First, we will consider the historical and theological context in which Ratzinger wrote on the topic of divine revelation. Subsequently, we will summarize major themes in Ratzinger's understanding of divine revelation, including the nature of revelation (what it is); the role of faith in the process of divine revelation; the relationships between revelation, Scripture, and Tradition; and other associated topics.[1]

HISTORICAL AND THEOLOGICAL CONTEXT

The modernist crisis of the late nineteenth and early twentieth centuries affected much of the discussion in Catholic theology at the time, including theology of divine revelation. In his encyclical *Pascendi Dominici Gregis*, Pope Pius X condemned modernism as "the synthesis of all heresies."[2] In that document, he highlights two major components of modernism: agnosticism and immanentism.

Agnosticism essentially denies the possibility of knowing God's existence, due to inherent limitations of the human mind. It rejects natural theology in principle. Agnosticism thus falls under the condemnation of Vatican I, which states, "If anyone says that the one, true God, our creator and lord, cannot be known with certainty from the things that have been made, by the natural light of human reason: let him be anathema."[3] Agnosticism, in this sense, also rejects the legitimacy of considering God as a historical subject, that is, as revealing himself in history.[4]

This latter error leads to immanentism. As Darrell Jodock explains, "Agnosticism is thus a negative position; immanentism

1. This chapter may be of particular relevance to those interested in studying the thought of Pope Benedict XVI, because it is a foundational element of his theology but—at the same time—an area not adequately explored in English-language works. Part of the reason for this is that his original, unapproved *Habilitationsschrift* from 1955, which dealt with divine revelation, was not published until 2009 as part of his collected works, which, as yet, is still not translated into English. Some of his other early and important works on divine revelation were likewise published well after they were originally written. Thankfully, some of these (although not all) have been made available in English translation. The paucity of English-language explications of Ratzinger's theology of divine revelation that take into account these seminal works on the topic render this chapter especially valuable for those interested in augmenting their understanding of his theological vision. For those interested in doing a deep dive into the topic, see Richard DeClue, "Joseph Ratzinger's Theology of Divine Revelation" (SThD diss., The Catholic University of America, 2021).

2. Pius X, *Pascendi Dominici Gregis* 39, encyclical letter, September 8, 1907, vatican.va.

3. First Vatican Council, *Dei Filius* 2, dogmatic constitution, April 24, 1870, vatican.va.

4. See Pius X, *Pascendi Dominici Gregis* 6.

is its positive correlate. Because the Modernists cannot appeal to external revelation to explain religion, they seek its sources instead 'in man,' in a 'movement of the heart' which is called 'sentiment.'"[5] For modernists, then, faith is not really a response to an objective self-revelation of God but has its roots within the human person; it is an internal feeling or sense of the divine. In this way, modernism's understanding of faith is highly subjective.

Counteracting this subjectivistic, modernist tendency, neo-Scholasticism emphasized the objective character of revealed truth. From this perspective, as Darrell Jodock notes, "the source of the supernatural was beyond history. It disclosed eternal truths that likewise were not subject to change. These truths could be found in the Bible, which the neo-scholastics interpreted as a handbook of theological axioms, and in tradition."[6] Accordingly, neo-Scholastic treatments of divine revelation were highly propositional; that is to say, revealed truth could be expressed in precisely worded propositions. Revelation was practically equated with doctrinal statements about specific truths.

This reified understanding of revelation—equating revelation with its revealed contents—was not entirely new. Some scholars posit that this view of revelation has its origin in Francisco Suárez, a Jesuit scholastic who lived from 1548 to 1617. Jean-Luc Marion explains Suárez's view: "If we ask what defines revelation, Suárez suggests in response that it requires only the single sufficient proposition of the revealed object, whether *or not* the one to whom it comes believes in it, and without mattering whether it comes from him directly through an inner, direct movement of God, or through an exterior intermediary."[7]

---

5. Darrell Jodock, ed., *Catholicism Contending with Modernity: Roman Catholic Modernism and Anti-Modernism in Historical Context* (Cambridge: Cambridge University Press, 2000), 4. See also Pius X, *Pascendi Dominici Gregis* 7.

6. Jodock, *Catholicism Contending*, 10.

7. Jean-Luc Marion, *Givenness and Revelation*, trans. Stephen E. Lewis (New York: Oxford University Press, 2016), 21. See also Francisco Suárez, *De Trinitate* 1.12.4, in *Opera Omnia*, ed. M. André (Paris: Ludovicu Vivès, 1857), 1:571.

While Ratzinger rejects modernism and affirms that there is objective content to divine revelation, he nevertheless thinks that such a neo-Scholastic approach is overly reductionistic to the other extreme. In a way typical of Ratzinger, he sought a more complete and balanced approach to the question that could hold two sides of the equation together in harmony. In this case, he sought to unify the subjective and the objective dimensions of divine revelation. In what follows, we will explore how he attempts to arrive at such a balance.

DIVINE REVELATION ITSELF

In our last chapter on theological anthropology, we discussed the twofold aspect of natural human knowledge: exterior sense data and some form of divine illumination that is necessary for the certitude of knowledge. In other words, there is an exterior and an interior dimension to the act of human knowing. This was true especially with respect to natural knowledge of God, whereby creation was understood as a reflection of its divine origin (God, the Creator) that coordinates with the mind's grasp of the eternal reasons coming from the divine light in order for man to grasp this reality. In a prelapsarian world, these exterior and interior witnesses functioned sufficiently to have a clear perception of the existence of the Creator. However, after the fall, creation's reflection of its Creator and the light of the mind both dimmed, making this perception more difficult.

In a speech written by Ratzinger (in German) but delivered by Cardinal Frings (in Italian) in Genoa, Italy (November 20, 1961), a further complication impinging upon natural knowledge of God is raised. The title of the speech could be rendered in English as "The Council and the Modern Thought-World." The text discusses the effects of modern technological advancements on man's ability to recognize God as the Creator. Ratzinger first notes man's relation to nature for the vast majority of human existence. "In the history of humanity, the encounter with nature was always one of the most important starting points of religious experience."[8] He then expresses the shift from earlier history to recent times. "In all previous cultures, man lived in a close and direct dependence on nature. In most of the occupations which were open to him he was led into a straightforward, direct encounter with nature as such. That has largely changed since the breakthrough of technology."[9] As Jared Wicks notes, "The world we now encounter," in contrast with former times, "bears the mark of human work and organization."[10]

If man's natural knowledge of God takes place by reasoning from effect to cause (from creation to the Creator), then the reduction of man's direct contact with creation inevitably reduces the mind's likelihood of perceiving the Creator. Concomitantly, the more one's daily environment is surrounded by human inventions, the more one is likely to see man himself as the creator. "He encounters not God's work, but the works of men."[11] As Wicks summarizes, "God was to be known through the things he made (Rom 1:20). But now we lack this significant source of religious existence, as shown by the decline of faith among modern industrial workers."[12]

Ratzinger repeats this concern about modern man's situation in his attempt to draft an introductory constitution for Vatican II that Frings had asked him to write. As Ratzinger remarks:

---

8. Joseph Ratzinger, "Das Konzil und die moderne Gedankenwelt," in JRGS 7/1, ed. Gerhard Ludwig Müller (Freiburg, DE: Herder, 2012), 81. Recall how Ratzinger's own frequent encounters with the beauty of the Bavarian landscape were sources of his own religious development, as discussed in chapter 1.

9. Ratzinger, "Das Konzil," 81.

10. Jared Wicks, "Six Texts by Prof. Joseph Ratzinger as *Peritus* before and during Vatican Council II," *Gregorianum* 89, no. 2 (2008): 257.

11. Ratzinger, "Das Konzil," 81.

12. Wicks, "Six Texts," 257.

For the human condition has been transformed in the brief interval of one century by striking advances in the natural sciences and by marvels of technological invention which human genius has produced with disturbing rapidity. As a consequence, the truth of God, the Creator of the world, seems almost inaccessible to people inhabiting a world largely made by themselves. This world no longer "shows forth the glory of God and the work of his hands" (Ps 18:1 Vulg.), but instead speaks of the glory of humans and of their genius.[13]

Such is the situation of the modern world, which is seeing a drastic decrease in belief in God and overall religiosity. No doubt, the ever-expanding reliance on man-made technology is one factor in this process.

Given the darkening of nature's reflection of the divine through the fall and the significant distance between man and nature due to enhanced technology, the external perceptions of God are radically reduced. At the same time, the fall also affected man's intellect, hindering the proper perception of God from the inside as well. Thus, a remedy is needed both on the external and on the internal levels. A new external witness and an additional interior illumination are required, in accordance with human epistemology. The "first book" (creation) needs to be augmented by a new book, and a new light must shine into the interiority of man to counteract his impeded intellect. It is worth repeating a quote given at the end of the last chapter here:

The deficiency of the "first book" demands a compensation, which is achieved through the addition of a second witness, the "book of scripture." However, this new book only remedies the objective deficiency, which consists in the eclipse of the mirror

13. Joseph Ratzinger, "A Draft of an Introductory Constitution of Vatican Council II," in Wicks, "Six Texts," 262.

> of creation. The subjective deficiency of the darkening of the human eye remains. It cannot be remedied through a new external witness but only through a new, internal light. . . . The illumination coming from God himself, which is a part of the human process of knowledge.[14]

Just as with natural human knowledge, supernatural knowledge involves both an external, sensible witness and a form of divine illumination working within the human subject. Both are crucial.

This duality of the external and the internal is a key element of Ratzinger's theology of divine revelation, which he derived from his studies of St. Bonaventure. In his original *Habilitationsschrift*, Ratzinger undertook a word study to determine precisely what Bonaventure understood by the term "revelation." In the process, Ratzinger noticed a connection with two other words: "apparition" and "manifestation." His analysis of these terms as used by St. Bonaventure is quite extensive and, indeed, often confusing due to very slight nuances. In his later works, Ratzinger does not maintain allegiance to the use of these three terms precisely as he reads them in Bonaventure. A full presentation is therefore neither necessary nor possible here. Nevertheless, there are certain elements of that discussion that remain important to his thought, particularly the relationship between apparition and revelation, as they relate to the external and internal witnesses mentioned above.

In Ratzinger's reading of Bonaventure, apparition and revelation work together to accomplish the manifestation, which is their inner goal. According to Ratzinger, apparition "is a becoming visible of a sensible sign for the presence of the Divine Person sent. It is assigned to sensible knowledge, but a sense-knowledge . . . which does not remain in itself, but points

---

14. Joseph Ratzinger, *Das Offenbarungsverständnis und die Geschichtstheologie Bonaventuras: Habilitationsschrift und Bonaventura-Studien*, in JRGS 2, ed. Gerhard Ludwig Müller (Freiburg, DE: Herder, 2009), 363–364.

beyond itself, which thus grasps its object not as something final but understands it as a sign that points to something greater."[15] Apparition, in the theological sense, means some sort of sensible sign that indicates the presence of a divine person. Some examples of apparitions of the Holy Spirit are the descent in the form of a dove at Jesus' baptism and the tongues of fire that appeared at Pentecost.[16] Another example could be the voice of the Father at the baptism of Jesus. For Bonaventure, writes Ratzinger, even "the historical existence of Jesus . . . is designated as *apparitio*."[17]

These sensible apparitions are important, but they are not sufficient. Using Jesus' life on earth as an example, "the *humanitas* is indeed accessible to the sensory vision, but not the *divinitas*: it discloses itself only in the 'revelatio.'"[18] Here, then, apparition corresponds to the exterior witness, while revelation is associated with the interior illumination. As Ratzinger himself suggests, revelation is "the inner complement of the *apparitio*."[19] As Eckart Schmidt confirms, "For Bonaventure, revelation occurs through a *verbum internum*, the divine Word, the *Logos*, which first—in order to adopt the diction of Bonaventure—must become sensible in an *apparitio*, i.e., in a *verbum externum*, but can arrive at the becoming-known of the divine only through the *revelatio*."[20]

Again, there is a twofold aspect to this process. The first aspect, apparition, is "an externally comprehensible 'historical' event—which however taken by itself alone is blind, empty of meaning, and therefore still no 'revelation,' no truly making-*known* of the

15. Ratzinger, *Offenbarungsverständnis*, 101.

16. See Ratzinger, 105.

17. Ratzinger, 105. See n. 52, where Ratzinger indicates that the Latin word *apparitio* is used to translate the Greek word for epiphany, whereas the Latin word *revelatio* translates the Greek for apocalypse. Therein lies some indication of the difference between apparition and revelation.

18. Ratzinger, 105–106.

19. Ratzinger, 101.

20. Eckart Schmidt, ». . . *das Wort Gottes immer mehr zu lieben« Joseph Ratzingers Bibelhermeneutik im Kontext der Exegesegeschichte der römisch-katholischen Kirche* (Stuttgart: Katholisches Bibelwerk, 2015), 53.

divinity."[21] The second aspect is the "inner self-disclosure of the divinity, which alone is revelation in the true sense and is given the name 'revelatio,' 'inspiratio,' 'illuminatio.'"[22] Here, we see revelation proper as synonymous with divine illumination rather than with exterior, sensible signs.

This equation of revelation with interior illumination rather than with external and sensible signs (e.g., the human face of Christ, Scripture, or specific doctrines), may seem strange, but Ratzinger insists that this is how St. Bonaventure himself understood revelation in the most proper and technical sense. One argument he uses in support of this interpretation comes from Bonaventure's *Commentary on the Sentences*. In a specific passage, Bonaventure argues that it is problematic to speak of demons receiving revelations from holy angels. "Bonaventure's argument can be summarized in three steps as follows: 1) 'revelation is a *"cognitio gratiae, non naturae* [graced, not natural cognition],"' but 2) 'the receptivity for grace has left the demons,' 3) 'and therefore a *"revelatio"* to the demons constitutes a contradiction.'"[23] Here, we see Bonaventure directly equating revelation with knowledge attained through grace, such that the content of the knowledge itself does not constitute revelation without the reception of grace from God that accompanies it.

For analogous reasons, Bonaventure differentiates revelation in the strict sense from mere divinely inspired predictions of future events. As Ratzinger explains, "To 'revelation' belongs the inner, faithful acceptance of what has been said, the knowledge of the '*pro me*' of the relevant prediction. Talk of real revelation can only exist where it does not remain in the external word but

---

21. Ratzinger, *Offenbarungsverständnis*, 106.

22. Ratzinger, 106.

23. DeClue, "Ratzinger's Theology of Divine Revelation," 144, quoting from Ratzinger, 86.

where it arrives at a true, inner contact with God, to an inner enlightening of the man addressed by God."[24]

This divine illumination is transformative, as Ratzinger notes when he contrasts two types of "revelation" in Bonaventure's thought: "*aliqua revelatio*" (revelation in some sense) versus "'*illa revelatio, in qua est animae illustratio per gratiam*' [that revelation, in which there is the enlightenment of the soul by grace]. The '*aliqua revelatio*' can proceed from angels as well, while true and real revelation proceeds not only from God alone, but also induces the inner transformation of man."[25] Thus, revelation properly speaking, for Bonaventure, is a divine action which illumines the human person who is thereby transformed by grace. Revelation is bound up with grace. The mere sensible reception of words or signs is not enough for revelation to truly take place. Grace is a necessary part of divine revelation, in St. Bonaventure's view.

Ratzinger adopts this same perspective in his later works, where he emphasizes that the theological virtue of faith is necessary for revelation (in the truest sense) to occur. He writes:

> For revelation always and only becomes a reality where there is faith. The unbeliever remains under the veil of which Paul speaks in 2 Corinthians 3. He can read scripture and know what it contains. He can even understand, purely conceptually, what is meant and how its statements cohere, yet he has no share in the revelation. Revelation is in fact fully present only when, in addition to the material statements which testify to it, its own inner reality is itself operative in the form of faith. Consequently revelation to some degree includes its recipient, without whom it does not exist. Revelation cannot

24. Ratzinger, 85–86.
25. See Ratzinger, 88–89.

be pocketed like a book one carries around. It is a living reality which calls for the living man as the location of its presence.[26]

Here, Ratzinger draws from his investigation of St. Bonaventure's understanding of divine revelation by including the receiving subject as part of divine revelation.

This approach makes sense when one understands revelation as God's self-communication. Communication takes place between persons. Without the recipient, no communication happens. The very term "revelation," etymologically speaking, denotes the removal of a veil. As Ratzinger indicated in the above quote, if one does not perceive the truth of the reality of what is being communicated, then the veil remains. Think of the many people who saw Jesus yet who did not believe—that is, did not perceive the divine reality in the human visage.

Conversely, Jesus' disciples were said to both see (with their bodily eyes) and believe (perceive through faith). Ratzinger thinks there is an important distinction here. Physical vision and faith have different formal objects. Yes, the external sign is part of the process, but revelation does not happen without the interior perception of the reality made possible by graced illumination and faithful reception. Verweyen summarizes this process as follows: "Bonaventure understands the appearance (*apparitio*), accessible to the senses, the external historical process, as a 'wake-up call' to the spirit. . . . Through such a wake-up call, it *prepares* for the revelation (*revelatio*), and after the revelation it awakens to love."[27]

In order for revelation to reach its terminus, then, the receiving subject must receive it in faith; otherwise, the mind remains darkened and the person is not transformed by what they are

---

26. Joseph Ratzinger, "Statement of the Problem," in Joseph Ratzinger and Karl Rahner, *Revelation and Tradition*, trans. W.J. O'Hara (New York: Herder, 1966), 36.

27. Hansjürgen Verweyen, *Ein unbekannter Ratzinger: Die Habilitationsschrift von 1955 als Schlüssel zu seiner Theologie* (Regensburg: Friedrich Pustet, 2010), 45. See also Ratzinger, *Offenbarungsverständnis*, 107.

hearing or seeing. They may look but not see, hear but not understand. As Ratzinger notes, "The receiving subject is always also a part of the concept of 'Revelation'. Where there is no one to perceive 'Revelation', no re-*vel*-ation has occurred, because no veil has been removed. By definition, revelation requires a someone who apprehends it."[28] Rudolf Voderholzer thus concludes that for Ratzinger, "a divine revelation only purely from the outside is not conceivable. Rather, the process of the acceptance of revelation as the becoming revealed *for* someone is always also considered along with this."[29]

Ratzinger himself offers a helpful summary of the essence of divine revelation: it is the "self-disclosure of God to men, to which the man of faith must—for his part—respond in order, then, in this self-disclosure of God, to make that same man a sharer in that indwelling of Christ, which is here called 'grace.'"[30] As Rowland explains, "Like von Balthasar, he [Ratzinger] holds that Revelation can only be mediated from a standpoint of 'engraced' participation within the horizon of faith. Otherwise, 'there are lights, but no Light; words, but no Word'."[31]

This heavy emphasis on the receiving subject, and hence on the subjective dimension of revelation, should not be taken as an indication of a modernist form of subjectivism, relativism, or immanentism. Ratzinger is not denying the importance of the external signs, the deeds and words, by which God communicates to man in salvation history. He is merely highlighting the fact that, without the graced interior illumination received in faith,

---

28. Joseph Ratzinger, *Milestones: Memoirs 1927–1977*, trans. Erasmo Leiva-Merikakis (San Francisco: Ignatius, 1998), 108. In this passage, Ratzinger acknowledges that he gained this insight from his study of St. Bonaventure.

29. Rudolf Voderholzer, "Der Grundduktus innerhalb der Fundamentaltheologie von Joseph Ratzinger," in *Zur Mitte der Theologie im Werk Joseph Ratzinger/Benedikt XVI.*, ed. Maximilian Heim and Justinus C. Pech, in *Ratzinger-Studien* (Regensburg: Friedrich Pustet, 2013), 6:47.

30. Ratzinger, *Offenbarungsverständnis*, 92.

31. Tracey Rowland, *Ratzinger's Faith: The Theology of Benedict XVI* (New York: Oxford University Press, 2008), 50. See also Joseph Ratzinger, *On the Way to Jesus Christ*, trans. Michael J. Miller (San Francisco: Ignatius, 2005), 64–65.

God's self-communication has not actually occurred. Thus, the objective and the subjective dimensions are both necessary. Once again, Ratzinger is attempting to avoid false dichotomies. Against the neo-Scholastics, Ratzinger insists that the receiving subject's faithful reception of the objective content is necessary. Against the modernists, however, Ratzinger affirms the objectivity of the contents of the faith, and thus secures the place of dogma in faith and theology.

In fact, in the approved version of his *Habilitationsschrift*, Ratzinger is clear to avoid the accusation of an overly subjectivistic view of revelation. "We might well ask," he writes, "whether such a view would not destroy the objectivity of revelation in favor of a subjective actualism."[32] He insists that this is not the case. As he contends:

> Such an idea has no foundation in the intellectual world of
> Bonaventure. For the deep meaning of Scripture in which we
> truly find the "revelation" and the content of faith is not left up
> to the whim of each individual. It has already been objectified
> in part in the teachings of the Fathers and in theology so that
> the basic lines are accessible simply by the acceptance of the
> Catholic faith, which—as it is summarized in the *Symbolum*—
> is a principle of exegesis.[33]

Here, we encounter yet another connection between areas of theology: revelation and ecclesiology.

While the receiving subject's reception in faith is part of Ratzinger's understanding of divine revelation, he also insists that faith is not a merely individualistic reality. "One has not grasped the heart of the act of faith if one constructs it as a relationship between a book and the thinking of an individual. Essentially it

32. Joseph Ratzinger, *The Theology of History in St. Bonaventure*, trans. Zachary Hayes (Chicago: Franciscan Herald, 1989), 66–67.

33. Ratzinger, 67.

is an act of union. . . . To the act of faith belongs—as part of its basic structure—the insertion of the individual into the Church, the community, the communality of that which unites and that which is united."[34]

The ecclesial dimension of faith helps secure the objectivity of faith. "The understanding which elevates the Scripture to the status of 'revelation' is not to be taken as an affair of the individual reader; but it is realized only in the living understanding of the Scripture in the Church. In this way the objectivity of the claim of faith is affirmed without any doubt."[35] Voderholzer confirms this balance of the objective and subjective dimensions of revelation through the ecclesial dimension of faith in Ratzinger's thought. He writes, "When Ratzinger speaks of this in his memoires, [that] revelation requires a someone to whom it becomes known, this is thus not first of all the isolated individual, but the great-subject Church, embedded in whose faith access to the encounter with the self-disclosing God and thereby revelation is possible also for the individual."[36]

Maximilian Heinrich Heim, who wrote his doctoral dissertation on Ratzinger's ecclesiology, also affirms the ecclesial notion of faith in Ratzinger's thought. As he remarks, "The Church is the trans-temporal subject of faith. . . . For this reason, she is also 'the condition for real participation in Jesus' *traditio.*'"[37] "Accordingly," Heim elaborates, "the individual does not believe out of

34. Joseph Ratzinger, "The Church and Scientific Theology," *Communio* 7, no. 4 (1980): 340.

35. Ratzinger, *Theology of History*, 67. See also Joseph Ratzinger, "Sources and Transmission of the Faith," *Communio* 10, no. 1 (Spring 1983): 20, where Ratzinger agrees with Johann Adam Möhler that "the Scripture cannot be separated from the living community in which, alone, it can be 'Scripture.'"

36. Rudolf Voderholzer, "Offenbarung und Kirche: Ein Grundgedanke von Joseph Ratzingers Habilitationsprojekt (1955/2009) und seine theologische Tragweite," in *Gegenwart der Offenbarung: Zu den Bonaventura-Forschungen Joseph Ratzingers*, ed. Marianne Schlosser and Franz-Xaver Heibl, in *Ratzinger-Studien* (Regensburg: Friedrich Pustet, 2011), 2:60–61. See also 67–68 and 70–71. See also Voderholzer, "Der Grundduktus," 46.

37. Maximilian Heinrich Heim, *Joseph Ratzinger: Life in the Church and Living Theology*, 2nd ed., trans. Michael J. Miller (San Francisco: Ignatius, 2005), 149. Here, Heim quotes from Joseph Ratzinger, *Dogma und Verkündigung* (Munich: Erich Wewel, 1973), 265.

his own resources but, rather, as Ratzinger stresses, always believes 'along with the whole Church'."[38] The Church, then, is part of the faithful reception of divine revelation. According to Ratzinger, Voderholzer explains, "the Church is co-recognized as constitutive for the occurrence of revelation."[39] Revelation is achieved only when it is received in faith, and this faith is the faith of the Church.

These considerations lead directly into the theme of our next section on the relationship between revelation, Scripture, and Tradition. There we will explore the relationship between the exterior witness and the internal illumination as well as the communal dimension of revelation more precisely.

REVELATION, SCRIPTURE, AND TRADITION

Revelation, Scripture, and Tradition are obviously related, yet unpacking the distinctions in their mutual relations is quite complex. This complexity is something that Ratzinger grappled with extensively. His explications are incisive, revealing a depth to the matter one might not have noticed before. Even if he does not come to a definitive answer on certain aspects of the problem, one still gains a greater appreciation for the nuances involved.

First, let us start with a fundamental assertion of Ratzinger regarding the relationship between revelation, on the one hand, and Scripture and Tradition, on the other. As mentioned in chapter 1, Ratzinger was highly critical of some of the preparatory schemas that were drafted before the commencement of the Second Vatican Council. In particular, he criticized the draft text on revelation, entitled *De Fontibus Revelationis* ("On the Sources

38. Heim, *Joseph Ratzinger*, 148. Here, Heim quotes from Joseph Ratzinger, "Kommentar zur These I-VIII," in *Die Einheit des Glaubens und der theologischer Pluralismus*, ed. Internationale Theologenkommission (Einsiedeln: Johannes, 1973), 36. See also Joseph Ratzinger, *Salt of the Earth: Christianity and the Catholic Church at the End of the Millennium*, trans. Adrian J. Walker (San Francisco: Ignatius, 1997), 34.

39. Voderholzer, "Der Grundduktus," 46.

of Revelation"). One of his chief complaints involves the very title itself.[40]

Ratzinger takes issue with Scripture and Tradition being called "sources" of revelation. He acknowledges that this phrasing had become common in theological manuals of the day. "But," he argues, "Trent itself did not speak this way and in Vatican I's text itself this way of speaking does not occur."[41]

Even more than the lack of precedence in the two prior ecumenical councils, Ratzinger takes issue with a fundamental misunderstanding about the relationship between revelation, Scripture, and Tradition that the title suggests. He astutely points out that referring to Scripture and Tradition as sources of revelation confuses the order of ontology (the metaphysical order of being or causality) with the order of knowledge. Ratzinger insists that "the formula is completely false if one looks at it on a metaphysical level."[42] The ontological order is exactly the opposite of what *De Fontibus Revelationis* implies. Divine revelation is "*the source* of Scripture and tradition, which however the schema called 'sources' (*fontes*) of revelation."[43] Revelation is ontologically prior to Scripture and Tradition. Scripture and Tradition flow from revelation, not the other way around.

Ratzinger acknowledges that human reason often works in reverse of the order of ontology, reasoning backward from effect to cause. Thus, *epistemologically*, one may see Scripture and Tradition as means of gaining access to revelation, but the metaphysical order must be understood properly to avoid a fundamental error.

40. See Thomas Söding, "Die Seele der Theologie: Ihre Einheit aus dem Geist der Heiligen Schrift in *Dei Verbum* und bei Joseph Ratzinger," *Internationale Katholische Zeitschrift Communio* 35, no. 6 (2006): 546. See also Joseph Ratzinger, "Observations on the Schema *De fontibus revelationis*," in Wicks, "Six Texts," 269–270.

41. Ratzinger, "Observations on the Schema," in Wicks, "Six Texts," 270. Ratzinger does admit in this same work that there is one section heading in a chapter on revelation from Vatican I that uses similar language, but he correctly notes that the actual contents of the document do not present the matter in that way.

42. Joseph Ratzinger, "Cardinal Frings's Speeches During the Second Vatican Council," *Communio* 15, no. 1 (Spring 1988): 137.

43. Wicks, "Six Texts," 242.

From this view, Ratzinger acknowledges that "if one understands it strictly on the epistemological level: we experience what revelation is from Scripture and tradition."[44] Or as Ratzinger phrases it elsewhere, "Scripture and Tradition are the two sources *of the knowledge* of revelation."[45]

In defense of his position, Ratzinger once again appeals to the theological tradition of the high Scholastics. "Scripture and tradition are *for us* sources from which we know revelation, but they are not *in themselves* its sources, for revelation is itself the source of Scripture and tradition. Accordingly, it was traditional in the Middle Ages to call Scripture *fons scientia* [source of knowledge], but never *fons revelationis* [source of revelation]."[46]

If revelation is the source of Scripture and Tradition, then another conclusion logically follows: Scripture and Tradition are *not* revelation itself. Yet again, Ratzinger appeals to a high Scholastic in his defense. "As far as I can see, at no time does Bonaventure refer to the Scriptures themselves as 'revelation.'"[47] Ratzinger reiterates this point in another work: "When . . . I tried to make a study of the way Revelation was treated in thirteenth-century theology, I collided with an unexpected fact: nobody in that period ever thought to call the Bible 'Revelation,' nor was it called 'source.'"[48]

In his critique of *De Fontibus Revelationis*, Ratzinger gives an indication of what revelation is in contrast to Scripture and Tradition. "For revelation is not something following upon Scripture and tradition, but is instead God's speaking and acting . . . the one source that feeds Scripture and tradition."[49] Even though this

---

44. Ratzinger, "Cardinal Frings's Speeches," 137. This statement relates to the related topics of biblical inspiration and inerrancy. Those issues are not directly addressed in this book. For a recent and thorough presentation of Ratzinger's thought on biblical inspiration, see Aaron Pidel, *The Inspiration and Truth of Scripture* (Washington, DC: The Catholic University of America Press, 2023).

45. Ratzinger, *Offenbarungsverständnis*, 67. Emphasis added.

46. Ratzinger, "Observations on the Schema," 270.

47. Ratzinger, *Theology of History*, 62.

48. Ratzinger, "Sources and Transmission of the Faith," 27.

49. Ratzinger, "Observations on the Schema," 270.

was written before *Dei Verbum*—indeed as an attempt to aid the council in working out a document that would become *Dei Verbum*—Ratzinger's definition here closely resembles the Dogmatic Constitution on Divine Revelation: "This plan of revelation is realized by deeds and words having an inner unity: the deeds wrought by God in the history of salvation manifest and confirm the teaching and realities signified by the words, while the words proclaim the deeds and clarify the mystery contained in them."[50] Ratzinger views revelation as God's own action in salvation history: his speaking and acting in order to reveal himself and his will to humanity. "Revelation means God's whole speech and action with man; it signifies a *reality* which scripture makes known but which is not itself simply identical with scripture. Revelation, therefore, is more than scripture to the extent that reality exceeds information about it. It might be said that scripture is the material principle of revelation . . . but that it is not revelation itself."[51]

There is a certain tension here with what Ratzinger wrote in his original *Habilitationsschrift*, where the external signs (e.g., God's deeds and words) were distinguished from revelation understood as the interior divine illumination received in faith. However, one ought to keep in mind that while his study of Bonaventure made a sharp distinction between apparition (the external witness) and revelation (as the internal witness of divine illumination), Ratzinger himself does not stick to that strict delineation in his own writings. To be sure, the interior illumination and the reception in faith are key elements for Ratzinger's understanding of the process of divine revelation. But he does not, in his independent works, deny the external words and deeds of God as part of that process. In fact, they are central.

50. Second Vatican Council, *Dei Verbum* 2, November 18, 1965, in *The Word on Fire Vatican II Collection*, ed. Matthew Levering (Park Ridge, IL: Word on Fire Institute, 2021), 18.

51. Ratzinger and Rahner, *Revelation and Tradition*, 35. See also Joseph Ratzinger, *Milestones*, 109: "If Bonaventure is right, then revelation precedes Scripture and becomes deposited in Scripture but is not simply identical with it. This in turn means that revelation is always something greater than what is merely written down."

But even here, Ratzinger appears to draw a distinction between God's words and deeds in salvation history, on the one hand, and the testimony given to them in Scripture, on the other. As Voderholzer relates, "The insight into the added value of revelation as historical event in comparison with its attestation in Sacred Scripture is fundamental for the fundamental theology of Joseph Ratzinger."[52] Thus, while Ratzinger is willing to say that God's deeds and words are revelation, he notes to the contrary that "it is a disastrous simplification time and again to designate Scripture plainly as 'revelation' . . . revelation does not simply equal Scripture, so that one could say simply 'in revelation is written.'"[53]

Perhaps even more starkly, Ratzinger contends that there can be instances where one has Scripture but does not have revelation proper. "There can be scripture without revelation."[54] This concept was alluded to earlier when Ratzinger spoke about a nonbeliever being able to read Scripture without perceiving the reality to which Scripture bears witness. In such cases, the veil remains, and revelation therefore has not taken place. For "revelation always and only becomes reality where there is faith."[55]

In this connection, St. Bonaventure sometimes equates revelation with an understanding of the spiritual sense of Scripture. "At times in the *Hexaemeron*, *revelatio* means the unveiling of the future. . . . More often, it is the hidden 'mystical' meaning of Scripture that is referred to as the hidden mystery of *revelatio*. *Revelatio*, therefore, effects a pneumatic understanding of

52. Voderholzer, "Der Grundduktus," 45. See also Rowland, *Ratzinger's Faith*, 50: "For him [Ratzinger] it is important to understand that the level of reality of the Revelation event is deeper than that of the proclamation event, which seeks to interpret God's action in human language."

53. Joseph Ratzinger, "Offenbarung—Schrift—Überlieferung: Ein Text des heiligen Bonaventura und seine Bedeutung für die gegenwärtige Theologie," *Trierer Theologische Zeitschrift* 67 (1958): 27. See also Aaron Canty, "Bonaventurian Resonances in Benedict XVI's Theology of Revelation," *Nova et Vetera* 5, no. 2 (2007): 266.

54. Ratzinger and Rahner, *Revelation and Tradition*, 36.

55. Ratzinger and Rahner, 36.

Scripture."[56] Within the context of Bonaventure's notion of the fourfold wisdom, revelation belongs to the category of multiform wisdom, "which consists in grasping the three-fold spiritual sense of Scripture—the allegorical, the anagogical and the tropological."[57] This is another example of how revelation goes beyond the mere words on the page; it involves a spiritual understanding through graced illumination. Ratzinger thus concludes, "'Revelation' is synonymous with the spiritual understanding of Scripture; it consists in the God-given act of understanding, and not the objective letter alone."[58]

Again, the external sign is still part of the process, according to the manner of human knowing; but it is not revelation pure and simple. "Only those who understand Scripture spiritually have a 'facies revelata.'"[59] Ratzinger continues, "This means that that which truly constitutes revelation is accessible in the word written by the hagiographer, but that it remains to a degree hidden behind the words and must be unveiled anew."[60]

Ratzinger concludes from this idea that *sola scriptura* is *de facto* impossible. "This non-coincidence of scripture and revelation makes it clear that quite apart from the question whether scripture is the sole material source or not, there can never really, properly speaking, be a *sola scriptura* in regard to Christianity."[61]

Consequently, Ratzinger does not accept the thesis of material sufficiency of Scripture proposed by Josef Rupert Geiselmann.[62] Ratzinger accepts certain portions of Geiselmann's work, but nevertheless, he thinks Geiselmann takes the theory

56. Ratzinger, *Theology of History*, 58–59.
57. Ratzinger, 62–63.
58. Ratzinger, 63.
59. Ratzinger, 63.
60. Ratzinger, 66.
61. Ratzinger and Rahner, *Revelation and Tradition*, 36.
62. See Josef Rupert Geiselmann, "Das Konzil von Trient über das Verhältnis der Heiligen Schrift und der nicht geschriebene Traditionen," in *Die mündliche Überlieferung*, ed. Michael Schmaus (Munich: Max Hueber, 1957), 123–206. For an autobiographical account of Ratzinger's interaction with Geiselmann's work, see Ratzinger, *Milestones*, 124–128.

too far. It is a nuanced criticism. Thus, a word about Geiselmann's theory must be given for the sake of clarity.

In post-Tridentine theology, it became common to speak about revelation being given *partly* in Scripture and *partly* in Tradition. The idea is that some truths revealed by God are conveyed through the Scriptures while others were only handed on in unwritten Tradition. Geiselmann undertook an investigation into the Council of Trent's actual teaching to see whether such an interpretation of Trent was warranted. Geiselmann concluded that this interpretation cannot be accurate, precisely because Trent had intentionally removed the *partly-partly* (*partim-partim*) expression in the final draft of its official teaching. In other words, Trent directly refused to bind Catholics to the position that revelation is partly given in Scripture and partly in Tradition.

Ratzinger sees Geiselmann's study of Trent as a legitimate advancement in the understanding of Tridentine doctrine.[63] In fact, this point was another reason that Ratzinger criticized *De Fontibus Revelationis*. That preparatory schema on revelation had tried to canonize the *partly-partly* concept of the material aspect of revelation by insisting that there were some truths that were known only through Tradition, apart from Scripture.[64] Ratzinger thought such a move was unwarranted, given that Trent intentionally refused to settle the matter and left open alternative understandings. As Wicks explains:

> Furthermore, the draft text overstepped proper bounds when it proposed giving conciliar ratification to the position that some parts of God's revelation come to us from the Apostles via tradition alone and not by Scripture. This would amount to censuring the contrary conclusion of J.R. Geiselmann of Tübingen,

63. See Ratzinger and Rahner, *Revelation and Tradition*, 33: "It seems to me quite indisputable that it [Geiselmann's thesis] represents in fact a considerable material advance."

64. See *De Fontibus Revelationis* 5, trans. Joseph A. Komonchak, "In Verbo Veritatis" blog, https://jakomonchak.files.wordpress.com/2012/09/de-fontibus-1-5.pdf.

drawn from the absence of the famous *partim-partim* phrasing from the Council of Trent's promulgated decree on the Gospel and its transmission.[65]

Ratzinger felt that Vatican II should follow Trent's decision to leave the question open. In other words, Catholic theologians should be allowed to maintain either that there are specific revealed truths only contained in Tradition or that Scripture is materially complete—that is, that Tradition does not supply any specific content in addition to Scripture.[66] Both theological opinions should be allowed to persist. "Tradition must not be depicted, as in *De fontibus*, as an autonomous source offering a plus of revealed content beyond scripture."[67]

On the other hand, Ratzinger does not think Geiselmann's solution is absolutely tenable either. Geiselmann's interpretation of Trent goes too far in the opposite direction, insofar as it insists that Trent taught the material sufficiency of Scripture. Ratzinger thinks that is also an inaccurate portrayal of the Council of Trent. Geiselmann had rooted his claim in comments made by Giacomo Nacchianti, who argued for material sufficiency at Trent. However, in rebuttal to Geiselmann, Ratzinger "cites the testimonies of Cervini and Massarelli that the bishops were scandalized by Nacchianti's position on the sufficiency of Scripture, calling him a 'lover of new things' and 'reprehensible to many.'"[68] From that evidence, it is a bridge too far to conclude that the Council of Trent formally taught what many of the very fathers of Trent rejected.

Thus, despite his appreciation for aspects of Geiselmann's

---

65. Wicks, "Six Texts," 242.

66. See Verweyen, *Unbekannter*, 32–34.

67. Jared Wicks, "Light from Germany on Vatican Council II," *The Catholic Historical Review* 99, no. 4 (Fall 2013): 734.

68. Joshua Brotherton, "Revisiting the *Sola Scriptura* Debate: Yves Congar and Joseph Ratzinger on Tradition," *Pro Ecclesia* 24, no. 1 (Winter 2015): 105n88. See also Ratzinger and Rahner, *Revelation and Tradition*, 77–78n22.

work, Ratzinger nevertheless thinks Geiselmann does not achieve the success he was aiming for. "He [Geiselmann] thought he had found the reconciliation of the Catholic principle with the Protestant principle of *sola scriptura*. He was mistaken."[69] In Ratzinger's estimation, material is never sufficient, and thus the very idea of "material sufficiency" of Scripture is meaningless. "The question has to be raised, after all, what from a Christian point of view, material sufficiency can mean. It is only the Christ-*reality* which is 'sufficient'."[70]

Ratzinger's thought on this matter involves the relationship between Scripture and Tradition, which is extremely nuanced. Scripture cannot be materially sufficient, because the matter of Scripture can only be understood correctly from within ecclesial Tradition. Drawing from the Tridentine council father Marcello Cervini, Ratzinger states, "Tradition refers to the *institutio vitae*, to the mode of realization of the word in actual Christian living. In other words, it is the form in which the word finds reality and without which the word would remain unreal."[71] Tradition is understood here in a broad sense; it includes all aspects of the Church's life. "Tradition is for Ratzinger the process—made possible and supported by the Holy Spirit—of the ever new appropriation and of the deepened understanding of the event of revelation attested to in scripture in the Church's consciousness of faith. . . . This process of ever new appropriation and deepened understanding . . . includes the liturgy, prayer, meditation, includes the Church's whole life of faith."[72] Without Tradition, the context of the whole of the Church's life, the material provided by Scripture is insufficient. Hence, material sufficiency is a fundamentally flawed concept.

As already stated, Ratzinger thinks that the Magisterium

69. Ratzinger, "Cardinal Frings's Speeches," 136.
70. Ratzinger and Rahner, *Revelation and Tradition*, 40.
71. Ratzinger and Rahner, 59.
72. Voderholzer, "Der Grundduktus," 49.

should allow the continuance of both opinions regarding the materiality of revelation—that is, whether Tradition adds any material *content* to Sacred Scripture. Yet the question remains: Which allowable opinion does Ratzinger himself hold? Answering that question is not as straightforward as one might hope. There are different places in Ratzinger's theological corpus that seem to advocate for one or the other position. Let us take a look at examples where both positions are put forward, before arriving at a conclusion.

In his original *Habilitationsschrift*, Ratzinger seems to hold that Tradition does not add any content to Sacred Scripture. He writes:

> One will certainly do well, however, not so much to grasp Tradition as a substantive principle alongside Scripture (which almost always happens in a false interpretation of Trent), as to find expressed in it, rather, simply the ecclesial bond of the word of Scripture. The proposition: alongside Scripture, Sacred Tradition is a source of "revelation" (= knowledge of revelation) implies therefore accordingly *in the first place* not that there is a stockpile of "truths of revelation" beyond Scripture, which is handed on further alongside Scripture; rather, it means that Scripture is not simply already "revelation" of God as a dead, historical book, which therefore would be accessible and "available" (!) to everyone, even to the profane reader, but on the contrary that it only becomes revelation in the hands of the living Church in her proclamation. In short, it could be expressed thusly: the proposition "Scripture and Tradition are the two sources of the knowledge of revelation" is synonymous with the other: Scripture is God's revelation only in the living Church of God.[73]

---

73. Ratzinger, *Offenbarungsverständnis*, 66–67.

Accordingly, Ratzinger says that "one may not define tradition as the communication of unwritten affirmations," arguing that "neither the Fathers nor pre-Tridentine scholastics held this position."[74] In fact, in defense of his argument, "he [Ratzinger] cites expressions of the 'two greatest' scholastics, Bonaventure and Thomas, who stress that all truths necessary for salvation are found in Sacred Scripture or can be attributed to it."[75]

In this connection, Ratzinger makes a distinction between material and formal principles. "Because the scholastics clearly set apart the formal principle 'revelation' from the material of Scripture, they could now conversely unselfconsciously assert a material *sola scriptura*, i.e., understand Scripture as the sole material principle of the faith, without having to attempt the questionable construction of material, oral traditions."[76]

Consequently, Ratzinger is loath to conceive of Tradition as a set of concrete teachings handed on from the Apostles in unwritten form. "History," he insists, "can name practically no affirmation that on the one hand is not in Scripture but on the other hand can be traced back even with some historical likelihood to the Apostles."[77]

Some theologians have argued that the canon of Scripture itself proves a material addition of Tradition to that of Scripture, since Scripture does not testify internally to its own table of contents. However, Ratzinger does not think this proves the notion of Tradition as doctrines handed on from the Apostles for one very simple reason: "The Church possessed no formulated communication left as its own legacy by the last living Apostle concerning which books should go together to make up Scripture."[78]

All these examples suggest that Ratzinger does hold that

---

74. Ratzinger, "Observations on the Schema," 275.

75. Verweyen, *Unbekannter*, 33.

76. Ratzinger, "Offenbarung—Schrift—Überlieferung," 27.

77. Ratzinger, "Observations on the Schema," 274.

78. Ratzinger, 274.

Scripture is the sole material principle of revelation—that is, that Tradition does not add supplementary contents to what is found in Scripture. In fact, Ratzinger raises and answers the question quite directly. "The question of whether certain express affirmations were transmitted from the beginning side by side with scripture, whether, therefore, there is a second material principle besides scripture, independent from the beginning, becomes quite secondary in comparison; but it would probably have to be answered negatively."[79] Voderholzer interprets Ratzinger's thought thusly: "Tradition is not a second material principle of revelation alongside Scripture but a mode of transmission of revelation through the Church."[80]

However, there are specific passages in Ratzinger's writings that seem to call this stance into question. For instance, in his "Observations on the Schema," Ratzinger says that "Scripture and Tradition are material principles of our knowing revelation."[81] Similarly, as part of his criticism of Geiselmann's thesis of scriptural material sufficiency, Ratzinger appeals to certain dogmas that he thinks call that thesis into question:

> Geiselmann himself, as a Catholic theologian, has to hold fast to Catholic dogmas as such, but none of them is to be had *sola scriptura*, neither the great dogmas of Christian antiquity, of what was once the *consensus quinquescacularis*, nor, even less, the new ones of 1854 and 1950. In that case, however, what sense is there in talking about the sufficiency of scripture? Does it not threaten to become a dangerous delusion with which we deceive first ourselves and then others . . . ? At least, in order to maintain both that scripture contains all revealed truth and that the dogma of 1950, for example, is a revealed

---

79. Ratzinger and Rahner, *Revelation and Tradition*, 46.
80. Voderholzer, "Offenbarung und Kirche," 66.
81. Ratzinger, "Observations on the Schema," 272.

truth, recourse has to be had to such a wide sense of the term "sufficiency" that the word loses all serious meaning.[82]

This argument seems to contradict his other statements. On the one hand, he argues that Scripture is not materially sufficient by pointing to the dogma of the Assumption as a prime example. On the other hand, he claims that Tradition does not contain revealed truths not found in Scripture. There is, then, a certain tension when one compares different passages from Ratzinger's writings.

Nevertheless, the preponderance of evidence suggests that generally speaking, Ratzinger does not see Tradition as a second, material source for the contents of revelation. Despite a couple of isolated passages that point in the opposite direction, Ratzinger most often agrees with the understanding of the Scholastics (i.e., Bonaventure and Aquinas) and the Church Fathers, namely, that Scripture is the one material source for the knowledge of revealed truth.

I think my reading of Ratzinger is further supported when one delves into how Ratzinger understands "Tradition." So far, we have focused on whether it adds any material to the contents of revelation. But it is more illuminating to ask what Tradition is according to Ratzinger. "Tradition," writes Ratzinger, "by its very nature is always interpretation, does not exist independently, but only as exposition, interpretation 'according to the scriptures'. . . . As 'tradition' . . . it must recognize that it is under an obligation to scripture and linked to it."[83] Tradition as interpretation of Scripture is a recurring theme in Ratzinger's work. In this vein, Ratzinger asks "whether a person can be a witness to tradition in any other way than by being a witness to the interpretation of Scripture, to the discovery of its true meaning. Perhaps, indeed, the wisdom of the pronouncements of Trent and of 1870

82. Ratzinger and Rahner, *Revelation and Tradition*, 33–34.
83. Ratzinger and Rahner, 47.

consists precisely in the fact that they allow tradition to bear upon scriptural interpretation; that they recognize the Fathers as the expression of tradition because they are revealers of the Bible."[84]

Tradition as interpretation of the Bible should not be understood in an overly academic sense. Speaking about Tradition, Ratzinger writes, "It is true that it is not interpretation in the sense of purely exegetical exposition, but in virtue of the spiritual authority of the Lord operative in the whole existence of the Church, its faith, life and worship."[85] Here again we see a broad understanding of Tradition as the entirety of ecclesial life. For the Church Fathers themselves, "Tradition was the insertion of Scripture into the living organism of the Church and the Church's right of possession of Scripture. . . . For them tradition is simply *scriptura in ecclesia* [scripture in the Church]."[86]

An important caveat needs to be noted here. Despite the fact that Ratzinger speaks about Tradition as interpretation of Scripture, he does not think that Tradition only exists *after* the finalization of the New Testament canon. Bernhard Körner explains, "As the Bible attests, for Ratzinger, Tradition is not only a process which temporally begins *after* Sacred Scripture but a process which can already be observed and is documented *within* Scripture."[87] In fact, Tradition is responsible for the biblical canon. "Scripture became Scripture through the tradition."[88]

When considering Ratzinger's various statements regarding the relationship between Scripture and Tradition, it becomes clear that for him, the two are inseparable. Without Tradition,

---

84. Joseph Ratzinger, *Principles of Catholic Theology: Building Stones for a Fundamental Theology*, trans. Mary Frances McCarthy (San Francisco: Ignatius, 1987), 138.

85. Ratzinger and Rahner, *Revelation and Tradition*, 47.

86. Ratzinger, "Observations on the Schema," 275.

87. Bernhard Körner, "Übereignung und die Kirche als Grundakt der Glaubenserkenntnis: Joseph Ratzinger im Vergleich mit Max Seckler," in *Zur Mitte der Theologie im Werk von Joseph Ratzinger/Benedikt XVI.*, ed. Maximilian Heim and Justinus C. Pesch, in *Ratzinger-Studien* (Regensburg: Friedrich Pustet, 2013), 6:70.

88. Joseph Ratzinger, *Called to Communion*, trans. Adrian J. Walker (San Francisco: Ignatius, 1996), 70.

Scripture cannot be read efficaciously, since it would be missing its lived, ecclesial context. At the same time, Tradition is fundamentally linked to Sacred Scripture. This coexistence of Scripture and Tradition leads Pablo Blanco Sarto to interpret Ratzinger's thought thusly: "Scripture and Tradition . . . do not form two different sources [of the knowledge of revelation], but just one in which both intimately unite."[89] This view of Scripture and Tradition reflects the teaching of *Dei Verbum*: "Hence there exists a close connection and communication between sacred tradition and Sacred Scripture. For both of them, flowing from the same divine wellspring, in a certain way merge into a unity and tend toward the same end."[90]

We have already seen that Ratzinger does not view Tradition as a set of doctrines existing alongside Scripture in unwritten form. Rather, for Ratzinger, Tradition is directly connected to the authority present within apostolic succession. Basing himself on his study of St. Bonaventure, Ratzinger states, "It is not the *content* handed over that matters here so much as the *act* of handing over."[91] In this context, Ratzinger contrasts Bonaventure's view of Tradition with more contemporary (mid-twentieth century) views. To highlight his point, he uses two different German terms to express each concept: *Übergabe* for Bonaventure's understanding and *Überlieferung* for the more contemporary approach. The former denotes the authoritative handing down from superior to subordinate, while the latter denotes the handing on from generation to generation.[92] "One could thus set the two concepts of Tradition, which loom in the background, against each other as the hierarchical-formal and as the historical-material. While

89. Pablo Blanco Sarto, *La Teología de Joseph Ratzinger: Una introducción* (Madrid: Pelícano, 2011), 85–86.

90. *Dei Verbum* 9. Note that *Dei Verbum* reflects the ontological priority of revelation as the source from which Scripture and Tradition flow, which corresponds precisely to Ratzinger's understanding and which he advocated for in his work related to the council.

91. Ratzinger, *Offenbarungsverständnis*, 212.

92. See Ratzinger, 212–213.

for the former, Tradition is given functionally, as a function of the *auctoritas* [authority], the latter sees it in specific historical content."[93]

For Ratzinger, then, Tradition is not fundamentally specific doctrines taught by the Apostles, but rather the authority divinely given to the Apostles and subsequently transmitted to their successors. There is at least one passage in *Dei Verbum* that suggests the same notion of identification between apostolic succession and Tradition. "But in order to keep the Gospel forever whole and alive within the Church, the Apostles left bishops as their successors, 'handing over' to them 'the authority to teach in their own place.' *This sacred tradition . . .*"[94] Here, the antecedent to "this sacred tradition" is the Apostles' act of handing on their authority to their successors.

Similarly, "Ratzinger maintains that *successio* and *traditio* were virtually synonymous terms in the early Church. In fact, he holds that they 'were expressed by the same word διαδοχη.' For Ratzinger, 'succession' highlights the personal dimension of tradition."[95] This complex unity of Tradition and succession goes back to the nascent Church. "Christians had already formulated the principle of *successio-traditio* before they yet understood the New Testament as 'Scripture'."[96] What is more, Tradition—as an ongoing reality—requires succession. Hence, Ratzinger is able to say that "*tradition*" is "guaranteed by *succession*."[97]

This understanding of Tradition is directly related to Ratzinger's dislike for the notion of Tradition as unwritten content. Ratzinger argues that the Fathers appealed to apostolic

---

93. Ratzinger, 214.

94. *Dei Verbum* 7 (emphasis added).

95. Richard G. DeClue, "Primacy and Collegiality in the Works of Joseph Ratzinger," *Communio* 35, no. 4 (Winter 2008): 652. The internal quote is from Joseph Ratzinger in Karl Rahner and Joseph Ratzinger, *The Episcopate and the Primacy*, trans. Kenneth Barker et al. (New York: Herder, 1962), 46.

96. Rahner and Ratzinger, *Episcopate and the Primacy*, 49.

97. Rahner and Ratzinger, 50. Emphasis added.

succession as the guarantee of authentic Tradition precisely to combat the Gnostics' claim that they possessed some unwritten tradition.[98] In the early Church, Tradition was not "exhaustive doctrines of apostolic origin"; rather, it was "the connection of the living faith with the authority of the Church, embodied in the episcopal succession."[99]

There is both a mystical and a hierarchical aspect to this understanding of Tradition. It relates to the Church as both having a concrete, visible structure as well as being a spiritual reality. "This permanent actualization of the active presence of the Lord Jesus in his People, brought about by the Holy Spirit and expressed in the Church through the apostolic ministry and fraternal communion, is what, in a theological sense, is meant by the term 'Tradition': it is not merely the material transmission of what was given at the beginning to the Apostles, but the effective presence of the Crucified and Risen Lord Jesus, who accompanies and guides in the Spirit the community he has gathered together."[100] "Tradition is not the transmission of things or words, a collection of dead things. Tradition is the living river that links us to the origins."[101]

Despite the amount of territory already explored, there is more that could and should be said about Ratzinger's theology of divine revelation. Most especially, we have left out one extremely important aspect of Ratzinger's theology of divine revelation: Christ as the highpoint of divine revelation. This lacuna is not an oversight but quite intentional. The connection between revelation and Jesus is so central to who Christ is and what he does that it ought to be treated as part of Ratzinger's Christology. Thus, this current chapter on revelation and the next chapter on

---

98. See DeClue, "Primacy and Collegiality," 653.

99. Rahner and Ratzinger, *Episcopate and the Primacy*, 40.

100. Benedict XVI, *Jesus, the Apostles, and the Early Church* (San Francisco: Ignatius, 2007), 26–27.

101. Benedict XVI, 28.

Christology belong together. In a way, this entire chapter has been a precursor to the fullest aspect of revelation, Jesus Christ himself, to be covered in chapter 6. There, the reader will encounter ways in which Ratzinger connects theology of revelation not just with anthropology but also with Trinitarian theology, Christology, and soteriology.

6

Christology and Soteriology

It is fitting that chapters 5 and 6 constitute the central portions of this book. Their physical centrality reflects their conceptual centrality. Revelation in Christ is the turning point of the *exitus-reditus* structure of history that we have referred to time and again. As Ratzinger states, "All reality is carried away in the great circular movement, which proceeds from God, and through Christ, the turning point of the world, all is again 'led back' to God."[1] In some sense, the Incarnation is at one and the same time the apex of the *exitus* and the beginning of the *reditus*. It is the high point of God's union with humanity that enables the rest of humanity to begin the journey back to God on the way to the eschaton. As Peter Hofmann relates, "Christ is the center and the goal of salvation history; the world is ordered to him in procession and return."[2]

This idea of the Incarnate Word as both the high point and middle point is confirmed by Pablo Blanco Sarto, who explicitly

---

1. Joseph Ratzinger, *Das Offenbarungsverständnis und die Geschichtstheologie Bonaventuras: Habilitationsschrift und Bonaventura-Studien*, in JRGS 2, ed. Gerhard Ludwig Müller (Freiburg, DE: Herder, 2009), 412.

2. Peter Hofmann, "Jesus Christus als Mitte der Geschichte: Der Einfluss Bonaventuras auf das Denken Joseph Ratzingers/Benedikts XVI. und dessen Bedeutung für die aktuelle Fundamentaltheologie," in *Zur Mitte der Theologie im Werk Joseph Ratzinger/Benedikt XVI.*, ed. Maximilian Heim and Justinus C. Pech, in *Ratzinger-Studien* (Regensburg: Friedrich Pustet, 2013), 6:85.

connects this notion with Jesus as the pinnacle of divine revelation. He notes that Ratzinger "situated revelation within the framework of the history of salvation, and the idea of God as person appears, and the center and summit of this revelatory action was occupied by the same Christ."[3] As Pope Benedict XVI himself said, "For St Bonaventure Christ was no longer the end of history . . . but rather its centre; history does not end with Christ but begins a new period."[4]

Similarly, these two middle chapters on divine revelation and Christology/soteriology constitute the turning point. Here, we move conceptually from the Trinity and that which proceeds forth from God to God's self-disclosure to man (above all in Christ), which in turn inaugurates man's return back to God through the Incarnation and saving work of Jesus Christ. Yet again, the conceptual unity of the order of chapters is evident.

At the end of the last chapter, we mentioned how, in Ratzinger's thought, Jesus Christ is the fullness of revelation itself. Accordingly, this chapter can be viewed—at least in part—as the conclusion of the previous chapter. We will return to that idea later. In order to do so effectively, however, we must also highlight how this chapter connects with an even earlier chapter: chapter 3 (on the Triune God).

If this chapter were a stand-alone work, then much of what was written in chapter 3—particularly the section entitled "God the Son, the Eternal Word"—would be part of this exposition as well. Therefore, this chapter should be read and understood in connection with chapter 3. In that chapter, we intentionally focused primarily on God the Son within the immanent Trinity. What was said there about God the Son is an important element of Ratzinger's Christology and hence must be viewed as part of this current treatment. Where Jesus comes from (the Father) and

3. Pablo Blanco Sarto, *La Teología de Joseph Ratzinger: Una introducción* (Madrid: Pelícano, 2011), 87.

4. Benedict XVI, "General Audience," March 10, 2010, vatican.va.

who he is eternally (God the Son) are determinative for his meaning and significance as man on earth. As already quoted in chapter 3, "That which makes Jesus important and irreplaceable in every age is precisely the fact that he was and is the Son, that in him God has become man."[5] That is why Benedict XVI's book on the infancy narratives, which he calls the "antechamber" to his *Jesus of Nazareth* series, begins with a chapter on where Jesus is from.[6]

A HIGH CHRISTOLOGY FROM ABOVE

This emphasis on the divine origin of the Eternal Word leads me to describe Pope Benedict XVI's Christology as "from above." His starting point for understanding who Jesus is and what he does for us is the second person of the Trinity. Similarly, because Jesus' divine nature is the key factor in understanding the efficacy of his humanity in Benedict XVI's thought, one could also describe his Christology as "high Christology."

That description is further justified when one considers how frequently Benedict XVI decries the movement associated with the search for the "historical Jesus" in opposition to the Christ of faith, as if the two were not one and the same reality.[7] That movement tended to downplay the claims to divinity as later accretions coming from the Church rather than from Jesus himself. The movement thus emphasized Jesus' humanity: a low Christology. It is partly in reaction to this that Benedict XVI is so keen on emphasizing the *truth* of the Gospel that Jesus is the Word made flesh.[8] As he writes, "This is also the point around which I will

---

5. Joseph Ratzinger, *The God of Jesus Christ: Meditations on the Triune God*, trans. Brian McNeil (San Francisco: Ignatius, 2008), 87.

6. See Benedict XVI, foreword and "'Where Are You From?'" in *Jesus of Nazareth*, vol. 3, *The Infancy Narratives*, trans. Philip J. Whitmore (New York: Image, 2012), xi, 1–13.

7. See Emery de Gaál, *The Theology of Pope Benedict XVI: The Christocentric Shift* (New York: Palgrave MacMillan, 2010), 87: "Ratzinger has repeatedly warned against divining an artificial opposition between the Christ of faith and the historic Jesus."

8. See the entire foreword to Benedict XVI, *Jesus of Nazareth*, vol. 1, *From the Baptism in the Jordan to the Transfiguration*, trans. Adrian J. Walker (New York: Doubleday, 2007), xi–xxiv.

construct my own book. It sees Jesus in light of his communion with the Father, which is the true center of his personality; without it, we cannot understand him at all, and it is from this center that he makes himself present to us still today."[9]

While Benedict takes the humanity of Jesus very seriously, he is always careful to emphasize Christ's divinity, and it is for this reason that I would describe Benedict XVI's Christology as "high Christology." To re-quote the rhetorical questions given in chapter 3, "If he [Jesus] was really only a man like any of us, what was happening then, and what happens now? Can one expect that an enthusiasm for a Jesus of that kind will last?"[10] Jesus' humanity is extremely significant with respect to his status as the apex of divine revelation as well as his saving work (soteriology). However, his humanity is only able to be meaningful in those ways *because* he is truly God the Son, the Eternal Word. "It is only if Jesus was God, only if God became man in him, that something actually took place in him."[11]

Thomas Rausch also concludes that Benedict XVI's Christology is "high Christology": "In many ways, the Gospel of John becomes the lens through which Benedict reads the Synoptic tradition. . . . Thus he is able to find a high Christology not just in John but in the Synoptics as well."[12] Richard Hays offers a similar perception: "Benedict's portrait of Jesus is strongly Johannine: grounded in high-christological claims that Jesus was one with God."[13] Rausch also offers comments suggesting that Ratzinger's Christology is "from above": "In his 1968 *Introduction to Christianity*, Ratzinger began his Christology not from

---

9. Benedict XVI, *Jesus of Nazareth*, 1:xiv.

10. Ratzinger, *God of Jesus Christ*, 87.

11. Ratzinger, 88.

12. Thomas P. Rausch, *Pope Benedict XVI: An Introduction to His Theological Vision* (New York: Paulist, 2009) 87–88.

13. Richard B. Hays, "Benedict and the Biblical Jesus," *First Things* 175 (Aug./Sept. 2007): 51. See also Rausch, *Pope Benedict XVI*, 99.

the Jesus of history but from the Apostles' Creed,"[14] which first highlights God the Son, eternally begotten of the Father, before moving toward the Incarnation. Similarly, Ratzinger's chapter on Jesus Christ in *The God of Jesus Christ* starts with the Niceno-Constantinopolitan Creed.[15]

The description of Benedict XVI's Christology as "'high Christology from above" is justified further when one considers the variety of contexts wherein he emphasizes the priority of the order of ontology (or metaphysics). We encountered it with respect to divine revelation in the previous chapter; we encounter it here in his Christology; and we will encounter it again in the following chapter on the Church, where ontological priority will be shown to be of special importance in Ratzinger's ecclesiology.

To begin our treatment of Ratzinger's Christology proper, I would like to demonstrate precisely how it relates to divine revelation. The following section, then, can be understood as a conclusion to the previous chapter as much as an initial section to this present chapter.

THE TRINITARIAN FOUNDATION AND CHRISTOLOGICAL CORE OF REVELATION[16]

One of Ratzinger's ongoing concerns is to maintain both metaphysics and history as important aspects of faith and theology. He is allergic to theological approaches that dismiss one or the other. The same is true with respect to divine revelation. "The event of revelation . . . is bound on the outside to certain historical institutions or processes," but "according to Bonaventure, the echelon of this revelation reaches very much deeper: for him, it is precisely a

14. Rausch, *Pope Benedict XVI*, 86.

15. See Ratzinger, *The God of Jesus Christ*, 59. The title of the first section of that chapter also emphasizes "from above": "Descendit de caelis—He came down from Heaven."

16. For more details on the Trinitarian foundation and Christological core of revelation, see Richard DeClue, "Joseph Ratzinger's Theology of Divine Revelation," (SThD diss., The Catholic University of America, 2021), 168–183.

metaphysical, or better, a cosmic event."[17] From these statements, Ratzinger immediately goes on to specify that the metaphysical character of this historical process is linked foundationally to the life of the Trinity. "Thus, the saint's [St. Bonaventure's] speculation about revelation reaches into the middle of his doctrine of the Trinity and finds there its real foundation."[18]

The key to seeing the link between the Trinity and divine revelation in history is to consider how human communication through language reflects the intra-Trinitarian communion. Of course, for both, *word* is central, hinting at the Christological core to be detailed later.

According to Ratzinger, Bonaventure presents three analogies between the Eternal Word and human words: *verbum intelligibile*, *verbum medium*, and *verbum sensibile*. As is typical of Bonaventure, this represents the expansion of an earlier "duality" into a "triad." He takes the first term (*verbum intelligibile*) and the last term (*verbum sensibile*) from Augustine but adds the middle term (*verbum medium*) to augment the analogical list. Here is what each of the terms means:

> The *verbum intelligibile* moves in the pure inwardness of the spirit and is identical with the thought process, the thinking appropriation of a thing; the *verbum sensibile* signifies the announcement, the sensible proclamation of the thought; it is the task of the *verbum medium* to manufacture the connection between the two; it is "the thinking of speech," thus that process, in which the pure thought is first inwardly formed into the word.[19]

Despite the fact that all three terms are analogously related to the Eternal Word, they do not do so equally. "The analogy to the

17. Ratzinger, *Offenbarungsverständnis*, 131.
18. Ratzinger, 131.
19. Ratzinger, 132–33.

Eternal Word . . . is in the proper sense at home in the intelligible word, though weakened in the two other forms of the word, and so reflects the triple mode of existence of the human word and at the same time the threefold form of the essence of the Eternal Word."[20]

The reason the intelligible word has the highest ranking in the list is because it corresponds to the Word's eternal procession from the Father, which is *who* the Word is in himself. Only secondarily is the Word also the one through whom all things were created (*verbum medium*) and the Incarnate Word (*verbum sensibile*). Ratzinger explains these three analogies in greater detail:

> It [the Word] is first of all Son, proceeding in eternal origin from the Father, God's interiority eternally comprehending itself; beyond this, however, it is "*archetypus mundi*," archetype of the world, not only in God's eternal thinking of himself, but simultaneously God's idea of the world [*Weltgedanke Gottes*], not only *conversio rationis ad se ipsam*, but also *conversio ad sensum*, thinking toward the external word and so medium of the creation of the world. Finally, however, it is also comparable to the *verbum sensibile*, the outwardly spoken word: God's Son made man. In the Incarnation, that process to which human thought is subjected in its becoming word—the union of the spirit with the sensibly comprehensible—analogously takes place with the Eternal Word.[21]

In the Incarnation, God the Son, the Eternal Word (*verbum intelligibile*), the one through whom all things were made (*verbum medium*), has become the concrete, sensible revelation of God

---

20. Ratzinger, 133.
21. Ratzinger, 133.

(*verbum sensibile*). Therefore, "the real salvation-historical process of revelation is thus . . . taken into this metaphysics of the Trinity."[22]

There cannot be a higher instance of divine revelation—of God's self-communication to man—than the Incarnation. Hence, revelation and Christology are inextricably linked. "In short, this means that 'Christ in the flesh,' the visible, historical Jesus and inclusively his entire visible life's work is designated as *revelatio*, as revelation of the divinity."[23] As de Gaál writes, "In the life of Jesus' human existence, God becomes tangible."[24] No greater and no more complete revelation could take place that would surpass that of Jesus Christ, the Incarnate Word. Hence, as Jared Wicks explains, "Ratzinger thought *De revelatione* should tell why revelation 'ends' with Christ's Apostles—namely, because it reaches in Christ such fullness that no more can be added."[25]

What is more, Jesus, the Incarnate Word, is not just the best and most complete instance of God's self-communication; he is the key for understanding all other instances of God's self-revelatory deeds and words, and thus also the key for grasping the entirety of Sacred Scripture, even the Old Testament. As Ratzinger insisted in his address to German-speaking bishops on the eve of Vatican II, "The whole Old Testament, not just some parts of it, speaks of Christ, for its intention is Christological and as such it is the basis and foundation of the Christian religion. But the whole Old Testament also has to pass through a Christological transformation and it then has force not from itself but

---

22. Ratzinger, 134.

23. Ratzinger, 104.

24. De Gaál, *Theology of Pope Benedict XVI*, 4.

25. Jared Wicks, "Light from Germany on Vatican Council II," *The Catholic Historical Review* 99, no. 4 (Fall 2013): 735. See also Joseph Ratzinger, "Brief von Joseph Ratzinger," in "Texte im Umfeld des Zweiten Vatikanischen Konzils," in *Mitteilungen Institut Papst Benedikt XVI.*, vol. 5 (Regensburg: Schnell & Steiner, 2012).

from Christ and in reference to Christ, who is the one who removes the veil that covered the face of Moses (2 Cor 3:12–18)."[26]

The idea that Christ is the unsurpassable instance of revelation as well as the key for understanding all of Scripture is reflected in the teaching of *Dei Verbum*, when it proclaims that Christ "is the mediator and fullness of all revelation."[27] As Ratzinger insists, "Revelation is not a collection of statements—revelation is Christ himself. *He* is the Logos, the all-embracing Word in which God declares himself and that we therefore call the Son of God."[28] De Gaál expresses this idea as follows: "On the basis of the Johannine Christ as *the* Logos, the rationality of Christianity is laid forth. . . . Therefore, Jesus Christ is rational *and* divine self-communication."[29]

In addition to being the revelation of God, Jesus Christ, the Incarnate Word, also reveals what it means to be man. The Christological dogmas affirm both elements. In Ratzinger's view, those dogmas are attempts to flesh out the rather simple affirmation that Jesus is the Christ, with all that that confession entails. "In other words, developed christological dogma acknowledges that the radical Christship of Jesus presupposes the Sonship and that the Sonship includes the Godship. . . . But it also acknowledges no less resolutely that in the radicality of his service Jesus is the most human of men, the true man, and it thus subscribes to the coincidence of theology and anthropology a correspondence in

---

26. Joseph Ratzinger, "Observations on the Schema *De fontibus revelationis*," in Jared Wicks, "Six Texts by Prof. Joseph Ratzinger as *Peritus* before and during Vatican Council II," *Gregorianum* 89, no. 2 (2008): 283.

27. Second Vatican Council, *Dei Verbum* 2, November 18. 1965, in *The Word on Fire Vatican II Collection*, ed. Matthew Levering (Park Ridge, IL: Word on Fire Institute, 2021), 18.

28. Joseph Ratzinger, *On the Way to Jesus Christ*, trans. Michael J. Miller (San Francisco: Ignatius, 2005), 82. See also Tracey Rowland, *Ratzinger's Faith: The Theology of Benedict XVI* (New York: Oxford University Press, 2008), 49.

29. Emery de Gaál, "Pope Benedict XVI's Early Contributions to Fundamental Theology—1955–61," *Josephinum Journal of Theology* 21, no. 2 (Summer/Fall 2014): 278.

which ever since then the truly exciting part of Christian faith has resided."[30]

In a similar vein, the third section of Ratzinger's alternate schema on divine revelation is titled "Jesus Christ: Revelation of God and Man." Speaking of Christ, Ratzinger writes, "In him the truth about God as well as that about man is revealed: it is revealed who man is; for he [man] comes from the Word of God, who created him, and he was created toward the Word of God, who loves him."[31] The Word of God is presented as both the origin and goal of humanity. Humanity is only fully understood in relation to the Word from whom he comes and toward whom he is ordered. "Thus, as understood by the patristic inspiration, Jesus Christ as 'the new Adam' is the paradigm for God creating humankind. Jesus Christ becomes the human being who is the summons for all human beings to live as children of God."[32] He is God and perfect man. As such, Jesus also provides a concrete witness to the truth about humanity. As de Gaál notes, "God's only begotten Son, Jesus Christ, demonstrates for every age again what genuinely fulfilled human existence is."[33] This understanding of Christ as revelatory for what it means to be human is reflected in *Gaudium et Spes*: "The truth is that only in the mystery of the incarnate Word does the mystery of man take on light. . . . Christ, the final Adam, by the revelation of the mystery of the Father and His love, fully reveals man to man himself."[34]

Jesus is able to reveal both God and man, because he is fully God and fully man. Additionally, he is able to reveal what man is precisely through the communion of his humanity with his

30. Joseph Ratzinger, *Introduction to Christianity*, trans. Mary Frances McCarthy (San Francisco: Ignatius, 1987), 211–212.

31. Joseph Ratzinger, "De voluntate Dei erga hominem," in JRGS 7/1, ed. Gerhard Ludwig Müller (Freiburg, DE: Herder, 2012), 178–179. For this translation, both the Latin and the German were considered.

32. De Gaál, *Theology of Pope Benedict XVI*, 81.

33. De Gaál, 1.

34. Second Vatican Council, *Gaudium et Spes* 22, December 7, 1965, in *The Word on Fire Vatican II Collection*, ed. Matthew Levering (Park Ridge, IL: Word on Fire Institute, 2021), 238.

divinity. To be sure, this includes the hypostatic union, the union of the two natures in the one divine person. But it is also true *existentially*. On this point, Ratzinger thinks that the Third Council of Constantinople is key even for understanding the earlier Council of Chalcedon. Ratzinger interprets Constantinople III thusly:

> The Council's answer is this: the ontological *union* of two faculties of will which remain independent within the unity of the Person means that, at the existential level, there is a *communion* . . . of the two wills. With this interpretation of union as communion, the Council sketches an ontology of freedom. The two "wills" are united in the way in which two wills can be united, namely, in a common affirmation of a shared value. In other words, what unites the two wills is the Yes of Christ's human will to the divine will of the Logos. Thus, in concrete terms—"existentially"—the two wills become a single will while remaining, at the ontological level, two independent realities. . . . In practice the Council is here applying the trinitarian model (with the mandatory ever-greater difference in the analogy) to Christology: the highest unity there is—the unity of God—is not the unity of unstructured, amorphous substance but unity by communion, a unity which both creates and is love. Thus the Logos adopts the being of the man Jesus into his own being and speaks of it in terms of his own I: "For I have come down from heaven, not to do my own will, but the will of him who sent me" (Jn 6:38). In the Son's obedience, where both wills become one in a single Yes to the will of the Father, communion takes place between human and divine being.[35]

---

35. Joseph Ratzinger, *Behold the Pierced One: An Approach to a Spiritual Christology*, trans. Graham Harrison (San Francisco: Ignatius, 1986), 91–92.

Here, Ratzinger is developing what he calls a "spiritual" Christology.[36] It includes the metaphysics of Chalcedonian Christology, of course, but it then proceeds to contemplate what that ontology means on the existential level, which is also a spiritual level, since it involves the human will of Christ acting in communion with his divine will. As Ratzinger formulates the history of the question: "Chalcedon had defined the ontological content of the Incarnation with its well-known formula of two natures in one Person. The Third Council of Constantinople, however, was faced . . . with the question: What is the spiritual content of such an ontology? Or, in more concrete terms: What does 'one Person in two natures' mean, for practical purposes, in real life? How can a person live with two wills and a dual intellect?"[37] The existential communion of the two wills is the answer.

This perspective also opens up the question of what it means to be in communion with Christ, the meaning of discipleship. While no other human is the Incarnate Word, God the Son, the communion between Christ's human will and his divine will provides the exemplar of how we, too, can be united with God in Christ, through loving obedience to the will of God the Father. In following this example, we can say with St. Paul, "it is no longer I who live, but it is Christ who lives in me" (Gal. 2:20).[38] In a real way, this view links Christology, divine revelation, theological anthropology, and soteriology together. Christ's personal union between divine and human natures becomes, in his human will's complete obedience to the divine will, the exemplar of what it means to be a fulfilled human being: one who lovingly says "yes"

---

36. For an in-depth presentation on Ratzinger's spiritual Christology, see Peter John McGregor, *Heart to Heart: The Spiritual Christology of Joseph Ratzinger* (Eugene, OR: Pickwick, 2016).

37. Joseph Ratzinger, *Pilgrim Fellowship of Faith: The Church as Communion*, trans. Henry Taylor (San Francisco: Ignatius, 2005), 80. This section of *Pilgrim Fellowship* (pp. 60–89) is from the same original German source as *Behold the Pierced One* (pp. 71–100), but the translations are independent with certain variations of phrasing in English.

38. See Ratzinger, *Behold the Pierced One*, 91.

to God. This also anticipates soteriology, insofar as man's salvation includes his transformation: becoming Christ-like, divinized.

The effectiveness of the lived reality of these truths is exemplified in the lives of the saints. Christ's own human life reveals the truth about human life. It shows humanity what is truly important, what the priorities should be. This revelation of what it means to be human is reflected in the lives of those who live according to the teachings and example of Christ. An authentic Christian life shows the beauty of humanity lived according to that which it was made for. For this reason, Ratzinger emphasizes the evangelical impact of a holy life. "I have often said that I am convinced that the true apologetics for the Christian message, the most persuasive proof of its truth, offsetting everything that may appear negative, are the saints."[39] The saints are signs that God's way, as revealed in Christ, is what truly perfects humanity. "Whether we think of Francis of Assisi, Teresa of Avila, Vincent de Paul, the Curé of Ars, Maximilian Kolbe: they are all examples of discipleship who show us the way to life, because they show us Christ."[40]

THE LIFE OF CHRIST, THE INCARNATE WORD

When it is said that Christ's humanity reveals what it truly means to be human, this must not be understood solely in reference to human nature and thereby abstractly. Becoming man includes the entirety of Jesus' life on earth. As Ratzinger insists, "The individual never possesses his life in its completeness in one single moment; even in the individual, life has a temporal extension, and it is only the totality of this temporal structure that makes him the man he is."[41] This means that in Jesus' case, all the var-

---

39. Ratzinger, *On the Way to Jesus Christ*, 38.
40. Ratzinger, 101.
41. Ratzinger, *God of Jesus Christ*, 69.

ious stages of his life are important: his childhood, adulthood, and death.[42]

The issue of childhood raises another important aspect to the Incarnation. In his divinity, Jesus is God the Son, eternally begotten of the Father. In his humanity, Jesus also came from other humans (consider his genealogy). Most especially, "He grew in the womb of a woman, from whom he received his flesh and his blood, his heartbeat, his gestures, his language. He received his life from the life of another human being."[43]

This other human being from whom Jesus received his human life should not be overlooked. For Ratzinger, the Blessed Virgin Mary has a key role to play in God's plan of salvation. For God's offer of salvation to become effective in the manner he desires, it calls for a response. Mary's *fiat* provides such a response. As Ratzinger writes:

> Indeed, the whole drama hangs on just this thread. For without Mary, God's entrance into history would not achieve its intended purpose. That is, the very thing that matters most in the Creed [the Incarnation] would be left unrealized—God's being a God with us, and not only a God in and for himself. Thus, the woman who called herself lowly, that is, nameless (Lk 1:48), stands at the core of the profession of faith in the living God, and it is impossible to imagine it without her. She is an indispensable, central component of our faith in the living, acting God. The Word becomes flesh—the eternal Meaning grounding the universe [*Sinngrund der Welt*] enters into her. He does not merely regard her from outside; he becomes himself an actor in her. It needed the Virgin for this to be possible, the Virgin who made available her whole person, that is, her embodied existence [*Leib*], her very self, as the place of

42. See Ratzinger, 70–84.
43. Ratzinger, 70.

God's dwelling in the world. The Incarnation required con-
senting acceptance. Only in this way do Logos and flesh really
become one.[44]

Mary is not irrelevant to the Christian mystery. She is an integral
part of it. In fact, Ratzinger points to a passage of Scripture that
he views as both a foretelling of the Church's future and a command: "'From henceforth all generations will call me blessed'—
these words of the Mother of Jesus handed on for us by Luke (Lk
1:48) are at once a prophecy and a charge laid upon the Church
of all times."[45] Mary is indeed the Mother of God, worthy of our
veneration. She is the one who assented to the Incarnation in
humble obedience to the will of God. In her, the Word became
flesh and was born in Bethlehem.

Jesus was a child, and his childhood has something to say
about us. "It is striking to note that Jesus himself finds it so important for human existence that we be children: 'Truly I say to
you, unless you turn and become like children, you will never
enter the kingdom of heaven' (Mt 18:3)."[46] Being a child does
not just pertain to infancy. Rather, being a child is part of what it
means to be human as such. This makes sense, since it is God *the
Son* who is the archetype of humanity; his sonship is a paradigm
for all men. This means, like Jesus, humans must accept that they
come from God, and that they have nothing on their own accord.
Humans live from others and therefore cannot have radical autonomy and complete independence. Being human means being
part of a family, as witnessed to by the Holy Family in Nazareth.[47]

The sonship of Christ, of being from the Father, pervades
the entirety of Jesus' life, even as an adult and throughout his

44. Joseph Ratzinger, "'Et Incarnatus Est de Spiritu Sancto ex Maria Virgine,'" in Hans
Urs von Balthasar and Joseph Ratzinger, *Mary: The Church at the Source*, trans. Adrian J. Walker
(San Francisco: Ignatius, 2005), 83.

45. Ratzinger, 61.

46. Ratzinger, *God of Jesus Christ*, 71.

47. See Ratzinger, 71–79.

public ministry. In his book *Behold the Pierced One*, Ratzinger sets forth several theses for our consideration. It is no accident that the very first thesis reads as follows: "According to the testimony of Holy Scripture, the center of the life and person of Jesus is his constant communication with the Father."[48] In this connection, Ratzinger points to several key moments in Jesus' ministry that were preceded by time with the Father in prayer: (1) the choosing of the Twelve, (2) Jesus' question about who people say that he is (leading to Peter's profession of faith), (3) the Transfiguration, and (4) Jesus' prayer on the Mount of Olives at the beginning of his Passion.[49] Throughout his public ministry, Jesus repeatedly goes off alone to pray. As Ratzinger says, "The apostolate has a theological *locus*, that it is the fruit of the dialogue between the Son's will and the Father's will."[50] His entire mission is to do the will of the Father, and hence communing with the Father is at the heart of all that Jesus says and does, including his willingness to suffer and to die, leading to the final stage of life involved in the Incarnation. "Jesus died praying. At the Last Supper he had anticipated his death by giving of himself, thus transforming his death, from within, into an act of love, into a glorification of God."[51]

The Incarnation is understood not merely as the one-time conception of Jesus in the womb of the Virgin Mary. Rather, it includes the totality of Jesus' earthly life, including his death on the cross. "In this world, living means dying. Hence, 'he became man' also means that he made his way toward death."[52] As Ratzinger states elsewhere, "The death of Christ simply fulfills what began

48. Ratzinger, *Behold the Pierced One*, 15. See also Joseph Ratzinger/Pope Benedict XVI, "Seven Theses on Christology and the Hermeneutic of Faith," *Letter & Spirit* 3 (2007): 190–192.

49. See Ratzinger, *Behold the Pierced One*, 18–21. See also Ratzinger, *God of Jesus Christ*, 80–82, where Ratzinger speaks about this same idea of prayer with respect to some of these same moments in Jesus' public life.

50. Ratzinger, *God of Jesus Christ*, 81.

51. Ratzinger, *Behold the Pierced One*, 22. See also Ratzinger/Benedict XVI, "Seven Theses," 194–196.

52. Ratzinger, *God of Jesus Christ*, 83.

at the Incarnation. The Son has taken up what is human and now carries it back to God."[53]

Jesus' death, however, is utterly unique. "The new death that Jesus dies leads to the tomb, but not to corruption. It is the death of death."[54] Jesus' death leads to Resurrection.

The discussion of the Incarnation, life, death, and Resurrection of Christ leads to the topic of soteriology: Christ's saving work. As already noted, the metaphysics of Christology is the basis for the efficaciousness of Jesus' saving activity. It is precisely as God-become-man that Jesus' life, death, and Resurrection lead to the remission of sin and a new life of grace for humankind.

SOTERIOLOGY

As we have seen, Ratzinger's Christology and soteriology are intimately linked. Who Jesus is and what he does form a unity. As Ratzinger puts it, "The Christian Yes to Jesus affirms that he is the Christ, that is, the one in whom person and work are identical."[55]

From this vantage point, Ratzinger attempts to unify two different approaches to Christology and soteriology: the theology of the Incarnation and the theology of the cross. The former is metaphysical, emphasizing the *being* of Jesus; the latter focuses on God's saving action through the cross and Resurrection.[56] The key to Ratzinger's solution is precisely to emphasize that Jesus' being and doing form a unity. As he writes:

> For we have found that the *being* of Christ ("Incarnation" theology!) is *actualitas*, stepping beyond oneself, the exodus of going out from self; it is, not a being that rests in itself, but

---

53. Joseph Ratzinger, "The New Covenant: A Theology of Covenant in the New Testament," trans. Maria Shrady, *Communio* 22, no. 4 (Winter 1995): 643.

54. Ratzinger, *God of Jesus Christ*, 99.

55. Ratzinger, *Introduction*, 210; see also 203.

56. See Ratzinger, 229.

the act of being sent, of being son, of serving. Conversely, this "doing" is not just "doing" but "being." . . . So at this point a properly understood Christology of being and of the Incarnation must pass over into the theology of the Cross and become one with it; conversely, a theology of the Cross that gives its full measure must pass over into the Christology of the Son and of being.[57]

For this reason, Ratzinger laments the historical separation of Christology and soteriology into two separate disciplines. Speaking of Christology and soteriology, he writes, "That the two questions parted company, that the person and his work were made the subjects of separate inquiries and treatises, led to both problems becoming incomprehensible and insoluble. A brief inspection of the manuals of dogmatic theology is sufficient to confirm how complicated the theories dealing with both problems were, because it had been forgotten that they can only be understood when considered together."[58] It is for this reason that this chapter covers both Christology and soteriology. Additionally, it will be our task to constantly emphasize their inner unity.

This persistent theme of unity enters into Ratzinger's understanding of soteriology itself. What does it mean to be redeemed, to be saved? As mentioned earlier in this book, salvation includes the reversal of the effects of sin. In particular, it heals the divisions that result from sin: humanity's separation from God, divisions between persons and peoples, and even the disintegration within the individual human person. Salvation, then, reestablishes the unity that was lost through sin. Following Henri de Lubac, Ratzinger articulates this point well:

57. Ratzinger, 230.
58. Ratzinger, 231.

The essence of original sin is the split into individuality, which knows only itself. The essence of redemption is the mending of the shattered image of God, the union of the human race through and in the One who stands for all and in whom, as Paul says (Gal 3:28), all are one: Jesus Christ. On this premise, the word *Catholic* became for de Lubac the main theme of all his theological speculation: to be a Christian means to be Catholic, means to be on one's way to an all-embracing unity. Union is redemption, for it is the realization of our likeness to God, the Three-in-One.[59]

Yet again we see the Trinitarian foundation of Ratzinger's thought, including its implications for theological anthropology and soteriology. To restore unity is to restore man's image and likeness to God, who is tri-unity. Additionally, the above quote foreshadows the next chapter on ecclesiology, as it points toward the Church as the sacrament of unity, both between God and man as well as the unity of the human race. What is more, the sacramental character of the Church connects both the unity of believers in Christ as well as the healing of the individual Christian through the grace of Christ's saving work as imparted through the sacraments. All of this, in turn, is oriented to the final, ultimate communion of God and humanity in the eschaton. Thus, Ratzinger's soteriology is most comprehensible within the framework of the entire mystery of faith. Once again, a holistic understanding of theology comes to the fore.

As already noted, Christology and soteriology go hand in hand here. Salvation includes the healing of the divisions wrought by sin. The Incarnation is essential to this process. "The incarnate Son is the 'communion' between God and men."[60] As such, Jesus makes the reestablishment of communion possible for others.

59. Joseph Ratzinger, *Principles of Catholic Theology: Building Stones for a Fundamental Theology*, trans. Mary Frances McCarthy (San Francisco: Ignatius, 1987), 49.

60. Ratzinger, *Behold the Pierced One*, 88.

"Jesus Christ opens the way to the impossible, to communion between God and man, since he, the incarnate Word, is this communion. He performs the 'alchemy' which melts down human nature and infuses it into the being of God."[61] In this sense, the Incarnation is part of soteriology, since it is God the Son's taking on the human nature that unites him with all of humanity, and it is God's union with humanity that constitutes salvation. Salvation, then, comes from union with Christ, who is *ontologically* the union between God and man.

As already discussed, the Incarnation includes the whole of Jesus' human existence, including his death. The question of the salvific efficacy of Jesus' death is perhaps one of the most important soteriological questions. It is one which many theologians have tried to answer, and it is one prone to misunderstanding. What precisely is Ratzinger's view of the cross?

Here, we will concur with Margaret Turek that Ratzinger holds to a theology of atonement.[62] Ratzinger sees Jesus' death as "a death in the context of his service of expiation, which desires to bring about reconciliation."[63] On this front, Ratzinger points to St. Paul's use of an early creedal statement: "For I handed on to you as of first importance what I in turn had received: that Christ died for our sins in accordance with the scriptures" (1 Cor. 15:3). Ratzinger finds the two qualifying statements about Jesus' death—that it was "in accordance with the scriptures" and "for our sins"—to be of particular importance. The fact that Jesus died in accordance with the Scriptures means that it was no historical accident but part of God's providential plan in salvation history. The fact that Jesus died for our sins is to be understood in relation

---

61. Ratzinger, 90. In our later treatments of ecclesiology and of sacraments, we shall see how Ratzinger ties this to the Eucharist, which he also does in the context from which this quote is taken.

62. See Margaret M. Turek, *Atonement: Soundings in Biblical, Trinitarian, and Spiritual Theology* (San Francisco: Ignatius, 2022).

63. Ratzinger, *God of Jesus Christ*, 96.

to the Songs of the Suffering Servant.[64] It is a death accepted *for us*, on our behalf, thus giving us hope. Jesus' death is "the fulfillment of a love in which God himself comes down to us, so as to draw us back up to himself. . . . It is a death in the context of his service of expiation—a death that achieves reconciliation and becomes a light for the nations."[65]

Several related issues come to the fore here: the reality and seriousness of sin, God's will to redeem us from sin as worked out in salvation history, and Christ's death as expiation for our sins (atonement).

Benedict XVI takes sin seriously. "The reality of evil and injustice that disfigures the world and at the same time distorts the image of God—this reality exists, through our sin. It cannot simply be ignored; it must be addressed."[66]

This view is not always popular in this day and age. A tendency to downplay the reality of sin has even affected some Christians' perception of Jesus. "Today in broad circles, even among believers, an image has prevailed of a Jesus who demands nothing, never scolds, who accepts everyone and everything, who no longer does anything but affirm us."[67]

Yet, the New Testament is clear: Christ came to save us from sin. The need for atonement requires the acknowledgment that sin is real and must be addressed if it is to be overcome. "The fifth petition of the Our Father," writes Benedict XVI, "presupposes a world in which there is trespass—trespass of men in relation to other men, trespass in relation to God. Every instance of trespass among men involves some kind of injury to truth and to love and is thus opposed to God, who is truth and love. How to

64. See Ratzinger, 95–96. See also Benedict XVI, *Jesus of Nazareth*, vol. 2, *Holy Week: From the Entrance into Jerusalem to the Resurrection*, trans. Philip J. Whitmore (San Francisco: Ignatius, 2011), 252.

65. Benedict XVI, *Jesus of Nazareth*, 2:253.

66. Benedict XVI, 2:232.

67. Ratzinger, *On the Way to Jesus Christ*, 7–8. See also Benedict XVI, *Jesus of Nazareth*, 1:159, where he speaks about the "trivialization of evil."

overcome guilt is a central question for every human life."[68] For-giveness implies the recognition of a prior guilt, a guilt that has consequences. "Guilt is a reality, an objective force; it has caused destruction that must be repaired. For this reason, forgiveness must be more than a matter of ignoring, of merely trying to forget. Guilt must be worked through, healed, and thus overcome."[69]

Additionally, humans cannot overcome their sins on their own. Benedict insists that "the very first thing we encounter is the limit of our power to heal and to overcome evil. We encounter the superior power of evil, which we cannot master with our unaided powers."[70] Thus, not only does Christ's atonement for our sins reflect the reality of sin, it also bespeaks our inability to overcome it on our own. If our sins are to be borne away, there must be another way, *the* way: Jesus Christ.

The question is: how is the guilt of sin to be overcome? The answer to this question is not simple. Great minds have elaborated responses to this question with mixed results. For many Christians today, St. Anselm's *Cur Deus Homo* has become the touchstone for soteriology.[71] While Ratzinger acknowledges that St. Anselm's work is deserving of admiration, he also thinks it can lead to distortions that give a false impression of atonement that is overly legalistic. This is especially true in "vulgarized" representations of Anselm's thought.[72] The result has been false understandings of atonement that have led many to ignore or to reject the notion altogether.[73]

One of the primary issues in certain presentations of atonement is the false depiction of God the Father with respect to Jesus'

68. Benedict XVI, *Jesus of Nazareth*, 1:157.

69. Benedict XVI, 1:158.

70. Benedict XVI, 1:159.

71. See Ratzinger, *Introduction*, 281: "The universal Christian consciousness in this matter is extensively influenced by a much-coarsened version of St. Anselm's theology of atonement."

72. See Ratzinger, 231–233.

73. See Turek, *Atonement*, 14–19. See also Benedict XVI, *Jesus of Nazareth*, 1:159: "The idea that God allowed the forgiveness of guilt, the healing of man from within, to cost him the death of his Son has come to seem quite alien to us today."

Passion and death. As Margaret Turek explains: "Ever since the seventeenth century, and indeed well into the twentieth, a trend arose among theologians and preachers to portray God the Father as a celestial child abuser vis-à-vis Christ crucified, as someone who unleashes violent fury on his Son for sins of which his Son is innocent."[74] This view of atonement puts God the Father and God the Son at odds with one another. The loving Son appears to be sacrificed to satisfy the bloodlust of his enraged Father. It is as if the Father's anger must furiously lash out until his emotions are pacified, as if the Father took enjoyment at meting out violence and pain upon Jesus. But this perspective greatly misunderstands the role of the Father and the Son in the work of atonement.

To be sure, the Scriptures do speak of God's wrath as a reaction to sin. However, God's wrath must not be understood as an antonym to love. Rather, God's wrath must be seen as an expression of divine love. Turek explains that "from the outset we must insist that God's wrath in the face of sin is not an independent power of destruction separate from or set in opposition to God's love. Rather, God's wrath is the form that God's love takes when it encounters whatever is opposed to and threatens the designs of his love, designs that boil down to bringing his beloved to beatitude and perfection as God's true filial image."[75] God despises sin because he loves us. Sin is contrary to what humanity was made for and is thus harmful to us. God does not remain indifferent to our sinfulness precisely because of his love.

The New Testament attests to this fact in one of the most oft-quoted passages: "For God so *loved* the world that he gave his only Son" (John 3:16, emphasis added). The Incarnation, Passion, and Death of the Incarnate Word is not the result of God's hatred toward humanity. Rather, it is motivated precisely by his enduring love for us, despite our sinful rejection of him. "But

74. Turek, 16.
75. Turek, 65.

God proves *his love* for us in that while we were still sinners Christ died for us" (Rom. 5:8, emphasis added). The mystery of atonement thus includes the reality of sin and its effects as well as God's love for humanity despite sin.

Jesus reveals the Father even on the cross. Jesus' love for us on the cross is a reflection of God the Father's love for us. Jesus came to do the work of the Father. In the process of atoning for human sin, the Father and the Son are united in their love for humanity. It is not the case that God the Son accepted crucifixion *so that* the Father's hatred could be pacified and changed into love. It was the Father's love for us that sent the Son, who loves us with the Father's love. The Father and the Son concur in the plan of atonement, which includes the willing sacrifice of Christ on the cross.

But how is it that Jesus' suffering and death atone for sins? We must understand Jesus' Passion in light of salvation history, as prefigured in the Old Testament, which Christ brings to fulfillment. One must understand that sin is more than a moral failure to uphold a law; it is a disruption of relationship. It is the refusal of the child to be the image of the Father's love. A relationship is thus broken. The effect of sin, then, is a disrupted relationship that is a true offense against God. As Turek insists, "The proper setting in which to understand sin is the covenant relationship,"[76] which is disrupted through sin. "As a consequence of persistent sin, the covenant relationship is ruptured, and sinners exist in a state of estrangement from God—and God, on his side, is forsaken."[77] The damage caused by sin must be dealt with if the relationship is to be restored.

In the Old Testament, we see the effect of Israel's repeated rejection of God's election to be his people (and thus a witness to God in the world). There is a separation between God and his people. The exiles experienced by the people of God are only the

76. Turek, 50–51.
77. Turek, 52–53.

external manifestation of the rupture between God and his people that sin has caused. The people are made to feel the absence of God as a result of their sin.[78] The effect of sin leads to the recognition that the sin was in fact sin, which then opens up the path to true contrition for the sin and a desire to turn back to God.

God does not remain indifferent to this situation. As already stated in chapter 3, divine impassibility does not mean that God is completely lacking in affect. The whole truth that God is love includes an affective dimension. God actually cares about our relationship with him. "God is the absolute and ultimate source of all being; but this universal principle of creation—the *Logos*, primordial reason—is at the same time a lover with all the passion of a true love."[79] This positive affectivity also implies the ability to suffer. God's love thus includes his ability to suffer. "So God is a sufferer because he is a lover; the entire theme of the suffering God flows from that of the loving God and always points back to it."[80]

As a lover who invites humanity to love him in return, God chooses to accept the suffering that results from our rejection. "God suffers. Why does he not impose his way on his creature with the strength of his omnipotence? . . . Because he does not want to obtain anything by force, but desires love . . . and thus leaves our freedom to say yes to his offering . . . or else to say no. . . . Man says no, and he even ridicules this weak God who seeks his consent. . . . Hence God's sadness and suffering."[81]

This fact is important, because it relates to the cost of sin and the forgiveness of sin. "Forgiveness exacts a price—first of all from

---

78. See Turek, 53–54.

79. Benedict XVI, *Deus Caritas Est* 10, December 25, 2005, vatican.va.

80. Ratzinger, *Behold the Pierced One*, 58.

81. Joseph Ratzinger/Benedict XVI, *On Love: Selected Writings*, ed. Pierluca Azzaro, trans. Michael J. Miller (San Francisco: Ignatius, 2020), 25–26, quoted in Turek, *Atonement*, 41n40. Turek notes that this text originates from a homily given by Ratzinger on December 12, 2003, "God's Weeping and the Promise of Victory."

the person who forgives."[82] In this case, God is willing to forgive us despite the suffering that our sinful rejection has brought. His love endures through our rejection. The atonement of our sins rests firmly on God's own prerogative to offer forgiveness.

Margaret Turek helps explain this dynamic in her book. She outlines various factors that are intrinsic to atonement. The first factor is God's sovereign initiative—that is, no atonement would be possible without God's willingness to forgive. Atonement, then, originates from God's merciful love.[83]

The divine initiative in the process of atonement is contrary to parallel notions in the history of world religions. "In other world religions, expiation usually means the restoration of the damaged relationship with God by means of expiatory actions on the part of men. . . . In the New Testament the situation is almost completely reversed. It is not man who goes to God with a compensatory gift, but God who comes to man, in order to give to him. He restores disturbed right on the initiative of his own power to love, by making unjust man just again, the dead living again, through his own creative mercy."[84] Hence, as St. Paul says, "All this is from God, who reconciled us to himself through Christ . . . that is, in Christ God was reconciling the world to himself" (2 Cor. 5:18–19).[85] It is not man who reconciles himself with God; it is God who reconciles man with him. Despite our rejection of God through sin, God extends his loving mercy toward us. Atonement begins from God's initiative.

Yet, as Turek notes, atonement cannot be complete through a one-sided act of forgiveness, for this would not actually restore the damaged relationship. If the relationship is to be restored, then the sinner must turn away from their sin. A change must occur in the beloved; the sinner must receive the forgiveness and return to

82. Benedict XVI, *Jesus of Nazareth*, 1:158.

83. See Turek, *Atonement*, 29–31.

84. Ratzinger, *Introduction*, 282.

85. See Ratzinger, 283.

being a loving child of God. Accordingly, Turek includes *"man's participation and willing collaboration"*[86] in her list of factors for atonement. The restoration of the relationship requires the positive response of the offender. God's loving forgiveness calls for a loving response.

In Turek's analysis, there are three components of this loving response that are required for atonement to take place. "The sinner must (1) turn *back* his heart toward God, (2) turn *away* from the evil deed(s), and (3) turn *around* the effects of sin."[87] This third part is particularly important for our discussion. Turning back toward God and away from one's sins is important, but there still remains the problem of the effects of those sins, which do not just disappear. "The converted sinner still has to bring his regenerated love to bear on the effects of sin. Sin is not merely walked away from; sin must be 'borne away.'"[88]

According to Turek, bearing away sin requires the loving endurance of the effects of sin. "We must note that the 'original meaning of *nasa awon* ("to bear away sin" in Hebrew) is not "to take away" or "remove" guilt, but . . . to take it *upon* oneself and to "carry" it', to endure its effects or consequent punishments. . . . Insofar as one is animated by the love of God in bearing the effects of sin, this suffering is expiatory."[89]

But these considerations are only a precursor to the issue of Christ's redemptive suffering. Between the willingness to lovingly bear the effects of sin and Jesus' saving work on the cross, there stands the issue of *vicarious* atonement. Vicarious atonement bespeaks a situation where an individual or a smaller group of

---

86. Turek, *Atonement*, 47. This is Turek's third factor in the process of atonement. Her second is "God's passionate involvement" (31). We have already treated that factor in speaking about God's suffering.

87. Turek, 55.

88. Turek, 55.

89. Turek, 55. She cites here Alfons Deissler, "Hingegeben für die Vielen," in *Mysterium Salutis*, (Einsiedeln: Benziger, 1967), 2:341.

individuals bears the effects of the sins of others for the sake of the others.

In Ratzinger's theology, the foundation for vicarious atonement is vicarious representation.[90] This idea is bound up with Ratzinger's concept of *pro-existence*, of *being for* others, most fully exemplified by Christ. There are other instances of vicarious representation, but they all take their pattern and efficacy from that of Christ. "In other words, the mystery of this vicariousness, given in Christ and forming the basis of all election, is carried out from Christ according to the will of God in a whole system of vicarious relationships throughout salvation history as its fundamental law."[91]

Vicarious representation is behind election. "Election is always, at bottom, election for others."[92] The elect are chosen for the sake of those who appear not to be elected. The few are called for the sake of the many. The connection to *pro-existence* is clear. As Christopher Ruddy explains, "This pro-existence . . . stands at the core of [Ratzinger's] Christology and ecclesiology."[93]

While vicarious representation reaches its apex (and, indeed, its inner power) in Christ, it is found throughout salvation history. Israel's election was meant to benefit the world around them. Their own failure to remain faithful to the covenant, however, also required redemption from within their ranks, involving intra-Israel vicarious representation. We see it with Moses and, perhaps most conspicuously, in the Suffering Servant passages of Isaiah.[94] The latter example also shows vicarious representation as vicarious atonement: "But he was wounded for our transgressions,

---

90. For a good explication of vicarious representation in Ratzinger's thought, see Christopher Ruddy, "'For the Many': The Vicarious-Representative Heart of Joseph Ratzinger's Theology," *Theological Studies* 75, no. 3 (2014): 564–584.

91. Joseph Ratzinger, *The Meaning of Christian Brotherhood*, 2nd English ed. (San Francisco: Ignatius, 1993), 79. See also Ruddy, "'For the Many,'" 567.

92. Ratzinger, *Christian Brotherhood*, 79.

93. Ruddy, "'For the Many,'" 568.

94. See Joseph Ratzinger, "Vicarious Representation," trans. Jared Wicks, *Letter & Spirit* 7 (2011): 210–216. See also Ruddy, "'For the Many,'" 568. See also Turek, *Atonement*, 76, 80.

crushed for our iniquities; upon him was the punishment that made us whole, and by his bruises we are healed" (Isa. 53:5).

Turek sees this passage as a clear reference to vicarious atonement. "At any rate, in the Suffering Servant of the Lord (Isaiah 53) we have an unambiguous instance of an individual who *vicariously atones*. The Servant bears the sin . . . of the many in their place (Isa. 53:11–12). The suffering is willingly assumed by the Servant, undergone in righteousness, and deliberately offered to God (53:10, 12). It renders righteous the unrighteous, cleanses them from sin, and brings about reconciliation (53:5, 11–12)."[95] In light of the cross, this passage clearly foreshadows Jesus' Passion and death. "Jesus Christ, himself innocent, is chosen to expiate the guilt of the world . . . to bear the fate of rejection which otherwise would befall all other men."[96] Since Christ himself is sinless (as God Incarnate), his acceptance of the effects of sin is not expiatory of any fault of his own, but rather, he bears them lovingly on behalf of all sinners. He accepts the effects of sin and thus bears them away for us. "Indeed," writes Turek, "the central claim of the New Testament is that the Old Testament promise of divine forgiveness has been finally fulfilled because in the Passion and death of Christ Jesus atonement has been definitively achieved (Mt 1:21; Lk 1:77; Acts 2:38; 5:31)."[97]

In this regard, Benedict XVI (along with early Christians) views the end of the temple sacrifices relatively soon after the death and Resurrection of Jesus as providentially noteworthy. It was already foreshadowed in the Old Testament. "The expectations expressed in the Prophets' critique of Temple worship . . . were now fulfilled: God did not want to be glorified through the sacrifices of bulls and goats, whose blood is powerless to purify and make atonement for men. The long-awaited but as yet undefined new worship had become a reality. In the Cross

95. Turek, *Atonement*, 80.
96. Ratzinger, *Christian Brotherhood*, 76.
97. Turek, *Atonement*, 96.

of Jesus, what the animal sacrifices had sought in vain to achieve actually occurred: atonement was made for the world. The 'Lamb of God' took upon himself the sins of the world and wiped them away."[98] Jesus' sacrifice on the cross fulfills the purpose of the Old Covenant sacrifices, which—of themselves—were only efficacious insofar as they anticipated and thus participated in Christ's once for all sacrifice.

One might ask, however, how the death of Jesus atones for the sins of the whole world. How does his acceptance of suffering and death redeem us? This is not easy for contemporary people to comprehend. Benedict XVI acknowledges that "the understanding of the great mystery of expiation is also blocked by our individualistic image of man. We can no longer grasp substitution because we think that every man is ensconced in himself alone. The fact that all individual beings are deeply interwoven and that all are encompassed in turn by the being of the One, the Incarnate Son, is something we are no longer capable of seeing."[99]

Despite the difficulty for modern people to perceive this reality, it is the truth. Man is not an isolated individual but a person in relation to others. Humans are communal beings, sharing in the same nature, which—through the Incarnation—God the Son also shares. God the Son was the one through whom humanity was created, and through his Incarnation, he is the one through whom our re-creation is made possible. Under Ratzinger's prefecture, the Congregation for the Doctrine of the Faith described it

---

98. Benedict XVI, *Jesus of Nazareth*, 2:230. Benedict continues: "The Temple sacrifices, the cultic heart of the Torah, were a thing of the past. Christ had taken their place." The criticism of the temple sacrifices, of course, is not absolute, for God himself had prescribed them. They could only have any relevance, however, as remote foreshadowings of and spiritual participations in the sacrifice of Christ. In themselves, the blood of animals is powerless to bring atonement. However, in a manner akin to accepting a penance in the sacrament of reconciliation, one makes an offering in union with the suffering of Christ as a means of uniting oneself to Christ and thus as a means of actively allowing his grace to be imparted to oneself. Apart from sincerity, however, the sacrifices are meaningless. That, too, is behind the prophets' disdain of the temple sacrifices: offering them without repentance is meaningless. The external act without the interior reality avails no one.

99. Benedict XVI, *Jesus of Nazareth*, 1:159–160.

this way: "One must recognize that the human person is created in the 'image and likeness' of God, and that the prototype of this image is *the Son* of God, in whom and through whom we have been created (cf. Col 1:16). . . . In this sense, the Fathers are perfectly correct in speaking of the divinization of man who, having been incorporated into Christ, the Son of God by nature, may by his grace share in the divine nature and become a 'son in the Son.'"[100]

Humanity was created in the image and likeness of God through God the Son, the *Logos*. Even by nature, then, the Son can be viewed as the unity of humanity. Therefore, in assuming our own human nature in time, he can also restore our unity with God and with one another. As man, he can offer himself vicariously to atone for our sins. His atonement, then, is a true sacrifice. He is the priest as the one who offers the sacrifice, and he is the victim (the Lamb of God) as the one offered. This is an act of divine love given freely for us.

But there is an important part of that last quote that must be kept in mind. We must be incorporated into Christ so that we can become the adoptive sons of God in the Son. Christ offered himself as a sacrifice for the salvation of all mankind, but one must accept the offer of restored and elevated relationship with God in order for salvation to be made effective. One must willingly be incorporated into Christ. The offer of salvation calls for a response. This theme leads us to the topic of our next chapter, the Church, and to the subsequent chapter on the sacraments, especially the parts about Baptism and the Holy Eucharist.

---

100. Congregation for the Doctrine of the Faith (henceforth CDF), "Letter to the Bishops of the Catholic Church on Some Aspects of Christian Meditation" 14–15, October 15, 1989, vatican.va. See also Turek, *Atonement*, 100–101, from which this quote is taken.

7

Ecclesiology

The topic of this present chapter—ecclesiology—naturally follows the Christology and soteriology presented in the previous chapter. For the Church is an effect of the salvation gained through the Incarnation, Passion, Death, and Resurrection of Jesus. Benedict XVI's theology of the Church also relates to his Trinitarian theology, theological anthropology, sacramental theology, and eschatology. Such relations will be pointed out throughout this chapter.

Ecclesiology studies the origin, nature (essence), and structure of the Church. Accordingly, this chapter will offer an overview of Benedict XVI's thought on those topics in that order. They are, of course, interrelated, so some overlap is to be expected. The topic of the structure of the Church will be divided into two separate sections: (1) the apostles and their successors and (2) the Church as local and universal. Within both of those sections, issues related to Petrine primacy will also be discussed.

THE ORIGIN OF THE CHURCH

In the last chapter, the question of the origin of Jesus was fundamentally important. Likewise, here, the origins of the Church are foundational. Where the Church comes from is key to understanding her nature and purpose. First and foremost, the Church is not the invention of human beings. As already prefigured in the last chapter, the Church is an effect of Christ's saving work. As such, it is the result of God's action. "For he [Jesus] came in order to gather together what was dispersed (cf. Jn 11:52; Mt 12:30). His entire work is thus to gather the new people."[1] In other words, Jesus' life and saving work bring back into unity that which had been separated through sin. To this point, Thomas Rausch writes, "From de Lubac, Ratzinger also drew his patristic understanding of the mystery of Christ as a mystery of unity that heals the separations and divisions that are the results of sin."[2]

The reference to the Church as the people of God reflects her divine origin: she is a people constituted by God through his call and election. This theme was a crucial aspect of Ratzinger's doctoral dissertation. As noted in chapter 1, he wrote on *The People and the House of God in Augustine's Doctrine of the Church*.[3] Aidan Nichols explains the difference between the two terms "people" and "house" of God in Ratzinger's work when he writes, "Augustine's reflections on the concept of faith will be vital for his understanding of the Church as *people* of God. By contrast, his concept of love is more important for his portrait of the Church as the *house* of God: the other wing of the diptych which the title of Ratzinger's thesis evokes."[4] Here, we will focus primarily on the notion of the Church as the people of God, which is one of the key concepts of the Church in *Lumen Gentium*.[5]

---

1. Joseph Ratzinger, *Called to Communion: Understanding the Church Today*, trans. Adrian Walker (San Francisco: Ignatius, 1996), 23.

2. Thomas P. Rausch, *Pope Benedict XVI: An Introduction to His Theological Vision* (New York: Paulist, 2009), 103.

3. Joseph Ratzinger, *Volk und Haus Gottes in Augustins Lehre von der Kirche*, in JRGS 1, ed. Gerhard Ludwig Müller (Freiburg, DE: Herder, 2011). For a succinct and helpful summary of Ratzinger's dissertation, see Aidan Nichols, *The Thought of Benedict XVI: An Introduction to the Theology of Joseph Ratzinger* (New York: Burns & Oates, 2005), 27–50.

4. Nichols, *Thought of Benedict XVI*, 33. Nicholas also points the reader to Joseph Ratzinger, "Der Weg der religiösen Erkenntnis nach dem heiligen Augustinus," in *Kyriakon II: Festschrift J. Quasten*, ed. P. Granfield and J.A. Jungman (Münster: Aschendorff, 1970), 553–564.

5. See Second Vatican Council, *Lumen Gentium* 9–17, November 21, 1965, in *The Word on Fire Vatican II Collection*, ed. Matthew Levering (Park Ridge, IL: Word on Fire Institute, 2021), 55–69.

First of all, the term "people of God" is sometimes prefixed with the qualifier "new": the new people of God. However, this usage should not evoke an absolute dichotomy between the people of the Old Covenant and that of the New. Rather, there is both continuity and newness. "The 'People of God,'" explains Heim, "therefore has significance in the history of theology, and this aspect of it, which points up the incompleteness of what is temporal and interprets God's workings in human history as the history of salvation that can be experienced in the world, reveals the unity of the Old and the New Testaments in the one People of God, which God himself calls."[6] Ratzinger does not see the new people simply as a separate reality occurring temporally posterior to the people of God in Israel. Rather, as Heim explains, "According to the Scripture verse 'Salvation is from the Jews' (Jn 4:22), the Church as the new People of God has an Old Testament lineage, and 'this heritage remains abidingly vital.'"[7] This is reflected in the fact that the Old Testament retains its status as Sacred Scripture. As we saw in the chapter on divine revelation, Ratzinger fundamentally insists upon the relation between the two Testaments as mutually illuminating. The New Testament (and the revelation in Christ to which it bears witness) is the fulfillment of the Old, which means it must be understood in relation to the Old and never apart from it.

In his dissertation, Ratzinger sees three uses of the term "people of God" in Augustine's mature work. First, Nichols explains, "It refers to Israel, which was a *populus* in the common or garden sense of the word, yet also had the special vocation to act as a sign of the coming 'true' People of God, the spiritual Church. And this is Augustine's second usage."[8] To "Israel" and "spiritual

6. Maximilian Heinrich Heim, *Joseph Ratzinger: Life in the Church and Living Theology*, 2nd ed., trans. Michael J. Miller (San Francisco: Ignatius, 2005), 335.

7. Heim, *Joseph Ratzinger*, 335. Here, Heim quotes from Joseph Ratzinger, *Many Religions—One Covenant* (San Francisco: Ignatius, 1999), 28.

8. Nichols, *Thought of Benedict XVI*, 44.

Church," there is a third application of the term people of God: "Augustine also . . . ascribes to the empirical Catholic Church that title which fully befits only her heavenly and eschatological counterpart."[9]

Thus, the visible Catholic Church can be referred to as the people of God, but it is a *pilgrim* people, not yet having arrived at the Promised Land of heaven. There is, then, an eschatological dimension of the Church understood as the people of God. Furthermore, the persistence of the chaff in the midst of the wheat must be called to mind. As Ratzinger remarks:

> Norbert Lohfink has shown that, even in the Old Testament, the designation "people of God" referred to the people of Israel not simply in their empirical setting but only at the moment in which they were addressed by God and answered his call. This is even more true in the New Testament: of herself, the Church is not a people but an exteriorly very heterogeneous society. This nonpeople can become a people only through him who unites them from above and from within: through communion with Christ. Without this christological mediation it would be presumptuous, if not actually blasphemous, for the Church to designate herself the "people of God."[10]

Here, we see the importance of the response to God's call and offer of grace in order to be truly incorporated into Christ and thus into his Church. It is only in Christ that the Church can be the people of God. Of course, this presupposes, too, that the Church has been established by God in Christ.

Ratzinger is convinced—contra various liberal and Marxist interpretations—that the New Testament clearly indicates Jesus' intent to establish the Church. The fact that he chose the Twelve

9. Nichols, 45.

10. Joseph Ratzinger, *Principles of Catholic Theology: Building Stones for a Fundamental Theology*, trans. Mary Frances McCarthy (San Francisco: Ignatius, 1987), 55.

is illustrative, since it harkens back to the twelve tribes of Israel. "In constituting the circle of Twelve, Jesus presents himself as the patriarch of a new Israel and institutes these twelve men as its origin and foundation."[11]

This view is confirmed through Jesus' institution of the Eucharist. On the night before he died, Jesus "transformed the Passover of Israel into an entirely new worship, which logically meant a break with the temple community and thereby definitively established a people of the 'New Covenant.' The words of institution of the Eucharist, whether read in the Markan or in the Pauline tradition, always have to do with the covenant event; they refer backward to Sinai and forward to the New Covenant announced by Jeremiah."[12] Hence, Jesus' establishment of the Church is situated within the whole of salvation history; indeed, it is shown to be the fulfillment of the Old Covenant through the establishment of the prophesied New Covenant. "With Passover and the Sinaiatic covenant ritual, the two founding acts whereby Israel became and ever anew becomes a people are taken up and integrated into the Eucharist."[13]

The Church's divine origin is also attested to in the Acts of the Apostles and its witness to Pentecost. As Ratzinger asserts, "Vehement wind and fire of the Holy Ghost establish the Church. The origin of the Church is not the decision of men; she is not the product of human willing but a creature of the Spirit of God."[14] On this front, Ratzinger insists that the final statements of the Apostles' Creed form an inherent unity. Ecclesiology is understood pneumatologically. "To summarize all this, we can now say

---

11. Ratzinger, *Called to Communion*, 25.
12. Ratzinger, 26.
13. Ratzinger, 27.
14. Ratzinger, 43.

that in our Creed the Church is understood in terms of the Holy Spirit, as the center of the Spirit's activity in the world."[15]

The Church is a theological reality. The Triune God is the origin of the Church. As Pablo Blanco relates, "Ratzinger repeats insistently that the mystery of God and the theology of the Trinity must be the measure and criterion of ecclesiology. The Church will thus be a mystery of communion with God—participation in the intra-trinitarian communion—and among all humanity."[16] Aidan Nichols offers a similar explication of Ratzinger's understanding, expressing how the Church reflects the unity of the Trinity. He writes, "This unity [of the Trinity] is mirrored in that of the Church where through the unifying force of love, which the Holy Spirit, *vinculum amoris* [bond of love], personally is, the many believers are ushered into the unity of the body of Christ."[17]

Here, we begin to see the relation between the origin of the Church and her nature. In what follows, the Church's essence will be considered in connection with the leitmotif of communion, which has its origin and end in the Trinity.

THE NATURE OF THE CHURCH

What is the Church? The beginning of an understanding is found in the origin of the term itself. The Latin term, *ecclesia*, is derived from the New Testament Greek word for church. In turn, the Greek term is used to render the Old Testament Hebrew word *qahal*, which essentially means "assembly of the people." This word, *qahal*, has a religious significance; it indicates the people of Israel gathered to receive and assent to God's proclamations. It harkens back to the gathering of Israel at Mount Sinai. After the diaspora,

---

15. Joseph Ratzinger, *Introduction to Christianity*, trans. Mary Frances McCarthy (San Francisco: Ignatius, 1987), 335.

16. Pablo Blanco Sarto, *La Teología de Joseph Ratzinger: Una introducción* (Madrid: Pelícano, 2011), 102.

17. Nichols, *Thought of Benedict XVI*, 44.

in which the Israelites became geographically scattered, the Jewish people began to hope and to pray for God to provide a new gathering and a new establishment of his people.[18] "It is thus clear what it means for the nascent Church to call herself *ecclesia*. By doing so, she says in effect: This petition is granted in us. Christ, who died and rose again, is the living Sinai; those who approach him are the chosen final gathering of God's people (cf., for example, Heb 12:18–24)."[19] The designation of the Church as *ecclesia* or *qahal* thus includes both "the continuity of the covenant in saving history" and "the newness of the mystery of Christ."[20]

The etymology of "church," understood in its historical and religious context, bespeaks both the divine origin of the Church (as God's gathering of his people) as well as the core of the Church's essence. The Church is the assembly of the people of God. As such, the Church is a *communion* of God's people with one another in their worship of God. Ratzinger thus sees both a vertical and a horizontal aspect to the Church's nature. The latter is rooted in the former. "Communion with God is the path to interpersonal communion among men."[21] As he writes elsewhere, "The Church is the dynamic process of horizontal and vertical unification. It is vertical unification, which brings about the union of man with the triune love of God, thus also integrating man in and with himself. . . . Only by the impulse power of vertical unification can horizontal unification, by which I mean the coming together of divided humanity, also successfully take place."[22]

18. See Ratzinger, *Called to Communion*, 30–31.

19. Ratzinger, 31.

20. Ratzinger, 32.

21. Joseph Ratzinger, *Behold the Pierced One: An Approach to a Spiritual Christology*, trans. Graham Harrison (San Francisco: Ignatius, 1986), 90.

22. Ratzinger, *Called to Communion*, 76. See also Joseph Ratzinger, *Pilgrim Fellowship of Faith: The Church as Communion*, trans. Henry Taylor (San Francisco: Ignatius, 2005), 72: "In communion . . . the horizontal dimension is the result of the vertical and can be understood at all only on that basis"; as well as Joseph Ratzinger, "Église universelle et Église particulière: la charge épiscopale," in *L'évêque et son ministère* (Vatican City: Urbaniana University Press, 1999), 27: "The Church is a dynamic process of horizontal and vertical fusion."

We see in this last quote the reestablishment of communion between God and man, between human persons, and even the integrity of the individual. Again, we see the Church understood as the effect of God's saving work, which unites what had been divided through sin. The individual and communal aspects of salvation are shown in their inner unity. Man, as the image of God, must live in *communion* with both God and with others who are in communion with God. Salvation is not merely individualistic.

Ratzinger approves of Henri de Lubac's thoughts on this matter: "The concept of a Christianity concerned only with *my* soul, in which I seek only *my* justification before God, *my* saving grace, *my* entrance into heaven, is for de Lubac that caricature of Christianity that, in the nineteenth and twentieth centuries, made possible the rise of atheism. . . . De Lubac, for his part, is convinced that Christianity is, by its very nature, a mystery of union."[23] That is why Ratzinger insists on the "we-structure"[24] of Christian faith.

It is helpful at this point to quote a passage from Ratzinger that aptly expresses this deep truth. Ratzinger insists that

> belief in the Trinity is *communio*; to believe in the Trinity means to become *communio*. Historically, this means that the "I" of the credo-formulas is a collective "I", the "I" of the believing Church, to which the individual "I" belongs as long as it believes. In other words, the "I" of the credo embraces the transition from the individual "I" to the ecclesial "I". In the case of the subject, the "I" of the Church is a structural precondition of the creed: this "I" utters itself only in the *communio* of the Church; the oneness of the believing subject is the necessary counterpart and consequence of the known "object".[25]

23. Ratzinger, *Principles*, 49.
24. See Ratzinger, 15–55.
25. Ratzinger, 23.

The communion of the Trinity is the origin and cause of ecclesial communion. As we already saw in the chapter on theological anthropology, this is deeply rooted in man's own nature as the image of God. Interpersonal communion is an essential aspect of what it means to be human and thus of what it means for humanity to be saved. Communion with God entails communion with his people, the Church.

Ratzinger turns to the Acts of the Apostles to delve more deeply into the meaning of the Church as *communion*. There, he sees Luke's depiction of the *"exemplary form of the Church of all ages,"*[26] thus revealing aspects of the Church's nature. In that passage, we read the following about the Church: "They devoted themselves to the apostles' teaching and fellowship, to the breaking of the bread and the prayers" (Acts 2:42).

First, ecclesial unity includes both doctrinal and institutional elements: they dedicated themselves to the *teaching* of the *Apostles*. As Ratzinger notes, "What fellowship with the apostles means is now specified as *'persistent remaining in the teaching of the apostles'*. Unity thus has a content that is expressed in teaching. *The teaching of the apostles is the practical mode of their abiding presence in the Church.* Thanks to this teaching, the future generations after the death of the apostles also remain in unity with them and thus constitute the same one, apostolic Church."[27] Ratzinger continues by connecting this with the importance of apostolic succession, which we will cover in a later section of this chapter.

For now, we can focus on the importance of communion with the Apostles within the New Testament itself. Even St. Paul, who was called by the risen Lord and who received direct revelation from him, exhibits the importance of remaining in doctrinal union with the Apostles. In Galatians, he points out that Peter,

---

26. Ratzinger, *Pilgrim Fellowship*, 63. The emphasis is original, but the bolded text of the original has been rendered in italics here for stylistic purposes. The same will be true of subsequent quotes from the same book.

27. Ratzinger, 63–64.

James, and John (the three "pillars" of the Church) extended to him and Barnabas the right hand of *koinonia* (communion or fellowship). This fact is important. "For him [St. Paul] too, Church unity is unthinkable without 'remaining in the teaching of the apostles', that is, in the apostolic structure of the Church."[28]

Here, we see "fellowship" linked with apostolic teaching, which includes both the content of apostolic teaching and the office of Apostles as such. Furthermore, English "fellowship" translates the New Testament Greek term *koinonia*, which means "communion." This communion is also sacramental, insofar as the Church dedicated itself to the breaking of the bread. "*Fellowship in the body of Christ and in receiving the Body of Christ means fellowship with one another.*"[29] Of course, the sacrament of Baptism is also important. According to St. Paul, Ratzinger explains, "Through baptism . . . we are inserted into Christ and united with him as a single subject; no longer many alongside one another, but 'one only in Christ Jesus' (Gal 3:16; 26–29)."[30] Here, we see Baptism as the means of incorporation into Christ that enables us to receive the grace of his sacrifice on the cross, which was mentioned at the end of the last chapter. Being incorporated into Christ through the sacraments is precisely how we receive the grace of Christ's atonement.

Connected to both the baptismal and Eucharistic aspects of ecclesial communion is the notion of the Church as the Body of Christ. Here, ecclesiology and Christology are shown again in their mutual relation. As Ratzinger insists, "It is entirely impossible to conceive of the New Testament's notion of the people of God apart from Christology, which in turn is no abstract theory

28. Ratzinger, 67.
29. Ratzinger, 69.
30. Ratzinger, *Called to Communion*, 33.

but a concrete event taking place in the sacraments of baptism and the Eucharist."[31]

With respect to the Eucharist, the Church is the Body of Christ by receiving the Body of Christ. This concept is attested to by St. Paul. "The cup of blessing that we bless, is it not a communion in the blood of Christ? The bread that we break, is it not a communion in the body of Christ? Because there is one bread, we who are many are one body, for we all partake of the one bread" (1 Cor. 10:16–17).[32]

Ratzinger expresses his gratitude to Henri de Lubac for elucidating this connection between the Eucharist and the Church, helping to inaugurate a resurgence of Eucharistic ecclesiology in the twentieth century. "Henri de Lubac in a splendid work of extensive scholarship made clear that the term *corpus mysticum* originally designated the most Holy Eucharist and that for Paul, as well as the Church Fathers, the notion of the Church as the body of Christ was inseparably bound to the notion of the Eucharist in which the Lord is bodily present and gives us his body to eat."[33]

Following St. Paul and de Lubac, Ratzinger is a strong advocate of Eucharistic ecclesiology. The Eucharist and the Church are so intimately connected that they cannot be understood apart from one another. In this vein, Ratzinger writes, "According to the Fathers, Eucharist and Church do not stand as two different things next to one another but fall thoroughly into one another."[34] As Ratzinger posits elsewhere, "The formula 'the Church is the Body of Christ' thus states that the Eucharist, in which the

31. Ratzinger, 33. Interestingly, the words following this quote connect the sacraments and Christology to Trinitarian theology: "In these sacraments, Christology opens up into the Trinity."

32. Here, I have altered the NRSV-CE translation by substituting "communion" for "sharing." I think this is justified, since the Greek word is *koinonia*, which, as we said, means "communion," and which better exemplifies the overall meaning of St. Paul's teaching. See also Ratzinger, *Pilgrim Fellowship*, 77, and Ratzinger, *Called to Communion*, 36.

33. Joseph Ratzinger, "The Ecclesiology of the Second Vatican Council," trans. Stephen W. Arndt, *Communio* 13, no. 3 (Fall 1986): 242.

34. Joseph Ratzinger, "Gemeinde aus der Eucharistie," in *800 Jahre St. Martini Münster*, ed. Werner Hülsbusch (Münster: Regensburg, 1980), 32.

Lord gives us his body and makes us one body, forever remains the place where the Church is generated. . . . In the Eucharist the Church is most compactly herself."[35]

Ratzinger also connects Baptism and the Eucharist directly to Jesus' death on the cross, harkening back to the creation of the first woman in Genesis. "The open side of the new Adam repeats the mystery of the 'open side' of man at creation: it is the beginning of a new definitive community of men with one another, a community symbolized here by blood and water, in which John points to the basic Christian sacraments of baptism and Eucharist and, through them, to the Church as the sign of the new community of men."[36]

Here, we see a connection between the Church as the Body of Christ with another motif: the Church as the Bride of Christ. The New Testament allusion to the creation of Adam and Eve as tied to the issuing forth of the Church from the side of Christ on the cross helps to explain the way in which the Church is the Body of Christ: "The Church is the Body, not by virtue of an identity without distinction, but rather by means of the pneumatic-real act of spousal love. Expressed in another way, this means that Christ and the Church are one body in the sense in which man and woman are one flesh, that is, in such a way that in their indissoluble spiritual-bodily union, they nonetheless remain unconfused and unmingled."[37] It is this nuptial understanding of the Church as the Body of Christ that stands behind the command for husbands to love their wives the way that Christ loves the Church. Ephesians directly connects this to Genesis 2:24, in which man and woman are said to become one flesh. Ephesians goes on to say, "This is a great mystery, and I am applying it to Christ and the church" (Eph. 5:32). Thus, in Pauline literature there is an emphasis on the Church as the Body of Christ by means of the

35. Ratzinger, *Called to Communion*, 37.
36. Ratzinger, *Introduction*, 241.
37. Ratzinger, *Called to Communion*, 39.

reception of the Holy Eucharist as well as an explanation that the Church is the Body of Christ *as* the Bride of Christ.

There is also a Marian aspect to Ratzinger's understanding of the Church as Body and Bride. He insists that "precisely the eucharistic-christological mystery of the Church indicated in the term 'Body of Christ' remains within the proper measure only when it includes the mystery of Mary: the mystery of the listening handmaid who—liberated in grace—speaks her *Fiat* and, in so doing, becomes bride and thus body."[38] In this way, Mary is a kind of archetype of the Church. She is also a prime example of what it means to be a member of the Body of Christ. Her faithfulness and humility are precisely the measure of her greatness. Her receptivity to the will of God is what all Christians are called to imitate. It is by following her example that the members of the Church may build up the Body of Christ, not only in terms of numerical quantity but also in the quality of sanctity.

Relatedly, Mary is also understood as a sort of personification of the Church as the fulfillment of the promises made to Israel as Daughter Zion. On this front, Ratzinger interprets the angel Gabriel's greeting to Mary in Luke 1:28 in light of Zephaniah 3:14–17. Ratzinger explains the connection as follows: "In these words a twofold promise is made to Israel, to the daughter of Zion: God will come as a savior and will pitch his tent in his people's midst, in the womb of the daughter of Zion. This promise is fulfilled to the letter in the dialogue between the Angel and Mary. Mary is identified with the people espoused by God, she is truly the daughter of Zion in person; in her the expectation of the definitive coming of God is fulfilled, in her the Living God makes his dwelling place."[39]

---

38. Joseph Ratzinger, "Thoughts on the Place of Marian Doctrine and Piety in Faith and Theology as a Whole," in Hans Urs von Balthasar and Joseph Ratzinger, *Mary: The Church at the Source*, trans. Adrian J. Walker (San Francisco: Ignatius, 2005), 26–27.

39. Benedict XVI, "The Faith of Mary," in *The Pope Benedict XVI Reader* (Park Ridge, IL: Word on Fire Institute, 2021), 221.

Mary also teaches us something important about the Church's nature vis-à-vis its structural component. It is important to consider these reflections before proceeding to the topic of ecclesial structure in the next two sections so that it can be understood more properly. Otherwise, as Ratzinger writes, "A purely structural ecclesiology is bound to degrade Church to the level of a program of action. Only the Marian dimension secures the place of affectivity in faith and thus ensures a fully human correspondence to the reality of the incarnate Logos."[40]

In this vein, Ratzinger reminds us that the Church tends to refer to herself in the feminine, and for good reason. As he writes:

> In contrast to the masculine, activistic-sociological *populus Dei* (people of God) approach, Church—*ecclesia*—is feminine. This fact opens a dimension of the mystery that points beyond sociology, a dimension wherein the real ground and unifying power of the reality Church first appears. Church is more than "people", more than structure and action: the Church contains the living mystery of maternity and of the bridal love that makes maternity possible. . . . When the Church is no longer seen in any but a masculine, structural, purely theoretical way, what is most authentically ecclesial about *ecclesia* has been ignored.[41]

Here, Ratzinger is insisting that the proper functioning of the authoritative, structural elements of the Church must be preceded and accompanied by the receptive, Marian dimension of faith. The hierarchy must hand on only after they have faithfully received what the Lord has given. The same is true for all the faithful,

---

40. Balthasar and Ratzinger, *Mary*, 27.
41. Balthasar and Ratzinger, 25.

who are called to imitate Mary's humble submission to the will of God, not begrudgingly but with the loving heart of Mary.

With those caveats in mind, we can proceed to the topic of ecclesial structure. The hierarchical structure of the Church, too, is a theological dimension of the Church as established by God. To this point, Ratzinger emphasizes that "the community of Jesus' disciples is not an amorphous mob. At its center are the Twelve, who form a compactly knit core."[42] We shall deal with the Church's organizational structure in two sections: (1) the Apostles and their successors and (2) the Church as local and universal.

CHURCH STRUCTURE: THE APOSTLES AND THEIR SUCCESSORS[43]

As already discussed, Ratzinger holds that the twelve Apostles were of the utmost importance to the nascent Church. The term "twelve Apostles" combines two concepts, each of which bears its own significance. "The Twelve," as mentioned before, is related to the hope for "a final restoration of the twelve tribes."[44] The office of the Twelve was thus the very first office to be established in the Church by Christ himself. As the Twelve, their primary role was to represent the status of the Church as the new people of God.[45]

The term "Apostles" adds a new element to their role. Meaning "one who is sent," the title "Apostle" signifies the missionary character of the Church. The Apostles' "mission is to carry the message of Christ 'to the end of the earth' (Acts 1:8), to go to all nations and to make all men his disciples (Mt 28:19)."[46] This fact

---

42. Ratzinger, *Called to Communion*, 24.

43. For a fuller explication of Ratzinger's thought on this topic, see Richard DeClue, "Primacy and Collegiality in the Works of Joseph Ratzinger," *Communio* 35, no. 4 (Winter 2008): 642–670.

44. Joseph Ratzinger, "The Pastoral Implications of Episcopal Collegiality," in *The Church and Mankind, Concilium* 1 (Glen Rock, NJ: Paulist, 1965), 40.

45. See Ratzinger, "Pastoral Implications," 41.

46. Ratzinger, *Pilgrim Fellowship*, 187.

also means that the final, eschatological "new people of God" is not limited to one nation. The new Israel is meant to be universal. As such, it is the fulfillment of the promise given to Abraham that, through his posterity, all nations would find blessing (see Gen. 22:18). "The twelve became the twelve apostles and thereby collectively shared in a worldwide mission to unite all peoples in Christ."[47]

While the Twelve form a collective group that symbolizes and effects the unity of the people of God while the Church spreads throughout the world, they are not an entirely egalitarian group. Within the New Testament, three members of the Twelve are given particular prominence: Peter, James, and John. "They alone are admitted to two moments of particular consequence—the Transfiguration and the Garden of Olives (Mk 9:2ff.; 14:33ff.); likewise only these three are permitted to witness the raising of Jairus' young daughter (Mk 5:37)."[48]

Among these three as among the Twelve at large, Simon Peter has his own preeminence. Jesus gives Simon the new appellation "Rock" (*Petrus*, *Kepha*, or *Cephas*) which is loaded with its own significance. Ratzinger notes that "to the eschatological sign of 'the twelve' is added the sign of the Rock which is likewise taken from the eschatological symbolism of Israel. From these resulted, after the resurrection of Christ, the twofold office: the office of the witnesses and the office of the *first* witness in which St. Peter figures in the resurrection accounts and in the lists of the apostles."[49]

Ratzinger insists that the special primacy of Peter is attested to throughout the New Testament: "It is immediately striking that all the major groups of texts in the New Testament are acquainted with the subject of Peter, which is thereby proven to be a topic of universal significance whose importance cannot

47. DeClue, "Primacy and Collegiality," 646.

48. Ratzinger, *Called to Communion*, 53–54.

49. Ratzinger, "Pastoral Implications," 51. See 1 Cor. 15:5; Luke 24:34; Mark 16:7; Mark 16:12; and Matt. 10:2–4.

be restricted to a particular tradition limited to one person or place."[50] The fact that Peter is shown to be of primary importance in Pauline literature, Johannine literature, and the synoptic Gospels alike indicates that Peter's special role within the Twelve was universally recognized from the beginning of the Church.[51] Even the liberal Protestant theologian Rudolf Bultmann acknowledges Peter's preeminence. Referring to Jesus' threefold command to Peter in John 21:15–19, Ratzinger writes, "No one less than R. Bultmann has stated plainly that in this text Peter is 'entrusted with the supreme leadership of the Church'."[52]

Similarly, Ratzinger again points to Bultmann as well as another liberal scholar, Adolf von Harnack, to show that his reading of another passage (Matt. 16:17–19) is not simply due to Catholic bias. Along with Bultmann and von Harnack, Ratzinger thinks that this passage bespeaks its Aramaic origins.[53] "The introductory phrase 'blessed are you' is Aramaic, as is the unexplained name Barjona, and, furthermore, the terms 'gates of the netherworld', 'keys of the kingdom of heaven', 'bind and loose', 'on earth and in heaven'. The play on the word 'rock' . . . does not work with complete success in Greek. . . . We can thus hear even through this pun the Aramaic word *kepha* and perceive the voice of Jesus himself."[54] Ratzinger thus holds firmly that Peter's primacy was instituted by Jesus himself and is therefore a divinely established office.

This pericope is perhaps the most famous one cited by

50. Ratzinger, *Called to Communion*, 49.

51. For several specific examples of how pervasive Petrine primacy is in the New Testament, see Ratzinger, 48–65. See also DeClue, "Primacy and Collegiality," 647–651.

52. Ratzinger, 52. Here, Ratzinger cites R. Bultmann, *Das Evangelium des Johannes*, 15th ed. (Göttingen: Vandenhoeck & Ruprecht, 1957), 552n3.

53. See Ratzinger, 60. There, Ratzinger cites von Harnack from J.R. Geiselmann, *Der petrinische Primat* (Münster: Aschendorff, 1927), 9. The quote is: "There are not many longer sections in the Gospels from which the Aramaic basis shines through in form and content so surely as from this tightly compact pericope." Ratzinger also cites Bultmann from the same work of Geiselmann, 51: "I cannot see that the conditions for its composition would have existed anywhere other than in the primitive community at Jerusalem."

54. Ratzinger, 60.

Catholic theologians and apologists arguing for Petrine primacy. The giving of the keys to Peter is of particular importance. It harkens back to Isaiah 22:22, which helps elucidate the meaning of the gesture and the authority that it imparts. To this point, Ratzinger writes:

> As the faithful steward of Jesus' message, Peter opens the door to the Kingdom of Heaven; his is the function of the door-keeper, who has to judge concerning admission and rejection (cf. Rev 3:7). In this sense, the significance of the reference to the keys clearly approximates the meaning of binding and loosing. This latter expression is taken from rabbinic language, where it stands primarily for the authority to make doctrinal decisions and, on the other hand, denotes a further discipli-nary power, that is, the right to impose or to lift the ban. The parallelism "on earth and in heaven" implies that Peter's deci-sions for the Church also have validity before God—an idea that also occurs in an analogous sense in Talmudic literature.[55]

Accordingly, Ratzinger believes that Jesus' giving of the keys to Peter indicates doctrinal and juridical authority, the exercise of which is binding on the Church, because it is held bound by God in heaven.

The fact that Peter and the Apostles were given special of-fices in the nascent Church is obviously important. However, the question arises whether and how their authority continues in the post-apostolic period. Hence, we come to the twin issues of apostolic and Petrine succession.

The first stage of apostolic succession occurs within the ap-ostolic period itself. The Apostles established bishops (*episkopoi*, overseers) in the churches they founded during their missionary activity. The Apostles thus gave these bishops authority to preside

55. Ratzinger, 63–64.

over the local church communities. At this point, there was a distinction between the local office of bishop and the universal office of Apostle. Speaking of the Apostles, Ratzinger writes, "The sphere of action allotted them is the world. Without any restriction as to locality, they work for the building up of the body of Christ, of the one People of God, of the one Church of Christ. The apostles were not bishops of particular local Churches but simply 'apostles' and were commissioned as such for work in the whole world and in the whole of the Church to be built up in the world."[56] By way of contrast, Ratzinger remarks, "In the initial phase, their [bishops'] position as bearers of responsibility for the local Churches is clearly subordinate to the catholic authority of the apostles."[57]

In light of this, there is a legitimate distinction to be made between an Apostle and a bishop. The Twelve were a unique group insofar as they were eyewitnesses to the Resurrection of Jesus. As Ratzinger notes, St. Paul "views the essence of apostleship as witness to the Resurrection."[58] Being an eyewitness to the Resurrection is not, in itself, sufficient to be considered an Apostle. A direct commission from Christ is also required. However, on both counts, St. Paul himself is able to be called an Apostle, without being a member of the Twelve. This fact "provides an early illustration of the possibility of someone's sharing in the apostolic mission without being one of the original twelve, which is of undoubted importance for the notion of apostolic succession."[59] As already mentioned, Paul's status as an Apostle included the expectation that he receive the acceptance of the Twelve, especially Peter, as affirmation of his authority.

But what about the post-apostolic era? Is the office and authority of the Apostles simply lost? Ratzinger's answer is rooted

56. Ratzinger, *Pilgrim Fellowship*, 187–188.
57. Ratzinger, *Called to Communion*, 85.
58. Ratzinger, 49.
59. DeClue, "Primacy and Collegiality," 646.

in the concrete history of the early Church: "The fact that in the difficult formative process of the postapostolic Church the place of the apostles was also finally adjudged to them [the bishops of the local churches] implies that they now assumed a responsibility whose scope transcended the local principle. It means that the catholic and missionary flame must not be extinguished even in this new situation. The Church cannot become a static juxtaposition of essentially self-sufficient local Churches. The Church must remain 'apostolic', that is to say, the dynamism of unity must also mold her structure."[60] In other words, the early Church saw the role of universal mission and authority of the Apostles as becoming part of the role of the bishops, who had received their authority from the Apostles initially.

What is more, Ratzinger notes that the concept of apostolic succession (and its correlative term Tradition) even predates the recognition of the existence of the New Testament: "Christians had already formulated the principle of *successio-traditio* before they yet understood the New Testament as 'Scripture'."[61] The existence of succession and Tradition was, in fact, a condition for the possibility of the recognition of the New Testament as Scripture.

Ratzinger continues to link succession and Tradition together by combating a false notion. Whereas the Gnostic heretics claimed to have a secret knowledge (a tradition) not known by others, the early Church understood that Tradition is intrinsically tied to the authority guaranteed by apostolic succession: it is not a secret but something visible. Tradition, for the early Church, was not a set of "exhaustive doctrines of apostolic origin"; rather, tradition was "the connection of the living faith with the authority

---

60. Ratzinger, *Called to Communion*, 85.

61. Joseph Ratzinger, "Primacy, Episcopate, and Apostolic Succession," in Karl Rahner and Joseph Ratzinger, *The Episcopate and the Primacy*, trans. Kenneth Barker et al. (New York: Herder, 1962), 49. Ratzinger also notes that the words "succession" and "tradition" were synonyms in the early Church. See *Episcopate and Primacy*, 46, and DeClue, "Primacy and Collegiality," 652.

of the Church, embodied in the episcopal succession."[62] The way one was guaranteed to be in the line of the teaching of the Apostles was to be in communion with the successors of the Apostles, the bishops. Thus, Ratzinger says, "Apostolic succession means first of all . . . *guaranteeing the continuity of the unity of the faith— in a continuity we call sacramental.*"[63]

Apostolic succession is a necessity. How else could one know whether they were remaining in communion with the apostolic faith and in the one Church established by Christ upon the Apostles? As Nichols explains, "Ratzinger enquires, how, unless obedience to the apostolic ministry is an intrinsic feature of the Church, we are to determine what counts . . . as 'pure' teaching and 'right' sacraments."[64] The visible, historical link between the Apostles and the bishops is crucial. There must be an objective, tangible diachronic unity within the Church.

Additionally, the collective character of the Apostles is maintained in their successors. Just as the Apostles constituted a group endowed with authority, so too, the bishops constitute a group. "The bishop himself did not succeed to a specific apostle, but to the apostolic group, with and through the episcopal college."[65] In other words, it is not the case that every bishop traces his lineage to one particular Apostle. Neither is it the case that an individual bishop stands in isolation. His ability to exercise his apostolic authority is connected to his communion with the college of bishops as a whole. Thus, in addition to the diachronic unity guaranteed by apostolic succession, there is synchronic unity among the bishops. "Since the office of the apostles is collegial and the bishops are the successors of the apostles, the bishops are also collegial insofar as their *collegium* has taken the place of the *collegium* of

62. Rahner and Ratzinger, *Episcopate and Primacy*, 50.

63. Ratzinger, *Pilgrim Fellowship*, 190.

64. Nichols, *Thought of Benedict XVI*, 139.

65. Joseph Ratzinger, "La collégialité, développement théologique," in *L'Église de Vatican II: Études autour de la Constitution conciliaire sur l'Église*, (Paris: Cerf, 1967), 3:774.

the apostles. And just as each apostle had his function by belonging to the others who together with him formed the apostolic community, so each bishop has his office only by belonging to the *collegium* which is the post-apostolic continuation of the apostles."[66] The local bishop, then, serves a dual purpose. He preserves the unity of the local church while also keeping it in communion with the universal Church. "A bishop's job is to preserve his community within the greater unity of the whole Church."[67]

The communal dimension of the episcopal office is thus clear. It extends across both time and space (diachronic and synchronic unity). "The bishop is not the bishop alone but only in the Catholic community of those who were bishops before him, are bishops with him, and will be bishops after him."[68]

Within the college of bishops—or, more precisely, within the communion of local churches—there are certain sees (dioceses) that have traditionally been recognized as having greater significance. In particular, the local churches known to have been directly connected with Apostles have had a special gravitas within the Church. These are called apostolic sees, which are "those sees where apostles had once worked or which had received apostolic letters. In other words not every see was apostolic, but only that limited number which stood in a unique and special relationship to the apostles."[69] These apostolic sees were touchstones of regional and universal communion between the local churches. The establishment of additional local churches in the post-apostolic era naturally required the communion of these new churches with apostolic churches. As Ratzinger notes, "The majority of bishops, those not in apostolic sees, succeed only by a circuitous route, i.e., through an apostolic see. . . . They are legitimately apostolic

---

66. Ratzinger, "Pastoral Implications," 43.

67. Nichols, *Thought of Benedict XVI*, 247.

68. Ratzinger, "Ecclesiology of the Second Vatican Council," 246. See also Ratzinger, *Pilgrim Fellowship*, 143.

69. Rahner and Ratzinger, *Episcopate and Primacy*, 55.

only because they are in communion with an apostolic see."[70] In another place, Ratzinger remarks, "These [apostolic sees] were the centres of apostolic witness, with which all other sees had to align themselves. Tertullian, for example, expresses this very clearly when he refers each area to its respective apostolic see."[71]

This issue of apostolic versus non-apostolic sees is directly tied to the question of primacy and of Petrine succession. Among the apostolic sees, there were three that were considered to have special primacy. "The word 'primatus' [primacy] . . . to my knowledge appears in connection with the Roman see for the first time in Canon 6 of the Council of Nicaea, where, however, it characteristically occurs in the plural and describes not only the function of Rome, but at the same time that of Alexandria and Antioch."[72] The basis of the primacy of these three sees was their shared connection to St. Peter. "We can add that Rome and Antioch were conscious of succeeding to the mission of Peter and that early on Alexandria was admitted into the circle of Petrine sees as the city where Peter's disciple Mark had been active."[73] The fact that the three Petrine sees were seen as having preeminence among the other apostolic sees certainly bespeaks the recognition of St. Peter's primacy among the Apostles.

Furthermore, among these three Petrine sees, Rome was considered the most exalted, since it was the place of St. Peter's (and St. Paul's) martyrdom. This fact is attested to in Eusebius of Caesarea's *Ecclesiastical History*, which was "a written record of the continuity of apostolic succession, which was concentrated in three Petrine sees—Rome, Antioch and Alexandria—among which Rome, as the site of Peter's martyrdom, was in turn

70. Rahner and Ratzinger, 56. See also DeClue, "Primacy and Collegiality," 655.

71. Rahner and Ratzinger, *Episcopate and Primacy*, 55.

72. Joseph Ratzinger, *Das neue Volk Gottes: Entwürfe zur Ekklesiologie* (Düsseldorf: Patmos, 1969), 122.

73. Ratzinger, *Called to Communion*, 71.

preeminent and truly normative."[74] Similarly, writes Ratzinger, "Irenaeus too envisages the Church as covered with a network of apostolic sees, among which the See of Peter and Paul [Rome] possesses unequivocal pre-eminence as the criterion of the succession-tradition."[75] Given the historical witness of ecclesiastical Tradition, Ratzinger concludes: "Among the apostolic sees, there is in turn *the* apostolic see, Rome, which bears approximately the same relation to the other apostolic sees as they do to those which are not directly apostolic. Thus, Rome is the final, proper, and self-sufficient criterion of Catholicity."[76]

Just like apostolic succession in general, Ratzinger thinks Petrine succession is necessary; both are based upon the structure established by Christ himself, and therefore, they are of divine right. This is the case, he insists, "because the Lord himself established, beside and together with the office of 'the twelve', also the special office of the Rock."[77] Over time, this recognition of Roman primacy based upon the connection with St. Peter (and St. Paul) was confirmed through historical experience. As Ratzinger notes, "In the fourth and fifth centuries there was consensus about the fact that Rome itself had kept free from heresy, that it was the place of an unaffected, guaranteed Tradition and therefore could be called upon in special measure as upholder of the right faith, as a measuring stick of undistorted Tradition."[78]

In fact, the Roman primacy was a key factor for the existence of Tradition itself. "The formative development of tradition and of the Church supposed the continuation of Peter's authority in Rome as an intrinsic condition."[79] In fact, Roman primacy

74. Ratzinger, *Called to Communion*, 69. See also D. Vincent Twomey, *Apostolikos Thronos: The Primacy of Rome as Reflected in the Church History of Eusebius and the Historico-Apologetic Writings of Saint Athanasius the Great* (Münster: Aschendorff, 1982).

75. Rahner and Ratzinger, *Episcopate and Primacy*, 55.

76. Rahner and Ratzinger, 57. See also Ratzinger, *Called to Communion*, 69: "Rome was the standard of the authentic apostolic tradition as a whole."

77. Ratzinger, "Pastoral Implications," 51.

78. Ratzinger, *Das neue Volk Gottes*, 127.

79. Ratzinger, *Called to Communion*, 72.

predates the New Testament canon and was crucial in the process of determining the canon. Ratzinger cites the liberal Protestant scholar Adolf von Harnack to confirm this fact: "Harnack, a witness who cannot be suspected of pro-Roman bias, has remarked in this regard that it was only at the end of the second century, in Rome, that a canon of the 'books of the New Testament' won recognition by the criterion of apostolicity-catholicity, a criterion to which the other Churches also gradually subscribed 'for the sake of its intrinsic value and on the strength of the authority of the Roman Church'," which leads Ratzinger to conclude that: "We can therefore say that Scripture became Scripture through the tradition, which precisely in this process included the *potentior principalitas*—the preeminent original authority—of the Roman see as a constitutive element."[80] The Petrine see of Rome, historically, was a major factor in the preservation of Tradition and in the solidification of the New Testament canon.

With the affirmation of both episcopal collegiality and Petrine/Roman primacy, the question arises: What is the relationship between them? Far from seeing them as opposed, Ratzinger holds that they are mutually constitutive and reciprocally illuminating. Ratzinger "thinks collegiality uncovers papal primacy's 'central theological significance' and may even 'make it more understandable to our Orthodox brethren'" and that papal primacy belongs to "'the official center of the collegiality of bishops.'"[81] This approach makes sense when one considers Peter both as one of the Twelve and as having a relative primacy within it.[82] Similarly, "Only communion with Rome gives them [bishops] Catholicity and that fulness of apostolicity without which they would not be true bishops," but "on the other hand, the episcopal see of

---

80. Ratzinger, 70–71.

81. DeClue, "Primacy and Collegiality," 661, quoting from Ratzinger, "Pastoral Implications," 51.

82. See Heim, *Joseph Ratzinger*, 451: "Just as Peter belongs to the company of the apostles and at the same time assumes a special role within it, so too the successor of Peter in the *communio* of the college of bishops."

Rome itself does not stand in isolation, devoid of relationships. It creates their Catholicity for other sees, but precisely for this reason it also needs Catholicity."[83] As the bishop of the local church of Rome, it is the task of the pope to foster the communion of the bishops of all the local churches throughout the world, thus safeguarding the universality and unity of the one Church.

Part of this unity is, of course, the orthodoxy of the faith professed by the bishops and their people. As we read in Scripture, Jesus says to Peter, "I have prayed that your own faith may not fail; and once you have turned back, you must strengthen your brothers" (Luke 22:32).[84] Unsurprisingly, then, Ratzinger affirms the Catholic dogma regarding the papacy, which he explains thusly:

> First, it is the certain teaching of the Church that the pope has immediate, ordinary, truly episcopal power of jurisdiction over the whole Church. The Vatican Council [Vatican I] calls the primacy of the pope the apostolic primacy, and the Roman See the apostolic see. Thus in the realm of doctrine the pope, in his official capacity, is infallible, his *ex cathedra* decisions being irreformable *ex sese* and not in virtue of the Church's subsequent confirmation. So far as *communio* is concerned, the other pillar of the Church, it follows that only he who is in communion with the pope lives in the true *communio* of the body of the Lord, i.e., in the true Church.[85]

This Petrine authority is the concrete means of manifesting and maintaining the unity of the one Church established by Christ, according to his will "that they may all be one" (John 17:21).

Despite the primacy of the pope and the extent of his authority, Ratzinger insists that "the primacy cannot be patterned

83. Rahner and Ratzinger, *Episcopate and Primacy*, 60.
84. See Ratzinger, *Called to Communion*, 53.
85. Rahner and Ratzinger, *Episcopate and Primacy*, 39.

on the model of an absolute monarchy as if the pope were the un-
restricted monarch of a centrally constituted, supernatural State
called Church."[86] In fact, he enumerates several important points
with respect to what papal primacy does not entail:

1. the pope cannot arrogate to himself the episcopal rights, nor
   substitute his power for that of the bishops;
2. the episcopal jurisdiction has not been absorbed in the papal
   jurisdiction;
3. the pope was not given the entire fulness of the bishops'
   powers by the decrees of the Vatican Council;
4. he has not virtually taken the place of each individual bishop;
5. he cannot put himself in the place of a bishop in each single
   instance, *vis-à-vis* governments;
6. the bishops have not become instruments of the pope;
7. they are not officials of a foreign sovereign in their relations
   with their own governments.[87]

Here, Ratzinger recognizes the true authority of bishops for their
own local churches. He also sees the college of bishops working
together for the good of the whole Church. The pope cannot and
should not do everything on his own. "The Petrine office, again,
would not be rightly understood, and would become ossified as
a monstrous exceptional case, if we were to load onto the person
occupying that office sole responsibility for enforcing the universal dimension of the apostolic succession."[88] There are other bishops and additional offices and ministries in the Church. While
the pope has a duty and thus the prerogative to be the point of
unity between them as well as to hold them accountable to the
apostolic faith, he cannot function alone. "The pope is dependent

86. Ratzinger, "Pastoral Implications," 51.
87. Ratzinger, "Primacy, Episcopate, and Apostolic Succession," in Rahner and Ratzinger,
Episcopate and Primacy, 41. See DeClue, "Primacy and Collegiality," 664.
88. Ratzinger, *Pilgrim Fellowship*, 202.

upon these ministries, and they on him, and, in the existence side by side of the two kinds of mission, the symphony of Church life comes to fulfillment. . . . The primacy of the successor of Peter is there to guarantee the presence of these essential components of Church life and to bring them into an ordered relationship with the structures of the local Church."[89]

This last quote leads us to our next topic: the Church as local and universal. Issues connected with that topic have already arisen, but we will elaborate upon them more completely in the following section.

THE CHURCH AS LOCAL AND UNIVERSAL[90]

As mentioned in the section on the Church's nature, Ratzinger's ecclesiology is thoroughly Eucharistic. He understands the Church and the Eucharist as two intrinsically related realities. Accordingly, his Eucharistic understanding of the Church informs his understanding of the relationship between the local church and the universal Church. Here, we will explore this theme with regard to the following topics: the full ecclesial quality of the local church, the one universal Church, and the papacy understood Eucharistically.

First, the term "local church," also known as the particular church, refers to the episcopal diocese (or equivalent term, such as eparchy). Ratzinger recognizes that "for the early Christians the word *ecclesia* meant first of all and most conspicuously the local Church. In other words, the Church is realized immediately and

---

89. Ratzinger, 202.

90. For a more comprehensive presentation of Ratzinger's thought on the relationship between the local and universal Church together with a direct comparison and contrast between him and the Orthodox bishop and theologian John Zizioulas, see Richard DeClue, "Eucharistic Ecclesiologies of Locality and Universality in John Zizioulas and Joseph Ratzinger," *Nova et Vetera* 12, no. 1 (2014): 77–103. In what follows, I draw from the work I did for that article, which in turn, derived from my SThL Thesis: Richard DeClue, "The Petrine Ministry within a Eucharistic Ecclesiology according to John Zizioulas and Joseph Ratzinger" (SThL thesis, The Catholic University of America, 2008).

primarily in the individual local Churches which are not separate parts of a larger administrative organization but rather embody the totality of the reality which is 'the Church'."[91] The main
point here is that each local church *is* the Church present in a
given place with all her essential elements. Thus, the local church
should not be understood as a piece of the one Church, the way
an arm is part of the human body. Rather, the local church is the
embodiment of the one Church in a given place.

The foundation of understanding the local church as possessing full ecclesial quality is the Eucharist. "The Eucharist joins
men together, not only with one another but also with Christ
thus making them Church. . . . [The] Church lives in eucharistic
communities."[92] Keep in mind that Ratzinger sees the diocese—
and not the parish—as the local church understood in this way.
The reason is that, even when the bishop is not present at the
parish Mass (or Divine Liturgy), the bishop is still in some way
the presider. The priest is a representative of the bishop and works
under the bishop's headship. That is why, for instance, the local
bishop is named in the Eucharistic Prayer. Communion under
the leadership and authority of the bishop is essential for the local
church as a Eucharistic community.

Additionally, the full ecclesial quality of the local church is
dependent upon its unity with the other local churches in the
one Church. A local church cut off from the others would not
possess the full reality of what it means to be church. Thus, the
communion of local churches is essential. The reason for this is
also tied to the Eucharist. An authentic Eucharistic community
cannot be an isolated community. As Ratzinger explains, "Christ
is wholly present everywhere, that is the one very important thing
the Council formulated in common with our Orthodox brethren. But he is only one everywhere, and therefore I can have the

---

91. Ratzinger, "Pastoral Implications," 44.
92. Ratzinger, "Ecclesiology of the Second Vatican Council," 242–243.

one Lord only in the unity that he himself is, in the unity with the others who also are his body and are to become it ever anew in the Eucharist."[93] As a consequence, Ratzinger says forcefully that "*the Eucharist is celebrated with the one Christ, and thus with the whole Church, or it is not being celebrated at all.*"[94] Once again we see the merging of Ratzinger's Christology, soteriology, ecclesiology, and sacramental theology, with *communion* being the common notion uniting them all.

In Ratzinger's view, the Eucharist gives the Church a dynamic of multiplicity and unity at the same time. He writes:

> [The] Church arises and exists through this, that the Lord communicated himself to men, walks in communion with them, and thus brings them into communion with one another. The Church is the communicating of the Lord with us, which at the same time creates the true communing of men with one another. Hence, [the] Church arises each time around one altar. Therefore, it is built up in local churches—"communities," since only a "community" can be the location of communication. Hence, it is at the same time, however, still only one in the multiplicity of communities, since there are not many bodies of the Lord but one single Christ, who is everywhere whole but is also everywhere only one.[95]

There is a simultaneity between the locality and universality of the Church that is akin to that of the Eucharist itself. By way of analogy, each Communion host is physically differentiable from every other host in time and space, and yet they are all the same person, Jesus Christ; likewise, each local church is differentiable

---

93. Ratzinger, 244.
94. Ratzinger, *Pilgrim Fellowship*, 106.
95. Ratzinger, "Gemeinde aus der Eucharistie," 32.

from the other local churches, but they are the same Church present in each locale. The same reality is present in each instance.

Correlative to the idea of the full ecclesial quality of the local church is Ratzinger's insistence upon the ontological reality of the one Church. The local church is the one Church present in a given place. Since the local churches are more than just parts of the one Church, so too the universal Church must not be understood as a mere aggregate of local churches. Rather, "The one Church is a theological entity, and not the subsequent empirical uniting of many churches."[96] The universal Church is truly one entity, one substantial reality that is present in each local church.

In fact, Ratzinger holds that the universal Church has metaphysical priority over the local churches. Christ established the one Church, which then makes herself present with her fullness in various places. As Ratzinger states, "What *first* exists is the one Church, the Church that speaks in all tongues—the *ecclesia universalis*; she then generates Church in the most diverse locales, which nonetheless are all always embodiments of the one and only Church. The temporal and ontological priority lies with the universal Church."[97] Ratzinger thinks this is patently evident. "The ontological precedence of the Church as a whole, of the one Church and the one body, of the one bride, over the empirical and concrete realizations in the various individual parts of the Church seems to me so obvious that I find it difficult to understand the objections raised against it."[98]

96. Ratzinger, *Pilgrim Fellowship*, 249.

97. Ratzinger, *Called to Communion*, 44. Ratzinger and Cardinal Walter Kasper famously engaged in a back-and-forth debate about this question. The relevant texts are as follows: Walter Kasper, "Zur Theologie und Praxis des bischöflichen Amtes," *Auf neue Art Kirche sein: Wirklichkeiten—Herausforderungen—Wandlungen* (Munich: Bernward bei Don Bosco, 1999), 32–48; Joseph Ratzinger, "Über die Ekklesiologie der Konstitution 'Lumen Gentium,'" *Die Tagespost*, March 2000, Beilage [Supplement], 8 [English = "The Ecclesiology of the Constitution on the Church, Vatican II, 'Lumen Gentium,'" *L'Osservatore Romano*, September 19, 2001, 5–8]; Walter Kasper, "On the Church: A Friendly Reply to Cardinal Ratzinger," *America* 184 (April 23–30, 2001): 8–14; Joseph Ratzinger, "The Local Church and the Universal Church: A Response to Walter Kasper," *America* 185 (November 19, 2001): 7–11; Walter Kasper, "From the President of the Council for Promoting Christian Unity," *America* 185 (November 19, 2001): 7–11.

98. Ratzinger, *Pilgrim Fellowship*, 134–135.

After all, the local churches are not self-generating. They are preceded by the one Church. "Ratzinger, without denying the full ecclesial quality of the local church, emphasizes the fact that each local church does not create itself, but rather receives its being from without, that is, from the universal Church, which is therefore prior to (temporally and ontologically) these local churches."[99]

The local churches cannot even give themselves their own bishops. Bishops from other local churches are necessary to consecrate a bishop for a new diocese or to replace a bishop in an already existing diocese. Hence, not only are they not self-generating, they are not self-sustaining. In principle, they cannot—of themselves—give themselves the Eucharist either, without first receiving a bishop and priests through the sacrament of Holy Orders that they received through the universal Church by the hands of the consecrating bishops not of that local church. "The fact that the sacrament of priestly service is requisite for the Eucharist is founded upon the fact that the congregation cannot give itself the Eucharist; it has to receive it from the Lord by the mediation of the one Church."[100] I summarize elsewhere that "there is first the one Church (quite real and concrete) established by Christ, which then goes forth into the world and makes herself present in various places in and through local churches, which are fully churches only because they have received from the one Church all the necessary elements (including baptism, holy orders, and most especially the Eucharist)."[101]

---

99. DeClue, "Eucharistic Ecclesiologies," 88.

100. Ratzinger, *Pilgrim Fellowship*, 143. See also Congregation for the Doctrine of the Faith, *Communionis Notio* 11, in *Origins* (June 15, 1992): "It is precisely the Eucharist that renders all self-sufficiency on the part of the particular Churches impossible. Indeed, the unicity and indivisibility of the eucharistic Body of the Lord implies the unicity of his mystical Body, which is the one and indivisible Church. From the eucharistic centre arises the necessary openness of every celebrating community, of every particular Church; by allowing itself to be drawn into the open arms of the Lord, it achieves insertion into his one and undivided Body." This document was issued under the prefecture of Joseph Ratzinger.

101. DeClue, "Eucharistic Ecclesiologies," 89.

Church structure, then, is closely tied to the Eucharist. As we will see in the next section, this includes universal structures or offices, such as the papacy.

THE POPE AND THE EUCHARIST

The unity of the local churches with one another and with the one Church is essential. This unity, as we have seen, is visibly manifest through the catholic communion of bishops with the bishop of Rome. For Ratzinger, this unity is essential to the Church and to the proper celebration of the Eucharist. As Heim explains, "Every celebration of the Eucharist inherently presupposes 'a visible, concrete . . . unity' as an essential structural element. Accordingly, the commemoration of the pope and the bishop in the Eucharistic Prayer during the Mass is not something incidental; rather, it is an expression of this unity, for it means, in Ratzinger's opinion, 'that we are truly celebrating the *one* Eucharist of Jesus Christ, which we can receive only in the *one* Church.'"[102]

From this perspective, the role of the pope can be understood Eucharistically. The Roman pontiff keeps the Church united throughout the world, thus ensuring that the various celebrations of the Eucharist are carried out in catholic communion, which is an essential attribute of the Eucharist and of the Church alike. By keeping the local churches within the communion of the entire Catholic Church, the pope thus enables the proper celebration of the Eucharist in the local churches.[103] The papal office is a Eucharistic office. As Paul McPartlan notes, "Long before he became Prefect for the Congregation, Joseph Ratzinger already held, as Battista Mondin neatly summarises, that 'the primacy of the pope

---

102. Heim, *Joseph Ratzinger*, 275.

103. For a similar idea, written to elaborate the theology proposed in *Communionis Notio*, see Paul McPartlan, *Sacrament of Salvation* (London: T&T Clark, 1995), 70: "The pope, in short, is here being understood as eucharistic guardian and guarantor, as one who primarily strengthens his brother bishops not just juridically but eucharistically."

does not primarily concern either orthodoxy or orthopraxy, but rather ortho-Eucharist.'"[104]

Papal primacy supports the presidency of each local bishop as well, so that he can be an authentic source of unity within his own diocese. "In other words, the bishop cannot stand in isolation, as a principle of unity simply in himself. A major function of his role *within* the local church is precisely to keep it united to the other local churches and with the whole Church. He does this, Ratzinger believes, precisely through his union with the other bishops as a member of the college of bishops,"[105] whose unity as a college is rooted in the primacy of the bishop of Rome, the Petrine see *par excellence*.

As a final note, this point is the major issue keeping the Eastern Orthodox churches separate from the Catholic Church. Interestingly, however, Ratzinger thinks that very little would need to change on an administrative level if the Orthodox and the Catholic Churches were to reestablish full communion with one another. "It becomes additionally clear that an extensive patriarchal 'autonomy' is compatible with the true essence of primacy, and perhaps the Eastern Churches would hardly need to change anything in terms of concrete juridical structure."[106]

104. McPartlan, *Sacrament of Salvation*, 70n7. McPartlan quotes from Battista Mondin, *Le nuove ecclesiologie* (Rome: Paoline, 1980), 171.

105. DeClue, "Eucharistic Ecclesiologies," 91.

106. Joseph Ratzinger, "Primat," in *Lexikon für Theologie und Kirche*, 2nd ed., ed. Josef Höfer and Karl Rahner (Freiburg, DE: Herder, 1963), 8:763. See also *Unitatis Redintegratio* 16.

8

Liturgy and Sacraments

The Church and the sacraments go hand in hand. That is why, in the Gospel of John, the Church is depicted as proceeding forth from the side of the crucified Lord. The water and blood flowing out of the pierced side of Christ are concrete symbols of the sacraments of Baptism and the Eucharist, which together—as sacraments of initiation—incorporate us into the Church, the Body of Christ as the Bride of Christ. Relatedly, we saw how Ratzinger understands the Church primarily from a Eucharistic perspective: the Church is most herself in the celebration of the Eucharistic sacrifice where she becomes the Body of Christ by receiving the Body of Christ. Furthermore, the Eucharist is properly celebrated within the communion of the whole Church. The Church is the proper locus of the sacred liturgy, and the Church is most fundamentally the people of God united through the grace of Christ in their worship of God (vertical communion), which unites them together with one another (horizontal communion).

In a very real way, the individual sacraments are particular means in which the grace of Christ is mediated to us through the Church. As such, they are also instances in which the salvific effect of communion with God, communion with each other, and even the restoration of communion with our own selves (making us whole, integral) is received. In other words, they are specific ways in which the salvation won for us by Christ is made accessible. It is for this reason that they are central to the Church's life, for bringing salvation to the world is the very purpose of the Church's existence.

Because of this, the liturgy and the sacraments are fundamentally important to Ratzinger. This stance is contrasted with a temptation to think that other struggles facing humanity are more pressing. Ratzinger raises that concern and responds to it in the preface to his book *Feast of Faith*. "Faced with the political and social crises of the present time and the moral challenge they offer to Christians, the problems of liturgy and prayer could easily seem to be of second importance. But the question of the moral standards and spiritual resources that we need if we are to acquit ourselves in this situation cannot be separated from the question of worship. . . . Concern for the proper form of worship, therefore, is not peripheral but central to our concern for man himself."[1]

It is precisely for this reason that the current chapter on liturgy and sacraments precedes the following chapter on moral theology. The basic idea is this: unless we are in right relationship with God, which right worship embodies and makes possible, we will be unable to live an authentically moral life. The grace obtained through the worship of God in the sacraments is what enables us to overcome our sinfulness and to live as children of God who reflect the holiness of God. It is not possible to solve moral—including political and social—problems without addressing the crux of man's immorality: sin, which is a destruction of our right relationship with God. God, and the proper worship of him, must be the priority, or nothing else will be rightly ordered.

Because Ratzinger's writings on the liturgy and sacraments are mostly about the Eucharist, that sacrament and its celebration will be our focus in this chapter. Nevertheless, we will begin

---

1. Joseph Ratzinger, *Feast of Faith*, trans. Graham Harrison (San Francisco: Ignatius, 1986), 7.

our considerations with a brief discussion of the three sacraments of initiation in their mutual relation. Then, we will discuss the origin and nature of the Eucharist before we delve into some of Ratzinger's thoughts regarding liturgical celebration, since the way the liturgy is conducted should flow from and reflect the reality of the Eucharist's essence. As Aiden Nichols puts it, "Establishing a healthy liturgical *practice* can only be done on the basis of a sound liturgical *theology*."[2]

SACRAMENTS OF INITIATION

In the Latin Church, the three sacraments of initiation, Baptism, Confirmation, and Eucharist, are given all at once to adult catechumens. In the Eastern Catholic and Eastern Orthodox Churches, all three sacraments of initiation are given during the same liturgy, not only to adults entering the Church but also to infants. That practice was universal in the early Church. For historical and largely practical reasons, that gradually changed in the Latin Church. Nowadays, the three sacraments of initiation for most Roman Rite Catholics are separated by several years, and in many cases, they are not received in the most fitting order. For instance, most Latin Catholics receive Confirmation sometime *after* their First Communion.

Benedict XVI, following the deliberations of a synod of bishops, urges us to rethink our pastoral practice in this regard. He insists that we consider the logical ordering of the sacraments of initiation with respect to our doctrinal understanding.

First, of course, there is the sacrament of Baptism, which is the first sacrament to be received. "The sacrament of Baptism, by which we were conformed to Christ, incorporated into the Church and made children of God, is the portal to all the

2. Aidan Nichols, *The Thought of Benedict XVI: An Introduction to the Theology of Joseph Ratzinger* (New York: Burns & Oates, 2005), 208.

sacraments."[3] The Christian sacrament of Baptism has its precursor in the baptism given by John the Baptist. John's baptism was a baptism of repentance, which included the intent to leave behind one's sinful ways to live a new life of righteousness before God. It included a confession as part of the ritual. "John the baptizer appeared in the wilderness, proclaiming a baptism of repentance for the forgiveness of sins. And people from the whole Judean countryside and all the people of Jerusalem were going out to him, and were baptized by him in the river Jordan, confessing their sins" (Mark 1:4–5). The administration of Baptism reflects this understanding. Immersion in water recalls both death—such as the waters of the flood—and the life-giving character of water exemplified in great rivers such as the Nile and the Jordan itself, where John's baptism was administered. Thus, Baptism represents both death and new life. "Immersion in the water is about purification, about liberation from the filth of the past that burdens and distorts life—it is about beginning again, and that means it is about death and resurrection, about starting life over again anew. So we could say that it is about rebirth."[4]

Due to the repentant character of Baptism, John the Baptist is surprised at Jesus' request to be baptized. Even we today might struggle to understand how the perfectly sinless God-man could enter into a ritual that signified one's repentance of sin. "Then Jesus came from Galilee to John at the Jordan, to be baptized by him. John would have prevented him, saying, 'I need to be baptized by you, and do you come to me?' But Jesus answered him, 'Let it be so now; for it is proper for us in this way to fulfill all righteousness.' Then he consented" (Matt. 3:13–15).

Benedict XVI offers an intriguing explanation of this scene. First, the pope notes that the precise word used for "now" expresses

---

3. Benedict XVI, *Sacramentum Caritatis* 17, post-synodal apostolic exhortation, February 22, 2007 (Washington, DC: United States Conference of Catholic Bishops, 2007).

4. Benedict XVI, *Jesus of Nazareth*, vol. 1, *From the Baptism in the Jordan to the Transfiguration*, trans. Adrian J. Walker (New York: Doubleday, 2007), 16.

a certain hesitancy: "This is a specific, temporary situation that calls for a specific way of acting."[5] Jesus does not need Baptism himself; he does it for us. Benedict's interpretation is reminiscent of the soteriology discussed in chapter 6. Jesus is associating himself with sinful humanity who need to be made righteous. His baptism is a means of vicariously representing us. "Jesus loaded the burden of all mankind's guilt upon his shoulders; he bore it down into the depths of the Jordan. . . . The whole significance of Jesus' Baptism, the fact that he bears 'all righteousness,' first comes to light on the Cross: The Baptism is an acceptance of death for the sins of humanity, and the voice that calls out 'This is my beloved Son' over the baptismal waters is an anticipatory reference to the Resurrection"; that is why, in other contexts, "Jesus uses the word *baptism* to refer to his death (cf. Mk 10:38; Lk 12:50)."[6] Jesus' baptism is the hermeneutical key for understanding Christian Baptism. In our own Baptism, we enter into the death of Christ in the hope of rising with him.

Baptism incorporates us into Christ, which—in turn—calls us to share in Jesus' *pro-existence*. As Roland Millare explains, "Communion with Jesus Christ redefines our identity; consequently, divinization marks the end of our exodus of love because communion with Christ enables the human person to enter into the dynamic of existing 'for' others."[7]

Baptism is, then, of fundamental importance in the life of faith, incorporating us into the Body of Christ, the Church. Yet, it is not the highpoint of Christian initiation. Indeed, as Pope Benedict teaches, Baptism "makes us part of the one Body of Christ (cf. *1 Cor* 12:13), a priestly people. Still, it is our participation in the Eucharistic sacrifice which perfects within us the gifts given to us at Baptism. . . . The Holy Eucharist, then, brings

5. Benedict XVI, *Jesus of Nazareth*, 1:17.
6. Benedict XVI, 1:18.
7. Roland Millare, *A Living Sacrifice: Liturgy and Eschatology in Joseph Ratzinger* (Steubenville, OH: Emmaus Academic, 2022), 104.

Christian initiation to completion and represents the center and goal of all sacramental life."[8] The Eucharist perfects the graces given in Baptism, which are a fruit of the cross and Resurrection. Thus, the Eucharist, too, is connected to the *pro-existence* of Christ. As Millare attests, "The call to a life of 'pro-existence' is a fulfillment of the Eucharistic personalism described by Ratzinger. The human person is called to live a life 'for' others. In view of the reality of the communion that the faithful received with Baptism, which is deepened by the Eucharist, Christians are called to live in communion with other people."[9] The Eucharist is therefore communal.

Because the Eucharist is seen as the apex and perfection of the sacraments of initiation, Benedict XVI asks whether the concrete practices within the Latin Church correspond most appropriately to the theological relation between the sacraments of initiation. If the Eucharist is the high point and perfection of the initiation process, then ideally, it should be the final sacrament of initiation to be received. Benedict thus calls upon bishops to consider their current practices, to examine whether they aptly reflect and correspond to the proper relation between these three sacraments. "Concretely, it needs to be seen which practice better enables the faithful to put the sacrament of the Eucharist at the center, as the goal of the whole process of initiation. In close collaboration with the competent offices of the Roman Curia, Bishops' Conferences should examine the effectiveness of current approaches to Christian initiation."[10] Again, the implied suggestion is that the sacrament of Confirmation be administered earlier, before First Communion, so that the Eucharist can rightly be perceived and experienced as the summit of Christian initiation for Catholics born into the faith as infants just as it is for those who convert as adults.

8. Benedict XVI, *Sacramentum Caritatis* 17.

9. Millare, *Living Sacrifice*, 106.

10. Benedict XVI, *Sacramentum Caritatis* 18.

THE ORIGIN AND NATURE OF THE EUCHARIST

At bottom, the Eucharist is the Church's participation in Christ's self-sacrifice, where the members of the Church offer themselves along with Christ to the Father in the Holy Spirit. As Ratzinger asserts, "The eucharistic prayer is an entering-in to the prayer of Jesus Christ himself; hence it is the Church's entering-in to the Logos, the Father's Word, into the Logos' self-surrender to the Father, which, in the Cross, has also become the surrender of mankind to him."[11] The celebration of the Eucharist enables us to enter into the Paschal Mystery. "Jesus is the *true* paschal lamb who freely gave himself in sacrifice for us, and thus brought about the new and eternal covenant. The Eucharist contains this radical newness, which is offered to us again at every celebration."[12]

It is important to note that the Eucharistic liturgy is not a man-made ceremony but a divinely instituted reality that we are commanded to enact. Furthermore, the liturgy is first of all God's action. As Nichols explains, "Where members of a group make themselves the true acting subject of the liturgy, both the common subject (the Church) and the transcendent Subject (God) disappear from view. People forget that the liturgy is *opus Dei*, the work of God. First and foremost it is he who is active in it, and we, the worshipers, become redeemed people only because that is so."[13] The liturgy is God's gift to us, a share in his saving grace that he has established. It is not something that we ourselves have invented to suit our own purposes.

Jesus, the Incarnate Word, God the Son, instituted the Eucharist at the Last Supper. Jesus explicitly connects the Last Supper to the Passover: "He said to them, 'I have eagerly desired to eat this Passover with you before I suffer'" (Luke 22:15). He then commanded the Apostles to continue to celebrate the Eucharist: "Then he took the loaf of bread, and when he had

11. Ratzinger, *Feast of Faith*, 37.
12. Benedict XVI, *Sacramentum Caritatis* 9.
13. Nichols, *Thought of Benedict XVI*, 214–215.

given thanks, he broke it and gave it to them saying, 'This is my body, which is given for you. Do this in remembrance of me'" (Luke 22:19). The Eucharist, then, was established by God, by Jesus himself, with the express desire that it continue in the life of the Church, in a way similar to the continued celebration of the Passover in Judaism.

The Passover is also tied to the Mosaic covenant on Mount Sinai, which is alluded to at the Last Supper. As Millare explains, "The words of institution from the Markan tradition refer explicitly to the Old Covenant of Mount Sinai (Exod 24) as all four accounts make reference to blood. As Moses sprinkled blood upon the altar at Mount Sinai he proclaimed, 'Behold the blood of the covenant which the LORD has made with you in accordance with all these words' (Exod 24:8)."[14] Thus, the Eucharist is also the enacting of a covenant. The result is "an utterly concrete—and corporeal—community with this incarnate human being, Jesus, and hence with his divine mystery."[15] This, of course, harkens back to the last chapter on ecclesiology: the Eucharist makes the Church, the people of the New Covenant in Jesus' Blood.

This raises an additional point. The Last Supper, while rooted in the Passover and the Old Covenant established at Mount Sinai, is also new. The old Passover required the sacrifice of a lamb to be eaten. "Jesus," however, Benedict explains, "celebrated the Passover without a lamb—no, not without a lamb: instead of the lamb he gave himself, his Body and his Blood."[16] In doing so, Jesus supplies that which a mere animal could never truly give: redemption. As Ratzinger relates, "'*This is my Body, this is my Blood*': these are expressions taken from the Israelite language of sacrifice, which designated the gifts offered in sacrifice to God in

14. Millare, *Living Sacrifice*, 69. Here, Millare quotes from Joseph Ratzinger, *Many Religions—One Covenant* (San Francisco: Ignatius, 1999), 58.

15. Ratzinger, *Many Religions*, 60. See also Millare, *A Living Sacrifice*, 70.

16. Benedict XVI, *Heart of the Christian Life: Thoughts on Holy Mass* (San Francisco: Ignatius, 2010), 89.

the Temple. If Jesus makes use of these words, then he is designating *himself* as *the true and ultimate sacrifice*, in whom all these unsuccessful strivings of the Old Testament are fulfilled. What had always been intended and could never be achieved in the Old Testament sacrifices is incorporated in him."[17]

Notice here that Ratzinger is attributing to Jesus the fulfillment not just of the Passover sacrifice but of all the sacrifices of Israel. Drawing from the groundbreaking scholarship of Hartmut Gese, Ratzinger points to a specific Old Covenant sacrifice that is particularly illuminating and strikingly related to the Eucharist: the *toda* sacrifice. What is *toda* exactly? Relevant to its connection with the Eucharist, it is a sacrifice of *thanksgiving*. As Ratzinger elaborates:

> Gese describes it like this: "The thanksgiving sacrifice presupposes a particular *situation*. If a man is saved from death, from fatal illness or from those who seek his life, he celebrates this divine deliverance in a service of thanksgiving which marks an existential new start in his life. In it, he "confesses" . . . God to be his deliverer by celebrating a thankoffering. . . . He invites his friends and associates, provides the sacrificial animal . . . and celebrates . . . together with his invited guests, the inauguration of his new existence. . . . In order to recall God's deliverance and give thanks for it, it is necessary to reflect on one's pilgrimage through suffering, to bring to mind the process of redemption.[18]

What is more, the *toda* sacrifice was prominent during Jesus' lifetime. Additionally, some of the Psalms are connected to the *toda* as to their living context. Four of these Psalms are referred to in the New Testament as testimonies to Christ. The results of Gese's

17. Joseph Ratzinger, *God Is Near Us: The Eucharist, the Heart of Life*, ed. Stephan Otto Horn and Vinzenz Pfnür, trans. Henry Taylor (San Francisco: Ignatius, 2003), 32.

18. Ratzinger, *Feast of Faith*, 55.

study is profound. As Ratzinger explains, "Gese analyzes Psalms 69; 51; 40:1–12 and 22—the great christological psalms of the New Testament. (Indeed, for the evangelists, Psalm 22 became a textbook on the Passion of Christ.) From the context revealed by Gese, it is clear that what we have here is not some retrospective application of Old Testament words to an event, transforming and 'theologizing' it: the Passion and Resurrection of Jesus *is toda*. It is the real fulfillment of the words of these psalms at a new depth."[19] In light of this, the very word *Eucharist* (which means thanksgiving) is abundantly appropriate. For through the Passion of Christ, in his death, we are given access to a new, resurrected life, for which we give thanks to Almighty God.

Furthermore, there are other aspects of the *toda* that correspond to the Eucharist. For one, "*Toda* is the only form of sacrifice which is concerned with unleavened bread."[20] Additionally, rabbinic tradition predicts that the *toda* is the sole, everlasting sacrifice. "The *toda* of Jesus vindicates the rabbinic dictum: 'In the coming (Messianic) time, all sacrifices will cease except the *toda* sacrifice. This will never cease in all eternity.'"[21] This rabbinic prognostication has come true *de facto*, since the temple sacrifices have ceased, while the Eucharist has continued and will forever continue.

Both the Passover and the *toda* include a sacrificial dimension as well as a meal dimension. In the twentieth century, scholars were divided on which dimension has the greater emphasis. Although Ratzinger was heavily influenced by Romano Guardini's work[22]—even using a title of one of Guardini's books as the title of his own (*The Spirit of the Liturgy*)—he parts ways with Guardini on this issue. Whereas Guardini had emphasized the Eucharist

19. Ratzinger, 54.
20. Ratzinger, 56.
21. Ratzinger, 58.
22. See Joseph Ratzinger, *The Spirit of the Liturgy*, trans. John Saward (San Francisco: Ignatius, 2000), 7.

as a meal, Ratzinger sees sacrifice as the primordial reality of the Eucharist. According to Ratzinger, "The idea of sacrifice unquestionably enters into the Last Supper event through the concept of 'blood of the covenant': the liturgy of the life and death of Jesus Christ is interpreted as a covenantal sacrifice, which adopts the Mosaic first step at a higher level and directs it to its authentic meaning."[23] The Last Supper anticipated the death of Christ on the cross, and it draws its meaning from Jesus' self-offering, his sacrifice. Millare explains that "the Eucharist re-presents the sacrifice of the Cross drawing the faithful into this sacrifice so that they might make the sacrificial love paradigmatic for their own lives."[24]

By contrast, while the Last Supper obviously took place within the setting of a meal, this specific dimension is not the core of the Eucharist, and the meal aspect has been significantly reduced. As Ratzinger shows, "The meal element is not simply excluded, for *eucharistia* is *also* (but not solely) the grace said before the sacred meal. But the meal symbolism is subordinated to a larger whole and integrated into it."[25] Rausch writes that Ratzinger "turns to the work of Joseph Jungmann to show that the basic structure of the Eucharist was not the meal. . . . Indeed, he argues that, after 1 Corinthians 11:20, the Eucharist was not referred to as a meal again until the sixteenth century."[26] For context, here is a fuller quote from the First Letter to the Corinthians: "When you come together, it is not really to eat the Lord's supper. For when the time comes to eat, each of you goes ahead with your own supper, and one goes hungry and another becomes drunk. What!

---

23. Joseph Ratzinger, *Theology of the Liturgy: The Sacramental Foundation of Christian Existence*, in *Joseph Ratzinger Collected Works*, ed. Michael J. Miller, trans. John Saward et al. (San Francisco: Ignatius, 2014), 11:212. See also Millare, *Living Sacrifice*, 71.

24. Millare, *Living Sacrifice*, 72. This view corresponds precisely to what was said in chapter 6 about how the communion between the human will and the divine will in Christ provides an exemplar for the disciples of Christ.

25. Ratzinger, *Feast of Faith*, 38.

26. Thomas P. Rausch, *Pope Benedict XVI: An Introduction to His Theological Vision* (New York: Paulist, 2009), 123–124. See Ratzinger, *Feast of Faith*, 36–37.

Do you not have homes to eat and drink in?" (1 Cor. 11:20–22). The argument—defended through Jungmann's study of ancient liturgical texts as well as by appeal to patristic sources—is that the Eucharist, since apostolic times, was no longer celebrated in the context of a full-fledged meal. Thus, as Ratzinger remarks, "The Last Supper is the foundation of the dogmatic content of the Christian Eucharist, not of its liturgical form."[27] He says a little later in the same text that "first of all it is clear that Jesus' command to repeat the action does not refer to the Last Supper as a whole at all, but to the specifically eucharistic action. Thus the Last Supper was not repeated, and this in itself caused a change in the overall structure and gave birth to a specifically Christian form. An ordinary meal precedes the eucharistic celebration; the eucharistic acts, now joined together, follow in the form of a distinct action, framed and heightened by the prayer of thanksgiving, *eucharistia*."[28] According to Ratzinger, the biblical theology of the liturgy as well as the entire history of the liturgy point to sacrifice as the primary essence of the liturgy over against the meal aspect.

Emphasizing meal over sacrifice debases the liturgy, in Ratzinger's view: "To speak of the Eucharist as the community meal is to cheapen it, for its price was the death of Christ."[29] The fundamental reality of the Eucharist is the participation and reception of Christ's self-sacrifice for our redemption.

To go a step further, Benedict XVI sees in the Eucharist not just a share in Christ but also a gift of the whole Trinity to us. "The Eucharist reveals the loving plan that guides all of salvation history (cf. *Eph* 1:10; 3:8–11). There the *Deus Trinitas*, who is essentially love (cf. *1 Jn* 4:7–8), becomes fully a part of our human

---

27. Ratzinger, *Feast of Faith*, 41.

28. Ratzinger, 42–43. See also Ratzinger, *Spirit of the Liturgy*, 78: "True, the Lord established the new reality of Christian worship within the framework of a Jewish (Passover) meal, but it was precisely this new reality, not the meal as such, that he commanded us to repeat."

29. Ratzinger, *Feast of Faith*, 65.

condition. In the bread and wine under whose appearances Christ gives himself to us in the paschal meal (cf. *Lk* 22:14–20; *1 Cor* 11:23–26), God's whole life encounters us and is sacramentally shared with us"; and God's life is one of loving communion: "God is a perfect communion of love between Father, Son and Holy Spirit."[30] Therefore, the Eucharist is a participation in Trinitarian communion; it gives us access to the vertical relationship with God that also draws us into communion with one another as the Church. As Ratzinger explains, "The sacrificial character of this meal has a twofold significance: it expresses communion with God, in whose sacrifice people are permitted to share, and communion among the participants; these two things correspond to the saving fact that *shalom* reigns among those who are in the sacrificial meal."[31] Here, the sacrament of the Eucharist is understood in direct connection with the Trinity, with Christology and soteriology, and with ecclesiology.

The Eucharist is also connected to eschatology. As Tracey Rowland remarks, Vatican II "emphasized that the earthly liturgy is an anticipation of the heavenly one, so that at the same time as it renews the Paschal mystery it anticipates the consummation of the work of redemption and the renewal of the cosmos at the end of time."[32] To understand this connection, it is helpful to consider the patristic triad of shadow, image, and reality. Millare explains that "typically, the shadow represents a type in the Old Testament that foreshadows an image in the New Testament. Reality represents what will be revealed by the eschaton and fulfills what is anticipated by the image. Ratzinger applies this patristic idea to liturgy."[33] In this vein, Ratzinger sees the liturgy as uniting past, present, and future. "If the essence of the past is not simply

---

30. Benedict XVI, *Sacramentum Caritatis* 8.

31. Ratzinger, *Feast of Faith*, 53.

32. Tracey Rowland, *Ratzinger's Faith: The Theology of Benedict XVI* (New York: Oxford University Press, 2008), 123–124.

33. Millare, *Living Sacrifice*, 77.

a thing of the past but the far-reaching power of what follows in the present, then the future, too, is present in what happens in the liturgy: it ought to be called, in its essence, an anticipation of what is to come."[34] What is celebrated in the Eucharist will reach its full reality in the eschaton, in the heavenly kingdom at the end of this present age. To this end, Ratzinger remarks, "The Christ-event and the growth of the Church out of all the nations, the transition from Temple sacrifice to universal worship 'in spirit and truth', is the first important step across the frontier, a step toward the fulfillment of the promises of the Old Testament. But it is obvious that hope has not yet fully attained its goal. The New Jerusalem needs no Temple because Almighty God and the Lamb are themselves its temple. . . . But this City is not yet here."[35] Applying this directly to the liturgy, Ratzinger continues, "This idea of the New Testament as the between-time, as image between shadow and reality, gives liturgical theology its specific form."[36]

Therefore, while the liturgy is a memorial (remembrance) of the sacrifice of Christ on Calvary (the past), it is also—as Benedict teaches—"a real foretaste of the eschatological fulfillment for which every human being and all creation are destined (cf. *Rom* 8:19ff.)."[37] Thus, "Eucharist is ordered to eschatology."[38] The very purpose of the sacrificial character of the Eucharist—communion with the cross of Christ—is precisely because of the cross' power to lead to Resurrection. Ratzinger explains it thusly: "The novel Christian reality is this: Christ's Resurrection enables man genuinely to rejoice. . . . That is why the Christian liturgy—Eucharist—is, of its essence, the Feast of the Resurrection, *Mysterium*

---

34. Ratzinger, *Theology of the Liturgy*, 33. See Millare, *Living Sacrifice*, 78: "The liturgy is inherently ('in its essence') eschatological."

35. Ratzinger, *Spirit of the Liturgy*, 54.

36. Ratzinger, 54.

37. Benedict XVI, *Sacramentum Caritatis* 30.

38. Ratzinger, *Feast of Faith*, 65.

Paschae. As such it bears within it the mystery of the Cross, which is the inner presupposition of the Resurrection."[39]

Through Christ's death and Resurrection, we too can come to eternal life, which is the *telos* of the Eucharist as a mysterious participation in the liturgy of heaven. "Consequently, every eucharistic celebration sacramentally accomplishes the eschatological gathering of the People of God. For us, the eucharistic banquet is a real foretaste of the final banquet foretold by the prophets (cf. *Is* 25:6–9) and described in the New Testament as 'the marriage-feast of the Lamb' (*Rev* 19:7–9), to be celebrated in the joy of the communion of saints."[40] When carried out properly, "Worship gives us a share in heaven's mode of existence. . . . In this sense, worship . . . has the character of anticipation. It lays hold in advance of a more perfect life and, in so doing, gives our present life its proper measure."[41] As Millare expresses it, "Communion with the *Logos* in the celebration of the liturgy enables a person to be contemporaneous with the eternal liturgy, in which every member of the communion of the Church and the communion of the saints participates."[42]

LITURGICAL PRACTICE

The above considerations about the essence of the liturgy are a necessary precursor to any authentic discussion of what ought to be done in practice. How the liturgy is celebrated should flow from and correspond to what the liturgy *is*. As we have seen in multiple other contexts, here too there is a primacy of ontology and the related primacy of truth over praxis. In a way analogous to

---

39. Ratzinger, 65.

40. Benedict XVI, *Sacramentum Caritatis* 31.

41. Ratzinger, *Spirit of the Liturgy*, 21.

42. Millare, *Living Sacrifice*, 207. Here, Millare is commenting on Ratzinger, *Theology of the Liturgy*, 43: The Eucharistic liturgy "brings heaven into the community assembled on earth, or, rather, it takes that community beyond itself into the communion of saints of all times and places."

sinful humanity's refusal to correspond to human nature as God created it, the refusal to worship in the liturgy after the pattern established by God and in a way that befits the heavenly realities made present in the liturgy is a failure to correspond to reality.

Hence, Ratzinger insists on the fact that the liturgy is no mere human invention. "Man himself cannot simply 'make' worship."[43] Rather, "real liturgy implies that God responds and reveals how we can worship him. In any form, liturgy includes some kind of 'institution'. It cannot spring from imagination, our own creativity—then it would remain just a cry in the dark or mere self-affirmation. Liturgy implies a real relationship with Another, who reveals himself to us and gives our existence a new direction."[44] The manner that the liturgy is celebrated ought to reflect these realities.

This current section of the chapter aims to provide just a brief overview of some of the specifics of this principle in relation to concrete practice. Topics to be touched upon include Church art and architecture, liturgical music, and the direction of prayer in the liturgy. Additionally, Ratzinger's understanding of active participation in the liturgy will be discussed. Finally, we will treat a key theme in Ratzinger's liturgical theology that connects it directly with his moral thought, which is treated in the next chapter.

First, one's understanding of the essence of the liturgy has its effects on one's understanding of the place of worship: the building in which it is to be celebrated. We have already seen that Ratzinger rejects the notion that the Eucharist is primarily a meal. He connects a misunderstanding on this point with practical mistakes with regard to ecclesial architecture. Speaking of "progressives" who emphasize the Eucharist as a meal, Ratzinger describes their (misguided) conclusion: "The watchword that emerges from such reflections is: desacralization. The Lord's Supper should once

43. Ratzinger, *Spirit of the Liturgy*, 21.
44. Ratzinger, 22.

more become a simple, human, everyday meal. And from that there followed, for instance, the conclusion that it is not really right to have a church building, but we should have a multi-purpose area, so that the Lord's Supper can truly be held in an everyday setting and not be elevated into a cultic ritual."[45] This mentality, Ratzinger believes, was carried out in practice in many places, which explains the banality of many contemporary church buildings. Thus, an accurate understanding of the essence of the liturgy has a direct impact on the question of churches' physical structure.

For Ratzinger, the architecture of a church building should keep in mind both the continuity with the Old Covenant and the newness of the New Covenant. The church building has its Old Covenant precursors in two different Jewish buildings: the synagogue and the temple. Central to both was the ark of the covenant (in the Holy of Holies in the pre-exilic temple) or its representative, the shrine of the Torah (in the synagogue). In this way, the synagogue was understood in connection with the temple.[46]

The synagogue was where "the service of the word was celebrated, the Holy Scriptures were read, the Psalms were sung, people joined in praising God, hearing the Word of God interpreted, and making petitions to God."[47] Obviously, the synagogue relates to the part of the liturgy referred to as the Liturgy of the Word. Structurally, the synagogue had two foci: the seat of Moses and, as already mentioned, the shrine of the Torah. In Christian

---

45. Ratzinger, *God Is Near Us*, 57.

46. See Ratzinger, *Spirit of the Liturgy*, 64–65. Particularly noteworthy here is how Ratzinger sees this connection between synagogue and temple as negating any sense of independence of the local community from the universal community, which is reminiscent of his understanding of the local and universal Church: "Now the furnishing of the synagogue with an 'Ark of the Covenant' does not in any way signify that the local community has become, so to speak, independent, self-sufficient. No, it is the place where the local community reaches out beyond itself to the Temple, to the commonality of the one People of God as defined by the one God" (65). For this chapter of his book, Ratzinger draws heavily from Louis Bouyer, *Architecture et liturgie* (Paris: Cerf, 1991); available in English as Louis Bouyer, *Liturgy and Architecture* (Notre Dame, IN: University of Notre Dame Press, 1967).

47. Ratzinger, *God Is Near Us*, 63.

architecture these two focal points are reflected in the bishop's chair (*cathedra*) and the throne of the Gospel.[48]

The temple was the place of sacrificial worship. Early Christians (before they were excluded by the Jewish communities) continued for a time to participate in the synagogue services. "After the Resurrection of Jesus," however, "his followers ceased to take part in the sacrificial cult in the Temple. . . . In place of the Temple there is the Eucharist, since Christ is the true Paschal Lamb; everything that took place in the Temple has been fulfilled in him."[49]

Accordingly, the church building has something that the synagogue did not have: an altar. For, in the Old Covenant, only the temple was the place for cultic sacrifice. Now, the Eucharist, which is primarily a sacrifice (as we have seen), necessitates an altar for the sacrifice.[50]

While in the Old Covenant there were two buildings that together served as the Jewish places of worship, in the New Covenant, there is one place that reflects both the synagogue and the temple. "Thus, in early church buildings, the liturgy has two places. First, the Liturgy of the Word takes place at the center of the building. The faithful are grouped around the *bema*, the elevated area where the throne of the Gospel, the seat of the bishop, and the lectern are located. The Eucharistic celebration proper takes place in the apse, at the altar, which the faithful 'stand around'. Everyone joins with the celebrant in facing east, toward the Lord who is to come."[51]

Later, we will discuss the geographic orientation of the buildings, but first, let us consider their ornamentation. Due to the commandment not to make graven images, some people have

---

48. See Ratzinger, *Spirit of the Liturgy*, 71–72.

49. Ratzinger, *God Is Near Us*, 63.

50. See Ratzinger, *Spirit of the Liturgy*, 70.

51. Ratzinger, 72. The last sentence in this quote already anticipates what will be said later about the direction of liturgical worship.

concluded "that only non-figurative, geometrical designs are permitted in the ornamentation of the sanctuary."[52] However, that is due to a misunderstanding as well as a degree of ignorance regarding the standard practice for synagogue decoration in the time of Jesus and beyond. As Ratzinger remarks, "In the Judaism at the time of Jesus and well into the third century, a much more generous interpretation of the image-question developed. . . . As a result of archeological discoveries, we now know that the ancient synagogues were richly decorated with representations of scenes from the Bible. They were by no means regarded as mere images of past events . . . but as a narrative (*Haggadah*), which, while calling something to mind, makes it present."[53] The ornamentation of Christian churches, then, is actually a point of continuity with the practice of the ancient Jewish faith. This practice was celebrated in the very early Church, as evidenced by the images present in the Christian catacombs.

In response to the iconoclast controversy, the seventh ecumenical council (Nicaea II, AD 787) "and all the following councils concerned with icons regard it as a confession of faith in the Incarnation and iconoclasm as a denial of the Incarnation, as the summation of all heresies."[54] Thus, there is a Christological basis for the use of sacred images as well, rooted in the fact that Christ has become man, has become Incarnate.

Relatedly, Ratzinger sees beauty as an appropriate aspect of the liturgy, corresponding to its very nature. Millare writes that "Ratzinger maintains the central role beauty plays in serving as an outward sign of the mystery of Christ and the heavenly Jerusalem present within the sacred liturgy."[55] Benedict XVI expresses this view in *Sacramentum Caritatis*. After referring to God's love as the "truest beauty," which is revealed especially through the Paschal

52. Ratzinger, 116.
53. Ratzinger, 116–117.
54. Ratzinger, 122.
55. Millare, *Living Sacrifice*, 212–213.

Mystery, he goes on to say, "The beauty of the liturgy is part of this mystery; it is a sublime expression of God's glory and, in a certain sense, a glimpse of heaven on earth. . . . Beauty, then, is not mere decoration, but rather an essential element of the liturgical action, since it is an attribute of God himself and his revelation."[56] Therefore, in a paragraph encouraging proper formation in the history of sacred art and architecture (specifically mentioning paintings and sculptures), Benedict XVI states plainly, "Everything related to the Eucharist should be marked by beauty. Special respect and care must also be given to the vestments, the furnishings and the sacred vessels, so that by their harmonious and orderly arrangement they will foster awe for the mystery of God, manifest the unity of the faith and strengthen devotion."[57]

In chapter 1 of this book, we saw how Ratzinger was enamored with the liturgy from a young age. Included in this was the awe-inspiring experiences of beautiful architecture and sacred images. No doubt, his own experience of how this beauty can lead one to God was formative for his theology of liturgy and sacred art as evidenced in his writings.

Of course, for Ratzinger, sacred music ought to be included in the discussion of liturgical beauty. "With regard to the singing of the Church, we notice the same pattern of continuity and renewal that we have seen in the nature of the liturgy in general, in church architecture, and in sacred images."[58]

Ratzinger begins a chapter on music and liturgy by pointing to the fact that some form of the word "to sing" is found 309 times in the Old Testament and thirty-six times in the New Testament. The first time that singing is mentioned in the Bible is after the crossing of the Red Sea, and thus in the context of the

---

56. Benedict XVI, *Sacramentum Caritatis* 35. It should be noted that Benedict XVI here also includes the manner of liturgical celebration (liturgical action) under the issue of beauty. The external, visible actions should—in a beautiful manner—reflect the heavenly realities being made present.

57. *Sacramentum Caritatis* 41.

58. Ratzinger, *Spirit of the Liturgy*, 139.

Exodus. The Resurrection of Christ is seen as the new Exodus and is thus also a cause for singing. Of course, the Psalms are another witness to the importance of singing in worship.[59] In fact, "The Church has been singing since the time of Jesus and the apostles, for they sang in the synagogue and brought that singing into the Church."[60] As Ratzinger says elsewhere, "Liturgy and music have been closely related to one another from their earliest beginnings."[61]

In principle, then, liturgical music is warranted: "The People of God assembled for the liturgy sings the praises of God. In the course of her two-thousand-year history, the Church has created, and still creates, music and songs which represent a rich patrimony of faith and love."[62]

However, the question arises: What kind of music befits the liturgy? From Ratzinger's perspective, "pop" and "rock" are not suitable. "Pop" music "is aimed at the phenomenon of the masses, is industrially produced, and ultimately has to be described as a cult of the banal. 'Rock', on the other hand, is the expression of elemental passions . . . in opposition to Christian worship."[63] As Nichols explains, "Nor can it [the liturgy] employ those modes of musical expression which belong essentially to political or erotic arousal, or the simple desire to entertain."[64] From this viewpoint, Benedict insists that one "cannot say that one song is as good as another. Generic improvisation or the introduction of musical genres which fail to respect the meaning of the liturgy should be avoided."[65]

In his book *The Spirit of the Liturgy*, Ratzinger outlines three

59. See Ratzinger, 136–139.

60. Ratzinger, *Feast of Faith*, 102.

61. Joseph Ratzinger, "Liturgy and Sacred Music," *Communio* 13, no. 4 (Winter 1986): 377. See also Nichols, *Theology of Benedict XVI*, 213.

62. Benedict XVI, *Sacramentum Caritatis* 42.

63. Ratzinger, *Spirit of the Liturgy*, 148. See also Ratzinger, *Feast of Faith*, 118–119.

64. Nichols, *Thought of Benedict XVI*, 217.

65. Benedict XVI, *Sacramentum Caritatis* 42.

principles for liturgical music, based on its need to be related to *logos*. First, liturgical music should be tied to the biblical witness of salvation history. "In liturgical music, based as it is on biblical faith, there is, therefore, a clear dominance of the Word; this music is a higher form of proclamation. . . . The biblical and liturgical texts are the normative words from which liturgical music has to take its bearings."[66]

Second, liturgical music should reflect its roots in the *logos* by exemplifying "an ultimate sobriety, a deeper rationality, resisting any decline into irrationality and immoderation."[67] As an example, he contrasts two types of music delineated by Plato: one that "draws senses into spirit and so brings man to wholeness. . . . It elevates the spirit precisely by wedding it to the senses, and it elevates the senses by uniting them with the spirit"; the other "drags man into the intoxication of the senses, crushes rationality, and subjects the spirit to the senses."[68] The former kind is appropriate; the latter is to be avoided.

This principle means that music itself must be transformed before being adopted into the liturgy. Ratzinger posits that "the taking up of music into the liturgy must be its taking up into the Spirit, a transformation which implies both death and resurrection. That is why the Church has had to be critical of all ethnic music; it could not be allowed untransformed into the sanctuary. . . . Pagan music often endeavors to elicit an ecstasy of the senses, but without elevating the senses into the spirit."[69] In this vein, while he affirms *Sacrosanctum Concilium* in its encouragement of allowing a place in the liturgy for musical traditions from various (especially missionary) lands, he complements it with the principle outlined in *Ad Gentes* that the customs and cultures of various places should be retained but also purified and elevated

66. Ratzinger, *Spirit of the Liturgy*, 149.
67. Ratzinger, 150.
68. Ratzinger, 150.
69. Ratzinger, *Feast of Faith*, 118.

through the Gospel. In other words, not just any cultural music is admissible in the liturgy. Music must be developed that is suited to the liturgy. He writes, "Not every kind of music can have a place in Christian worship. It has its standards, and that standard is the Logos."[70]

Third, since the Incarnate Word is the meaning of the whole universe, there is a cosmic and communal dimension to liturgical music, which joins in the song of the angels, exemplified especially in the trisagion: "Holy, Holy, Holy." Ratzinger thinks this principle is reflected in the mathematics of music as elaborated by St. Augustine, who appealed to Pythagoras: "The beauty of music depends on its conformity to the rhythmic and harmonic laws of the universe."[71]

Benedict XVI applies these principles in his encouragement for one specific type of music, at least in the Roman Rite. "I desire, in accordance with the request advanced by the Synod Fathers, that Gregorian chant be suitably esteemed and employed as the chant proper to the Roman liturgy."[72] There is a reason for this. It must be remembered that Gregorian chant was created precisely *for* the liturgy. It is a liturgical genre that flows from a liturgical context and, in this way, is particularly suited for it. Something similar can be said for other types of sacred music. When speaking about the ability to purify cultural music traditions so that they may be suitable for the liturgy, Ratzinger exhorts us to recall that such a process took place in Europe. He finds it frustrating that a push for "inculturation" has been accompanied by some sort of disdain for European inculturation. "It is strange however that, in their legitimate delight in the new openness to other cultures, many people seem to have forgotten that the countries of Europe also have a musical inheritance which 'plays a great part in their religious and social life'! Indeed,

70. Ratzinger, *Spirit of the Liturgy*, 151.
71. Ratzinger, 152.
72. Benedict XVI, *Sacramentum Caritatis* 42.

here we have a musical tradition which has sprung from the very heart of the Church and her faith."[73] That last part is crucial. Much of traditional European liturgical music was not the mere cultural appropriation of music into the liturgy. Over centuries, European culture itself was Christianized; it became a *Christian* culture and as part of that process developed specifically *Christian* art forms, including liturgical music. The Christianization of the culture in many ways preceded the generation of the rich artistic and musical patrimony of the European Church, which is why it is particularly befitting the liturgy. In fact, Ratzinger contends, "Next to the saints, the art which the Church has produced is the only real 'apologia' for her history."[74] Ratzinger is careful to note that he is not equating European church music with the music of the Church absolutely speaking, but he is holding up that rich history as an example of how proper purification of music can take place before adopting it in the liturgy, and, along with *Sacrosanctum Concilium*, is exhorting the Church to preserve that rich patrimony and not toss it aside.[75]

There is an aspect of liturgical music that connects to the issue of the direction of liturgical worship. In agreement with St. Jerome, Ratzinger affirms that "liturgical music must be humble, for its aim is not applause but 'edification'. It is appropriate that in church, unlike the concert hall, the musician is for the most part not seen."[76] This notion is embodied in the practice of having a choir loft in the back of the church, so that the musicians themselves do not become a distracting focal point but rather serve a truly supporting role.

Here, we see a connection between the architecture of the church building and the appropriate direction of liturgical prayer. The mix of synagogue and temple elements of the church directly

73. Ratzinger, *Feast of Faith*, 125.
74. Ratzinger, 124.
75. See Ratzinger, 125–126.
76. Ratzinger, 120.

tie into liturgical movement and orientation. The twofold structure of the liturgy renders it fitting to have a twofold directionality of the liturgy. Ratzinger writes, "It was also important clearly to distinguish the place for the Liturgy of the Word from the place for the properly Eucharistic liturgy. For the Liturgy of the Word is about speaking and responding, and so a face-to-face exchange between proclaimer and hearer does make sense. . . . On the other hand, a common turning to the east during the Eucharist Prayer remains essential."[77]

Ratzinger has very strong thoughts about this latter liturgical direction. He sees the postconciliar emphasis on the priest facing the people (*versus populum*) as based on historical inaccuracies tied to a faulty emphasis on the meal aspect of the Liturgy of the Eucharist. He also points out that this postconciliar practice has no basis in *Sacrosanctum Concilium* itself, which does not mention such a change at all. Additionally, the new practice had led to a new form of clericalism that makes the priest the center of attention.[78] Thus, the *versus populum* posture is based upon misunderstandings and has negative consequences. "The turning of the priest toward the people has turned the community into a self-enclosed circle. In its outward form, it no longer opens out on what lies ahead and above, but is closed in on itself."[79]

In Ratzinger's opinion, this orientation is contrary to the theological significance of the Liturgy of the Eucharist. "There is only one inner direction of the Eucharist, namely, from Christ in the Holy Spirit to the Father. . . . The original meaning of what

---

77. Ratzinger, *Spirit of the Liturgy*, 81. N.b.: Here, one could reasonably conclude that Ratzinger approves of the liturgical change in the Novus Ordo in which the Scriptures are read from an ambo, facing the people, rather than from the altar, facing away from the people. In contrast, he is clear that he does not prefer the change of the direction of the Liturgy of the Eucharist.

78. See Ratzinger, 77–80. See also Ratzinger, *Feast of Faith*, 142: "This misunderstanding alone can explain the sweeping triumph of the new celebration facing the people, a change which has taken place with amazing unanimity and speed, without any mandate (and perhaps for that very reason!)."

79. Ratzinger, *Spirit of the Liturgy*, 80.

nowadays is called 'the priest turning his back on the people' is, in fact—as J.A. Jungmann has consistently shown—the priest and people together facing the same way in a common act of trinitarian worship."[80] The meaning of this posture is also tied to the understanding of the Church as the pilgrim people of God, and hence to ecclesiology. The liturgical direction is a matter of "priest and people facing in the same direction, knowing that together they were in a procession toward the Lord. They did not close themselves into a circle; they did not gaze at one another; but as the pilgrim People of God they set off for the *Oriens*, for the Christ who comes to meet us."[81]

As the description of this posture—*ad orientem*—suggests, the traditional direction of the Liturgy of the Eucharist was facing east, priest and people alike. The geographical layout of St. Peter's Basilica meant that in order to face east, the priest was also facing in the direction of the people. This fact has been misconstrued in modern times as indicating that the people and priest should face each other. But there is a fundamental detail that proves this wrong. Quoting Bouyer, Ratzinger writes, "As Professor Cyrille Vogel has recently demonstrated it, the only thing ever insisted upon, or even mentioned [before the sixteenth-century], was that he [the priest] should say the eucharistic prayer, as all the other prayers, facing East. . . . Even when the orientation of the church enabled the celebrant to pray turned toward the people, when at the altar, we must not forget that it was not the priest alone who, then, turned East: it was the whole congregation, together with him."[82]

Why east? While other religions direct their prayers toward a

---

80. Ratzinger, *Feast of Faith*, 140.

81. Ratzinger, *Spirit of the Liturgy*, 80. See also, Ratzinger, *Feast of Faith*, 142, where he talks about *versus populum*, "in which priest and people face each other in a dialogue relationship. This does express one aspect of the Eucharist. But the danger is that it can make the congregation into a closed circle which is no longer aware of the explosive trinitarian dynamism which gives the Eucharist its greatness."

82. Louis Bouyer, *Liturgy and Architecture*, 55–56, quoted in Ratzinger, *Spirit of the Liturgy*, 79.

particular city, the universality of Christianity means that it should not be directed toward a single terrestrial spot. Rather, wherever the liturgy is celebrated, it is appropriate to face east because of its cosmic and eschatological significance. As Ratzinger explains:

> For the true location and the true context of the eucharistic celebration is the whole cosmos. "Facing east" makes this cosmic dimension of the Eucharist present through liturgical gesture. Because of the rising sun, the east—*oriens*—was naturally both a symbol of the Resurrection (and to that extent it was not merely a christological statement but also a reminder of the Father's power and the influence of the Holy Spirit) and presentation of the hope of the parousia. Where priest and people together face the same way, what we have is a cosmic orientation and also an interpretation of the Eucharist in terms of resurrection and trinitarian theology. Hence it is also an interpretation in terms of parousia, a theology of hope, in which every Mass is an approach to the return of Christ.[83]

Early in Christianity, there developed the practice of putting a cross on the eastern wall of the building where people gathered. This practice eventually developed into the practice of placing a cross on the altar. As a result, the symbolism of the cross and the meaning of facing east gradually united.[84] In a church that is not built facing east, the cross can still serve the same meaning of liturgical *orientation*, what some call "liturgical east," even if it is not exactly geographically east. "Where a direct common turning toward the east is not possible, the cross can serve as the interior

---

83. Ratzinger, *Feast of Faith*, 140–141. See also Millare, *Living Sacrifice*, 204. Millare and I both present the same block quote with a similar introduction about the cosmic and eschatological meaning of the *ad orientem* posture. I did not read this part of Millare's book until after I had written my own discussion of this quote. We both thus independently present the same material in this instance (as in other instances).

84. Ratzinger, 141–143.

'east' of faith."[85] For this reason, Ratzinger thinks that even if the priest is facing the people (which is obviously not his theological preference), then "the cross could be placed on the altar in such a way that both priest and people can see it. At the eucharistic prayer they should not look at one another; together they ought to behold him, the Pierced Savior (Zech 12:10; Rev 1:7)."[86]

Millare offers a helpful summary of the multifaceted meaning of *ad orientem* during the Liturgy of the Eucharist: "The eastern direction, which coincides with the direction in which the sun rises, is a symbol simultaneously of the Lord's Resurrection and the hope of the Lord's Second Coming. Worship *ad orientem* is cosmological, Christological, and eschatological. The unified orientation of the people with the priest celebrant in the same direction also underscores the unity of the Body of Christ [and is thus ecclesiological] in worship of the Father, through the Son, in the Holy Spirit."[87] In a very real way, then, the *ad orientem* posture reflects many different aspects of the essence of the liturgy, and consequently it is a praxis truly rooted in and reflective of the truth of the nature of the liturgy.

Additionally, it is important to highlight that Ratzinger's understanding of *ad orientem* includes the congregation. Far from excluding the laity, their role in facing with the priest is incorporated into the symbolism of the gesture, adding content to the posture's meaning. The people are not being ignored by the priest; rather, they are worshiping along with him. Of course, this relates directly to our next and final topic for this section: the meaning of active participation in the liturgy.

In *Sacrosanctum Concilium* 14, the Second Vatican Council urged as a primary principle of liturgical reform the "full and

---

85. Ratzinger, *Spirit of the Liturgy*, 83.

86. Ratzinger, *Feast of Faith*, 144. See also Ratzinger, *The Spirit of the Liturgy*, 83: The cross "should stand in the middle of the altar and be the common point of focus for both priest and praying community."

87. Millare, *Living Sacrifice*, 205.

active participation by all the people." Ratzinger thinks the council was correct in doing so, but he calls for a reflection on what active participation means and does not mean. "Unfortunately, the word was very quickly misunderstood to mean something external, entailing a need for general activity, as if as many people as possible, as often as possible, should be visibly engaged in action."[88] Active participation was falsely equated with frenetic activity and a multiplication of special roles for people to play within the liturgical celebration.

But this view, Ratzinger thinks, cannot be the authentic meaning of the text. For one, if active participation is meant to be for *all*, then it cannot refer to a multiplicity of special roles, because then there would have to be a special role for every single person, which is impossible. On the contrary, Ratzinger insists, "The word 'part-icipation' refers to a principle action in which everyone has a 'part'."[89] In other words, active participation does not mean having several different roles that need to be filled by separate individuals; it means that *all* are called to actively participate in the *same* liturgical action.

What is more, Ratzinger thinks that active participation does not primarily refer to an *external* activity. "No external participation and creativity is of any use unless it is a participation in this inner reality, in the way of the Lord, in God himself."[90]

If active participation does not mean some external, physically tangible role, then what does it refer to? Ratzinger contends that "the real liturgical action, the true liturgical act, is the *oratio*, the great prayer that forms the core of the Eucharistic celebration, the whole of which was, therefore, called *oratio* by the Fathers."[91] What full and active participation means, then, is first and foremost that all the faithful ought to be intently praying, not just

88. Ratzinger, *Spirit of the Liturgy*, 171.
89. Ratzinger, 171.
90. Ratzinger, *Feast of Faith*, 150–151.
91. Ratzinger, *Spirit of the Liturgy*, 172.

with audible words (although *oratio* does connote a public and solemn proclamation) but with their minds and hearts. Furthermore, this prayer is—in its depths—the active acceptance of what *God* is doing. Thus, Ratzinger states, "The real 'action' in the liturgy in which we are all supposed to participate is the action of God himself. . . . True, the Sacrifice of the Logos is accepted already and forever. But we must still pray for it to become *our* sacrifice, that we ourselves, as we said, may be transformed into the Logos (*logisiert*), conformed to the Logos, and so be made the true Body of Christ."[92] Active participation, then, means consciously praying to God in acceptance of the sacrifice of Christ, offering ourselves along with Christ to the Father, so that God's action may be effective in us through his transforming grace. Without that, no liturgical "role" has any significance.

Benedict XVI has repeated this understanding in his official teaching. "It should be made clear that the word 'participation' does not refer to mere external activity during the celebration. In fact, the active participation called for by the Council must be understood in more substantial terms."[93] In support of his interpretation, he offers several quotes from *Sacrosanctum Concilium* 48. The whole paragraph is as follows:

> The Church, therefore, earnestly desires that Christ's faithful, when present at this mystery of faith, should not be there as strangers or silent spectators; on the contrary, through a good understanding of the rites and prayers they should take part in the sacred action conscious of what they are doing, with devotion and full collaboration. They should be instructed by God's word and be nourished at the table of the Lord's body; they should give thanks to God; by offering the Immaculate Victim, not only through the hands of the priest, but also with

92. Ratzinger, 173.
93. Benedict XVI, *Sacramentum Caritatis* 52.

him, they should learn also to offer themselves; through Christ
the Mediator, they should be drawn day by day into ever more
perfect union with God and with each other, so that finally
God may be all in all.[94]

Notice that none of the things enumerated refers to a special role
to play by individuals. All the examples of what active participation means refer to the entire congregation. Part of the "active" participation is actually a conscious "reception" (of God's
word and of the Eucharist). It includes consciously offering Jesus
and oneself to the Father. Interiority is at the core of what active
participation means: interiorizing and spiritually (with mind and
will) aligning oneself with the sacred mysteries in humble openness to transformation in Christ.

WORSHIP ACCORDING TO THE LOGOS

An important concept in Benedict XVI's theology of liturgy that
connects with both his understanding of active participation as
well as with the next chapter on morality is *logiké latreía* (spiritual
worship or worship according to the *logos*). Ratzinger draws this
term from St. Paul's Letter to the Romans: "I appeal to you therefore, brothers and sisters, by the mercies of God, to present your
bodies as a living sacrifice, holy and acceptable to God, which is
your spiritual worship [*logikén latreían*]" (Rom. 12:1).

Active participation in the liturgy has been described first
and foremost as an interior, spiritual (intellectual and volitional)
participation in the prayer addressed to the Father that includes
the active reception of God's offer of grace to us. This participation enables us to be transformed through the grace of Christ
in such a way as to become holy. This transformation ought to

94. Second Vatican Council, *Sacrosanctum Concilium* 48, December 4, 1963, in *The Word on Fire Vatican II Collection*, ed. Matthew Levering (Park Ridge, IL: Word on Fire Institute, 2021), 177–178.

lead to a change in the way we live. Hence, Benedict XVI opens the third and final part of *Sacramentum Caritatis*, "The Eucharist, a Mystery to Be Lived," with a consideration of *logiké latreía*. "Here," he says, "the eucharistic celebration appears in all its power as the source and summit of the Church's life, since it expresses at once both the origin and the fulfillment of the new and definitive worship of God, the *logiké latreía*."[95] By offering our own bodies—our own lives—as a sacrifice to God, we enact what is celebrated in the Eucharist in imitation of Christ's own self-offering to the Father. "Christianity's new worship includes and transfigures every aspect of life. . . . Christians, in all their actions, are called to offer true worship to God. Here the intrinsically eucharistic nature of Christian life begins to take shape. The Eucharist, since it embraces the concrete, everyday existence of the believer, makes possible, day by day, the progressive transformation of all those called by grace to reflect the image of the Son of God (cf. *Rom* 8:29ff.)."[96]

Here, we see the Christological and soteriological aspect of liturgy. As Millare explains: "Every member of the Body of Christ is drawn into the pro-existence of Christ. Hence, the liturgy as a *logiké latreia* is the heart of Ratzinger's theology of liturgy that represents the full implication of the primacy of *logos* for the liturgy and the *ethos* of charity that flows forth from this liturgical *logos*."[97] The loving sacrifice of Christ is something we are called to participate in and to live *for* others. Hence, charity is at the core of proper worship: love of God and love of neighbor. The Eucharist is the sacrament of charity precisely because our reception of the charity of Christ's sacrifice leads to our own charity. As Millare notes, "The liturgy is described by Ratzinger above all as a

---

95. Benedict XVI, *Sacramentum Caritatis* 70.

96. *Sacramentum Caritatis* 71.

97. Millare, *Living Sacrifice*, 171. Here, the main title of Millare's book is seen as an obvious reference to Romans 12:1, bespeaking the importance of this passage in Ratzinger's theology.

logiké latreia; subsequently, the self-giving of Christians becomes identical with Christ's own sacrifice."[98] Our worship of God in the celebration of the sacrifice of the divine liturgy is to be echoed and lived in our daily lives, which means that it leads to morality, a supernatural morality, which we will discuss in the next chapter.

98. Millare, 172. Here, Millare points the reader to Ratzinger, *Theology of the Liturgy*, 34.

9

Morality

Logiké latreía connects liturgical worship with the Christian life, which ought to conform to the mysteries celebrated and received in the liturgy. As Millare explains, "Christians must conscientiously make the choice to enter into communion with the sacrifice of Christ during the liturgy and beyond it in everyday life."[1] A proper understanding of the liturgy and of the sacraments includes their connection to right living—that is, the moral life.

TRUTH, FREEDOM, AND CONSCIENCE

Characteristically, Ratzinger presents his views on morality in conversation with common perspectives found in contemporary culture. Accordingly, we will first outline Ratzinger's understanding of modern approaches to the question of truth, freedom, and conscience before offering Ratzinger's response, which links authentic freedom to truth, especially to metaphysical truth. Yet again, it will become clear how there is a primacy of ontology in Ratzinger's thinking. The link between freedom and truth sets the stage for a proper understanding of conscience, clarifying what it means and what it does not mean.

The question of truth has arisen time and again throughout

---

1. Roland Millare, *A Living Sacrifice: Liturgy and Eschatology in Joseph Ratzinger* (Steubenville, OH: Emmaus Academic, 2022), 175.

this book. It is a persistent theme in Benedict XVI's writings. In particular, he has repeatedly lamented common currents of thought regarding truth in this day and age. Three elements of contemporary approaches to the question of truth, which can be combined in various ways, are: scientific reductionism, agnosticism, and relativism. For him, errors about truth and the ability to know the truth lead to significant mistakes in moral reasoning.

We have already discussed Ratzinger's opposition to an epistemology that reduces knowledge only to that which can be known through the hard sciences by way of their empirical methods. Sadly, such scientific reductionism (or scientism) is common nowadays, and it has implications for moral thinking. As Ratzinger notes, "Natural science has nourished a skepticism with regard to everything which cannot be explained or proved by its exact methods: all such things seem in the end to be a mere subjective assignment of value which cannot pretend to be universally binding."[2]

This tendency to reduce knowledge to the hard sciences includes the loss of metaphysics. While discussing the concept of reason related to moral theology, Ratzinger writes that "discussion is occurring in a context that is not only post-metaphysical but also a-metaphysical" and then proceeds to ask, "How could such a post-metaphysical reason construct a moral vision? Certainly no longer by recognizing moral principles inscribed in being."[3] In other words, reducing knowledge of the truth to the observations and calculations of the empirical sciences leads many to assert that we cannot know *moral* truth but can only have personal opinions about what is moral or immoral behavior.

Thus, at least with respect to morality, contemporary culture

<hr/>

2. Joseph Ratzinger, "Truth and Freedom," trans. Adrian J. Walker, *Communio*, 23, no. 1 (Spring 1996): 16.

3. Joseph Ratzinger, "The Renewal of Moral Theology," in *Joseph Ratzinger in "Communio,"* vol. 1, *The Unity of the Church* (Grand Rapids, MI: Eerdmans, 2010), 189; original English translation was published in *Communio* 32, no. 2 (Summer 2005).

often presupposes agnosticism: a denial of the ability to know truth. "The modern attitude toward truth is summed up most succinctly in Pilate's question, 'What is truth?' Anyone who maintains that he is serving the truth by his life, speech and action must prepare himself to be classified as a dreamer or as a fanatic."[4]

In this way, scientism leads to agnosticism with regard to moral truth, which in turn leads to moral relativism.[5] Moral relativism asserts that there is no absolute, objective moral truth. What is good or bad is a matter of one's perspective, and it is thus relative to the individual and their perceptions of what has value. As Ratzinger famously stated (with lament) in his homily during the Mass for electing the Roman pontiff, "We are building a dictatorship of relativism that does not recognize anything as definitive and whose ultimate goal consists solely of one's ego and desires."[6]

When truth is dismissed, the intellect is left out of the equation, and the result is that the will dominates. What one wants becomes the source of value judgments, including moral judgments. The main value underlying all the rest, therefore, is individual freedom. "In the mind of contemporary man, freedom appears to a large extent as the absolutely highest good, to which all other goods are subordinate. . . . Values which compete with freedom, or which might necessitate its restriction, seem to be fetters or 'taboos,' that is, relics of archaic prohibitions and fears."[7]

This view largely dominates modern views of society and politics. Nowadays, "We tend to think of freedom as the true good of

---

4. Ratzinger, "Truth and Freedom," 16–17.

5. See D. Vincent Twomey, *Pope Benedict XVI: The Conscience of Our Age* (San Francisco: Ignatius, 2007), 107: Ratzinger "attributes the contemporary denial of objectivity in moral (or ethical) questions to a consequence of the widespread denial of transcendence, namely, the reduction of reason to empirical or quantitative rationality. Relativism also poses the greatest of threats to the body politic."

6. Joseph Ratzinger, Homily at the Mass "Pro Eligendo Romano Pontifice," April 18, 2005, vatican.va.

7. Ratzinger, "Truth and Freedom," 16.

human beings. . . . We think today that respect for the freedom of the individual makes it utterly wrong for the state to decide the question of truth—and this in turn means we do not think it possible for a community as such to discern truth, and thus truth about what is good. . . . The concept of 'truth' has in fact moved into the zone of antidemocratic intolerance. It is not now a public good, but something private."[8] In this line of thinking, "The modern concept of democracy seems indissolubly linked to that of relativism."[9] Thus, the question of truth is seen as either impossible or, at best, undesirable.

In response to a society that mockingly asks "What is truth?" while exalting freedom as the highest good, Ratzinger asks back, "What is freedom?"[10] Is the modern conception of freedom really free? And what is the basis of it being lauded as the highest value, if values are relative?

Before offering his own perspective, Ratzinger presents a typical response to this question. After quoting Karl Marx's definition of freedom, Ratzinger writes, "This is exactly the sense in which average opinion spontaneously understands freedom: as the right and the opportunity to do just what we wish and not to have to do anything which we do not wish to do. Said in other terms: freedom would mean that our own will is the sole norm of our action and that the will not only can desire anything but also has the chance to carry out its desire."[11]

In this ideological context, a specific notion of conscience comes into play. As we have said, the denial of truth leads to an emphasis on the will, which in turn correlates with a subjective view of conscience. "Conscience appears here as the bulwark of freedom in contrast to the encroachments of authority

8. Joseph Ratzinger, "What Is Truth? The Significance of Religious and Ethical Values in a Pluralistic Society," in *Values in a Time of Upheaval*, trans. Brian McNeil (San Francisco: Ignatius, 2006), 55.

9. Ratzinger, "What Is Truth," 55.

10. Ratzinger, "Truth and Freedom," 17.

11. Ratzinger, 17.

on existence."[12] Conscience becomes a declaration of one's autonomy. In the modern era, the idea of freedom of conscience over and against authority was initially directed against the Church, particularly with the writings of Martin Luther. Interestingly, Luther himself limited this opposition to the religious context. "Every time it was extended into a political program, as in the Peasant War and the Anabaptist movement, Luther vigorously opposed it."[13]

However, a further stage eventually arose via the so-called Enlightenment. While there are somewhat divergent versions of the notion of freedom over against authority in the Enlightenment, there are still some main characteristics that can describe the general tendency. Ratzinger explains, "The element specific to the Enlightenment and to modernity in this line of thought may be seen in the notion that the juridical claim of nature vis-à-vis the existing forms of government is above all a demand that state and other institutions respect the rights of the individual. Man's nature is above all to possess rights against the community, rights which must be protected from the community: institution seems to be the polar opposite of freedom, whereas the individual appears as the bearer of freedom, whose goal is seen as his full emancipation."[14] From this perspective, the community is only of relative value. It is the individual that matters. "In this way, the freedom of the individual to order his own life is declared to be

12. Joseph Ratzinger, "Conscience and Truth," EWTN, ewtn.com. This article was originally the keynote address at the Tenth Bishops' Workshop of the National Catholic Bioethics Center, on "Catholic Conscience: Foundation and Formation," given in February 1991. Another version is printed in Ratzinger, *On Conscience* (San Francisco: Ignatius, 2007), 11–42.

13. Ratzinger, "Truth and Freedom," 20.

14. Ratzinger, 22. For divergent versions of Enlightenment understandings, Ratzinger points to what he calls the "Anglo-Saxon" view (based on the idea of natural rights and supportive of constitutional democracies) and Rousseau's program calling for absolute autarchy. While the former view has some concept of "nature" (even if a defective one), the latter is explicitly antimetaphysical, even to the point of being against reason (and will?) as an enemy of freedom. Nietzsche develops along Rousseau's path. See Ratzinger, 20–22.

the real goal of societal life. Community has no value whatever in itself but exists only to allow the individual to be himself."[15]

In this view, conscience stands on the side of the individual over against any authority that might impinge upon one's personal sovereignty. For modern man, "Conscience stands on the side of subjectivity and is the expression of the freedom of the subject. Authority, on the other hand, appears to him as the constraint on, threat to and even the negation of freedom."[16] Conscience is here reduced to an individual's claim of self-assurance about what is right. "Thus," writes Ratzinger, "there could be at best the subject's own truth, which would be reduced to the subject's sincerity."[17] From this vantage point, only the individual can truly judge the morality of his own actions. "The ultimate competence of the subject . . . is thus expressed in a certain conception of conscience, according to which man is the measure of himself. . . . His subjective conscience is what has the last and decisive word."[18] Here, conscience is seen as an appeal of the individual over against authority or other outside influences. The right—or even duty—to act according to one's conscience is hereby viewed as a claim against external interference.

This last point, the duty to follow one's conscience, has influenced certain strands of Catholic moral thought in ways that Ratzinger finds disturbing. Because there are elements of traditional Catholic moral theology that speak about the need to follow one's conscience, even if it is erroneous, some thinkers have drawn further inferences that put ignorance on par with saving grace. Ratzinger describes a couple of encounters he had with fellow academics about this issue that illustrate this attitude.

About the first example, Ratzinger recalls how "a senior colleague . . . expressed the opinion that one should actually be

15. Ratzinger, "What is Truth," 54.
16. Ratzinger, "Conscience and Truth."
17. Ratzinger.
18. Ratzinger, "Renewal of Moral Theology," 193.

grateful to God that He allows there to be so many unbelievers in good conscience. For if their eyes were opened and they became believers, they would not be capable, in this world of ours, of bearing the burden of faith with all its moral obligations. But as it is, since they can go another way in good conscience, they can reach salvation."[19]

A similar perspective was applied in a dispute among colleagues that took place at a later date. The topic was the justifying power of an erroneous conscience. One interlocutor objected (rightly!) to the notion of the salvific efficacy of an erroneous conscience, since it would lead to the conclusion that we should expect to see convinced members of the Nazi SS in heaven, because they acted fully in accordance with their convictions. Another interlocutor responded, indicating that we should accept that conclusion without hesitation. The argument runs thusly: "There is no doubting the fact that Hitler and his accomplices who were deeply convinced of their cause, could not have acted otherwise. Therefore, the objective terribleness of their deeds notwithstanding, they acted morally, subjectively speaking. Since they followed their albeit mistaken consciences, one would have to recognize their conduct as moral and, as a result, should not doubt their eternal salvation."[20] Ratzinger was appalled by both examples just described.

Before we delve into Ratzinger's response to these attitudes along with his conception of the relationship between truth, freedom, and conscience, we should point out one difference between these two examples of (misguided) Catholic thinkers and the fully modern conception of conscience. In these two examples, the dialogue partners are not denying that there is an objective truth about morality, as do the moderns. Neither are they agnostic about the ability to know moral truth. Here, they

19. Ratzinger, "Conscience and Truth."
20. Ratzinger.

are discussing instances in which one is following one's *objectively wrong* conscience but is thereby likely saved by doing so, despite the enormous extent of the error.

Like the moderns, however, in this case, too, conscience is being separated from truth. While there may be instances in which following an erroneous conscience puts one in a state of inculpable ignorance, does this really equal the grace of knowing the truth? Is it just as firm a ground for confidence in salvation? Ratzinger thinks not.

Speaking about the second real-life example given above, Ratzinger states, "Since that conversation, I knew with complete certainty that something was wrong with the theory of justifying power of the subjective conscience, that, in other words, a concept of conscience which leads to such conclusions must be false. For, subjective conviction and the lack of doubts and scruples which follow therefrom do not justify man."[21]

In fact, for Ratzinger, being completely self-certain when one is objectively wrong does not bespeak a morally upright state of existence. Rather, it is a sign of spiritual death. He found in the work of Albert Gorres a voice articulating his own thoughts. "Gorres shows that the feeling of guilt, the capacity to recognize guilt, belongs essentially to the spiritual make-up of man. . . . Whoever is no longer capable of perceiving guilt is spiritually ill, a 'living corpse, a dramatic character's mask,' as Gorres says. 'Monsters, among other brutes, are the ones without guilt feelings.'"[22] Further, "No longer seeing one's guilt, the falling silent of conscience in so many areas is an even more dangerous sickness of the soul than the guilt which one still recognizes as such."[23]

The reason for Ratzinger's diagnosis of spiritual illness here is precisely the fact that a conscience that is silent and calm before the reality of factual guilt does not correspond to the *truth*

21. Ratzinger.
22. Ratzinger.
23. Ratzinger.

of things. It cannot be spiritually healthy to fail to perceive moral reality.

Furthermore, Ratzinger proffers an explanation as to why someone may be guilty even if they are following their erroneous conscience. We should not be so quick to assume that others or ourselves are actually *inculpably* ignorant; one may be guilty for having an erroneous conscience in the first place. "Man can see the truth of God from the fact of his creaturehood. Not to see it is guilt. It is not seen because man does not want to see it. The 'no' of the will which hinders recognition is guilt. The fact that the signal lamp does not shine is the consequence of a deliberate looking away from that which we do not wish to see."[24]

Here, we see the application of what we encountered in a previous chapter. Ratzinger had approvingly pointed to Augustine, who draws from the Gospel: "Blessed are the pure in heart, for they will see God" (Matt. 5:8). This passage encapsulates the Augustinian and Franciscan emphasis on the effects of the will on the intellect. Sometimes one does not perceive the truth, because one has already chosen not to see it. It is *impurity* of heart that can lead to a faulty conscience. Thus, Ratzinger is able to conclude, "Certainly, one must follow an erroneous conscience. But the departure from truth which took place beforehand and now takes its revenge is the actual guilt which first lulls man into false security and then abandons him in the trackless waste."[25]

Here, we can already begin to see Ratzinger's understanding of the relationship between truth, freedom, and conscience. For him, they must go together. To put it briefly, the point of the conscience is not first and foremost to justify our autonomy against external authorities (even if it may on occasion serve that capacity). The purpose of conscience is to awaken us to the truth that we do not create, thus enabling us to act in accordance with that

24. Ratzinger.
25. Ratzinger.

truth, even when it may not be what we personally *desire* in the moment. Our freedom, then, is not to do what we want; freedom is the ability to do what we ought, because it corresponds to the truth of our being. Conscience and truth, then, are not opposed to freedom; they make freedom possible. "Freedom without truth is no freedom at all."[26]

In the chapter on creation and theological anthropology, we already encountered a foreshadowing of this position. In particular, we saw how Sartre saw freedom conceived of as separate from the truth of being (as detached from metaphysics) as a form of hell rather than a type of salvation. "For Sartre, the human being is pure existence, without essence. What he is and what he ought to be are not determined. One must define humanity anew out of the nothingness of an empty freedom. The idea of freedom here has been taken to its most radical extreme: no longer mere emancipation from tradition and authority, but now emancipation from the idea of 'man' as a creature, emancipation from one's own nature, complete indeterminacy that is open to everything. But this very freedom appears simultaneously to be hell; to be free means to be damned."[27]

Sartre is revealing the unavoidable conclusion drawn from the separation of freedom from truth and metaphysics. If one follows this presupposition, Ratzinger asks,

> How free is the will after all? And how reasonable is it? Is an unreasonable will truly a free will? Is an unreasonable freedom truly freedom? Is it really any good? In order to prevent the tyranny of unreason must we not complete the definition of freedom as the capacity to will and to do what we will by placing it in the context of reason, of the totality of man? . . . It is

26. Ratzinger, "Truth and Freedom," 24.
27. Joseph Ratzinger, "Freedom and Constraint in the Church," chapter 10 in *Church, Ecumenism, and Politics: New Endeavors in Ecclesiology*, trans. Michael J. Miller et al. (San Francisco: Ignatius, 2008), 182.

obvious that the question of truth is implicit in the question of the reasonableness of the will and of the will's link with reason.[28]

In other words, if there is no truth about morality, no objective standards for values, then what is the basis for elevating freedom to the highest value in the first place? If freedom is not correlated with truth in any way, then it is arbitrary. But if it is completely arbitrary, how free is it? If it is just following momentary impulses with no real rhyme, reason, or meaning behind them, then is it really freedom at all? Furthermore, if freedom conceived in this way were to be absolutized, then how would society function? If freedom is solely the fulfillment of the individual's desires, then how could there be an objective standard to mediate between individuals' competing desires?

This last question is directly connected to Ratzinger's understanding of the metaphysical truth of humanity and how it relates to freedom. To be like God is, in a very real way, the essence of human fulfillment. The problem with modern, liberal conceptions of the human person is that they have a faulty notion of the divine. Again, for Ratzinger, everything flows from and leads back to the Trinity. As Ratzinger notes:

> The implicit goal of all of modernity's struggles for freedom is to be at last like a god who depends on nothing and no one, and whose own freedom is not restricted by that of another. Once we glimpse this hidden theological core of the radical will to freedom, we can also discern the fundamental error. . . . To be totally free, without the competing freedom of others, without a "from" and a "for"—this desire presupposes not an image of God, but an idol. The primal error of such a radicalized will to freedom lies in the idea of a divinity conceived as a pure egoism. The god thought of in this way is not a God, but an

28. Ratzinger, "Truth and Freedom," 17.

idol. Indeed, it is the image of what the Christian tradition would call the devil—the anti-God—because it harbors exactly the radical antithesis to the real God. The real God is by his very nature entirely being-for (Father), being-from (Son), and being-with (Holy Spirit). Man, for his part, is God's image precisely insofar as the "from," "with," and "for" constitute the fundamental anthropological pattern. Whenever there is an attempt to free ourselves from this pattern, we are not on our way to divinity, but to dehumanization, to the destruction of being itself through the destruction of the truth.[29]

When man places the ultimate value on his own individual will (keeping it detached from truth and metaphysics) over and against everyone else, then he has not, in fact, attained the goal of his existence but rather destroyed his own participation in the truth of his being as the *imago Dei*.

Ratzinger insists that man cannot escape the metaphysical truth of what human perfection is. Any moral thought that ignores man's ontology can only lead to doom. The elevation of individual freedom divorced from truth to the highest value is reflective of a false conception of God. True human perfection requires living in a manner reflective of the true God, who is the loving communion of Father, Son, and Holy Spirit, whose perfection and freedom are rooted precisely in mutual relation. As Ratzinger contends, "The foregoing has made it clear that freedom is tied to a measure, the measure of reality—to the truth. Freedom to destroy oneself or to destroy another is not freedom, but its demonic parody. Man's freedom is shared freedom, freedom in the conjoint existence of liberties which limit and thus sustain one another. Freedom must measure itself by what I am, by what we are [hence metaphysics]—otherwise it annuls itself."[30]

29. Ratzinger, 28.
30. Ratzinger, 28.

Ratzinger draws an important conclusion from these reflections: "This means that in order to understand freedom properly we must always think of it in tandem with responsibility. . . . Increase of freedom can no longer lie simply in giving more and more latitude to individual rights—which leads to absurdity and to the destruction of those very individual freedoms themselves. Increase in freedom must be an increase in responsibility."[31]

Moral responsibility is itself tied to the truth of man's nature. As Ratzinger posits, "There is a common truth of a single humanity present in every man. The tradition has called this truth man's 'nature.' Basing ourselves on faith in creation, we can formulate this point even more clearly: there is one divine idea, 'man,' to which it is our task to answer. In this idea, freedom and community, order and concern for the future, are a single whole. . . . Responsibility would thus mean to live our being as an answer—as a response to what we are in truth."[32]

In this connection, conscience is important because, when it is properly formed with a pure heart, it aids in the perception of the truth of things. It challenges one to conform one's moral decisions to the reality perceived.

On this front, Ratzinger draws from the tradition to distinguish two levels of conscience. According to Twomey, Ratzinger attains "the recovery of what might be described as the ontological level of conscience, which in the Middle Ages was known as *synderesis* . . . as distinct from *conscientia*, the level of judgment, that is, conscience in the narrow sense of the term."[33] Ratzinger insists that the two levels must be seen both in their proper relation and in their proper distinction; failing to see either their connection or their difference results in serious mistakes.[34]

31. Ratzinger, 30.

32. Ratzinger, 32.

33. Twomey, *Conscience of Our Age*, 122.

34. See Joseph Ratzinger, "The Two Levels of Conscience," in *The Pope Benedict XVI Reader* (Park Ridge, IL: Word on Fire Institute, 2021), 326. This text is an excerpt from the same piece cited earlier as "Conscience and Truth" as it appeared in *On Conscience*, 30–38.

In recuperating the Scholastic notion of *synderesis*, Ratzinger makes a slight, terminological modification. He prefers to use the term *anamnesis* instead of *synderesis*. The latter derives from *stoicism*, while the former is Platonic, meaning recollection or memory. Given his philosophical preferences, this choice is not much of a surprise. But it also corresponds to the primacy of Scripture in his theology. As Twomey describes the term *anamnesis*, "It is a term, moreover, that is close to biblical thought, such as when Saint Paul describes in Romans 2:14–15, the law that is written into our hearts. This ontological level of conscience was central to tradition from Saint Basil the Great and Saint Augustine to the mediaeval mystics and the Schoolmen such as Saint Thomas Aquinas. . . . It is [also] central to the thought of Cardinal Newman."[35]

What exactly does *anamnesis* mean in this context? Following the use of St. Basil and St. Augustine, Ratzinger posits that "the first so-called ontological level of the phenomenon conscience consists in the fact that something like an original memory of the good and true (they are identical) has been implanted in us, that there is an inner ontological tendency within man, who is created in the likeness of God, toward the divine."[36] As a metaphysical component of human nature, this *anamnesis* is interior to man's being. In the words of Rowland, "Ratzinger believes that God inscribed 'instructions for use' objectively and indelibly in his creation and, consequently, 'nature, and with it precisely also man himself, so far as he is part of that created nature, contain that morality within themselves'. For the Church 'the language of *nature* is also the language of *morality*'."[37]

---

35. Twomey, *Conscience of Our Age*, 122. See also Ratzinger, "Two Levels," 326: "It is not only linguistically clearer and philosophically deeper and purer, but *anamnesis* above all also harmonizes with key motifs of biblical thought and the anthropology derived from it."

36. Ratzinger, "Two Levels," 327.

37. Tracey Rowland, *Ratzinger's Faith: The Theology of Pope Benedict XVI* (New York: Oxford University Press, 2008), 77. Here, Rowland quotes from Joseph Ratzinger, *The Ratzinger Report* (San Francisco: Ignatius, 1985), 91, 97.

Just as human nature is one, so too, when perceived properly, *anamnesis* is common to all men. "It is 'the window that opens up to man the view of the truth common to us all that establishes and sustains us and so makes community of decision and responsibility possible due to the common ground of perception'."[38] Despite being in the interiority of each person, then, this level of conscience is also objective; it is not the result of personal taste, preferences, or wishes; it is the capacity to perceive the truth of things as they really are.

As a capacity or capability, this *anamnesis* is able to grow or decay. Not everyone at every stage of life recognizes the truth implanted within us with the same clarity. As Ratzinger explains, "The anamnesis instilled in our being needs . . . assistance from without so that it can become aware of itself. But this 'from without' is not something set in opposition to anamnesis but is ordered to it. It has maieutic function, imposes nothing foreign, but brings to fruition what is proper to anamnesis, namely, its interior openness to truth."[39]

These words remind me of the twofold element of divine revelation discussed in chapter 5: the exterior and interior witnesses. In this new context, too, there is an external appearance—perhaps a word of moral exhortation—that awakens us to the truth. This helps explain why one can be converted through moral teaching, when one recognizes the profundity of the truth within it. The capacity to perceive this truth is not just a matter of logical deduction, but the external expression gives clarity to the reality that was already there but ill-perceived.

Relatedly, Ratzinger sees this *anamnesis* as a reason for successful missionary activity. "The gospel may, indeed must, be proclaimed to the pagans, because they themselves are yearning for

---

38. Twomey, *Conscience of Our Age*, 124. Here, Twomey quotes from Joseph Ratzinger, *Wahrheit, Werte, Macht: Prüfsteine der pluralistischen Gesellschaft* (Freiburg, DE: Herder, 1993), 32.

39. Ratzinger, "Two Levels," 329.

it in the hidden recesses of their souls (see Isa. 42:4). Mission is vindicated, then, when those addressed recognize in the encounter with the word of the gospel that this indeed is what they have been waiting for."[40] Ratzinger thinks the "God-fearers" encountered by the Israelites and Paul's success with his mission to the Gentiles are examples of this. "Their proclamation encountered an antecedent basic knowledge of the essential constants of the will of God."[41]

We turn now to the second level of conscience, sometimes referred to simply as *conscientia*, which can unfortunately give the impression that it is the only thing meant by conscience to the neglect of the first, ontological level just discussed. This second level is "that of judgment and decision": "The act of conscience applies this basic knowledge [of repugnance to evil and attraction to good] to the particular situation."[42] In other words, the truth about the good perceived through the *anamnesis* informs our concrete moral decisions through our judgment of what we ought to do in a given case. "Though Ratzinger does not advert to it," opines Twomey, "conscience here would seem to be closely related to the virtue of prudence."[43] Not to act in accordance with the truth presented by *anamnesis* is to fail in *conscience*. That is why the appeal to personal subjectivity and autonomy does not justify one's actions absolutely. "The guilt lies somewhere else, not for judging something right that is in fact objectively wrong, but deeper, 'in the desolation of my being that makes me insensible to the voice of truth and its appeal to my inner self'."[44] As in the earlier context, so too here the will comes into play. "Whether something is recognized or not depends too on the will, which can block the way to recognition or lead to it. It is dependent,

40. Ratzinger, 327–328.
41. Ratzinger, 328.
42. Ratzinger, 330.
43. Twomey, *Conscience of Our Age*, 127.
44. Twomey, 127. Here, he quotes from Ratzinger, *Wahrheit, Werte, Macht*, 58.

that is to say, on an already formed moral character, which can either continue to deform or be further purified."[45]

This reference to the possibilities of deformation or purification alludes to the themes to be discussed in our next chapter on eschatology. There, as here, an ontological understanding of the human person is central to the notions of salvation and damnation. Hence, Ratzinger's moral thought can be viewed in relation to both anthropology and eschatology, precisely insofar as our moral formation and ethical actions here and now anticipate—positively or negatively—our eternal destiny. For both our moral character and our salvation or damnation pertain to what we become. They relate to one another as do formal and final causality in metaphysics.

Here, we encounter the ontological and eschatological essence of virtue. According to the *Catechism of the Catholic Church*, "A virtue is an habitual and firm disposition to do the good. It allows the person not only to perform good acts, but to give the best of himself. The virtuous person tends toward the good with all his sensory and spiritual powers; he pursues the good and chooses it in concrete actions. 'The goal of a virtuous life is to become like God.'"[46] Thus, the individual virtues are means of living up to our nature as the image of God and, when bolstered by supernatural grace, to attain to the likeness of God. Our moral lives bring us closer or further away from the goal of our existence: heavenly beatitude. "Leading a virtuous life leads to God."[47] It is clear, then, that moral theology is directly connected

---

45. Ratzinger, "Two Levels," 331.

46. *Catechism of the Catholic Church* 1803. Here, the Catechism quotes from St. Gregory of Nyssa, *De beatitudinibus* 1.

47. Jacquelyn Lindsey, introduction to Benedict XVI, *The Virtues*, ed. Jacquelyn Lindsey (Huntington, IN: Our Sunday Visitor, 2010), 9. This work is a collection of excerpts from Pope Benedict XVI's homilies, addresses, and encyclicals that address the theological and cardinal virtues. This volume is recommended for those who want to see how Benedict XVI's moral thought is worked out with respect to the individual virtues. For a presentation of how to apply Pope Benedict XVI's understanding of the theological virtues to everyday life, see Matthew J. Ramage, *The Experiment of Faith: Pope Benedict XVI on Living the Theological Virtues in a Secular Age* (Washington, DC: The Catholic University of America Press, 2020).

to eschatology. Accordingly, we will unpack Benedict's eschatology in the next chapter.

10

Eschatology

In the last chapter, we encountered Pope Benedict XVI's moral theology. We saw how he insists that morality must be tied to the truth of our being, that it has an ontological basis. Like everything in this book, the foundation of ontology is the Triune God. Hence, living a morally upright life means to live a life according to the call to be holy, the way God is holy. The virtues are particular ways to embody the holiness that we are called to. Only by possessing the virtues (cardinal and theological) can we *be* that which we are meant to be forever in heaven. As we have seen repeatedly, this is not only an individual reality; we are called to *communion* with God and with our fellow human beings. Living this call here and now is a means of already living, in time, the beginnings of the eschaton, our final end, and this moral, holy life is thus a preparation for entering into the finality of life everlasting.

Hence, morality relates directly to the topic of this tenth and final topical chapter. Here, we will explore major themes in Benedict XVI's eschatology. In what follows, we will consider: death and immortality; the intermediate state; resurrection; and hell, purgatory, and heaven (including the communion of saints).

DEATH AND IMMORTALITY

Before Ratzinger gives his own explication of his theology of death and immortality, he opens with brief summaries of contemporary approaches to the issue. First, he writes about the view that biblical and Greek thought are opposed to one another on this matter. From this perspective, Plato's dualism is portrayed as contrary to the biblical record.

In the Platonist view, materiality is inherently bad, and it therefore sees death as the liberation of the immaterial soul from corporeality. "Death, then, is the great moment when the gates of that prison house [the body] are flung wide open and the soul steps forth into that freedom and immortality which are its by right. Death is man's true friend, his liberator from the unnatural chains of matter."[1] Explaining the Greek understanding further, Ratzinger writes that "the Greek conception is based on the idea that man is composed of two mutually foreign substances, one of which (the body) perishes, while the other (the soul) is in itself imperishable and therefore goes on existing in its own right independent of any other beings. Indeed, it was only in the separation from the body, which is essentially foreign to it, so they thought, that the soul came fully into its own."[2]

This soul-body dualism is then purported to be at odds with the Bible. "In biblical thought, by contrast, man is seen in his undivided wholeness and unity as God's creature and cannot be sliced down the middle into body and soul."[3] Rejecting Plato's premise of dualism, some argue, should lead Christians to reject the idea that only the body dies. Instead, they posit the

1. Joseph Ratzinger, *Eschatology: Death and Eternal Life*, 1st ed., trans. Michael Waldstein (Washington, DC: The Catholic University of America Press, 1988), 73.

2. Joseph Ratzinger, *Introduction to Christianity*, trans. Mary Frances McCarthy (San Francisco: Ignatius, 1987), 349.

3. Ratzinger, *Eschatology*, 74. See also Ratzinger, *Introduction*, 349: "The biblical train of thought, on the other hand, presupposes the undivided unity of man; for example, Scripture contains no word denoting only the body (separated and distinguished from the soul), while conversely in the vast majority of cases the word soul, too, means the whole corporeally existing man."

hypothesis of "total death." Ratzinger summarizes their perspective thusly: "Language itself indicates this truth, for we say 'I will die,' not 'My body will die.' You can't get away from the totality of death: it devours you, leaving nothing behind. . . . The immortality of the soul must be firmly rejected as an idea which goes against the grain of biblical thought."[4] The rejection of the immortality of the soul on this basis has been espoused particularly in twentieth-century Lutheran thought. "In reality, so it is said, this idea [of the immortality of the soul] expresses a thoroughly un-Christian dualism."[5]

Some proponents of this position nevertheless find hope via Jesus' Resurrection, even if precise accounts of how the two are reconcilable are left unattended. Immortality, from this perspective, has nothing to do with a quality of the soul that makes it immortal. Rather, immortality is the result of divine action: "Immortality results not simply from the self-evident inability of the indivisible to die but from the saving deed of the lover who has the necessary power: man can no longer totally perish because he is known and loved by God."[6]

Other proponents of the "total death" perspective take a further step. "Arguing that the ideas of both immortality *and* resurrection are entirely peripheral in the Jewish Scriptures, they find the same conviction of the 'totality' of death in the (hypothetically reconstructed) 'Q' community."[7]

Against this backdrop, Ratzinger proffers his own understanding. Acknowledging the limits of Greek philosophy, he nevertheless finds a way to reconcile Platonism and Christianity. As Nichols attests, "Faithful to his early work on Augustine, Ratzinger insists that Platonism had, and has, much to offer

4. Ratzinger, *Eschatology*, 74.

5. Ratzinger, *Introduction*, 347.

6. Ratzinger, 350. See also Pablo Blanco Sarto, *La Teología de Joseph Ratzinger: Una introducción* (Madrid: Pelícano, 2011), 272.

7. Aidan Nichols, *The Thought of Benedict XVI: An Introduction to the Theology of Joseph Ratzinger* (New York: Burns & Oates, 2005), 168. See also Ratzinger, *Eschatology*, 74–75.

Christianity, by way of assisting the latter's 'philosophical unfolding'. Yet he also holds that the Church has much to do in order to 'correct and purify' Plato's intention."[8]

As already seen in our consideration of Ratzinger's understanding of the relationship between philosophy and theology, here too, Ratzinger thinks that Christianity can cleanse aspects of Plato's thought, rather than throw it out altogether as completely incompatible. "There is indeed a profound divergence between Plato and Christianity. Yet this should not blind us to the possibilities of a philosophical unfolding of the Christian faith which Platonism offers. These possibilities are rooted in a deep affinity on the level of fundamental formative intention."[9] Pablo Blanco sees a similar attempt at a synthesis in *Introduction to Christianity*. He writes, "For him [Ratzinger], a complementarity exists between both doctrines—the one, biblical, the other, Greek—, despite the logical difficulties of understanding between both perspectives."[10]

To start this discussion, Ratzinger compares the biblical concept to dualistic notions, highlighting some fundamental differences. First, he notes that both views hold to an idea of human immortality, but they differ in their understanding thereof. He reiterates that the dualist conception sees the body and the soul as having separate fates: the body dies and the soul lives on and that is all. They go their separate ways, so to speak. Contrary to this, Ratzinger argues that "the idea of immortality denoted in the Bible by the word 'resurrection' is an immortality of the 'person,' of the *one* creation 'man'."[11] Elaborating further on this point, Pablo Blanco notes that "linking 1 Cor 15:50 with Jn 6:63, Ratzinger concludes that the 'resurrection of the flesh' is the resurrection of

8. Nichols, *Thought of Benedict XVI*, 169.

9. Ratzinger, *Eschatology*, 79.

10. Blanco, *Teología de Joseph Ratzinger*, 272. See Ratzinger, *Introduction*, 348: "One can only arrive at an answer if one inquires carefully into the real intentions of the biblical testimony and at the same time considers anew the relation between the biblical and the Greek ideas."

11. Ratzinger, *Introduction*, 350.

the whole person . . . and not only of the bodies."[12] The biblical revelation about resurrection precludes a false dualism that sees the body as a mere prison, impeding the soul from its perfected state. Rather, resurrection is something positive for the soul as well as the body. As Emery de Gaál explains, "Christian hope in the resurrection of the flesh prohibits disparaging corporeal life."[13]

Second, the *basis* of immortality is different in the Greek and biblical notions. In the view of ancient philosophy, the soul is immortal by its very nature; there is something about the soul that makes it incapable of death. In a way that parallels Christianity's corrections to the purely philosophical conception of God, Ratzinger points to the *relational* basis of man's immortality as a different foundation. As Verweyen explains, "It would be unbiblical to speak of an immortality grounded in the essence of the soul itself. Soul is, rather, the connecting point set by God for the communion with human beings endowed by him already from the beginning of creation."[14] In the Bible, according to Ratzinger:

> It is a question of a "dialogic" immortality (= awakening!); that is, immortality results not simply from the self-evident inability of the indivisible to die but from the saving deed of the lover who has the necessary power: man can no longer totally perish because he is known and loved by God. All love wants eternity, and God's love not only wants it but effects it and is it. . . . Immortality as conceived by the Bible proceeds, not from the intrinsic power of what is in itself indestructible, but from being drawn into the dialogue with the Creator. . . . Because the Creator intends, not just the soul, but the man physically existing in the midst of history and gives *him* immortality.[15]

12. Blanco, *Teología de Joseph Ratzinger*, 273. See Ratzinger, *Introduction*, 356–358.

13. Emery de Gaál, *The Theology of Pope Benedict XVI: The Christocentric Shift* (New York: Palgrave MacMillan, 2010), 276.

14. Hansjürgen Verweyen, *Joseph Ratzinger–Benedikt XVI.: Die Entwicklung seines Denkens* (Darmstadt: WBG, 2007), 74.

15. Ratzinger, *Introduction*, 350.

Here, we again see *relationality* and *communion* as fundamental aspects of Ratzinger's view of immortality. As Nichols explains, "The upshot of these reflections was that life, real life, means communion, whereas death, the heart of death, is the absence of relationship."[16] It is man's relationship with God that is the basis of immortality and not simply a necessary quality of an immaterial soul.

This relational and communal dimension of immortality is extended to the interpersonal character of humanity as well, which is Ratzinger's third point of comparison. "To the soul as conceived by the Greeks, the body, and so history, too, is completely exterior; the soul goes on existing apart from them and needs no other beings in order to do so."[17] The Christian view, based upon the biblical testimony, is quite different. "There is no such thing as a private, unsocial repose of the soul,"[18] explains de Gaál. For Ratzinger, the fact that "the awakening is expected on the 'Last Day', at the end of history, and in the company of all mankind indicates the communal character of human immortality, which is related to the whole of mankind. . . . For man understood as a unity . . . fellowship with his fellowmen is constitutive; if *he* is to live on, then this dimension cannot be excluded."[19]

That is why the "communion of saints" is an article of faith in the Creed. Immortality is not simply a question pertaining to each individual person separately; it is not that a man continues to exist in himself in isolation from all others. Rather, human immortality is fully *human*, which, as we have repeatedly seen, is essentially *communal*, precisely as the image of God who is

---

16. Nichols, *Thought of Benedict XVI*, 170. The context for this quote is Ratzinger's reflection upon ancient Israel's realization that the concept of death and its realm, Sheol, held by primitive peoples, could not be the full story. In that faulty conception, God is not in Sheol nor worshiped there, which is an unacceptable limitation on God with respect to his creation. See Nichols, *Thought of Benedict XVI*, 169–170.

17. Ratzinger, *Introduction*, 351.

18. De Gaál, *Theology of Pope Benedict XVI*, 283.

19. Ratzinger, *Introduction*, 351.

communal. Even before the "Last Day," Ratzinger sees room for the communal nature of humanity postmortem. De Gaál reports that "Ratzinger introduces the vision originally expressed by Origen in his seventh homily on the book of Leviticus of all the dead waiting in solidarity together with the risen Christ. This serves as proof for his theory of the individual's relationship in solidarity with his fellow human beings well beyond this life. This is enlarged then to include solidarity with all of history, that is, with people of all ages."[20]

As one might expect, in addition to the Trinitarian foundation of Ratzinger's presentation, there is a Christological core. It is in Christ that man's destiny is fully revealed, and it is in communion with Christ that we are given access to eternal life. "As one would expect of a Christian," writes de Gaál, "Ratzinger's eschatology is eminently Christological, and it contains a rarely reached intensification toward Christ: eschatology can only be made sensible in light of Jesus Christ awaiting each individual believer on Judgment Day."[21] Christ is the means of man's relationship with God. Ratzinger notes, "The Old Testament by itself ultimately leaves the question about the future of man in the air. Only with Christ, the man who is 'one with the Father', the man through whom the being 'man' has entered into God's eternity, does the future of man definitely appear open. . . . Christ is man, completely; to that extent the question of who we men are is present in him."[22]

Once more, we see here how Ratzinger connects various areas of dogmatic theology together: eschatology is linked with Christology, which is determinative for anthropology. It is also connected to the sacraments, as Nichols elucidates: "Whenever someone enters into Christ's life, through baptismal faith and the

---

20. De Gaál, *Theology of Pope Benedict XVI*, 278.
21. De Gaál, 276.
22. Ratzinger, *Introduction*, 351.

banquet of the Eucharist, he enters straight away into the 'space of unconditional life'."[23]

Ratzinger adds to the Christological understanding of immortality, referring back to his notion of the dialogic character of the biblical understanding. "But if the dialogue of God with man means life, if it is true that God's partner in the dialogue himself has life precisely through being addressed by him who lives forever, then this means that Christ, as God's Word to us, is himself 'the resurrection and the life' (Jn 11:25). It also means that the entry into Christ known as faith becomes in a qualified sense an entry into that being known and loved by God which is immortality: 'Whoever believes in the Son *has* eternal life' (see Jn 3:15; 3:36; 5:24)."[24]

Points of agreement and compatibility between Greek and biblical thought on the issue of immortality may seem impossible, given the stark contrasts that have already been established. Ratzinger poses some serious questions to himself in this regard. Is his approach, even if supported by biblical evidence, too cut off from man's nature (essence)? "Does this view not make immortality into a pure grace, although in reality it must fall to man's lot by virtue of his nature as man? . . . Must we not hold fast, precisely for the sake of the humanity of the Christian faith, to natural immortality, for the reason that a continued existence conceived in purely Christological terms would necessarily slide into the miraculous and mythological?"[25] Perhaps surprisingly, Ratzinger answers "yes" to these questions.

This affirmative response may seem quite confusing. Earlier, Ratzinger appeared to reject the notion that man is immortal by virtue of his essence in favor of the communal/dialogical character of human immortality. Nevertheless, Ratzinger insists that "the two definitions are not in the least contradictory; they simply

23. Nichols, *Thought of Benedict XVI*, 172.
24. Ratzinger, *Introduction*, 352.
25. Ratzinger, 354.

express the same thing in different modes of thought. For 'having a spiritual soul' means precisely being willed, known, and loved by God in a special way; it means being a creature called by God to an eternal dialogue and therefore capable for its own part of knowing God and of replying to him. What we call in substantialist language 'having a soul' we will describe in a more historical, actual language as 'being God's partner in a dialogue'."[26]

In a manner paralleling Christianity's correction to the philosophical understanding of God, Ratzinger is basically saying that the biblical data helps correct and augment the notion of man's natural immortality. There is an immortal element to man's spiritual nature as such. "But, on the other hand, it also needs to be complemented if we are not to fall back into a dualistic conception that cannot do justice to the dialogic and personalistic view of the Bible."[27] In other words, Ratzinger sees the dialogic and interpersonal dimension as part of man *qua* man. "What really makes man into man? . . . The distinguishing mark of man, seen from above, is his being addressed by God, the fact that he is God's partner in a dialogue, the being called by God. . . . The immortality that, precisely because of its dialogic character, we have called 'awakening' falls to the lot of man, *every* man, as man, and is not some secondary 'supernatural' addition."[28] Ratzinger reiterates this point in *Eschatology*: "Being referred to God, to truth himself, is not, for man, some optional pleasurable diversion for the intellect. When man is understood in terms of the formula *anima forma corporis* [the soul is the form of the body], that relationship to God can be seen to express the core of his very essence. As a created being he is made for a relationship which entails indestructibility."[29]

Here, Ratzinger is favoring a close connection between nature

26. Ratzinger, 355.
27. Ratzinger, 355.
28. Ratzinger, 354.
29. Ratzinger, *Eschatology*, 154.

and the supernatural end of man, for "in the last analysis one cannot make a neat distinction between 'natural' and 'supernatural': the basic dialogue that first makes man into man makes a smooth transition into the dialogue of grace known as Jesus Christ. How could it be otherwise if Christ actually is the 'second Adam', the real fulfillment of that infinite longing that arises from the first Adam—from man in general?"[30]

In brief, the Greek philosophical conception of human immortality tended toward a dualism between body and soul. This dualism could partly be attributed to its inability to foresee the possibility of the resurrection of the body, which is only known through divine revelation. Thus, the biblical view helps correct the overly dualist conception of Greek philosophy. At the same time, the philosophical conclusion that the human spirit as such must have an immortal character was correct, although incomplete. Again, the biblical witness helps to correct and augment this perception. Yes, the human spirit does have an immortal character, precisely because the human spirit is called by God to an eternal dialogue: a true everlasting relationship. "It is not a relationless being oneself that makes a human being immortal, but precisely his relatedness, or capacity for relatedness, to God. . . . [This] constitutes what is deepest in man's being. It is nothing other than what we call 'soul.'"[31] The Greeks could not have known that aspect of the problem, but their intuitions were correct to a degree; the soul's ontology was created precisely to make immortal union with God possible.

Furthermore, the Christian understanding is able to fathom the *communal* dimension of human immortality. It is not just an isolated individual, a separated soul, that lives forever; the real goal is the *communion of saints* in communion with the Triune God. Since that is the reason humanity was created, *from the*

30. Ratzinger, *Introduction*, 356.
31. Ratzinger, *Eschatology*, 155.

outset, one can say that man is immortal by nature, but only because that nature was created for this supernatural union. Here, grace is understood as perfecting nature as such; the second Adam is the true fulfillment of the hope of the first Adam and thus of every man.

THE INTERMEDIATE STATE

Before we delve into questions about hell, purgatory, and heaven as well as the resurrection, we must discuss the more general issue of the intermediate state. By intermediate state is meant the existence of the human person after death but before resurrection. As Ratzinger poses the question, "If the 'Last Day' is not to be identified with the moment of individual death but is accepted as what it really is, the shared ending of all history, then the question naturally arises as to what happens 'in-between.'"[32]

Some recent theologies simply deny the existence of an intermediate state, precisely in order to avoid conflict with their rejection of the idea of the immortality of the soul (separated from the body). One such approach advocates for a type of "resurrection in death" perspective, in which a person's death ends their connection to the timeline of the present age and leads them directly into what, from our earthly perspective, we consider to be the end of time. Ratzinger summarizes this view as follows: "Death signifies leaving time for eternity with its single 'today.' Here the problem of the 'intermediate state' between death and resurrection turns out to be a problem only in seeming. The 'between' exists only in our perspective. In reality, the 'end of time' is timeless. The person who dies steps into the presence of the Last Day and of judgment, the Lord's resurrection and the parousia."[33]

Ratzinger calls this view into question by asking whether it

32. Ratzinger, 119.
33. Ratzinger, 107–108.

305

is truly possible for the person who has died to enter into eternity, understood as timelessness, as such. He asks, "Can an eternity which has a beginning be eternity at all? Is it not necessarily non-eternal, and so temporal, precisely because it had a beginning? Yet how can one deny that the resurrection of a human being has a beginning, namely, after death?"[34]

One such proponent of "resurrection in death" theology, Gerhard Lohfink, who is aware of this dilemma, seeks to connect his view to the medieval notion of *aevum*, a special mode of time distinct from both earthly time and eternity. "Lohfink sees that death leads not into pure timelessness but into a new kind of time proper to created spirits."[35]

Ratzinger takes issue with this view, because it seems to involve a contradiction. "The point of this construct is the claim that on the other side of death history is already complete. . . . But this is just what can hardly be reconciled with the continuation of history. History is viewed as simultaneously completed and still continuing"; furthermore, "one can hardly ignore the fact that the message of resurrection 'on the third day' posits a clear interim period between the death of the Lord and his rising again. And, more importantly, it is evident that early Christian proclamation never identified the destiny of those who die before the Parousia with the quite special event of the resurrection of Jesus."[36] Additionally, Lohfink's view seems to misunderstand the category of time. As de Gaál explains, "Ratzinger argues that time is not primarily a physical reality but an anthropological category, formed by human relationships. Closely allied with this notion is the objection of devaluing history."[37]

Commencing his own response to the question, Ratzinger appeals to ancient Tradition. Nichols explains, "Belief in the

34. Ratzinger, 109.
35. Ratzinger, 110.
36. Ratzinger, 111.
37. De Gaál, *Theology of Pope Benedict XVI*, 278.

existence of an 'inter-mediate state' was firmly entrenched in inter-testamental Judaism, as a variety of documents, from the book of Enoch and Fourth Ezra to diverse early rabbinic texts can testify. In the New Testament and the Fathers, all the images that Jews created for the inter-mediate state recur: Abraham's bosom, Paradise, the Tree of Life, water, light, and so on."[38] The difference is that these images are now applied to Christ himself.[39]

Ratzinger eventually turns to the patristic era as well as to magisterial texts in support of his position. While the immediate post-apostolic period did not specify an explicit doctrine of the immortality of the soul per se, "The Jewish matrix of Christianity provided the Church with a tradition which held it to be self-evidently certain that the dead do not return to nothingness but await the resurrection in 'Hades,' in a manner appropriate to their form of life"; and later, turning to the likes of Clement and Origin, whose works were somewhat pivotal in their offer of unique perspectives, Ratzinger notes that "even for these two Alexandrians and their intellectual posterity, the condition of the dead remains an intermediate state."[40]

After going through a series of magisterial texts that speak about the resurrection of the self-same bodies that we possess now, Ratzinger turns to a particularly noteworthy intervention by Pope Benedict XII in the papal bull *Benedictus Deus* (1336). Quoting that document, Ratzinger writes, "'Even before their re-unification with their bodies and the general judgment . . . they are and will be in heaven,' so that they 'see the divine nature in an immediate vision, face-to-face, without the mediation of any creature.'"[41]

Nichols fleshes out the significance of this papal bull, which "maintained, in accordance with the tradition, that there is still

---

38. Nichols, *Thought of Benedict XVI*, 172–173. See also Ratzinger, *Eschatology*, 120–122.

39. See Ratzinger, *Eschatology*, 130.

40. Ratzinger, 133.

41. Ratzinger, 136.

something provisional about the state of the separated soul. Reunification with the body, and final judgment, are yet to come."[42] Nichols then proceeds to summarize two of Ratzinger's central points. "First, not even death can destroy life with Christ. Secondly, before the final 'resurrection of the flesh' that life is incomplete."[43]

At this point, however, a question raised earlier returns with full force. If the soul and the body cannot simply be bifurcated into two separate substances, then how are we to understand the possibility of human immortality in a time period between a person's bodily death and the resurrection at the end of time? Ratzinger admits that formulating a solution was no easy task in the history of theology. The answer must hold together seemingly contrary realities. On the one hand, it requires an anthropology that sees man—body and soul—as a unity. On the other hand, "This anthropology was also obliged to distinguish within man between an element that perishes and an element that abides—though in such a way that the path toward the resurrection, the definitive reunification of man and creation, remained open. In sum, the anthropology desired should weld together Plato and Aristotle precisely at the points where their doctrines were mutually opposed. There was a need to take over Aristotle's teaching on the inseparable unity of body and soul, yet without interpreting the soul as an entelechy."[44]

Here, Ratzinger gives credit to the genius of St. Thomas Aquinas. While drawing from Aristotle, Aquinas nevertheless develops the latter's thought in a way that Aristotle himself would not have considered. "Thomas' wonderful contribution to Christian anthropology lay in his showing how the spirit could be *both* personal *and* the form of matter."[45] That which is the form of the

42. Nichols, *Thought of Benedict XVI*, 174. See Ratzinger, *Eschatology*, 139.
43. Nichols, 174. See Ratzinger, *Eschatology*, 147.
44. Ratzinger, *Eschatology*, 148.
45. Nichols, *Thought of Benedict XVI*, 174. See Ratzinger, *Eschatology*, 149.

human body is also spirit and, as such, makes a human being a person. And as we have seen repeatedly, Ratzinger understands "person" as an intrinsically relational category. Because man's soul is also spirit, that means it is capable of entry into relationship with God and thereby capable of immortality.[46]

It is not the material of human corporeality, then, that constitutes man's identity. His enduring identity is found else-where, in his spiritual soul. "Matter as such cannot provide the underpinning for man's continuing identity. . . . Thus a duality distinguishing the constant from the variable factors in the make-up of man is necessary. . . . Hence the indispensability of the body-soul distinction."[47] At the same time, "Christian tradition . . . which reached its climax . . . with the work of Thomas . . . has conceived this duality in such a way that it is not dualistic but rather brings to light the worth and unity of the human being as a whole."[48] Ratzinger elaborates on Aquinas' position later on: "Both soul and body are realities only thanks to each other and as oriented toward each other. . . . The soul can never completely leave behind its relationship with matter. . . . If it belongs to the very essence of the soul to be the form of the body then its ordination to matter is inescapable."[49] Therefore, while in the intermediate state, the soul is still ordered toward the body, and—as we saw in the papal bull *Benedictus Deus*—there is, prior to the resurrection, an incompleteness even with respect to the souls enjoying the beatific vision. "Here," notes Nichols, "we see emerging an 'anthropological logic' which shows the resurrec-tion to be a postulate of human existence."[50]

Let us sum up a couple of the major points treated thus far. Due to its potential to be unified with God in personal

46. See Ratzinger, *Eschatology*, 149.
47. Ratzinger, 158.
48. Ratzinger, 158–159.
49. Ratzinger, 178–179.
50. Nichols, *Thought of Benedict XVI*, 178.

relationship, the human soul is capable of perduring after bodily death. "As a creature, by its very essence, the person is created in a relationship that includes otherness [being in relation to another] and indestructibility."[51] Nevertheless, as Aquinas insists, it retains its ordering toward a body, and therefore, its separation from a material body is not its final state; it is an intermediate state that awaits the resurrection, which is the topic of our next section.

RESURRECTION

Because the soul is properly the form of the body, a condition of separation from the body cannot be understood as whole, perfect, or complete. This factor helps explain the need for resurrection.

But the question arises: What exactly is resurrection? And what is a resurrected body? In characteristic fashion, Ratzinger develops his position in contrast with opposing views common in his day. He stands against those who deny that there will be a "Last Day" (i.e., an end to history in the current state) and deny that the resurrection has anything to do with matter. As an example, Greshake insisted that matter is intrinsically incapable of being perfected, and thus has no part in whatever "resurrection" means.[52]

Also characteristic of Ratzinger, he turns to Scripture, Tradition, and the Fathers to develop his own view. First, he turns to 1 Corinthians 15:35–53. There are two aspects to this passage that are important for our present discussion. On the one hand, Paul affirms the bodily resurrection on the basis of his encounter with the risen Christ; on the other hand, based on this same experience, Paul does not view the resurrection as mere resuscitation. "And this means that Paul was decidedly opposed to the prevailing Jewish view whereby the risen body was completely identical

51. Blanco, *Teología de Joseph Ratzinger*, 276.
52. See Ratzinger, *Eschatology*, 166–168.

with the earthly body and the world of the resurrection simply a continuation of the world of the present. Such ideas were utterly shattered by encounter with the risen Lord."[53] As Nichols elaborates, "Paul embraces a 'pneumatic realism', which should be contrasted both with physicalist realism and with spiritualism."[54]

Ratzinger sees commonality between Paul and John on this point: "They emphatically assert the resurrection in its bodiliness."[55] At the same time, "That the resurrection state is quite different from our present conditions of life is resoundingly affirmed."[56]

Appealing to the early Tradition, Ratzinger relies on the work of Georg Kretschmar, who showed that the Western Creed, in its nascence, referred to the "resurrection of the flesh" rather than "of the dead." Speaking of this phrasing, Ratzinger writes, "We meet it in Tertullian, where it appears as an aspect of the tradition handed down in the Roman see, and indeed can trace its fortunes there from Hippolytus to the Apostles' (or 'Old Roman') Creed."[57] Similarly, in a work Ratzinger thinks is most likely written by St. Justin Martyr, we read, "If the gospel of salvation is proclaimed to humanity, then salvation is also proclaimed to the flesh."[58]

Ratzinger thinks the Church's stance on this question has a reasonable basis. "The Church's rejection of Valentinus resulted from her conviction that God is faithful to his *whole* creation. In the healing activity of Jesus, this faithfulness was made known as a fidelity not least toward the body, toward this earth which God has made."[59] Precisely as the salvation of humanity and of the

---

53. Ratzinger, 169.

54. Nichols, *Thought of Benedict XVI*, 176.

55. Ratzinger, *Eschatology*, 171.

56. Ratzinger, 172.

57. Ratzinger, 172. N.b.: Ratzinger immediately continues to make an important caveat to the phrase 'resurrection of the flesh': "Thanks to its Jewish roots, this phrase indicates the salvation of the human creature, or of creation, in its entirety."

58. *De resurrectione* 8, quoted in Ratzinger, 174.

59. Ratzinger, 175.

world, the consummation at the end of history must include the essential elements of what the human body and his environment consist of, even if raised to a new, more perfected state of existence than is currently the case. The materiality of creation was *good*, and therefore ought to be understood as entirely compatible with the eschatological fulfillment of creation. As Ratzinger argues, "An everlasting, unrelated and therefore static juxtaposition of the material and spiritual worlds contradicts the essential meaning of history, the creation of God and the word of Scripture."[60]

There are limits to what we can say about the resurrected body and the new earth to come. But there are certain things that we can and ought to affirm. Ratzinger concludes, "The new world cannot be imagined. Nothing concrete or imaginable can be said about the relation of man to matter in the new world, or about the 'risen body.' Yet we have the certainty that the dynamism of the cosmos leads toward a goal, a situation in which matter and spirit will belong to each other in a new and definitive fashion. This certainty remains the concrete content of the confession of the resurrection of the flesh even today, and perhaps we should add: especially today."[61]

HELL, PURGATORY, AND HEAVEN

As the last section of this chapter on Ratzinger's eschatology, we shall consider his thoughts about two possible final states for the human person (hell and heaven) and one temporary state (purgatory) that could be a precursor to final admittance into heaven. We shall treat them in the same order that Ratzinger does: hell, purgatory, heaven.

To start, Ratzinger does not mince words. At the very beginning of his section on hell, he comes right out of the gate

60. Ratzinger, 192.
61. Ratzinger, 194.

speaking directly and plainly: "No quibbling helps here: the idea of eternal damnation, which had taken ever clearer shape in the Judaism of the century or two before Christ, has a firm place in the teaching of Jesus, as well as in the apostolic writings. Dogma takes its stand on solid ground when it speaks of the existence of Hell and of the eternity of its punishments."[62]

This is not to say that Ratzinger does not appreciate the motivation behind the likes of Origen (and the Church Fathers who followed his logic), who expected universal salvation at the end of time. He even perceives a certain beauty in the Buddhist myth of the Bodhisattva that refuses to enter into paradise (Nirvana) until hell is empty. "Nevertheless," notes Verweyen, "Ratzinger, in the end, relentlessly holds fast to the tradition prevailing in the 'wider Church' [*Großkirche*]."[63]

The authenticity of the dogma regarding hell is not just a fact that must be accepted despite apparent irrationality. Ratzinger perceives a fundamental rationale undergirding the doctrine of hell: "God's unconditional respect for the freedom of his creature."[64] Referring once again to the *exitus-reditus* structure of the world and salvation history, Ratzinger makes an important observation. "'The *exitus* or, better, the free creative act of God does, in fact, look toward the *reditus*, but this does not mean that the reclamation of the created being is already achieved, but rather that the autonomous creature . . . responds'—from freedom—'to the love of God.'"[65]

While man does not create the ascent into loving union with God, he does have the freedom to accept or to reject the offer. As Verweyen explains, "The God-given freedom of the creature

---

62. Ratzinger, 215.

63. Verweyen, *Joseph Ratzinger*, 75.

64. Ratzinger, *Eschatology*, 216.

65. Joseph Ratzinger, "El fin del tiempo," in J.B. Metz, J. Ratzinger, and E. Goodman Thau, *La provacación del discurso sobre Dios* (Madrid: Trotta, 2001), 29–30, quoted and translated from Blanco, *Teología de Joseph Ratzinger*, 282.

opposes the assertion of universal reconciliation."[66] God is a lover who *pro*-poses to his beloved; he does not *im*-pose himself upon us. Ratzinger holds that "heaven reposes upon freedom, and so leaves the damned the right to will their own damnation."[67] Each human person has the right, and thus the ability, to accept or to reject God. As Blanco summarizes, "It is the dynamic of freedom, of the call of God and of the free response on the part of man."[68]

This free decision will eventually reach finality. As Ratzinger expounds, "The irrevocable takes place, and that includes, then, irrevocable destruction. The Christian man or woman must live with such seriousness and be aware of it."[69]

Ratzinger takes hell seriously, because he takes humanity—and human freedom—seriously. In addition, the gravity of the cross exemplifies just how serious the possibility of rejecting God really is. The only remaining question is "whether in this event [of the cross] we are not in touch with a divine response able to draw freedom precisely as freedom to itself."[70] That is what we hope for, but it cannot be the necessary conclusion of any rational system demanding that all be saved *de jure*. Any philosophy or theology rejecting the possibility of hell is contrary to the faith. At best, Ratzinger believes, hope "must place its petition into the hands of its Lord and leave it there. The doctrine of everlasting punishment preserves its real content. The idea of mercy . . . must not become a theory. Rather is it the prayer of suffering, hopeful faith."[71]

That is as far as Ratzinger is willing to go on the extent of hope for the salvation of others. He does not dare to venture as far

---

66. Verweyen, *Joseph Ratzinger*, 75.
67. Ratzinger, *Eschatology*, 216.
68. Blanco, *Teología de Joseph Ratzinger*, 282.
69. Ratzinger, *Eschatology*, 217.
70. Ratzinger, 217.
71. Ratzinger, 218.

as his friend Hans Urs von Balthasar.[72] Rather, "Ratzinger devotes the bulk of his attention to a more securely founded dogmatic topic, that of Purgatory."[73]

Even though purgatory might be more doctrinally secure than the hope for universal salvation, it is not without controversy. Ratzinger is well aware of the ecumenical difficulties—with both Protestants and Eastern Orthodox—that the Catholic teaching on purgatory represents. "Ratzinger insisted, nevertheless, on the Christian genesis of the idea of purgatory, as much in the East as in the West."[74] Accordingly, Ratzinger traces the origins and development of the doctrine in a helpful way, fleshing out the fundamental content of the doctrine that permanently remains.

Ratzinger admits from the start that the definitive form of the doctrine of purgatory was not achieved until two medieval (reunion) councils, Lyon (1274) and Ferrara-Florence (1439), as well as at the Council of Trent (1545–1563).[75] However, he does a masterful job of showing how the various components of the doctrine are present much earlier in Tradition. As Nichols explicates, "From a history-of-religions standpoint, it crystallised out of the materials offered by three sources: Late Antique sensibility, Judaism and Christianity. The common element is the idea of a suffering on the part of the dead that may be lightened through prayer."[76]

For Ratzinger, the concept of purgatory clarifies the question of the intermediate state in connection with anthropology and Christology. "In this doctrine, the Church held fast to one aspect of the idea of the intermediate state, insisting that, even if one's fundamental life-decision is finally decided and fixed in

---

72. See Verweyen, *Joseph Ratzinger*, 76. Verweyen thinks it is "odd" or "curious" (*merkwürdig*) that Ratzinger does not engage in any direct dispute with Balthasar on this topic in this context.

73. Nichols, *Thought of Benedict XVI*, 184.

74. Blanco, *Teología de Joseph Ratzinger*, 283.

75. Ratzinger, *Eschatology*, 218–219.

76. Nichols, *Thought of Benedict XVI*, 184–185. See also Ratzinger, *Eschatology*, 222–223.

death, one's definitive destiny need not necessarily be reached straight away. It may be that the basic decision of a human being is covered over by layers of secondary decisions and needs to be dug free."[77]

This description contains an ontological dimension. It is not merely a question of whether or not one has been "saved" in a purely juridic or extrinsic sense but whether one has yet *become* the saint one is meant to be and thus capable of entering into heaven. Heaven is not just a place but a mode of existence. Hence, there needs to be a transition—even for the justified—from a state of weakness with remaining sinful inclinations to the perfect life of the blessed, of the sinless and perfectly virtuous. That is why purgatory is understood as a *purification* process, which is exactly how those three aforementioned councils describe it.[78]

This understanding has its roots in early Judaism. In 2 Maccabees 12:32–46, we encounter the lauded practice of offering prayers and sacrifice (i.e., sin offerings) for fallen soldiers so that their sins may be wiped away.[79] "The equivalent practice," writes Benedict XVI, "was readily adopted by Christians and is common to the Eastern and Western Church."[80] As Ratzinger notes, "In the material presented by the Strack-Billerbeck collection, part of which goes back to the second century of the Christian era, there are clear signs of the idea of an intermediate Gehenna, understood as a purgatory where souls, in their atoning suffering, are prepared for definitive salvation."[81]

Born in the second century and dying in the early third century, both Tertullian (in the West) and Clement of Alexandria (in the East) testify to elements of the purgatory doctrine. Tertullian,

77. Ratzinger, *Eschatology*, 219.

78. See Ratzinger, 220.

79. See Ratzinger, 220. See also Benedict XVI, *Spe Salvi* 48: "Early Jewish thought includes the idea that one can help the deceased in their intermediate state through prayer (see for example 2 Macc 12:38–45; first century BC)."

80. Benedict XVI, *Spe Salvi* 48.

81. Ratzinger, *Eschatology*, 221.

who wrote a work about the martyrdom of St. Perpetua, relays a story about a dream St. Perpetua had about her deceased brother, Dinocrates. In brief, the dream saw him suffering, which induced her to pray tirelessly for him. Afterward, she had another dream showing him as happy and healed of a wound. Coupled with this story, Tertullian sees Matthew 5:25–26[82] as a hint at what we call purgatory, although he takes this in a rigorist direction that posits it as necessary for all who are to be saved. Cyprian of Carthage (d. 258) draws from this outlook but in a new, less rigorist, more pastoral context.[83] Ratzinger explains Cyprian's view thusly:

> He asserted a definitive salvation for those who have died in faith, and notably for the martyrs. He was similarly clear about the definitiveness of Hell. His actual pastoral problem concerned the well-intentioned but weak, average Christians who did not find the strength to accept martyrdom in times of persecution. . . . The saying found in Matthew 5, 26 offered Cyprian an occasion for thinking through a possible continuation of penance in the afterlife. . . . Certainly they cannot, in their present condition, enter into definitive communion with Christ. Their denial, their half-heartedness, stands in the way. But they are capable of purification. The penitential way of purification exists not only in this world but in the world to come.[84]

This view reflects the metaphysical aspect of the issue mentioned earlier. Purgatory bespeaks the need to be purified in order to be fit for the kingdom. If one were still plagued by moral weakness and sinful inclinations in heaven, then it would not be paradise

---

82. "Come to terms quickly with your accuser while you are on the way to court with him, or your accuser may hand you over to the judge, and the judge to the guard, and you will be thrown into prison. Truly I tell you, you will never get out until you have paid the last penny."

83. See Ratzinger, *Eschatology*, 222–223.

84. Ratzinger, 224.

for oneself or for the others present there. Heaven means sharing in God's own life and thus existing without any sinful dispositions. Insofar as concupiscence is present at the moment of death, further purification is needed *ontologically* to be in a state of heavenly bliss.

In addition to Matthew 5:25–26, there is 1 Corinthians 3:10–15, which stands as a classic "proof text" for the doctrine of purgatory.[85] Verse 15 of this pericope speaks of being saved but only as through fire, a fire of judgment that saves. St. Clement of Alexandria understands this image in terms of the Greek concept of *paideia* and, accordingly, views this fire as purifying and educating. "The process of man's pneumatic purification, that catharsis which will fit him for God, begins with baptism and reaches into eternity."[86]

Clement shares this aspect with the Western tradition. "In Clement as in the Western writers, the penance imposed by the Church is the concrete starting point. For him as for them, such penance is a process which can and often must continue beyond the gate of death. For him as for them, this process points up the difference between someone's valid fundamental decision, whereby he is accepted in grace, and the defective permeation of the effects of that decision throughout the being of the whole person."[87] Here, too, there is a metaphysical element to this concept. "The idea of purification after death: 'turns out to be, in this context, something of a mediating metaphysical link between the Platonic idea of the soul's immortality and the Resurrection.'"[88]

In addition to the metaphysical dimension of Clement's view, there is also a communal, ecclesial aspect. "The process of

---

85. See Nichols, *Thought of Benedict XVI*, 185–186. See also Ratzinger, 225.

86. Ratzinger, 225.

87. Ratzinger, 226.

88. Ratzinger, 225. Here, Ratzinger quotes from Klaus Schmöle, *Läuterung nach dem Tode und pneumatische Auferstehung bei Klemens von Alexandrien* [*Münsterische Beiträge zur Theologie* no. 38] (Münster: Aschendorff, 1974), 135.

purification is, on all its levels, an activity of reciprocal caring."[89] Accordingly, "Ratzinger notes that . . . death does not destroy, or even disrupt, the anchoring of a person in the Church."[90]

Clement's perspective continued in the work of Origen as well as in Gregory Nazianzen (d. 390). With so many Fathers in the East as much as in the West attesting to the ideas signified by purgatory, one may wonder how the Orthodox began to disagree with the Catholic understanding. Ratzinger traces the divergence to St. John Chrysostom (d. 407), whom the Eastern churches followed ever since. The background was Origen's doctrine of the restoration of all things (*apokatastasis panton*), which included a reference to purging fire. Chrysostom strongly opposed Origen's view of the restoration of all things and, in the process, threw out the notion of the purifying fire that he associated it with.[91]

The result is an Orthodox perspective that retains elements of the Catholic understanding but minus the purifying/atoning element, which was present in the earlier patristic writings. Ratzinger explains the Orthodox view as follows:

> The intermediate state, "Hades," applies to everyone in the period between death and resurrection. But this state contains "various levels of happiness and unhappiness," which correspond to the different levels of justification and sanctification of the faithful on earth. The saints intercede for their brethren here on earth, and we may call on them for their intercession.

89. Ratzinger, 225.

90. Nichols, *Thought of Benedict XVI*, 185. See Ratzinger, *Eschatology*, 227: "Even when they have crossed over the threshold of the world beyond, human beings can still carry each other and bear each others' burdens. They can still give to each other, suffer for each other, and receive from each other. More clearly at Alexandria [and hence in the East!] than in the Western tradition, this conviction rests on the Pauline–Johannine belief that the real frontier runs not between earthly life and not-life, but between being with Christ, on the one hand, and, on the other, being without him or against him."

91. See Ratzinger, *Eschatology*, 227. See also Nichols, *Thought of Benedict XVI*, 185: "But because this idea of the purifying fire had become linked in the Eastern Christian mind with the Origenistic notion of *apokatastasis*, general restoration, it was combatted by Chrysostom whose doctrine became and remains official in the Orthodox churches."

Through the Eucharist, through prayer and almsgiving, the living can bring "respite and refreshment" to the souls in Hades. However, the "unhappiness" to be alleviated by such actions is not taken to include a purifying or atoning suffering.[92]

Thus, Eastern Orthodox accept the notion of praying and offering sacrifices for the dead who are in an intermediate state, which can alleviate some of their unhappiness, which is very close to the Catholic perspective but with a subtle (although important) difference. As Benedict XVI explains in *Spe Salvi*, "The East does not recognize the purifying and expiatory suffering of souls in the afterlife, but it does acknowledge various levels of beatitude and of suffering in the intermediate state. The souls of the departed can, however, receive 'solace and refreshment' through the Eucharist, prayer and almsgiving."[93]

What, for Ratzinger, is the enduring content of the Catholic doctrine of purgatory? "His explication," posits Blanco, "goes along the lines of the necessary purification also after death."[94] As with so many theological topics, Ratzinger understands this purification Christologically. Alluding to the fire mentioned in 1 Corinthians 3:15, he asserts that "purgatory is understood in a properly Christian way when it is grasped christologically, in terms of the Lord himself as the judging fire which transforms us and conforms us to his own glorified body."[95] It is Christ himself, then, who purifies the souls in purgatory, removing any dross that remains in them that is incompatible with heavenly glory.

Once again, this process is conceived of metaphysically. He posits that purgatory is "the inwardly necessary process of

92. Ratzinger, 228. Here, Ratzinger draws from J.N. Karmiris, "Abriss der dogmatischen Lehre der orthodoxen katholischen Kirche," in P. Bratsiotis, *Die orthodoxe Kirche in griechischer Sicht*, 2nd ed. (Stuttgart: Evangelisches Verlagswerk, 1970), 113–117.

93. Benedict XVI, *Spe Salvi* 48.

94. Blanco, *Teología de Joseph Ratzinger*, 283.

95. Ratzinger, *Eschatology*, 229.

transformation in which a person becomes capable of Christ, capable of God and thus capable of unity with the whole communion of saints"; he then adds that the need for such a process should be obvious: "Simply to look at people with any degree of realism at all is to grasp the necessity of such a process."[96]

For Ratzinger, this does not in any way negate the effectiveness of grace. Rather, it demonstrates it; it is precisely the working of grace within us that takes place in purgatory, overcoming any remaining resistance to that grace that we may possess. "Man is the recipient of the divine mercy, yet this does not exonerate him from the need to be transformed. Encounter with the Lord *is* this transformation. It is the fire that burns away our dross and re-forms us to be vessels of eternal joy. This insight would contradict the doctrine of grace only if penance were the antithesis of grace and not its form, the gift of a gracious possibility."[97] As Pablo Blanco expresses it, "It is a question, then, of sifting through the hay, the wood, and the straw that St. Paul speaks of in 1 Cor. 3:10–15, in order to reach the gold, the silver, and the precious stones of the grace of Christ."[98]

Interestingly, this purifying element, not shared by the Eastern Orthodox, may be for many people the most acceptable component of the doctrine, while, on the other hand, the part the Orthodox do accept—the ability for those on earth to intercede effectively for those in purgatory—may be the most difficult aspect for people to grasp. Ratzinger himself raises this question explicitly before offering his response. "And how can a third party enter into that most highly personal process of encounter with Christ, where the 'I' is transformed in the flame of his closeness?

96. Ratzinger, 230–231. Note that in the first part of this quote, there is once again the notion of Christ as the source of vertical and horizontal communion, that is, union of God with man and of men with one another.

97. Ratzinger, 231.

98. Blanco, *Teología de Joseph Ratzinger*, 284.

321

Is not this event which so concerns the individual that all replacement or substitution must be ruled out?"[99]

To answer this question, Ratzinger once more appeals to the communal character of human nature. "Yet the being of man is not, in fact, that of a closed monad. It is related to others by love or hate, and, in these ways, has its colonies within them. My own being is present in others as guilt or as grace. We are not just ourselves; or, more correctly, we are ourselves only as being in others, with others and through others."[100] Human beings are intimately involved with one another; their lives interpenetrate, for good or for ill. "So," writes Benedict XVI, "my prayer for another is not something extraneous to that person, something external, not even after death. In the interconnectedness of Being, my gratitude to the other—my prayer for him—can play a small part in his purification."[101] In short, the same reason we can pray and offer sacrifices for one another here on earth is maintained across the boundaries of death. "The belief that love can reach into the afterlife, that reciprocal giving and receiving is possible, in which our affection for one another continues beyond the limits of death—this has been a fundamental conviction of Christianity throughout the ages and it remains a source of comfort today."[102]

In brief, the Catholic doctrine of purgatory consists in two major elements. First, after death, some of the elect need purification before entering the heavenly repose. This takes place through an encounter with Christ, represented by the image of the purifying fire. Due to the communal character of humanity and the continuation of relationship with those who have gone before us, we are able—on earth—to offer prayers and sacrifices to God on behalf of the souls in purgatory, after the same manner we are able

99. Ratzinger, *Eschatology*, 231.
100. Ratzinger, 232.
101. Benedict XVI, *Spe Salvi* 48.
102. *Spe Salvi* 48.

to do so for those still living. The Body of Christ is not divided, even by death.

Understanding purgatory as a process of purification for entrance into heaven already anticipates fundamental elements of heaven. Heaven is not, first and foremost, a *place*; rather, it denotes something about the being of the saint; it is ontological. "Heaven is not, then, 'above' in a spatial but in an essential way."[103] The saint is truly, metaphysically, and morally free from all sin and inclination to sin. It is an unimpeded participation in the divine life.

Of course, this is mediated through Christ. As Nichols relates, "If Purgatory is to be 'christologically determined', so must Heaven be also. Heaven's existence, for Ratzinger, depends upon the fact that Christ as God is also man, and has made 'space for human existence in the existence of God himself'. By being with Christ we find the locus of our existence as human beings in God."[104]

Being with Christ means being with the one who is eternal self-donation to the Father and whose Paschal Mystery continues to abide in his person. Thus, reflecting the eschatological dimension of the liturgy discussed in chapter 8, "Heaven, as our becoming one with Christ, takes on the nature of adoration. . . . And so worship, in its heavenly, perfected form, entails an immediacy between God and man which knows no setting asunder. This is what theological tradition calls the vision of God."[105] In heaven, "God totally permeates the whole man with his plenitude and his utter openness. God is 'all in all,' and thus the human person enters upon his boundless fulfillment."[106]

Of course, as to be expected from all that has been said before in this book, heaven is not just a matter of individual perfection.

103. Ratzinger, *Eschatology*, 237.
104. Nichols, *Thought of Benedict XVI*, 186. See also Ratzinger, *Eschatology*, 234.
105. Ratzinger, *Eschatology*, 234.
106. Ratzinger, 235.

Blanco explains, "The Christian heaven—the highest end of the human person—is personal and interpersonal, individual and relational."[107] As we saw in the chapter on ecclesiology, the Church is an aspect of salvation. The relational character of heaven is ecclesial. It is union with Christ, yes, "but the total Christ, Head and members. If heaven depends on being with Christ, then it must entail a co-being with all those who are members of his body."[108] As Ratzinger writes, "Heaven is a stranger to isolation. It is the open society of the communion of saints, and in this way the fulfillment of all human communion. This is not by way of competition with the perfect disclosure of God's Face, but, on the contrary, is its very consequence."[109]

Yet again, we see the horizontal communion of men, of the Church, as a salvific effect of the vertical communion with God gained through communion with Christ, who is God and man. Only in this way can heaven truly be reflective of Trinitarian life, for the Trinity is a communion. The saints thus form a *communion* in the shared communion of divine life and love. As Pablo Blanco neatly summarizes, "In the final part of his treatise on eschatology, Ratzinger insisted again on this Trinitarian and Christological character of Christian beatitude: it will consist in the definitive union with the Trinity through Jesus Christ and his Church. The Trinitarian, Christological, and ecclesiological—together with the already mentioned existential and personalistic—dimensions are intimately united in this explication."[110]

As the original goal of creation itself, heaven also has a cosmic aspect. "In particular, by announcing a new heaven and a new earth, the Bible makes it clear that the whole of creation is destined to become the vessel of God's Glory. All of created reality is to be drawn into blessedness. The world—God's creature—is

---

107. Blanco, *Teología de Joseph Ratzinger*, 284.

108. Nichols, *Thought of Benedict XVI*, 186. See also Ratzinger, *Eschatology*, 235.

109. Ratzinger, *Eschatology*, 235.

110. Blanco, *Teología de Joseph Ratzinger*, 284.

what the Scholastics would call an 'accidental' element in the final joy of the redeemed."[111] While it is union with God through the beatific vision that constitutes the essence of heaven, the glory of God will also be perceptible through the perfection of the whole world, which will thus be a part of the happiness of heavenly bliss. The eschaton is truly the redemption and supernatural elevation of creation, including its material aspect, up to and including the resurrected bodies of the saints.

In order to be complete, all of this must be realized. Ratzinger therefore concludes that "the individual's salvation is whole and entire only when the salvation of the cosmos and all the elect has come to full fruition. For the redeemed are not simply adjacent to each other in heaven. Rather, in their being together as the one Christ, they *are* heaven."[112]

111. Ratzinger, *Eschatology*, 237.
112. Ratzinger, 238.

Conclusion

The Unity of Benedict XVI's Theology

Throughout his vast theological corpus, Pope Benedict XVI shows that Trinitarian theology, theological anthropology, Christology, soteriology, ecclesiology, sacramental theology, moral theology, and eschatology are all inherently related. The key concept for Benedict's theology and the entirety of our Catholic faith is communion. God is the eternal communion of three divine persons, and consequently, relational communion is an inherent aspect of being itself. God created in order to bring this creation into communion with himself. In particular, God created human beings in his image and likeness, that is, as spiritual beings capable of knowing and loving and therefore capable of intentional communion. Sin is the antithesis of communion. It divides us from God, from one another, and even from ourselves. Salvation, in turn, must heal the divisions created on these three levels.

By becoming man, God the Son brings divinity and humanity together in an unsurpassable unity. Through his Incarnation and redemptive death, Jesus inaugurates the way for man to once again be in communion with God. This vertical communion with God also serves as a means of bringing men into communion with one another. Thus, salvation in Christ generates the Church, which—as Vatican II affirms—is like "a sacrament . . . a sign and instrument both of a very closely knit union with God and of the unity of the whole human race."[1] Through the sacraments of

---

1. Second Vatican Council, *Lumen Gentium* 1, November 21, 1964, in *The Word on Fire Vatican II Collection*, ed. Matthew Levering (Park Ridge, IL: Word on Fire Institute, 2021), 47.

initiation, we are incorporated into this Church; we thereby enter into communion with God and with the whole Church as well as receive the graces necessary to live holy lives. In this way, our worship of God enables us to love God and our neighbor, fulfilling Christ's twofold command of love. Ultimately, our living of morally upright and holy lives is ordered toward heaven, where we become members of the communion of saints. Since heaven is a share in divine life, and divine life is precisely loving communion, heaven is the loving communion of man with God and with the entire communion of saints. Communion, in the end, is founded upon the Trinity, centered on Christ, with the Church as the principal effect, and the eternal communion of saints as the ultimate goal. The Triune God is all in all.

Bibliography

Adams, Marilyn McCord, and Richard Cross. "Aristotelian Substance and Supposits." *Proceedings of the Aristotelian Society, Supplementary Volumes* 79 (2005): 15–72.

Balthasar, Hans Urs von. *The Theology of Karl Barth*. Translated by Edward T. Oakes. San Francisco: Ignatius, 1992.

Benedict XVI. *Creation and Evolution: A Conference with Pope Benedict XVI in Castel Gandolfo*. San Francisco: Ignatius, 2008.

———. *Deus Caritas Est*. Encyclical letter, December 25, 2005, vatican.va.

———. "Faith, Reason, and the University: Memories and Reflections." Apostolic Journey of His Holiness Benedict XVI to München, Altötting, and Regensburg, September 12, 2006, vatican.va.

———. "General Audience." February 27, 2008, vatican.va.

———. "General Audience." March 10, 2010, vatican.va.

———. "General Audience." January 30, 2013, vatican.va.

———. "Grace and Vocation without Remorse: Comments on the Treatise *De Iudaeis*." *Communio* 45 (Spring 2018): 163–184.

———. *Great Teachers*. Huntington, IN: Our Sunday Visitor, 2011.

———. *Heart of the Christian Life: Thoughts on Holy Mass*. San Francisco: Ignatius, 2010.

———. *Jesus, the Apostles, and the Early Church*. San Francisco: Ignatius, 2007.

Benedict XVI. *Jesus of Nazareth*. Vol. 1, *From the Baptism in the Jordan to the Transfiguration*. Translated by Adrian J. Walker. New York: Doubleday, 2007.

———. *Jesus of Nazareth*. Vol. 2, *Holy Week: From the Entrance into Jerusalem to the Resurrection*. Translated by Vatican Secretariate of State. San Francisco: Ignatius, 2011.

———. *Jesus of Nazareth*. Vol. 3, *The Infancy Narratives*. Translated by Philip J. Whitmore. New York: Image, 2012.

———. *The Pope Benedict XVI Reader*. Edited by Daniel Seseske. Park Ridge, IL: Word on Fire Institute, 2021.

———. *Sacramentum Caritatis*. Post-synodal apostolic exhortation, February 22, 2007, vatican.va.

———. *Spe Salvi*. Encyclical letter, November 30, 2007, vatican. va.

———. *Verbum Domini*. Post-synodal apostolic exhortation, September 30, 2010, vatican.va.

Benedict XVI and Peter Seewald. *Last Testament: In His Own Words*. Translated by Jacob Phillips. London: Bloomsbury, 2016.

———. *Light of the World: The Pope, the Church, and the Signs of the Times*. Translated by Michael J. Miller and Adrian J. Walker. San Francisco: Ignatius, 2010.

Blanco Sarto, Pablo. *La Teología de Joseph Ratzinger: Una introducción*. Madrid: Pelícano, 2011.

Bonagura, David. "Joseph Ratzinger/Benedict XVI's Christology of Jesus' Prayer and Two Contemporary Theological Questions." *Nova et Vetera* 12, no. 1 (2014): 287–306.

Brotherton, Joshua. "Revisiting the *Sola Scriptura* Debate: Yves Congar and Joseph Ratzinger on Tradition." *Pro Ecclesia* 24, no. 1 (Winter 2015).

Cahill, Brendan J. *The Renewal of Revelation Theology (1960–1962): The Development and Response to the Fourth Chapter of the Preparatory Schema "De deposito Fidei."* Rome: Editrice Pontificia Università Gregoriana, 1999.

Canty, Aaron. "Bonaventurian Resonances in Benedict XVI's Theology of Revelation." *Nova et Vetera* 5, no. 2 (2007).

Catechism of the Catholic Church. 2nd ed. Libreria Editrice Vaticana, 1994.

Congregation for the Doctrine of the Faith. *Communionis Notio: A Letter to the Bishops of the Catholic Church on Some Aspects of the Church Understood as Communion.* June 15, 1992, vatican.va.

———. *A Letter to the Bishops of the Catholic Church on Some Aspects of Christian Meditation.* October 15, 1989, vatican.va.

DeClue, Richard. "Eucharistic Ecclesiologies of Locality and Universality in John Zizioulas and Joseph Ratzinger." *Nova et Vetera* 12, no. 1 (2014): 77–103.

———. "Joseph Ratzinger." In *The New Apologetics: Defending the Faith in a Post-Christian Era*, edited by Matthew Nelson, 106–111. Park Ridge, IL: Word on Fire Institute, 2022.

———. "Joseph Ratzinger's Theology of Divine Revelation." SThD dissertation, The Catholic University of America, 2021.

———. "The Petrine Ministry within a Eucharistic Ecclesiology according to John Zizioulas and Joseph Ratzinger." SThL thesis, The Catholic University of America, 2008.

———. "Primacy and Collegiality in the Works of Joseph Ratzinger." *Communio* 35 (Winter 2008): 642–670.

De Lubac, Henri. *Medieval Exegesis: The Four Senses of Scripture.* Vol. 1. Translated by Mark Sebanc. Grand Rapids, MI: Eerdmans, 1998.

Gaál, Emery de. "Pope Benedict XVI's Early Contributions to Fundamental Theology—1955–1961." *Josephinum Journal of Theology* 21, no. 2 (Summer/Fall 2014).

———. *The Theology of Pope Benedict XVI: The Christocentric Shift*. New York: Palgrave MacMillan, 2010.

Geiselmann, Josef Rupert. "Das Konzil von Trient über das Verhältnis der Heiligen Schrift und der nicht geschriebene Traditionen." In *Die mündliche Überlieferung*, edited by Michael Schmaus, 123–206. Munich: Max Hueber, 1957.

Hays, Richard B. "Benedict and the Biblical Jesus." *First Things* 175 (August–September 2007).

Heim, Maximilian Heinrich. *Joseph Ratzinger: Life in the Church and Living Theology*. 2nd ed. Translated by Michael J. Miller. San Francisco: Ignatius, 2005.

Hellín, Francisco Gil. *Dei Verbum: Constitutio dogmatica de Divina Revelatione. Concilii Vaticani II Synopsis in ordinem redigens schemata cum relationibus necnon Patrum orationes atque animadversionis*. Vatican City: Libreria Editrice Vaticana, 1993.

Hofmann, Peter. "Jesus Christus als Mitte der Geschichte: Der Einfluss Bonaventuras auf das Denken Joseph Ratzingers/Benedikts XVI. und dessen Bedeutung für die aktuelle Fundamentaltheologie." In *Ratzinger-Studien*, vol. 6, *Zur Mitte der Theologie im Werk Joseph Ratzinger/Benedikt XVI.*, edited by Maximilian Heim and Justinus C. Pech. Regensburg: Friedrich Pustet, 2013.

Jodock, Darrell, ed. *Catholicism Contending with Modernity: Roman Catholic Modernism and Anti-modernism in Historical Context*. Cambridge: Cambridge University Press, 2000.

Kasper, Walter. "From the President of the Council for Promoting Christian Unity." *America* 185 (November 19, 2001): 7–11.

———. "On the Church: A Friendly Reply to Cardinal Ratzinger." *America* 184 (April 23–30, 2001): 8–14.

Kasper, Walter. "Zur Theologie und Praxis des bischöflichen Amtes." In *Auf neue Art Kirche Sein: Wirklichkeiten—Herausforderungen—Wandlungen*, 32–48. Munich: Bernward bei Don Bosco, 1999.

Kerr, Fergus. *Twentieth-Century Catholic Theologians: From Neoscholasticism to Nuptial Mystery*. Malden, MA: Blackwell, 2007.

Koch, Kurt. "Ein konsequenter Papst des Konzils: Joseph Ratzinger—Benedikt XVI. und das Zweite Vatikanum." *Internationale Katholische Zeitschrift: Communio* 43, no. 4 (2013).

Körner, Bernhard. "Übereignung und die Kirche als Grundakt der Glaubenserkenntnis: Joseph Ratzinger im Vergleich mit Max Seckler." In *Ratzinger-Studien*, vol. 6, *Zur Mitte der Theologie im Werk Joseph Ratzinger/Benedikt XVI.*, edited by Maximilian Heim and Justinus C. Pech. Regensburg: Friedrich Pustet, 2013.

Levering, Matthew. "Jesus and Metaphysics: Knowledge of God according to Joseph Ratzinger/Pope Benedict XVI." *Josephinum Journal of Theology* 21, no. 2 (Summer/Fall 2014).

Lindsey, Jacquelyn. Introduction to Benedict XVI, *The Virtues*, edited by Jacquelyn Lindsey. Huntington, IN: Our Sunday Visitor, 2010.

López, Antonio. "God the Father: A Beginning without Beginning." *Communio* 36 (Summer 2009): 219–258.

———. *Surnaturel: études historiques*. Paris: Aubier, 1946.

Marion, Jean-Luc. *Givenness and Revelation*. Translated by Stephen E. Lewis. New York: Oxford University Press, 2016.

McGregor, Peter John. *Heart to Heart: The Spiritual Christology of Joseph Ratzinger*. Eugene, OR: Pickwick, 2016.

McPartlan, Paul. *Sacrament of Salvation*. London: T&T Clark, 1995.

Millare, Roland. *A Living Sacrifice: Liturgy and Eschatology in Joseph Ratzinger*. Steubenville, OH: Emmaus Academic, 2022.

Nichols, Aidan. *The Thought of Benedict XVI: An Introduction to the Theology of Joseph Ratzinger*. New York: Burns & Oates, 2005.

Pasnau, Robert. "Divine Illumination." *The Stanford Encyclopedia of Philosophy* (Spring 2020 edition). Revised February 10, 2020. Edited by Edward N. Zalta. https://plato.stanford.edu/archives/spr2020/entries/illumination/.

Perry, Tim, ed. *The Theology of Benedict XVI: A Protestant Appreciation*. Bellingham, WA: Lexham, 2019.

Pidel, Aaron. *The Inspiration and Truth of Scripture*. Washington, DC: The Catholic University of America Press, 2023.

Pius X. *Pascendi Dominici Gregis*. Encyclical letter, September 8, 1907, vatican.va.

Ramage, Matthew J. *Dark Passages of the Bible: Engaging Scripture with Benedict XVI and St. Thomas Aquinas*. Washington, DC: The Catholic University of America Press, 2013.

———. *The Experiment of Faith: Pope Benedict XVI on Living the Theological Virtues in a Secular Age*. Washington, DC: The Catholic University of America Press, 2020.

———. *From the Dust of the Earth: Benedict XVI, the Bible, and the Theory of Evolution*. Washington, DC: The Catholic University of America Press, 2022.

———. *Jesus, Interpreted: Benedict XVI, Bart Ehrman, and the Historical Truth of the Gospels*. Washington, DC: The Catholic University of America Press, 2017.

Ratzinger, Joseph. "Assessment and Future Prospects." In *Looking Again at the Question of the Liturgy with Cardinal Ratzinger: Proceedings of the July 2001 Fontgombault Liturgical Conference*, edited by Alcuin Reid. Farnborough, UK: Saint Michael's Abbey Press, 2003.

Ratzinger, Joseph. *Behold the Pierced One: An Approach to a Spiritual Christology*. Translated by Graham Harrison. San Francisco: Ignatius, 1986.

———. "Biblical Interpretation in Conflict: On the Foundations and the Itinerary for Exegesis Today." In *Opening up the Scriptures: Joseph Ratzinger and the Foundations of Biblical Interpretation*, edited by José Granados et al. Grand Rapids, MI: Eerdmans, 2008.

———. "Brief von Joseph Ratzinger." In "Texte im Umfeld des Zweiten Vatikanischen Konzils," in *Mitteilungen Institut Papst Benedikt XVI.*, vol. 5, 13–16. Regensburg: Schnell & Steiner, 2012.

———. *Called to Communion*. Translated by Adrian J. Walker. San Francisco: Ignatius, 1996.

———. "Cardinal Frings's Speeches During the Second Vatican Council." *Communio* 15, no. 1 (Spring 1988).

———. *Church, Ecumenism, and Politics: New Endeavors in Ecclesiology*. Translated by Michael J. Miller et al. San Francisco: Ignatius, 2008.

———. "The Church and Scientific Theology." *Communio* 7, no. 4 (1980).

———. "La collégialité, développement théologique." In *L'Église de Vatican II: Études autour de la Constitution conciliaire sur l'Église*, vol. 3. Paris: Les Éditions du Cerf, 1967.

———. "Commentary on Introductory Article and Chapter I of *Gaudium et Spes*." In *Commentary on the Documents of Vatican II*, vol. 5, edited by Herbert Vorgrimler, translated by W.J. O'Hara. New York: Herder and Herder, 1969.

———. "Concerning the Notion of Person in Theology." Translated by Michael Waldstein. *Communio* 17 (Fall 1990): 439–454.

Ratzinger, Joseph. "Conscience and Truth." Keynote address of the Tenth Bishops' Workshop of the National Catholic Bioethics Center, February 1991, ewtn.com.

———. *Credo for Today: What Christians Believe.* Translated by Michael J. Miller et al. San Francisco: Ignatius, 2009.

———. *Das neue Volk Gottes: Entwürfe zur Ekklesiologie.* Düsseldorf: Patmos, 1969.

———. *Daughter Zion: Meditations on the Church's Marian Belief.* Translated by John M. McDermott. San Francisco: Ignatius, 1983.

———. *Der Gott des Glaubens und der Gott der Philosophen: Ein Beitrag zum Problem der theologia naturalis.* Munich: Schnell & Steiner, 1960.

———. "Der Weg der religiösen Erkenntnis nach dem heiligen Augustinus." In *Kyriakon II: Festschrift J. Quasten*, edited by P. Granfield and J.A. Jungman, 553–564. Münster: Aschendorff, 1970.

———. "The Dignity of the Human Person." In *Commentary on the Documents of Vatican II*, vol. 5, edited by Herbert Vorgrimler, translated by W.J. O'Hara. New York: Herder and Herder, 1969.

———. "Discorso introduttivo alla III giornata del Simposio di Newman." *Euntes Docete* (1990): 432–433. Translated and quoted in Andrzej Proniewski, "Joseph Ratzinger's Philosophical Theology of the Person," *Rocznik Teologii Katholickiej* 17, no. 3 (2018): 222–223.

———. *Dogma and Preaching: Applying Christian Doctrine to Daily Life.* Edited by Michael J. Miller. Translated by Michael J. Miller and Matthew J. O'Connell. San Francisco: Ignatius, 2011.

———. "The Ecclesiology of the Second Vatican Council." Translated by Stephen W. Arndt. *Communio* 13 (1986).

Ratzinger, Joseph. "Église universelle et Église particulière: la charge épiscopale." In *L'évêque et son ministère*. Vatican City: Urbaniana University Press, 1999.

———. "Einleitung." In *Einleitung und Kommentar zum Vorwort und zu Kapitel I, II und VI der Offenbarungskonstitution "Dei Verbum*," in *Lexikon für Theologie und Kirche*. Erg.-Bd. II, 1967.

———. *Eschatology: Death and Eternal Life*. 1st ed. Translated by Michael Waldstein. Washington, DC: The Catholic University of America Press, 1988.

———. *Faith and the Future*. Chicago: Franciscan Herald, 1971.

———. "Faith, Philosophy and Theology." *Communio* 11, no. 4 (Winter 1984).

———. *Feast of Faith*. Translated by Graham Harrison. San Francisco: Ignatius, 1986.

———. "The Feeling of Things, the Contemplation of Beauty." Message, August 24–30, 2002, vatican.va.

———. "Gemeinde aus der Eucharistie." In *800 Jahre St. Martini Münster*, edited by Werner Hülsbusch. Münster: Regensburg, 1980.

———. *God Is Near Us: The Eucharist, the Heart of Life*. Edited by Stephan Otto Horn and Vinzenz Pfnür. Translated by Henry Taylor. San Francisco: Ignatius, 2003.

———. *The God of Jesus Christ: Meditations on the Triune God*. Translated by Brian McNeil. San Francisco: Ignatius, 2008.

———. "Gratia praesupponit naturam: Erwägungen über Sinn und Grenze eines scholastischen Axioms." In *Einsicht und Glaube: Festschrift für Gottlieb Söhngen zum 70. Geburtstag*, edited by Joseph Ratzinger and Heinrich Fries, 135–249. Freiburg: Herder, 1962.

———. "The Holy Spirit as Communio: Concerning the Relationship of Pneumatology and Spirituality in Augustine." *Communio* 25 (Summer 1998): 324–337.

Ratzinger, Joseph. "Homily at the Mass '*Pro Eligendo Romano Pontifice*,'" April 18, 2005, vatican.va.

———. *'In the Beginning . . .': A Catholic Understanding of the Story of Creation and the Fall*. Translated by Boniface Ramsey. Grand Rapids, MI: Eerdmans, 1995.

———. *Introduction to Christianity*. Translated by Mary Frances McCarthy. San Francisco: Ignatius, 1987.

———. *Joseph Ratzinger: Gesammelte Schriften*. 16 vols. Edited by Gerhard Ludwig Müller. Freiburg: Herder, 2008–2020.

———. "Liturgy and Sacred Music." *Communio* 13, no. 4 (Winter 1986).

———. "The Local Church and the Universal Church: A Response to Walter Kasper." *America* 185 (November 19, 2001): 7–11.

———. *Many Religions—One Covenant*. San Francisco: Ignatius, 1999.

———. *The Meaning of Christian Brotherhood*. 2nd English edition. San Francisco: Ignatius, 1993.

———. *Milestones: Memoirs 1927–1977*. Translated by Erasmo Leiva-Merikakis. San Francisco: Ignatius, 1998.

———. *The Nature and Mission of Theology: Approaches to Understanding Its Role in the Light of Present Controversy*. Translated by Adrian J. Walker. San Francisco: Ignatius, 1995.

———. "The New Covenant: A Theology of Covenant in the New Testament." Translated by Maria Shrady. *Communio* 22 (Winter 1995).

———. "Offenbarung—Schrift—Überlieferung: Ein Text des heiligen Bonaventura und seine Bedeutung für die gegenwärtige Theologie." *Trier Theologische Zeitschrift* 67 (1958).

———. *On Love: Selected Writings*. Translated by Michael J. Miller. San Francisco: Ignatius, 2020.

Ratzinger, Joseph. *On the Way to Jesus Christ*. Translated by Michael J. Miller. San Francisco: Ignatius, 2005.

————. "The Pastoral Implications of Episcopal Collegiality." In *The Church and Mankind. Concilium* 1. Glen Rock, NJ: Paulist, 1965.

————. *Pilgrim Fellowship of Faith: The Church as Communion*. Translated by Henry Taylor. San Francisco: Ignatius, 2005.

————. "Primat." In *Lexikon für Theologie und Kirche*, 2nd ed., vol. 8, edited by Josef Höfer and Karl Rahner. Freiburg: Herder, 1963.

————. *Principles of Catholic Theology: Building Stones for a Fundamental Theology*. Translated by Mary Frances McCarthy. San Francisco: Ignatius, 1987.

————. "The Renewal of Moral Theology." In *Joseph Ratzinger in "Communio,"* vol. 1, *The Unity of the Church*. Grand Rapids, MI: Eerdmans, 2010.

————. "Schöpfungsglaube und Evolutionstheorie." Quoted in Christoph Schönborn, Foreword to *Creation and Evolution: A Conference with Pope Benedict XVI in Castel Gandolfo*, translated by Michael J. Miller, 7–23. San Francisco: Ignatius, 2008.

————. "Seven Theses on Christology and the Hermeneutic of Faith." *Letter & Spirit* 3 (2007): 189–209.

————. "Sources and the Transmission of the Faith." *Communio* 10, no. 1 (Spring 1983): 17–34.

————. *The Spirit of the Liturgy*. San Francisco: Ignatius, 2000.

————. *Theological Highlights of Vatican II*. Translated by Henry Traub et al. New York: Paulist, 2009.

————. *The Theology of History in St. Bonaventure*. Translated by Zachary Hayes. Chicago: Franciscan Herald, 1989.

Ratzinger, Joseph. *Theology of the Liturgy: The Sacramental Foundation of Christian Existence.* In *Joseph Ratzinger Collected Works*, vol. 11, edited by Michael J. Miller, translated by John Saward, Kenneth Baker, Henry Taylor, et al. San Francisco: Ignatius, 2014.

―――. "Truth and Freedom." Translated by Adrian J. Walker. *Communio* 23 (Spring 1996): 16–35.

―――. *Truth and Tolerance: Christian Belief and World Religions.* Translated by Henry Taylor. San Francisco: Ignatius, 2004.

―――. "Über die Ekklesiologie der Konstitution 'Lumen Gentium.'" *Die Tagespost*, March 2000.

―――. *Values in a Time of Upheaval.* Translated by Brian McNeil. San Francisco: Ignatius, 2006.

―――. "Vicarious Representation." Translated by Jared Wicks. *Letter & Spirit* 7 (2011): 209–220.

Ratzinger, Joseph, and Hans Urs von Balthasar. *Mary: The Church at the Source.* Translated by Adrian J. Walker. San Francisco: Ignatius, 2005.

Ratzinger, Joseph, and Karl Rahner. *The Episcopate and the Primacy.* Translated by Kenneth Barker et al. New York: Herder and Herder, 1962.

―――. *Revelation and Tradition.* Translated by W.J. O'Hara. New York: Herder and Herder, 1966.

Ratzinger, Joseph, and Peter Seewald. *Salt of the Earth: Christianity and the Catholic Church at the End of the Millennium: An Interview with Peter Seewald.* Translated by Adrian J. Walker. San Francisco: Ignatius, 1997.

Rausch, Thomas P. *Pope Benedict XVI: An Introduction to His Theological Vision.* New York: Paulist, 2009.

Resch, Felix. "Der Gott des Glaubens und der Gott der Philosophen: Zur fundamentaltheologischen Bedeutung der philosophischen Gotteslehre in Joseph Ratzingers Bonner Antrittsvorlesung (1959)." In *Mitteilungen Institut Papst Benedikt XVI.*, vol. 7, edited by Rudolf Voderholzer et al. Regensburg: Schnell & Steiner, 2014.

Rowland, Tracey. *Benedict XVI: A Guide for the Perplexed*. New York: T&T Clark, 2010.

———. *Ratzinger's Faith: The Theology of Benedict XVI*. New York: Oxford University Press, 2008.

Ruddy, Christopher. "'For the Many': The Vicarious-Representative Heart of Joseph Ratzinger's Theology." *Theological Studies* 75, no. 3 (2014): 564–584.

Schindler, David L. "The Person: Philosophy, Theology, and Receptivity." *Communio* 21 (Spring 1994): 172–190.

Schmidt, Eckart. »*... das Wort Gottes immer mehr zu lieben« Joseph Ratzingers Bibelhermeneutik im Kontext der Exegesegeschichte der römisch-katholischen Kirche*. Stuttgart: Katholisches Bibelwerk, 2015.

Seewald, Peter. *Benedict XVI: An Intimate Portrait*. Translated by Henry Taylor and Anne Englund Nash. San Francisco: Ignatius, 2008.

———. *Benedict XVI: A Life*. Vol. 1. Translated by Dinah Livingstone. London: Continuum, 2020.

Söding, Thomas. "Die Seele der Theologie: Ihre Einheit aus dem Geist der Heiligen Schrift in *Dei Verbum* und bei Joseph Ratzinger." *Internationale Katholische Zeitschrift Communio* 35, no. 6 (2006).

Suárez, Francisco. *De Trinitate*. In *Opera Omnia*, vol. 1, edited by M. André. Paris: Ludovicu Vivès, 1857.

Thomas Aquinas. *Summa theologiae*.

Turek, Margaret M. *Atonement: Soundings in Biblical, Trinitarian, and Spiritual Theology*. San Francisco: Ignatius, 2022.

Twomey, D. Vincent. *Apostolikos Thronos: The Primacy of Rome as Reflected in the Church History of Eusebius and the Historico-Apologetic Writings of Saint Athanasius the Great.* Münster: Münsterische Beiträge zur Theologie, 1982.

―――. *Pope Benedict XVI: The Conscience of Our Age.* San Francisco: Ignatius, 2007.

Vall, Gregory. *Ecclesial Exegesis: A Synthesis of Ancient and Modern Approaches to Scripture.* Washington, DC: The Catholic University of America Press, 2022.

Vatican Council I. *Dei Filius.* Dogmatic constitution, April 24, 1870, ewtn.com.

Vatican Council II. *De Fontibus Revelationis.* Translated by Joseph A. Komonchak. https://jakomonchak.files.wordpress.com/2012/09/de-fontibus-1-5.pdf.

―――. *Gaudium et Spes.* In *The Word on Fire Vatican II Collection*, 215–337. Park Ridge, IL: Word on Fire Institute, 2021.

―――. *Lumen Gentium.* In *The Word on Fire Vatican II Collection*, 45–149. Park Ridge, IL: Word on Fire Institute, 2021.

―――. *Unitatis Redintegratio.* In *The Word on Fire Vatican II Collection: Declarations and Decrees*, 133–167. Elk Grove Village, IL: Word on Fire, 2023.

Verweyen, Hansjürgen. *Ein unbekannter Ratzinger: Die Habilitationsschrift von 1955 als Schlüssel zu seiner Theologie.* Regensburg: Friedrich Pustet, 2010.

―――. *Joseph Ratzinger–Benedikt XVI.: Die Entwicklung seines Denkens.* Darmstadt: WBG, 2007.

Voderholzer, Rudolf. "Der Grundduktus innerhalb der Fundamentaltheologie von Joseph Ratzinger." In *Ratzinger-Studien*, vol. 6, *Zur Mitte der Theologie im Werk Joseph Ratzinger/Benedikt XVI.*, edited by Maximilian Heim and Justinus C. Pech. Regensburg: Friedrich Pustet, 2013.

Voderholzer, Rudolf. "Offenbarung und Kirche: Ein Grundgedanke von Joseph Ratzingers Habilitationsprojekt (1955/2009) und seine theologische Tragweite." In *Ratzinger-Studien*, vol. 2, *Gegenwart der Offenbarung: Zu den Bonaventura-Forschungen Joseph Ratzingers*, edited by Marianne Schlosser and Franz-Xaver Heibl. Regensburg: Friedrich Pustet, 2011.

Wicks, Jared. "Light from Germany on Vatican Council II." *The Catholic Historical Review* 99, no. 4 (Fall 2013).

Wicks, Jared. *Prof. Ratzinger at Vatican II: A Chapter in the Life of Pope Benedict XVI.* New Orleans: Loyola University Press, 2012.

——. "Six Texts by Prof. Joseph Ratzinger as *Peritus* before and during Vatican Council II." *Gregorianum* 89, no. 2 (2008).

Index